Subverting Patriarchy

Berg Monographs in German Literature

General Editors:
Jeffrey Sammons and Keith Bullivant

Subverting Patriarchy
Feminism and Fantasy in the Works of Irmtraud Morgner

ALISON LEWIS

BERG PUBLISHERS
Oxford / Washington, D.C.

First published in 1995 by
Berg Publishers Limited
Editorial offices:
150 Cowley Road, Oxford, OX4 1JJ, UK
13590 Park Center Road, Herndon, VA 22071, USA

© Alison Lewis 1995

Library of Congress Cataloging-in-Publication Data

A catalogue record for this book is available from the Library of Congress.

British Library Cataloguing in Publication Data

A catalogue record for this book is available from the British Library.

ISBN 0 85496 322 7

Printed in the United Kingdom by WBC Book Manufacturers, Mid-Glamorgan.

Contents

Acknowledgments

I am particularly grateful to Anthony Stephens, who read all of the earlier drafts of this work, for his continued encouragement and support. He has been a great source of inspiration over the years and this book would not have been possible without his generous help and advice. I am also indebted to Rita Felski for her helpful criticisms and detailed comments on early drafts as well as for her friendship throughout the project which provided a productive forum for the exchange of ideas. My thanks also go to Patricia Herminghouse and Sigrid Weigel who provided useful comments on the manuscript. Finally, I owe a special thanks to Herbert Meier whose unflagging support and patience helped me sustain momentum and faith in the project from beginning to end.

For financial assistance during this time I am indebted to the University of Adelaide whose repeated assistance in the form of scholarships and travel grants made much of the initial research possible. The University of Western Australia also provided crucial financial aid in the final stages of the project, providing me with an opportunity to assess many of the changes that had occurred in the new unified Germany. I am also appreciative of the support of my colleagues at the University of Western Australia and Queensland University of Technology where I was employed for most of the time spent writing the book.

Earlier versions of this book have appeared in *Southern Review* (Australia), and parts of chapter 5 have appeared in *The German Quarterly*.

Introduction

The use of fantasy by contemporary feminist writers represents a relatively new and little explored form of feminist intervention. One of the most innovative examples in recent feminist fiction of the use of fantastic forms is the work of East German author Irmtraud Morgner. Little known outside German-speaking countries, her experiments with forms of the fantastic offer one of the most comprehensive and extensive examples of a feminist critique of the history of patriarchal institutions and practices to emerge out of second wave feminist movements.[1] Writing under conditions of severe political and cultural repression during the last two decades of the reign of the ruling socialist party in the former German Democratic Republic, Morgner's unique brand of fantastic realism is potent testimony to both the subversive nature of a literature of fantasy and the transgressive power of feminist writing. Although her works can be considered subversive both in terms of their immediate political effect and the aesthetic form they adopt, it is this latter sense, the textual and structural strategies her

---

1. The term feminist is somewhat problematic when applied to Morgner since she herself repeatedly rejected the label in interviews. She maintained that as a communist she did not need to be a feminist as well since the sweeping social changes brought about by the socialist revolution automatically envisaged the abolition of all forms of exploitation, including those based on gender: "Does that make me a feminist? I have no reason to be a communist on the one hand and a feminist on the other." See Irmtraud Morgner, "Weltspitze sein und sich wundern, was noch nicht ist," *Kürbiskern* no. 1 (1978): 98. In interviews with West German feminists she declined to call herself a feminist on the grounds that the term apoliticized and trivialized women's struggles for equality: "I do not like the word 'feminist' because for me it has a fashionable, unpolitical ring to it, because it provokes the assumption that the 'coming to humanity' of woman could only be a matter for women." Morgner, "'Produktivkraft Sexualität souverän nutzen': Ein Gespräch mit der DDR-Schriftstellerin von Karin Huffzky," in *Grundlagentexte zur Emanzipation der Frau*, ed. Jutta Menschik (Cologne: Pahl-Rugenstein, 1976), 328. Morgner repeatedly affirms her belief in the socialist revolution and its relevance for women, despite her caustic critiques that socialism has not lived up to its expectations. In an interview in 1976 she remarked: "The first major step in the liberation of women is the socialist revolution. And then there remains a lot of hard work to do." Morgner, "Das eine tun und das andere nicht lassen: Interview mit Ursula Krechel," *Konkret* no. 8 (1976): 44.

texts deploy to subvert dominant representations of the patriarchal real, that shall be the major focus of this book.

Once dismissed as merely irrational and escapist, fantasy can no longer be regarded as a subject unworthy of serious literary study.[2] Periodically marginalized and banished as realism's "other," fantasy has most recently been interpreted as a telling indication of that which a particular culture is most at pains to keep hidden. Freed from the derogatory epithets that frequently characterized the reception of non-mimetic forms of representation in the German- and English-speaking cultures of the twentieth century,[3] fantasy has established itself as an infinitely rich and varied form of cultural expression. The return of fantasy as a modernist writing practice and an object of critical inquiry marks in various ways a "return of the repressed"[4] that does not merely celebrate the triumphant re-emergence of those forms of life and artistic expression a particular culture has sought to suppress; its return serves at the same time to undermine the values of the dominant culture and to actively subvert its claims to truth and power. Often thought to resurface periodically in times of excessive reliance on

2. Among the most influential studies of fantasy as a genre are Tzvetan Todorov, *The Fantastic: A Structural Approach to a Literary Genre*, trans. Richard Howard (Ithaca: Cornell UP, 1975); Rosemary Jackson, *Fantasy: The Literature of Subversion* (London: Methuen, 1981); W.R. Irwin, *The Game of the Impossible: A Rhetoric of Fantasy* (Illinois: University of Illinois Press, 1976); and Kathryn Hume, *Fantasy and Mimesis: Responses to Reality in Western Literature* (London: Methuen, 1981).

3. In both the GDR and the Federal Republic of Germany the influence of Lukács and his vehement attacks on romanticism, expressionism, and the avant-garde has been powerful in perpetuating the marginalization of forms of modernist prose. Lukács's legacy was, of course, much stronger in the GDR where the party adopted his model of socialist realism and the guidelines laid down by Zhadanov at the First Congress of Soviet Writers in Moscow in 1934 for a socialist cultural politics. Lukácsian terms such as decadence, schematism, formalism, and subjectivism were all applied with monotonous regularity to works of fantasy throughout the first few decades of the GDR and even up until the 1980s. English literary criticism has likewise been dismissive of many forms of fantasy on the grounds that many works aim at escaping the human condition or hark back to a "nostalgic, humanist vision." The revival in interest in forms of fantasy is closely connected to the impact of psychoanalytic theory on traditional literary studies and the influence of feminism and post-structuralism.

4. See Jackson, *Fantasy*, 63–72; Terry Lovell, *Consuming Fiction* (London: Verso, 1987), 62; Franco Moretti, *Signs Taken for Wonders: Essays in the Sociology of Literary Forms*, trans. Susan Fischer, David Forgacs, and David Miller (London: Verso 1988), 98–104.

the powers of reason,[5] modern fantasy can be read as the critical conscience of the twentieth-century's blind adherence to abstract rationality and instrumental reason. Its emergence can be seen therefore as a response to the legitimation crisis of the project of the Enlightenment. And yet fantasy itself is borne out of the very same impulse that sustained the Enlightenment: it too strives to demystify absolute and falsifying truths, to counter myth with Enlightenment and, in turn, to reveal Enlightenment as myth.[6] Not surprisingly, the recurrent appearance of forms of literary fantasy has been linked to historical periods of severe cultural repression.[7] Fantasy can articulate dissatisfaction and frustration with particular historical and social conditions while also fueling hopes for better worlds and for social transformation. It strives to make visible those aspects of a society – those censored desires and taboos – that a particular culture is unable to assimilate and must therefore repress. Fantasy gives expression to a culture's blind spots, to its silences and its gaps. It challenges the real, explores the limits of what can be said and calls into question prevailing assumptions about the nature of social reality. It subverts official or public versions of the truth by opposing dominant ideologies with alternative truths, counter-myths, and other histories. It is therefore inherently concerned with the limits of ideology.

Contemporary feminist fantasy is similarly concerned with the exploration of ideology through its commitment to revealing the ideology of *gender*. The burgeoning body of works by feminist writers that employ elements of fantasy is evidence of the extensive possibilities that experimentation with fantasy offers feminist writers in the late twentieth century. Feminists have adapted a varied range of forms that, for the purposes of this study, will be subsumed under the term "fantasy," though they range from fairytale, science fiction, horror, and gothic, to works about utopias and dystopias. This stock of traditional genres has provided feminists with a fertile source of material from which to formulate oppositional ideologies and to question the construction of women's experience in dominant narratives. Certainly by no means

5. See Jackson, *Fantasy*, 21.
6. The theory proposed here comes close to what Horkheimer and Adorno called the "dialectic of the Enlightenment." See Max Horkheimer and Theodor W. Adorno, *Die Dialektik der Aufklärung* (Frankfurt/Main: Fischer, 1969), 7–8.
7. Jackson, *Fantasy*, 179.

all contemporary works of fantasy by women are written from a self-consciously feminist perspective that is sustained at all levels of the text; some unwittingly reinscribe the traditional gender hierarchy they are attempting to dismantle in what are often nostalgic, mystificatory texts celebrating myths of the eternal feminine. Others are more radical in their critiques of patriarchal society, exposing the fundamental contradictions and gender imbalances that permeate every aspect of women's lives while taking care not to fall into the traps of essentialism. The works of Irmtraud Morgner belong to this latter group of feminist fantasy whose predominant impulse is transgressive rather than escapist, critical rather than celebratory. Morgner's works bear comparison with the novels of Joanna Russ, Ursula Le Guin, Marge Piercy, and Barbara Frischmut, although it has been suggested that in their use of the supernatural they come perhaps closest to the novels of Toni Morrison and Maxine Hong Kingston.[8]

Like many twentieth-century women's texts, Morgner's works are engaged in a cultural practice that consciously aims to expand the choice of narrative patterns organizing the cultural and ideological inscription of women's experience.[9] Morgner's novels doubtless share much in common with these works in their use of intertextuality to articulate dissent with the construction of women in narrative. Like the conventional ending of the "heroine's text" in much nineteenth-century fiction that culminated in either death or marriage for the heroine,[10] the range of narrative options available to East German women writers was similarly restricted by the dominance of the socialist realist plot. Certainly, death was rarely an acceptable option for the resolution of social and personal conflicts in the East German novel, and marriage ceased to provide the sole focus and telos of narrative. Yet the trajectories of the female heroines in socialist realist fiction tended to follow remarkably predictable and uniform paths down the road to personal fulfillment and social commitment. Although these

---

8. Angelika Bammer, "Trobadora in Amerika," *Irmtraud Morgner: Texte, Daten, Bilder*, ed. Marlis Gerhardt (Darmstadt & Neuwied: Luchterhand, 1990), 203–4.
9. Rachel Blau DuPlessis, *Writing Beyond the Ending: Narrative Strategies of Twentieth-Century Women Writers* (Bloomington: Indiana UP, 1985), esp. 1–19.
10. See Nancy K. Miller, *The Heroine's Text: Readings in the French and English novel, 1722–1782* (New York: Columbia UP, 1980); and DuPlessis, *Writing Beyond the Ending*, 3–4.

narratives pay tribute to women's increasing autonomy and growing visibility in public life with their abundance of stories about the emancipatory effects of work, they still severely curtail the narrative possibilities open to women in their continued emphasis on the heterosexual romance plot and the inevitably harmonious resolution of the contradictory trajectories of the quest and romance. However, Morgner's writing practice differs in the crucial sense that her aesthetic practice evolved as a response to cultural and literary conventions that limited women's cultural expression not merely by virtue of their normative power. Many of the narrative patterns that Morgner sought to disrupt were nothing short of prescriptive.[11] For this reason, Morgner's use of narrative to "write beyond the ending" by challenging the "ideological scripts" imbedded in dominant narrative forms represents a special case in the history of twentieth-century women writers.[12]

The existence of strict literary censorship in former Eastern bloc countries adds a further dimension to her transgressive use of narrative. While permitted to be published in her own country – albeit with considerable delay[13] – Morgner was continually at risk of invoking the displeasure and disapproval of the ruling cultural and literary elite throughout her writing career.[14] The gay abandon

11. The guidelines for authors and critics were laid down regularly at the conferences held by the Writers' Union (Schriftstellerverband der DDR), an organization that came under the close control of the Socialist Unity Party. Although these guidelines were broadened or relaxed from time to time, the original dictates of socialist realism remained extremely powerful and could be invoked at any time to condemn works that were thought to take liberalizing tendencies too far. The Eighth Party Congress of the Socialist Unity Party held in 1971 was one such important turning point in the reception of non-realist modes of writing that also marked a watershed in the development of women's fiction.

12. The term "writing beyond the ending" is taken from Rachel Blau DuPlessis, *Writing Beyond the Ending*, 4–5.

13. *Gustav der Weltfahrer* for example was written in 1967/68 for the Eulenspiegelverlag who originally commissioned the work but did not publish it. It was eventually published by the Aufbau publishing house in 1972. See Eva Kaufmann, "Der Hölle die Zunge rausstrecken . . .": Der Weg der Erzählerin Irmtraud Morgner," *Weimarer Beiträge* 30 (1984): 1531.

14. Although Morgner was never expelled from the Writers' Union and never experienced the sort of recriminations that many of her colleagues did, the response by the literary establishment of the GDR, particularly in the reviews published in the official journals of the party, made it clear that her form of fantasy may have been tolerated but never met with official approval.

with which she defied the dictates of socialist realism and the blithe lack of concern with which she proceeded to expand her early forays into what became her own distinctive brand of fantastic realism are both evidence of the subversive potential of her works within the immediate political context of the former GDR.[15] However, the indifferent or ambiguous response to Morgner's works by East German critics was not so much due to the offensive political and ideological content of her novels – although there is certainly ample evidence of comments in her works that could easily be construed by the party as being directly subversive or counter-revolutionary. Rather, it appeared to be her own particular idiosyncratic use of form that unsettled her critics, a form, moreover, that until the 1970s had been thoroughly discredited by the GDR cultural establishment for its anti-socialist, anti-realist connotations and its citations of the "irrational" cultural heritage. The use of a disreputable literary tradition coupled with the undeniable feminist intent of her writing only served to exacerbate the lukewarm response her works provoked from within the GDR.

However, as I shall be arguing, the subversive potential of her works cannot be defined solely in terms of the political effects of her texts – although the history of the reception of her works is obviously an important consideration. The subversiveness of her writing can be seen instead to lie in its challenge to literary convention at the level of formal innovations and the deployment of intertextuality. Thus, her explorations of the subversive potential of a marginalized literary tradition to articulate an all-encompassing feminist critique of the history of women's oppression make Morgner's works much more than a curious relic of one of the most repressive eras in the history of the twentieth

---

15. The extent to which her works met with the disapproval of the censorship authorities is not yet fully known, as no history of the various stages of the production of her works has yet been written. It is also dangerous to criticize writers such as Morgner and Christa Wolf for not conforming to some absolute standard of what constitutes genuine or false subversion simply because they chose not to leave the GDR. As Martin Jay has remarked, the distinction between real and pseudo-subversion is contextual and cannot be judged according to "some ultimate standard of subversiveness" (Martin Jay, "Force Fields: Who's Afraid of Christa Wolf? Thoughts on the Dynamics of Cultural Subversion," *Salmagundi* 92 (1991): 52).

century. Her use of the fantastic as a means to expose the all-pervasive nature of patriarchy serves as an instructive example of how feminists can utilize narrative and genre as powerful tools of cultural criticism. Since the end of state socialism has only removed one particularly oppressive form of patriarchal domination, the nature of Morgner's concerns will continue to be of relevance to women for as long as prevailing gender hierarchies hold sway in Western societies. Indeed, many of the obstacles faced by East German women still await women in the West, as many of the conditions created by state socialism for women, such as full employment and the implementation of positive discrimination programs, have yet to be realized in most late-capitalist societies.

While Morgner's works can be considered disruptive in terms of both political effect and textual practice, the emphasis in the following will be on the textual strategies and narrative devices Morgner employs in her works to disrupt the institutions and discourses of patriarchy. It is her strategic deployment of a wide range of fantastic narrative devices, her interweaving of history and myth, of fiction and documentary, of Greek mythology, medieval legends, and contemporary socialist mythology that forms the basis of her feminist critique of the dominant myths of patriarchal history. Fantasy is thus used to give expression to women's frustrations with the limitations and insufficiencies of patriarchal culture – in Morgner's case with socialist patriarchy – by exposing through a multitude of fantastic techniques of estrangement, ironic inversion, and doubling the oppressive and intractable nature of patriarchal ideologies.

The impetus of the fantastic in Morgner's works is at once critical and compensatory. Morgner's fantasy challenges stereotyped accounts of women's reality and the dominant discourses that construct women's experience in late modernity. She challenges, for instance, the official party accounts of women's emancipation and the Marxist discourses that pronounced the "woman question" as having been singlehandedly solved with the advent of socialism. Recourse to supernatural instruments or figures also provides a means of transcending social and political limitations impeding the process of women's emancipation.

Morgner's novels belong to a small group of texts published by East German women writers in the 1970s and 1980s that make use of fantasy to foreground the fundamental contradictions inherent in women's daily working lives.[16] The decision to depart from realist forms of literary representation stems from a refusal to shore up the multiple contradictions lived by women in modern industrial societies in a homogenizing unitary vision of social reality. As a result of the political and economic imperative to mobilize all women of working age into the work force during the first few postwar decades, women in the GDR found themselves forced to "do a man's job" during the day while still performing traditional female "reproductive" work in the family at night. The new stereotype of the emancipated working woman that was propagated at all political and cultural levels during the 1950s and 1960s meant that women were required to perform traditional female duties in the family as wife and mother *in addition* to participating actively in the community and the work force. The myth of the new female socialist personality necessitated the harmonizing of two essentially "non-synchronous" ideals.[17] However, as Morgner points out, equal rights are not much use to women if it means they have twice as many duties as well.[18]

These contradictions of working life under socialism where women were officially considered men's equals in the work force while still having to service their husbands and families in private found expression in a number of feminist stories via the intrusion of a fantastic subtext into what are otherwise realist narratives. As visible and tangible proof of those forces that the realist text can no longer contain, this fantastic subtext can be read as the *non dit* of the realist text with its positive working heroine, its obligatory happy end, and its often facile resolution of conflicts – a text not unlike the one women in the West are accustomed to finding in popular fiction and culture. The inclusion of the other side of women's social lives necessarily explodes the myth of the superwoman who excels effortlessly in her career and in the home – unless, of course, she has the help of magic. They challenge, moreover, the common feminist notion that women's full

---

16. The most well-known stories are Charlotte Worgitzky, "Karriere Abgesagt," *Vieräugig oder Blind* (Berlin/GDR: Buchverlag Der Morgen, 1978), 69–82; and Monika Helmecke, "Lauf Weg! – Kehr um!" *Klopfzeichen* (Berlin/GDR: Verlag Neues Leben, 1979), 76–87.
17. For Bloch's theory of "non-synchronicity" ("Ungleichzeitigkeit") see Ernst Bloch, *Erbschaft dieser Zeit* (Frankfurt/Main: Suhrkamp, 1962), 45ff.
18. Morgner, "'Produktivkraft Sexualität souverän nutzen,'" 331.

participation in the work force substantially alters women's status in patriarchal societies.

Morgner's texts can be seen as giving shape to the once hidden and censored text of a female "political unconscious" that earlier narratives dealing with women's inroads into male-dominated professions and the emancipatory effects of work had suppressed. The concept of a "political unconscious" was originally conceived by Fredric Jameson to designate the determining social and political forces at work in the production of literary texts.[19] Realist texts typically suppress these contradictions at a textual level, the political significance of this textual unconscious generally only coming to the fore in the hermeneutic process. While the texts under discussion here no longer suppress references to their conditions of production and all explicitly incorporate this "political unconscious" into the text in the form of fantastic narratives (that provide the necessary support for women's survival in the everyday), the concept seems particularly pertinent in relation to the status of the fantasy narrative in Morgner's works. The primary purpose of the introduction of the fantastic is indeed the uncovering of a repressed and censored narrative that charts the continued subordination of women in the private sphere, in the work place, and in the domains of historical and scientific inquiry. The foregrounding of this subtext exposes previous realist accounts of women's participation in the work force as being patriarchal myths founded on the suppression of the truth about the continued discrimination against women in both public and private spheres.

Despite the specificity of many of Morgner's concerns, her works of fantasy clearly belong to a larger body of feminist work that has emerged out of second wave feminist movements. In broad terms, they participate in the feminist project of demystifying androcentric views and giving expression to alternative discourses on femininity, motherhood, and sexuality. They seek to counter closed monological truths about femininity and its function in dominant philosophical systems with multiple truths and stories about women and the construction of the feminine. They combat doctrine and orthodoxy with a feminine heterodoxy; they respond to dogma and blind faith in modern secular religions with heresy and

---

19. Fredric Jameson, *The Political Unconscious: Narrative as a Socially Symbolic Act* (London: Methuen, 1981), 20.

irreverence. In particular, they oppose Marxist dogma with insights gained from feminist analysis. In light of the demise of Eastern European socialist societies, Morgner's repeated public commitment to the principles of socialism may at first glance appear to present a stumbling block in a post-communist age. Her critical rereadings of Marxist philosophy, however, and in particular her insights into the inadequacies of orthodox Marxist solutions to the "woman question," feed into more general debates within feminism about the usefulness of Marxist categories of analysis for questions of gender.

Finally then, Morgner's works belong to the movement in international feminism that argues for the reintroduction of a notion of irreducible sexual difference. Morgner is one of a number of prominent East German women to give voice to her growing dissatisfaction with the prevailing interpretation of women's emancipation as a process of abolishing all differences between the sexes. Christa Wolf summarized this shift in feminism away from the notions of sameness when she protested in 1968 that women had been encouraged to identify with an antiquated ideal of masculinity for far too long, thus denying all sense of a feminine difference. It can no longer be the aim of a politics of emancipation, she argued, to erase all markers of sexual difference by encouraging women to become more like men.[20]

The following analysis of the diverse aspects and multiple uses of fantastic narrative techniques in Morgner's works focuses on her two major works of fantasy, the first two and only completed volumes of the Salman trilogy, *Leben und Abenteuer der Trobadora Beatriz nach Zeugnissen ihrer Spielfrau Laura* (1974) (*Life and Adventures of the Troubadour Beatriz as Chronicled by her Minstrel Laura: Novel in Thirteen Books and Seven Intermezzos*)[21] and *Amanda: Ein Hexenroman* (1983) (*Amanda: A Witch Novel*).[22] Since all the motifs and themes of her earlier shorter novels are to be found in

20. Christa Wolf, *Lesen und Schreiben: Neue Sammlung* (Darmstadt & Neuwied: Luchterhand, 1980), 93–94.
21. Irmtraud Morgner, *Leben und Abenteuer der Trobadora Beatriz nach Zeugnissen ihrer Spielfrau Laura* (Berlin/GDR: Aufbau; Darmstadt & Neuwied: Luchterhand, 1976). All further references to this work will appear in the text after the abbreviation [TB].
22. Morgner, *Amanda: Ein Hexenroman* (Berlin/GDR: Aufbau, 1983; Darmstadt & Neuwied: Luchterhand, 1983). All further references to this work will appear as [A].

more developed form in *Trobadora Beatriz* and *Amanda,* Morgner's other works of fantasy – *Hochzeit in Konstantinopel* (1968) (*Wedding in Constantinople*), *Gauklerlegende: Eine Spielfraungeschichte* (1970) (*Legend of a Jester: A Story of a Female Minstrel*), and *Die wundersamen Reisen Gustavs des Weltfahrers: Lügenhafter Roman mit Kommentaren* (1972) (*The Amazing Travels of Gustaf The World-Traveler: A Novel of Tall-stories with Commentary*)[23] – will only be analyzed in relation to the two larger novels. A discussion of the published fragments of the uncompleted third volume in the Salman trilogy, as well as her censored novel *Rumba auf einen Herbst* (1965/1992) (*Rumba to an Autumn*) rediscovered and published after her death, will likewise be incorporated into the analysis of the two completed volumes.[24]

While Morgner's oeuvre obviously constitutes a unique case in the history of contemporary feminist writing, this study aims to situate Morgner's contribution to the formulation of a feminist aesthetic and her fictional treatment of feminist themes in the broader context of contemporary Anglo-American, French, and German feminist writing and second wave feminism. At the same time attention will be paid to the cultural specificity of the works under discussion. Many interpretations have tended to read statements issued by East German authors in public forums far too literally, unaware of the rhetorical imperative to pay lip service to Marxist doctrine that impeded many author's ability to speak truthfully. East German writers have been often accused of not being sufficiently radical in their judgments of patriarchy, or of neutralizing the caustic edge of their critiques.[25] Such charges are

23. Morgner, *Hochzeit in Konstantinopel* (Berlin/GDR, 1968; Darmstadt & Neuwied: Luchterhand, 1979). All further references to this work will appear in the text as [HK]. Morgner, *Gauklerlegende: Eine Spielfraungeschichte* (Berlin/ GDR, 1970; Darmstadt & Neuwied: Luchterhand, 1982); *Die wundersamen Reisen Gustavs des Weltfahrers: Lügenhafter Roman mit Kommentaren* (Berlin/ GDR: Aufbau, 1972; Darmstadt & Neuwied: Luchterhand, 1981). All references to this work will appear in the text as [GW].
24. See Morgner, *Die Hexe im Landhaus: Gespräch in Solothurn: Mit einem Beitrag von Erica Pedretti* (Zurich & Villingen: Raureif, 1986); *Der Schöne und das Tier: Eine Liebesgeschichte* (Darmstadt & Neuwied: Luchterhand Literaturverlag, 1991); and *Rumba auf einen Herbst* (Hamburg: Luchterhand Literaturverlag, 1992). All references to this work will appear in the text as [RH].
25. See for example Maureen McNeil, "Being Reasonable Feminists," *Gender and Expertise,* ed. Maureen McNeil (London: Free Association Books, 1987), 48–52.

based on, at best, a lack of sensitivity towards the very different processes and patterns of reading and writing in the GDR and, at worst, a poor understanding of the cultural and political determinants governing the production and consumption of literary texts in the former GDR. In order to avoid the sort of homogenizing and colonizing modes of reading that result in a denial of cultural difference, this study will attempt to preserve the singularity of Morgner's works at the same time as it reads these texts within the global framework of Western feminist movements and the institutions of late modernity.

It seems important, therefore, to be reminded yet again of the fact that particular aesthetic choices presented quite concrete political risks – albeit of varying degrees – for former East German authors. While it is by now a truism that all narrative is a "socially symbolic act"[26] and that no narrative convention is "neutral, purely mimetic, or purely aesthetic,"[27] there are certain social and historical constellations under which narrative becomes a relatively harmless social activity, and others under which it becomes a courageous gesture of defiance. Formal innovations or radical textual politics do not constitute in themselves radical or revolutionary politics; an estimation of their political effectiveness can only be adjudicated in relation to dominant cultural practices and their respective contexts of production and reception. But by the same token, the choice of a particular aesthetic form cannot be considered to be only a political rather than a literary act, say, purely a vehicle for political commentary or a tactic to avoid censorship. As vehicles and tactics, literary practices have their own materiality, their particular histories, and their own "ideology of form."[28] It follows therefore that while Morgner's techniques for subverting the truth claims of the dominant culture are obviously shaped in some measure by the constraints and norms of institutionalized censorship, her literary techniques cannot be collapsed onto this political function. It is certainly true that criticism expressed either obliquely or in estranged form provided a common means of thwarting the censorship bodies in their epistemological drive to ascertain the ideological thrust of authorial intent or the precise (political)

26. See Jameson, *The Political Unconscious*, passim.
27. DuPlessis, *Writing Beyond the Ending*, 2.
28. Jameson, *The Political Unconscious*, 76.

meaning of a text. Texts that favored multiple perspectives, used historical allegories, or extrapolated from the present often escaped censure simply because the texts' ultimate meaning could not be distilled with sufficient unambiguity to warrant censoring. Yet in a fashion similar to works produced in the West, the literary forms developed by writers under censorship draw on a finite stock of romantic, modernist, and avant-garde traditions. Although one main motive for choosing a modernist style may be its effectiveness in evading the censor, one should be wary of an approach that regards narrative tropes as mere transparent devices that require decoding in order to disclose their hidden meaning, or in this case, their covert political agenda. Any attempt to reduce aesthetic devices to mere reflex reactions to forms of institutional control must therefore be seen as dubious if it cannot account for the literariness of the literary product in question.

A discussion of censorship must also include reference to one further peculiarity of feminist fiction produced in the former GDR: the social and political functions specifically assigned to all literature in former communist countries. Under the strict control of party organizations, literature played a crucial role in the dissemination of socialist ideas and doctrines and in the education of the populace. Yet despite the complete colonization of all facets of life by the organs of the party, the observation still holds true that literature was nonetheless able to perform the function of a critical alternative public sphere.[29] Since the demise of the GDR in 1989, this critical service has come under considerable scrutiny, in particular during the so-called "literature debate" of 1990 sparked off by the ill-timed publishing of Christa Wolf's short novel *Was Bleibt*[30] detailing her experiences with the East German "Stasi." At the heart of the matter seemed to be the perceived need on the part of the West German literary establishment to strip the entire corpus of East German literature of its "dissident bonus" and to retrospectively brand all works by East German authors as a state literature hopelessly compromised and corrupted by its association with the ruling cultural authorities. In this climate of literary

29. See David Bathrick, "Kultur und Öffentlichkeit," *Literatur der DDR in den siebziger Jahren*, ed. P.U. Hohendahl and P. Herminghouse (Frankfurt/Main: Suhrkamp, 1983), 59.
30. Wolf, *Was Bleibt: Erzählung* (Frankfurt/Main: Luchterhand Literaturverlag, 1990).

witchhunts, it must serve as a timely reminder that the officially sanctioned and protected public spheres of literature and culture provided one of the few permissible forums for critical dialogue. In the absence of such alternative public spheres in the 1970s and 1980s as an autonomous women's movement and a popular women's press to promote debate on feminist issues, it was largely left to women's literature to perform the function of a feminist public sphere. Literature provided a crucial avenue for the identification of feminist strategies of intervention and the experimentation with strategies of feminine resistance. As part of this service they provided, the works by East German feminist writers were often engaged in the reception of themes central to the aims of international feminism during the 1970s and 1980s.

Despite the extreme popularity of works by feminist authors marketed under the rubric of "fantasy," very few critical studies have yet to address the complex relationship between textual practice and oppositional politics as it relates to the problem of a feminist aesthetic.[31] Like much of the literature on fantasy itself, feminist literary criticism has on the whole suffered from a tendency to lift aesthetic practices out of the multiple historical, social, and literary contexts that shape these writings. The production of feminist texts of fantasy must be considered therefore against the background of a great diversity of social movements and cross-cultural knowledges, that is, as simultaneously being part of local and global contexts. The writings of any one author of feminist fantasy participate in both local and transnational contexts; they respond to historical, political, and economic determinants present at a national or geo-political level at any given time, as well as forming part of broader global contexts such as international feminism, literary modernism, and late modernity.

Chapter 1 will investigate the relationship between fantasy and feminism and the ways in which feminist writing, following the example of Morgner, can usefully avail itself of the subversive possibilities of an aesthetic of fantasy. Chapter 2 will examine how encounters with the fantastic in *Trobadora Beatriz* provide the impetus for an assessment of women's lack of autonomy in modern

---

31. One notable exception to this tendency is the work of Rita Felski, *Beyond Feminist Aesthetics: Feminist Literature and Social Change* (Cambridge, Massachusetts: Harvard UP, 1989), esp. 158–59.

society through a critical look at the status of women as objects of exchange. The focus of chapters 3, 4, and 5 will be on the way in which Morgner's texts, in particular *Trobadora Beatriz*, subvert the androcentric bias of the generic traditions and patterns of the romance, the Bildungsroman, and the medieval epos. In chapter 6 a further master narrative structuring the multiple narrative strands of *Trobadora Beatriz* will be identified in the quest for sexual liberation. This quest for sexual liberation and the concern with a feminist politics of the body gives way in *Amanda* to a preoccupation with the "body politic" that calls for new and different strategies of feminine resistance. Chapters 7 and 8 will investigate how the assistance of a diverse range of fantastical, mythological, and contemporary female figures is mobilized in the interests of the survival of the human race and the feminization of politics. Finally, chapter 9 will focus on Morgner's "unreal" solution to the complex and fraught question of female subjectivity via an exploration of her innovative model of split subjectivity. The implications of the feminist alternatives elaborated in Morgner's texts together with her strategies of resistance will be assessed with respect to their effectiveness as a feminist aesthetic of subversion.

1
Feminism and Fantasy

Social Reality and the Power of Miracles

In 1979, in an essay entitled "Why are Americans afraid of Dragons," Ursula Le Guin, the American author of numerous works of fantasy and science fiction, asks the question why so many highly technological societies are persistently "antifantasy."[1] The fundamental moral disapproval of fantasy she detects in the contemptuous, suspicious reactions of her fellow Americans to fantastic literature is the result, she contends, of a systematic repression of the powers of the imagination and all that modern, technological societies have come to associate with the world of fantasy and the human imagination. Many modern societies, she continues, have learned to suppress the imagination and dismiss its products as childish and somehow effeminate, or as unprofitable and possibly sinful.[2] She issues a word of warning to those who would deny both the beneficial and pleasurable aspects of fantasy:

> Those who refuse to listen to dragons are probably doomed to spend their lives acting out the nightmares of politicians. We like to think we live in daylight, but half the world is always dark; and fantasy, like poetry, speaks the language of the night.[3]

These words could equally serve as a motto for the works of East German proponents of fantasy such as Irmtraud Morgner, whose impassioned pleas for an injection of fantasy and imagination into the daily lives of the citizens of the former German Democratic Republic must now seem rather prophetic in light of the end of state

---

1. Ursula Le Guin, "Why are Americans afraid of Dragons," in *The Language of the Night: Essays on Fantasy and Science Fiction*, ed. with introduction Susan Wood (New York: G.P. Putnam's Sons, 1979), 40.
2. Ibid., 41–42.
3. Ibid., 11.

socialism in Eastern Europe and the demise of East Germany as a separate state. Morgner's insistence from *Amanda* onward on the need to revive a positive tradition of heresy as a means of preserving the "possible of the day after tomorrow" (A. 246) is a warning that indirectly alludes to the "impossible" of the present. Those who fail to listen to dragons and close their minds to the dreams of future possibilities may well be doomed to perpetuate the nightmares and shortcomings of the present. If the citizens of the former GDR had maintained a keener sense of alternative possibilities and had not relinquished their belief in dragons and miracles, the seemingly impossible events of November 1989 may have belonged to the realm of the possible somewhat sooner than they actually did. Of course, the events that were to befall the people of the GDR late in 1989 could not have been anticipated by Morgner herself, for not even she would ever have imagined the dissolution of the GDR as a communist state being within the realm of possibility.

Morgner was not to live to experience the end of the socialist experiment: she died in May 1990 only several months after the collapse of the Honecker regime. Her dire predictions throughout the 1980s and the urgency of her pleas for a greater space for utopian dreaming and feminine fantasy now seem more than merely prophetic; the importance of these qualities in a post-communist age has certainly not diminished. More than ever before women's imagination and creativity is vital if the women of the GDR are not to forfeit many of the gains made in the forty years of socialist rule. In the wake of unification, it is once again women's reserves of imagination and patience that are required to ensure their survival. In the economic, political, and social upheavals of a unified Germany, Morgner's recipe for fueling faith in the future can provide women with a powerful blueprint for the future. If the very real and concrete benefits of socialism are not to be lost entirely, it may well be those well-developed qualities of witchcraft and sorcery that will guarantee women will not be the losers in the long and painful process of unification.

An unshaken belief in the power of miracles and fantasy is, according to Morgner, a means of staving off the threat of stagnation and imposed immobility; it encourages faith in the possibility of social change and therefore in the improvement of existing conditions for women. Fantasy and a belief in the impossible is a survival strategy. For both Morgner and Le Guin the world of the imagination provides a crucial counter-weight to modern society with its increasingly exclusive reliance on rationality, abstraction, and calculable and quantifiable values. Fantasy can act as a corrective to an increasing trend towards the instrumentalization of human needs and reason.

Both Morgner and Le Guin argue that fantasy can be more "realistic" than many realist accounts of social reality. The cognitive value of non-realist forms of prose was recognized by Christa Wolf in 1968 when she remarked that the reality of this century has succeeded in confounding people's wildest dreams. In an age where reality itself is increasingly "more fantastic than any product of the imagination" and "its cruelty and marvelousness is not to be surpassed through invention," fantasy becomes a more appropriate mode of representing the concerns of the modern world.[4] Morgner made a similar assertion in an interview with Ekkehart Rudolph in 1974 when she remarked that her prose should be understood as a form of realism, specifically as a form of socialist realism, as she regarded herself a socialist. She emphatically denied any incompatibility between the fantastic aspects of her work and the aims of a realist aesthetic, proclaiming her use of fantasy as being merely another variant of realism.

While comparable in thrust to Le Guin's assertion that "fantasy is true,"[5] Morgner's defense of fantasy as a realistic mode of representation differs in one important respect: her insistence on realism is also a polemic attack on prescriptive conceptions of socialism realism as propagated during the early anti-fascist years of reconstruction and the concomitant exclusion of all non-mimetic literary forms from the socialist realist canon. By maintaining that her brand of fantasy is in reality another form of socialist realism simply because she considers herself to be a committed socialist, she in effect makes a mockery of the attempts of the literary establishment to lay down poetic guidelines for the construction of socialist literature. Morgner's disclaimer concerning her use of fantasy is further motivated by a central paradox that continued

---

4. Wolf, *Lesen und Schreiben*, 17.
5. Le Guin, "Why are Americans afraid of Dragons," 44.

to beleaguer all forms of formal innovation in the GDR. To gain acceptance into the realist canon, a poetics of fantasy had to minimize those aspects that deviated too radically from prevailing literary norms, stressing instead the lines of continuity and convergence with the dominant aesthetic. The condition for the inclusion of works of feminist fantasy and other non-mimetic modes of writing into the realist canon was paradoxically the rhetorical erasure of their markers of textual difference, that is, precisely those formal features that distinguish fantasy as transgressive and subversive vis-à-vis dominant modes of realism. While the *gestus* of fantasy evident in Morgner's works is at once transgressive and subversive with respect to prevailing notions of reality, at the same time this transgression is one that always returns to the world of the real and to the notion that the real is a point of departure. The reasons for Morgner's strategic denial of the specific textual and ideological features that characterize her use of fantasy are to be found in part in the history of the reception of utopian and fantasy fiction in the GDR and its peculiar androcentric bias.

Socialist Realism, Fantasy, and Science Fiction

Since the formation of the German Democratic Republic as a separate republic in 1949, works of fantasy fiction epitomized the marginalized "other" of socialist realism, as did the literary innovations of modernism, expressionism, surrealism, and the avant-garde. Works that deviated too radically from Zhadanov's cultural politics of socialist realism, relentlessly enforced in the GDR in the postwar Stalinist years, were branded variously as decadent, schematist, formalistic, and subjectivistic. Reformulated by Zhadanov at the First Congress of Soviet Writers (Allunions-kongress) in Moscow in 1934, Lukács's model of classical realism was reduced to the doctrine of the positive exemplary hero of the revolution and socialist production. Thus, his argument for a critical appropriation of classical realism in a socialist literature was drowned out by the more persuasive cries from other voices calling for the working classes to become immediate heirs to the cultural heritage of German classicism. Accordingly, writers were expected to storm the heights of German classicism, appropriating the bourgeois cultural heritage for socialism and the working classes.[6] Realism thus became functionalized in the services of the ideological education and indoctrination of the working masses to the economic and political goals of the party. Literature was enlisted in the name of cultural politics in a type of "cultural planned economy"[7] that resulted, in its first two decades, in a proliferation of works set in the spheres of production, from the factory novels and literary reportages of the 1950s to the so-called "arrival novels" of the 1960s.

Until the end of the 1960s, the use of fantasy had been largely restricted to popular literature, most notably the science fiction and factory sabotage novels of the Cold War period. It was in fact not until well after the Party Congress that entire works employing science fiction and fantasy motifs such as Franz Fühmann's "Die Ohnmacht" (1974), Anna Seghers's *Sonderbare Begegnungen* (1973), Christa Wolf's "Selbstversuch: Traktat zu einem Protokoll" (1972), and Morgner's *Hochzeit in Konstantinopel* (1968) began to appear, lending credence to the use of fantasy in serious literature as a legitimate means of articulating constructive social criticism. It was therefore primarily as an estrangement effect that the use of fantasy first gained acceptance.

A significant step in the development of feminist fantasy was the gradual rehabilitation of "progressive" aspects of the German Romantic tradition during the 1970s. The discovery of the emancipatory and socially critical impulses of Romantic writers such as Jean Paul, E.T.A. Hoffmann, and Hölderlin by Christa Wolf and others provided an important impetus for the experimentation with Romantic themes and the exploration of Romantic figures.[8] The influence of such discredited modernist writers as Kafka was of further significance in encouraging East German women writers to explore the realms of fantasy. Anna Seghers's strong anti-

6. Robert Karl Mandelkow, "Die literarische und kulturpolitische Bedeutung des Erbes," in *Hansers Sozialgeschichte der deutschen Literatur: Die Literatur der DDR*, Vol. 11, ed. Hans-Jürgen Schmitt (Munich: Carl Hanser, 1983), 92–99.
7. John Milfull, "Die Literatur der DDR," in *Geschichte der deutschen Literatur vom 18. Jahrhundert bis zur Gegenwart, 1945–1980*, vol. III/2, ed. Viktor Žmegač (Königstein/Ts.: Athenäum, 1984), 594.
8. See Patricia A. Herminghouse, "Die Frau und das Phantastische in der neueren DDR-Literatur: Der Fall Irmtraud Morgner," in *Die Frau als Heldin und Autorin*, ed. Wolfgang Paulsen (Bern: Francke, 1979), 263; Herminghouse, "Die Wiederentdeckung der Romantik: Zur Funktion der Dichterfiguren in der Neueren DDR-Literatur," in *DDR-Roman und Literaturgesellschaft*, ed. Jos Hoogeveen and Gerd Labroisse (Amsterdam: Rodopi, 1981), 217–48.

Lukácsian stance on the role of realism also helped lend credence to a more Brechtian notion of realism, seen as the commitment to changing social reality though aesthetic techniques of alienation, that aim to dissect the illusory appearance of reality and reveal the socio-historical "causal nexus" beneath it. The use of fantasy as a form of Brechtian alienation that holds up a critical mirror to the fascist past and aspects of the socialist present gained currency throughout the 1970s, providing the socially critical intention was clearly constructive and the "partisanship" of the author was not in doubt.

Fantasy was construed by many writers as a form of "play" or "playfulness" in recognition of the Schillerian notion that the aesthetic realm is a domain of play. The concept of play remained, on the whole, heavily indebted to Brechtian notions of alienation, and its sole function was generally seen by male writers and critics to lie in its cognitive value. Ideally, fantasy as alienation had to engage productively with reality rather than provide a means of escape. Escapist literature had, since the founding of the GDR, been closely identified with the culture industry in the West and the resulting trivialization and commodification of art and literature under capitalism. Alienation, understood primarily in terms of creating a greater critical distance on reality, was held to make social conditions more transparent; by leading the reader away from reality into fantasy and fairytale worlds, a socialist realist use of fantasy was ultimately supposed to return the reader to the social realm with fresh insights and constructive suggestions.

In the 1960s and 1970s a number East German writers and critics emphasized the compatibility of fantasy with the ideals of socialism through a reinterpretation of fantasy as a practical-mimetic form of cognition. Fantasy and the human imagination were an "ideal force of production,"[9] it was thought, and could be harnessed to human ends and a rational and scientific world view in a productive way. Many theorists of fantasy curried favor with orthodox Marxist notions of productivity in order to prove the compatibility of an aesthetics of fantasy with Marxist notions of rationality and the "scientific-technological revolution." Since Engels proclaimed the death of all utopias in 1882 in *Socialism:*

---

9. Günther K. Lehmann, *Phantasie und künstlerische Arbeit: Betrachtungen zur poetischen Phantasie* (Berlin/GDR, Weimar: Aufbau, 1966), 6.

Utopian and Scientific (*Die Entwicklung des Sozialismus von der Utopie zur Wissenschaft*), models of future or alternative societies have been regarded within Marxism with the suspicion duly afforded all revisionist tendencies within Marxist theory. Historical materialism no longer saw any need for the earlier unscientific social utopias of the likes of Saint-Simon, Fourier, and Owen; since Marx had placed Hegel's idealist philosophy firmly back on its feet, humanity was no longer reliant on utopian ideas for change. Change was to be brought about instead through real, material transformations in the economic base of society by means of the class struggle and not through fanciful ideas of better worlds embedded in people's heads.[10]

A materialist view of history, these East German successors to Marx and Engels argued, could afford to dispense entirely with the concept of utopia because socialism itself was on the way to becoming the living incarnation of all utopias past and present. Today this seems highly ironic considering the ways in which literary utopias and dystopias have in fact anticipated many of the more unsavory aspects of twentieth-century socialist societies. For many, however, socialism meant the death of all utopias. Socialism had effectively monopolized the future; it was itself the only possible utopia and the Soviet Union its only permissible concrete realization.[11] Throughout the utopia debates in the GDR during the second half of the 1950s it was Lenin's and Engels's condemnation of utopias that set the tone for the reception of utopian literature, scoring a short-lived victory over the revisionism of Bloch's concept of "the Principle of Hope." Against the reproach of unscientificity and schematism, Bloch argued instead for the value of dreams, hopes, and wishful thinking, "the force of disciplined thinking, the salt of concrete anticipation," as a legitimate factor in the progress of a society towards socialism.[12] Despite Bloch's fall from grace in the mid-1950s, his emphasis on the present and its utopian

---

10. Frederick Engels, *Socialism: Utopian and Scientific*, trans. Edward Aveling, *Collected Works*, vol. 24 (London: Lawrence & Wishard, 1989), 306.
11. See Horst Heidtmann, *Utopisch-phantastische Literatur in der DDR: Untersuchungen zur Entwicklung eines unterhaltungsliterarischen Genres von 1945–79* (Munich: Wilhelm Fink, 1982), 138.
12. Ernst Bloch, "Naturstimme und Klarheit," in *IV Schriftstellerkongreß. Januar 1956. Protokolle*, vol. 2, ed. Deutscher Schriftstellerverband (Berlin: Aufbau, 1956), 84, quoted in Heidtmann, *Utopisch-phantastische Literatur in der DDR*, 143.

moments as forms of concrete anticipation provided a strong impetus to writers such as Morgner and Wolf in their attempts to rehabilitate notions of subjectivity and the validity of subjective hopes and ideals.

The 1960s witnessed the beginnings of a more favorable climate for the reception and production of non-realist literary forms in the discovery of the value of "scientific dreaming." The explosion in scientific knowledge and technological know-how towards the end of the reconstruction period, coupled with advances in nuclear space technology most visible in the launching of Sputnik, contributed to the myth of the wonders of the "scientific-technological revolution." Literature, in particular science fiction, was now thought to be best used to encourage faith in the miracles of technology, to inform readers of its benefits, and to encourage participation in its projects. As Alexander Stephan remarked, the postwar technological revolution acted as a kind of magic wand designed to conjure up utopian images of the future and to instill faith in socialism.[13]

The euphoria at the dawn of a new scientific age in the expansion of socialism into outer space also found expression in numerous works by established writers, most notably in Christa Wolf's *Der geteilte Himmel* (1963). But its most enthusiastic proponents were to be found among the writers of popular fiction, especially popular science fiction, who were among the first writers to popularize elements from the traditions of fantasy and utopian fiction. This popular literature was characterized chiefly by its claim to base its prognoses about the future of socialism on sound scientific evidence. "Real fantasy" or "utopian-scientific literature" became the socialist equivalent of what was marketed in Western countries as science fiction. "Real fantasy" claimed to situate its futuristic models "within the realm of known findings," never departing too far from the firm ground of well-founded scientific and technological evidence.[14] Scientific verisimilitude remained one of the author's main responsibilities if science fiction was to fulfill its epistemological function as a means of stimulating new knowledge about the universe and not become trivial trash.

13. Alexander Stephan, "Die wissenschaftlich-technische Revolution in der Literatur der DDR," *Der Deutschunterricht* 30, no. 2 (1978), 21.
14. Heidtmann, *Utopisch-phantastische Literatur in der DDR*, 145.

Socialist science fiction was entrusted with the important task of educating its readers in the central role of science and technology along the socialist road to Utopia. Socialist science fiction conceived of its mission in fundamentally different terms from its counterparts in the West. Writers of science fiction (and, increasingly, the authors of poetry and other fiction) were called upon to correct the "bourgeois decadent" bias against technological progress present in much Western science fiction and to participate in the struggle for the "true humanization" of science and technology.[15] In their works, writers were to allay readers' fears about the potentially negative effects of technology and to encourage optimism and faith in the rationality of technological progress. The relative importance given the positive portrayal of technological progress in the literature of the late 1950s and early 1960s was proportional to the supremacy of the "scientific-technological revolution" in official party rhetoric and in political discourse in the Eastern bloc at this time. In the same way that the figure of the robot became socialism's best friend, "men's companion and helper," technology too became humanity's "helper" in the quest for a socialist future.[16]

The prevailing discourses of science and technology during this period were patently androcentric in their bias, allowing little or no room for the expression of sexual difference. The literature of "real fantasy" was similarly informed by the dominant discourses of sexism, which envisioned only a subordinate place for women within the grand scheme of a technological socialist future. Women, although indirectly and implicitly the beneficiaries of the technological revolution, simply did not figure in this process as active subjects. They were in fact little more than helpers themselves in this quest, much like the robots only less reliable and less efficient, albeit if more human. In most works of popular science fiction women are featured as being little more than objects of male erotic fantasies, titillating diversions in the quest to conquer

---

15. Adolf Sckerl, *Wissenschaftlich-phantastische Literatur. Anmerkungen zu ihrem Wesen und ihrer Entwicklung, Überlegungen zum Umgang mit ihr in unserer Gesellschaft* (Berlin/GDR: Arbeitsmaterial für die literaturpropagandistische Arbeit im Kulturbund der DDR, ed. by Der Kulturbund der DDR, Präsidialrat, Zentrale Komission Literatur, 1976), 126ff.
16. Dieter Wuckel, *Science Fiction: Eine illustrierte Literaturgeschichte* (Leipzig: Edition Leipzig, 1986), 225–28.

the heavens for socialism. Occasionally women did in fact figure as protagonists but the images of femininity tended to remain confined to existing female stereotypes. In a few cases the female figures succeeded in breaking down conventional images, but these women merely reversed gender stereotypes, and female scientists or space explorers were generally portrayed in heavily masculinized terms. Furthermore, the science fiction of the 1950s and 1960s was characterized by pre-pubescent attitudes towards sexuality and eroticism that it had inherited as a legacy from the proletarian-revolutionary prose of the Weimar Republic years.[17]

Women writers who sought to correct the sexism and androcentric bias of popular literary forms found themselves challenging much more than the female stereotypes in popular representations. They sought to question many of the fundamental assumptions underpinning the techno-fetishism of the postwar period, examining the implications for women, for their sexuality, and for their forms of creativity. If the quest for a scientific socialist future was one that only envisaged a masculine subject, then the validity of the quest itself ought to be called into question as an appropriate model for women.

Eroticism, the Female Imagination, and Creativity

Morgner's novels represent some of the first novels in the GDR to raise questions about the relationship between the sexes and to lament the lack of eroticism in socialist everyday life as well as in popular visions of the future. Her early novels are a response to the prudery of much socialist literature and to the exclusive reliance on the powers of reason and rationality. She calls for an injection of eroticism into everyday life as a means of humanizing technology and its applications. Eroticism remains, she argues, the one domain where affirmative action programs have had little success. She sees eroticism as "the last male bastion" (TB. 112) and its antiquated customs and sexual practices one of the main hurdles in the liberation of women from traditional roles. The use of fantasy in Morgner's works is closely connected to the unleashing of female desire and eroticism and the stimulation of the female creative

17. See Heidtmann, *Utopisch-phantastische Literatur in der DDR*, 119–20.

imagination. The discovery of the productive and creative potential of female eroticism acts as a catalyst for releasing the female imagination and the revaluation of invisible, traditionally neglected forms of female productivity. In all of Morgner's novels from 1965 onward (including *Rumba auf einen Herbst*) the intrusion of eccentric or fantasy figures into the rational and thoroughly rationalized worlds of working women triggers off quests for subjectivity and self-realization, which are mainly actualized through the liberating act of reading other women's texts.

The encounter with the supernatural and the impossible provides the impetus for a critical review of dominant notions of productivity and reproductivity typically resulting in experimentation with alternative modes of creativity. In *Rumba auf einen Herbst* Karla conducts an imaginary conversation with two women who mysteriously appear one afternoon from the blue piano in her living room. The two women – prototypes for Laura and Beatriz in *Trobadora Beatriz*[18] – encourage Karla to confront her dissatisfaction with her marriage and give vent to her anger at the years of sacrifice forced on her by child-bearing and -minding. In *Hochzeit in Konstantinopel* Morgner presents a feminine alternative to masculinist forms of "scientific fantasy" in the "poetic fantasy" of Bele's twenty-one one-hundred-and-one-good-night-stories. The figure of Sheherezade from the Arabian Nights is used by Morgner as a powerful symbol of women's stifled creativity, who in the original version is galvanized into action by the pending threat of death. In *Hochzeit in Konstantinopel* and *Gauklerlegende* both female protagonists Bele and Wanda take refuge from the excessive empiricism of their cold, rational, and unimaginative lovers by narrating Sheherezade-like stories. In this way they attempt to rescue a creative space of their own and to ward off the deadly effects of an extreme reliance on science and reason. Female creativity is seen as marginal to mainstream scientific inquiry, and its fruits are often trivialized, neglected, or simply overlooked. Morgner vehemently rejects any suggestion that her use of fantasy is peripheral to the major concerns of society, insisting on the validity of both scientific and non-scientific modes of apprehending

18. Doris Jahnsen, "'Eingeklebt aus Ernst und Spaß und Übermut' – Der Bezug von 'Rumba auf einen Herbst' zu den späteren Romanen Irmtraud Morgners," in *Rumba auf einen Herbst*, 356.

reality. "Bele is not only a narrator of tall-stories! And there is no counterpoint in the sense of an opposition, there are two possible sides to our cognition of the world."[19] She refuses to accept the classification of feminine fantasy as the irrational opposite or trivial feminine "other" of (male) scientific fantasy, insisting on the complementarity and thus the necessary existence of both forms of cognition.

In her earlier works as well as in *Trobadora Beatriz* Morgner incorporates the concrete effects of encounters with the fantastic into the structure of the narratives through the device of a frame narrative in which a female narrator and reader of the manuscript, who is also in part a co-author of the texts, is introduced. Surprisingly, the role of this narrator is not to correct falsehoods but to reinvent the stories: "The stories were partly refabricated" (HK. 191). With the exception of *Gauklerlegende*, the novels can be read as the direct products of the unleashed creative energies of the female imagination. The texts, in this way, offer potent testimony to the emancipatory and creative potential of fantasy. Even *Gustav der Weltfahrer*, nominally about the untapped potential of the proletarian imagination, thematizes the peripheral status of female creativity and the imagination in the footnote references to the suppressed "false" fruits of the female imagination. Because, according to Morgner, official historiography has always been the history of the rulers, and the majority of the male population has been expropriated, then "the female half of humanity" has been doubly expropriated.[20] The subtext of the story about the unleashing of the proletarian imagination, which only emerges in the footnotes of the text, tells the previously untold story of the continued exploitation of the wives of working-class men – "the slaves of the slaves." The story submerged in the footnotes is the anonymous and invisible history of the "conquered," those women who cooked the "victory banquet" and fed those workers who built Thebes and the Great Wall of China in Brecht's poem "Questions of a Reading Worker."

In *Gustav der Weltfahrer* Morgner demonstrates how the glorification of the figure of the proletarian effectively marginalizes women and their specific forms of creativity and cultural

19. Morgner, "Interview mit Joachim Walther," *Weltbühne* 32 (1972): 1012.
20. Morgner, "Rede auf dem VII Schriftstellerkongreß," *Protokolle*, vol. 2, ed. Schriftstellerverband der DDR (Berlin, Weimar: Aufbau, 1974), 112.

production. Female desire has only merited a place in the footnotes of history and in the margins of Morgner's text, in the footnotes supplied by the female narrator. The tentative inclusion of questions of gender in the footnotes to the main text marks the beginnings of the foregrounding of the hidden or submerged subtext of a female "political unconscious" that emerges in Morgner's main novels after 1973. The desires and demands of the wives of those exemplary proletarian men, which are only allowed to disrupt the text through the timid intrusion of footnotes in *Gustav der Weltfahrer*, are gradually afforded more space in the social realm, intruding further in the later novels as the imaginary enclaves become more necessary to women's survival.

Subverting the Patriarchal Real

In many works by contemporary feminist authors the use of fantasy and science fiction serves as a form of cognitive estrangement by which the authors aim to reveal the intractability of the logic of patriarchy and its practices. The fantastic works to demystify the naturalness of social conventions by offering an ironic and critical examination of contemporary gender relations. At the same time, the fictional worlds of fantasy must seem sufficiently similar to existing worlds to encourage readers to see themselves in the mirror the fantasy text holds up to society. If the fictional world is either too far removed from the concerns of the world of the reader or too superior to present worlds, the effect of estrangement can frequently be compensation or wish-fulfillment rather than critical engagement with the insufficiencies of the real.[21] The result is the creation of another world that does not invite a critical reassessment of the status quo but rather indulgence in a remote and distant realm that offers instead an escape from the pressures and burdens of the real. Morgner makes frequent use of science fiction topoi as an ironic form of the inversion of reality to provoke recognition of antiquated sexual and social practices in several stories, but the fantastic impulse in her works cannot be adequately summarized by the concept of estrangement or escapism alone. Fantasy does

21. See Anne Cranny-Francis, *Feminist Fiction: Feminist Uses of Generic Fiction* (Cambridge: Polity, 1990), 78.

not merely invert or "make strange" aspects of the social world by displacing the real onto a hypothetical future or past in order to bring it more sharply into focus. Instead, it can be seen as transgressing the limits of the dominant social and political order, exposing at every turn the ideological and socially contingent nature of patriarchal social and sexual relations.

Rosemary Jackson locates the subversive potential of fantasy in its ability to interrogate unitary, monological ways of seeing by introducing confusion and uncertainty regarding the precise nature of social reality. Fantasy "subverts dominant philosophical assumptions which uphold as 'reality' a coherent, single-viewed entity."[22] Here, Jackson adapts the theses developed by Mikhail Bakhtin in his study of the novel from its origins in Menippean satire to its twentieth-century variants. For Bakhtin, the modern novel as represented in the paradigmatic works of Dostoevski is a form of dialogic discourse that challenges monologic or authoritarian discourses striving to restrict the heterogeneity of voices and opinion in the social realm. Encoded in Bakhtin's study of the genealogy of fantasy in the modern novel is of course a hidden political agenda in the indictment of the authoritarian political, cultural, and aesthetic discourses of Soviet socialism. Dialogism in the context of the Soviet Union and other Eastern bloc countries dominated by Stalinist aesthetic orthodoxy is quite clearly both a politically and aesthetically subversive activity. The orthodoxy that Bakhtin's dialogism undermines is more than a set of consensual aesthetic assumptions shared by a particular epoch or literary movement, as it becomes in Jackson's account of the interrogation of bourgeois norms: it is a politically motivated and centrally controlled form of poetic dogma that provides the main target of the dialogic form. Jackson herself is quick to point out that she is not proposing a poetics of fantasy as a form of revolutionary politics, despite stating in her concluding remarks that "[s]tructurally and semantically, the fantastic aims at dissolution of an order experienced as oppressive and insufficient."[23] If fantasy is in itself not a "socially subversive activity"[24] as Jackson argues, then its subversiveness must hinge instead on its ability to

---

22. Jackson, *Fantasy*, 48.
23. Ibid., 180.
24. Ibid., 14.

undermine dominant representations of what constitutes the "real" and to call into question dominant ideological assumptions about the nature of this order.

Although aware of the affirmative nature of much nineteenth-century fantasy, Jackson seems reluctant to consider subversion as anything more than a mere formal possibility of texts. In the final analysis, then, her remarks appear to reinforce a strict division of labor between politics and representation, history and form, thus disallowing the possibility that fantasy might constitute both an aesthetically and a politically radical act within a particular set of social and historical co-ordinates. Quite clearly, Jackson's context is limited to works of fantasy produced "in the secularized, materialistic world of modern capitalism."[25] What is lacking in her account, it would seem, is a more rigorous contextualization of fantasy as a literary genre that would allow for the possibility that fantasy may well constitute a "socially subversive" form of cultural intervention within different historical and political contexts.

Notably absent from Jackson's account, moreover, is any consideration of the ways in which the norms of the dominant order or ideological formation are inherently gendered. Her otherwise excellent overview remains remarkably blind to the possibility of feminist writing that utilizes forms of fantasy to subvert a dominant order that is perceived to be phallocentric and oppressive to women. Her focus on canonical works from French, German, Russian, and English literary traditions has prevented an examination of the ways in which feminist writers have drawn on and modified motifs and topoi from the fantasy canon to challenge phallocentric assumptions about consensus views of reality. Although aware of the different relationship men and women have to the dominant culture, she "makes little attempt to map the generic differences she detects onto gender differences."[26]

Most recent studies of fantasy, Jackson's included, rely heavily on the notion of a consensual reality that the fantastic seeks to disrupt and overturn. Most contemporary theorists seem in agreement that the fantastic can be defined as the representation of that which lies outside the parameters of normal experience in its refusal to accept prevailing definitions of the "real." Both

25. Ibid., 17.
26. Lovell, *Consuming Fiction*, 63.

Jackson and Kathryn Hume seem to agree with W.R. Irwin that "a fantasy is a story based on and controlled by an overt violation of what is generally accepted as possibility," "a transgression of that which is normally taken to be real or within the limits of the possible."[27] Fantasy, in particular much of the literature marketed in the West under the rubric "fantasy," as well as much of the science fiction published in the GDR, is, of course, far from subversive in its uncritical reproduction of the dominant ideologies of the systems in which it was produced. Nor does much of what is loosely termed "fantasy" necessarily by definition always extend the limits of the possible. In many cases, an initial transgression of the limits of the real is followed by a strict adherence to prevailing societal conventions and codes that is anything but subversive. The same can be said of feminist appropriations of fantasy. As Cranny-Francis readily acknowledges, many women writers do not explore the limits of the patriarchal real and often reproduce dominant ideologies of race, gender, and class, or alternatively, discredited essentialist notions of femininity in their works.[28]

There are, however, serious problems with definitions of fantasy that are grounded in notions of a consensus reality that the fantastic defies or confounds. A theory of the fantastic that is aware of the impact of gender on the construction of the real must challenge the very idea of a consensus reality, subjecting such supposedly gender-neutral concepts as objective reality and subjective experience to critical scrutiny. A feminist theory of fantasy needs therefore to focus on the ways in which feminist fantasy dispels the illusion of a single coherent view of reality shared by both sexes alike. It needs to stress the significance of gender in determining what constitutes normal experience and the limits of the real. The parameters of the real, of the thinkable and utterable may in fact differ radically from one sex to the other, as must, therefore, perceptions of what is real and possible.

Morgner questions the assumption that there exists a shared perception of reality common to both sexes, exposing the concept of a consensus reality as a myth perpetuated by dominant interest

---

27. W.R. Irwin, *The Game of the Impossible: A Rhetoric of Fantasy* (Illinois: University of Illinois Press, 1976), 4; Jackson, *Fantasy*, 14; Hume, *Fantasy and Mimesis*, 13–21.
28. Cranny-Francis, *Feminist Fiction*, 1.

groups in society. In all her works she thematizes the gendered nature of prevailing perceptions of empirical events and experiences in the different responses of her characters to fantastic events. Whilst the men in Morgner's novels remain on the whole oblivious to most of the supernatural occurrences in the novels, the impossible events and supernatural characters that intrude into the lives of the women are initially perceived by the women involved as violations of the social and political order. They are violations not of a universally applicable reality but of what is constructed in official and political discourses as an accurate objective representation of women's social reality. A fantastic event or character in Morgner's works must be elucidated therefore in strictly gender-specific terms. A fantastic event has on the whole no presence for the majority of male characters in the novels and can thus be defined in terms of the structural and ideological features by which it challenges official androcentric representations of women's emancipation, their history, and their experience.

A fantastic character or event thus becomes by definition something that is afforded no official or recognized place in the dominant (socialist) discourses that structure and organize women's reality in public and private life. Rephrasing Jackson's definition to include considerations of gender, fantasy can be said to exist as the "underside" of a realism that privileges masculine ways of seeing and knowing; it gives utterance to those aspects pertaining to women that are absent within the dominant political and cultural discourses. Feminist fantasy inverts prevailing distinctions between the visible and the invisible, the real and the unreal, by rendering problematic consensus views on what constitutes visibility in society. It also aims to highlight the dominant interests served by such distinctions between valid and invalid social experience and permissible and impermissible perceptions. It achieves this by challenging the accepted norms and standards of classifying empirical data, by calling into question the dominant modes of categorizing experiences into real/unreal, possible/impossible. Feminist fantasy can be said to enter into a dialogue with patriarchal assumptions and ideologies, scrutinizing their claims to truth and incorporating "that dialogue as part of its essential structure."[29]

29. Jackson, *Fantasy*, 36.

Todorov's structuralist analysis of the workings of post-Romantic fantasy also makes the hesitation between the real and unreal a central linchpin of his study of the fantastic. He reduces the structural features of fantasy to the fulfillment of three basic narrative conditions, organized around the moment of uncertainty governing the interpretation of a fantastic event. The first condition is concerned with the hesitation experienced by the reader between a rational interpretation of an unnatural occurrence (such as in the case of dreams, hallucinations, madness, or other phenomena with natural causes) and a supernatural explanation (ghosts, witches, monsters, vampires, devils). In the first case, which Todorov defines as the "uncanny," the reader resolves the uncertainty by eventually opting for a solution that leaves the laws of the rational world intact; the unnatural phenomenon is explained as being a mere illusion or a figment of the protagonist's imagination. By contrast, where the reader explains the unnatural event in terms of a supernatural cause, the text can be classified as operating in the "marvelous" mode (e.g., in fairytales and ghost stories). The "marvelous" transcends or contradicts the "laws of nature as experience has taught us to recognize them,"[30] requiring a willing suspension of disbelief. However, Todorov stipulates that only those works in which the hesitation is sustained throughout the entire length of the narrative by either the reader or one of the characters (as the second condition) can be classified as belonging to the pure fantastic. The fantastic exists therefore only at the interface of two genres, the uncanny and the marvelous, the privileged middle term of a continuum.

Todorov's introduction of the category of hesitation, with its focus on the moment of undecidability and uncertainty in the classification of an event that, according to all natural and social laws, is impossible, is a useful means of differentiating between gender-specific forms of the reception of fantastic events. For Morgner, the interpretability of unusual or unnatural events is determined primarily by the gender of the observer. Questions of gender, absent from Todorov's and Jackson's accounts, are for Morgner fundamental to the functioning of the fantastic and play a significant role in deciding the dominant mode of a segment of text. For the men in Morgner's texts the fantastic is either simply

---

30. Todorov, *The Fantastic*, 24–28.

uncanny or non-existent; if a rational explanation is not immediately on hand, the male observer goes in search of one. Thus, when Heinrich Fakal in *Amanda* witnesses what is generally thought to be the ascension of Laura as a witch, he at first obstinately resists the idea that a flying woman could be possible. As a rule, the male observer (with the exception of Heinrich) steadfastly refuses to question his belief in the rationality of the empirical world. Even Laura's father still adheres unswervingly to his belief in the predictability of the scientific age, despite first-hand empirical evidence to the contrary. Consequently, he refuses to acknowledge the existence of miracles even after his wife, Olga, has been granted a sleeping-beauty-like repose by the "lovely Melusine" for at least 259 years to await "better times for womankind" (A. 583). Not even the presence of Olga's sleeping body in his garden shed is sufficient to shake the foundations of his scientific *Weltanschauung* (A. 584).

For the women in Morgner's novels the moment of hesitation becomes a measure of the degree to which they too have become indoctrinated by rational modes of thinking. They invariably hesitate when confronted by a fantastic event or the appearance of a supernatural figure, often running through a mental checklist of all the possible natural and physical causes for the apparition before eventually accepting the supernatural as a necessary part of everyday life. When Penthesilea appears to Laura in *Trobadora Beatriz* on her way from the Eleusinian fields of Hades to the upperworld of the Round Table, Laura assumes she is a charlatan, recalling a recent newspaper report which warned of the deceptions of a female confidence-trickster. She checks her purse to see if any money is missing; only when she discovers the parcel with the title "Stories from Hades along with amazing prospects opened up by research in the area of animate matter" does she accept Penthesilea's visit as real.

Similarly, when the "lovely Melusine" appears to Laura for the first time in *Trobadora Beatriz*, Laura attributes the dragon-like figure at first to the hallucinatory effects of eating lentils as she wonders what legitimate place a sphinx could possibly have in the GDR. Only once she has confirmed the reality of the sphinx, even checking her legal status as a resident, does she finally come to accept the possibility of miracles and begrudgingly cooperates in Melusine's scheme for helping the working women of her country.

Although Laura admits that there is no place for ghosts in her philosophy of life, the appearance of Beatriz has made her open to suggestion and she readily accepts the fact that "consistency was not absolutely necessary for a philosophy of life" (TB. 181). She soon comes to realize that the supernatural has always been a necessary part of her life; after all, the miracles women perform on a daily basis are themselves sufficient proof that "witchcraft has long been integrated into our daily lives."[31]

Valeska, in the "Glad Tidings" contained in the twelfth book of *Trobadora Beatriz*, also initially passes off her transformation into a man as a momentary aberration in sensory perception caused by "caffeine hallucinations" (TB. 428). She then entertains the possibility that magic might well be at work and that she could be the victim of a "nasty trick" inflicted on her as an "act of revenge through sorcery" (TB. 428) by her lover, Rudolf, for not pandering to his misogynistic wishes. The women's hesitation is in each case fleeting; the existence of miracles as "paths of least resistance" (TB. 424) is welcomed without exception by women of all generations for whom magic and the impossible seem the only means of survival. Trained in coping effortlessly with radical changes at close quarters, Valeska even adapts with relative ease to a change of sex. By the same token, real occurrences are often perceived by women to be so unbelievable, so fantastic and grotesque, that they experience difficulty believing they are happening. Therefore, when the Chief Devil visits Laura in the guise of a television correspondent in *Amanda*, and it becomes obvious he is not part of "Laura's imagination" (A. 394), she too wonders if she is not the victim of a belated "carnival prank" (A. 421).

Where women resolve the issue of uncertainty, the text could be described as entering into the marvelous mode once the moment's hesitation has passed. The marvelous exists, however, only for the women who are willing to believe that the supernatural is possible and accept the conditions and terms of this new order. The segments of the text that are in the marvelous mode for women are often simultaneously in the uncanny mode from the point of view of the male protagonists. The text thus oscillates between the marvelous and the uncanny depending on the gender of the

---

31. ". . . was beweist, daß die Hexerei längst in unseren Alltag integriert ist." Morgner, "Interview mit Eva Kaufmann," *Weimarer Beiträge* 30 (1984): 1499.

observer. For example, when Laura is visited as a child by Frau
Holle in *Amanda*, her playmate, Gerhard, appears not to notice
anything at all unusual and remains unaware of the exchange
taking place between the two women. In the earlier novels most
male characters (with the exception of the Gustafs in *Gustav der
Weltfahrer*) are simply oblivious to supernatural occurrences.
Hubert, in *Gauklerlegende*, is blissfully ignorant of the fact that
Wanda, his lover, is sleeping with a medieval jester during a
scientific conference on game theory. He is also unaware of the
conjuring tricks Rade performs to amuse Wanda in the conference
lecture-theater during the talks on zero sum game theory. In
Trobadora Beatriz, Valeska's lover, Clemens, fails to realize that the
flesh he is eating is the product of sorcery, and Rudolf at the end of
the novel apparently does not seem to notice his wife has changed
into a man when he returns from Moscow. In *Amanda*, Tenner
likewise remains unaware of the alchemical experiments being
conducted in his kitchen or any of the supernatural feats that Vilma
and Laura perform.

At the end of *Amanda* there are signs that a radical transformation
of society is taking place, as the various witnesses to the sight of a
woman flying on a broom attempt to reach a consensus on the
interpretation of what initially seems to all present a rationally
impossible event. The majority of those who witness Laura's
"Defenestration" either deny that it happened or settle for a rational
explanation. These rational explanations are themselves a paranoid
blend of the real and the fantastic with their invocation of Cold War
rhetoric. For instance, the flying woman is thought to be a creation
of Western propaganda and is explained in terms of the on-going
ideological warfare between the two superpowers. Another equally
fanciful theory invented to account for the unidentifiable flying
woman is the suspicion that the consistency of the eyewitness
accounts is itself a result of the age-old military strategy of mass
hypnosis deployed by an enemy who will stop at nothing (A. 579).
Heinrich Fakal, although deeply troubled by the phenomenon, tries
to explain it by reference to "the category of jokes that have a
stabilizing effect on the system" disseminated occasionally by the
leading daily newspaper *Neues Deutschland*. In the meantime,
however, he secretly hopes that it turns out to be an "April Fools'
Day joke of a new kind" (A. 570). Despite all attempts to rationalize
the phenomenon of a witch on a broom, the sheer number of reports

from eyewitnesses ensures that the event cannot be ignored. Of those present, ninety-eight admit it happened and eight school pupils, seven students, and one hundred and two adults deny it. Of those who deny the occurrence only three are women.

The eyewitness accounts from those who claim to have seen a woman fall from a balcony and then disappear into thin air are nonetheless sufficient to cause concern to the People's Police, who become alarmed at the absence of a corpse. Quasi-religious or chiliastic explanations of the older generation are quickly dismissed, but the non-religious reports, particularly from the students at the Humboldt University, cause the ideologues at the University considerable consternation. Unaware of the momentous import of their testimonies, the students report "that they were pleased to have finally experienced something which could not be explained by natural laws" (A. 560–61). Any belief in the supernatural, however, is perceived by the police to be even more subversive than religious revisionism. Openness towards the supernatural is immediately suspected as a covert means of drumming up support for the dead Laura Salman, "an unknown train driver" and the fictional hero of *Trobadora Beatriz*. It is feared that the sympathies for the death of Laura Salman could be fueled by "a certain subliminal oppositional mood" (A. 561). This sympathy for the death of Laura is interpreted by the University administration as part of an international conspiracy to annex East German women writers for the purposes of Western propaganda and ideological warfare. Amanda's fall from the window is compared with the Prague Defenestration that triggered off the Thirty Years' War; Morgner thus implies the event could have far-reaching revolutionary consequences.

Instrumental Rationality and the Suppression of Feminine Fantasy

Jackson has suggested it may be possible to read fantasy as "the inverse side of reason's orthodoxy"[32] that erupts during periods of extreme reliance on the powers of reason. Yet Jackson's account does not take into consideration the ways in which a feminist

32. Jackson, *Fantasy*, 21.

poetics of fantasy might be concerned with revealing precisely how the instrumentalization of rationality has served to discriminate against women and their interests. Like many other theories of the fantastic, her investigation does not pursue the question of gender in relation to fantasy's ability to interrogate reason's hold on social reality. A feminist theory of the fantastic needs to be able to account for the ways in which gender structures the individual's relationship to rationality. Women have traditionally found themselves identified with irrationality and with reason's inverse, and have frequently been thought to possess a greater affinity with those forces reason strives to overcome. Although feminist criticism has investigated the link between masculinity and rationality, few works have applied these insights to the use of fantasy by women writers.

Morgner's poetics of fantasy clearly conceives of itself as a critique of instrumental rationality and the extreme fetishization of scientific reason in the postwar era from the point of view of those groups in society who have suffered most at the hands of "reason's orthodoxy." She is not so much concerned with revealing the rationalist world view as arbitrary, or even as masculine, but as an ideological construct that has been instrumental in marginalizing other modes of knowledge traditionally practiced by such subordinate groups in society as women. She sees the global arms race, the development of weapons of mass destruction, and the damage to the environment as all being part of the culmination of this rationalist world view.

Todorov has noted that the literature of the fantastic is "nothing but the bad conscience of this positivist era."[33] Feminist fantasy could justifiably be termed the critical conscience of an empiricist era that privileges public spaces over private, scientific forms of knowledge over practical forms, and masculine forms of cognition over feminine. Yet feminist fantasy does not necessarily pit irrationality against rationality or replace modern scientific knowledge with traditional feminine forms of cognition. Feminist fantasy is also not necessarily anti-rational; as Irène Bessière has remarked, fantasy can include an investigation of the limits of reason from a rationalist point of view without advocating a return

---

33. Todorov, *The Fantastic*, 168.

to pre-rational modes of thinking.[34] Bessière contends that the tension present at the heart of the fantastic text is not so much a result of the hesitation experienced between two possible explanations, but stems instead from the incompatibility of two opposing orders or two possible "economies."[35] She sees literature of the fantastic as characterized by a dualist and antinomical structure that sets in motion an oscillation between a supernatural and a natural "economy."[36]

The fantastic in Morgner's works springs from the incompatibility of a masculine empiricist economy with a feminine one; the irreconcilability of the two orders becomes immediately apparent when women begin to challenge the received wisdom of "reason's orthodoxy." Whilst Morgner's anxiety about the dehumanizing effects of the instrumentalization of reason is articulated in decidedly feminist terms, her concerns are in themselves not gender-specific. Her criticisms of instrumental rationality and the techno-fetishism of the space age are shared by many of her male colleagues; Heiner Müller and Peter Hacks, for instance, share many of Morgner's misgivings about the suppression of the human imagination in modern industrial societies. The interest among both East and West German writers in the progressive, critical potential of fantasy as a form of resistance to rationalism and utilitarianism rehearses many of the antibourgeois criticisms of German Romanticism and its attacks on the perversion of Enlightenment values by the rising middle classes. As such, these critiques do not imply a wholesale rejection of the tradition of Enlightenment thought but merely a repudiation of the instrumentalization of Enlightenment values as manifest in forms of utilitarianism and the narrow application of Enlightenment principles to art.

Müller identifies the main function of art as its ability to mobilize the imagination, given that "capitalist society, but basically every modern industrial society, the GDR included, is an industrial state that tends to instrumentalize the imagination, in any case to throttle

---

34. Irène Bessière, *Le Récit Fantastique: La Poétique de L'incertain* (Paris: Librairie Larousse, 1974), 59–62.
35. Ibid., 57.
36. Ibid., 32.

it."[37] Fantasy literature seeks to undo the processes of reification, which Heiner Müller sees as a defining feature of both capitalist and socialist industrialized societies. The interest in the liberating effects of myth among East German writers such as Morgner and Müller, along with such West German writers as Günter Grass, clearly stems from a common desire to salvage the aesthetic domain from the clutches of an abstract and instrumental rationality that is seen to stifle spontaneous, subjective expression. The rediscovery of the value of creatively rewriting traditional myths is interpreted by Petra Reuffer as "always a sign of sensitivity towards the crisis of self-understanding of abstract and instrumental rationality," which sees itself as transcending superstition and myth in a higher form of cognition.[38] In their recourse to myth and poetic fantasy these writers can be seen as responding to the remark made by Adorno in his "Aesthetic Theory" that art is "too deeply steeped in rationality."[39] According to Adorno, the great deception perpetrated in the name of such heirs to Enlightenment values as revolution, humanity, and socialism has been the erroneous and falsifying identification of all so-called irrational currents of thought with fascism.[40] The return to fantasy provides an important means of restoring those aspects of human activity that one-dimensional reason has repressed, excluded, or discarded.[41]

Morgner's attempts to mobilize fantasy are more specifically concerned, however, with the unleashing of poetic fantasy in the form of women's fantasies and creative imagination. A central thesis of all her novels remains the commitment to the amelioration of women's situation in industrial societies through the liberation

37. Heiner Müller, "Gespräch mit Bernard Umbrecht," in *Rotwelsch* (Berlin/BRD: Merve, 1982), 111: "Wenn man davon ausgeht, daß die kapitalistische Gesellschaft, aber im Grunde jede moderne Industriegesellschaft, auch die DDR, ein Industriestaat ist und die Tendenz hat, Phantasie zu instrumentalisieren auf jeden Fall zu drosseln."
38. "immer Anzeichen für eine Sensibilität gegenüber der Krise des Selbstverständnisses der abstrakten und instrumentellen Ratio," in Petra Reuffer, *Die unwahrscheinlichen Gewänder der anderen Wahrheit: Zur Wiederentdeckung des Wunderbaren bei Günter Grass und Irmtraud Morgner* (Essen: Die blaue Eule, 1988), 38.
39. Theodor W. Adorno, *Aesthetische Theorie, Gesammelte Schriften*, vol. 7 (Frankfurt: Suhrkamp, 1970), 487.
40. See Adorno, *Aesthetische Theorie*, 88–90 quoted in Reuffer, *Die unwahrscheinlichen Gewänder der anderen Wahrheit*, 27–30.
41. Reuffer, *Die unwahrscheinlichen Gewänder der anderen Wahrheit*, 443–44.

of the productive forces of the female imagination and sexuality. If the processes of reification and instrumentalization are to be undone in postwar European societies, she argues, the suppressed fantasies and fruits of women's imagination must be reharnessed and redirected to productive rather than destructive ends. Morgner argues for liberating a type of "practical-intellectual form of apprehending the world," something she claims has been in decline since the Scientific Revolution of the Renaissance. She postulates a practical-intellectual form of cognition as a means of correcting the prevailing forms of "scientific cognition," which she sees as having reached an impasse in the 1980s in the threat of a nuclear holocaust. The cultivation of alternative modes of knowledge, referred to by Marx as the "artistic," the religious, and the "practical-intellectual," falls then to women who historically had privileged access to these suppressed forms of knowledge (A. 353).

Morgner's criticisms of the history of the Enlightenment are indebted to the tradition of cultural critique pioneered by the Frankfurt School. She is not merely concerned with demonstrating the negative dialectic of the Enlightenment but also with revealing the domination of women and the suppression of feminine forms of knowledge as an integral part of this dialectic. The Enlightenment's vision of technical mastery over the world of nature and the power of mythical thinking must be seen as particularly problematic when nature is encoded as feminine and science and technology as masculine. Many of the fantastic devices in Morgner's works can be seen as strategies for subverting the identification of women with nature and for claiming an active role for women in the quest for the mastery of the future. She establishes links between this tendency to equate women with nature and more insidious forms of gender discrimination that continue to prevent women from achieving true equality in scientific professions, despite formal and legal guarantees of equality. While affirmative action programs facilitated women's entry into traditionally male-dominated professions in science and technology in the GDR during the postwar period, as indeed they continue to do today in most Western democracies, outmoded notions of women's inherent closeness to nature presented a massive stumbling block for women. The unresolved contradictions between women's traditional role in society and the need to enlist women in scientific and technological professions effectively stymied attempts to free women from their subordinate role in the official quest for technological mastery of the future. The quest for a scientific future remained a male-driven and -dominated enterprise, with women privileged to preside, at most, as companions and assistants, but never as autonomous historical subjects of this struggle for a better future.

Metonymical and Metaphorical Fantasy

By far the most popular form of contemporary feminist fantasy is secondary world fantasy in which writers construct an alternative world removed in space and time from their own, something that is explicitly or implicitly a displaced form of commentary on aspects of the writers' own society.[42] This form of fantasy resembles what Jonathan Culler has described as metaphorical fantasy. Metaphorical fantasy worlds are, according to Culler, ones that are "immediately recognized as different from our own but analogous to it."[43] The fantastic in Morgner's texts, however, is not confined to the extrapolation of a known world in the creation of a secondary or "metaphorical" world. Morgner's use of fantasy seems to correspond more to the type of fantasy fiction Culler terms metonymical fantasy. Defined as "a portion of our own which we have not yet encountered," a metonymical world signals a deviation from the existing world and hence the possibility of a transformation of the present one.[44] In all of Morgner's works of fantasy, the fantastic or supernatural exists in a relationship of metonymical contiguity to the real world, tangenting on the real, interfering and intervening in its events yet never totally displacing or replacing it. The law of metonymy, one which guarantees the independence of terms rather than the mutual exclusivity of terms, can be identified as the basic principle governing the relationship of the fantastic to the real in Morgner's texts.

The segments of the narrative in which the fantastic dominates introduce a heterogeneous mixture of female characters, from stock supernatural figures such as dragons and witches; mythical women

---

42. Cranny-Francis, *Feminist Fiction*, 77.
43. Jonathan Culler, "Literary Fantasy," *Cambridge Review* 23 (1973): 32.
44. Ibid.

from folklore in sphinxes and sirens; Greek Goddesses in Demeter and Persephone and Arke, the daughter of Gaia; to medieval figures such as Beatriz de Dia and the "lovely Melusine" who lead a twilight existence between the realms of fairytale, legend, and history. Although these figures are said to inhabit a mythological other world – situated somewhere "between Caerleon on the Usk and the future" (TB. 445), the mythical seat of King Arthur and his Round Table that Greek Goddesses have conquered in a victory for the matriarchy – this other world exists as a parallel world to the main narrative spaces, which are set in the GDR in the 1970s and 1980s. These other mythical worlds play a supportive role, a form of legendary and historical help for the working women of the GDR.

Like Joanna Russ's *The Female Man* and Marge Piercy's *Woman on the Edge of Time*, each of the main female characters in Morgner's works can be defined primarily in terms of their function with respect to "plot-spaces,"[45] that is, in terms of the narrative spaces they are permitted to inhabit. Each female character exists predominantly within the confines of a particular geo-political space within which she is permitted to move. The spaces Morgner's women occupy and the political and ideological frontiers they are able to cross are highly significant and display a measure of the range of utopian perspectives open to the particular women in the text. These political spaces correspond to narrative spaces or separate strands within the narrative, and stand in a complementary relationship to one another. As a "transgressor of boundaries/borders," the character of Beatriz is described as someone who can cross barriers of all kinds: she can inhabit the past, present, and the future, leap forwards in time, leap sideways in space, moving freely between Eastern and Western Europe and between communist and capitalist systems. But she is also a transgressor of the limits of ideologies, of the ideology of sexism, socialism, and feudal patriarchalism.

The narrative spaces Beatriz inhabits are primarily the spaces of the romance or the medieval courtly romance. Characterized by her mobility with respect to official limits and borders of all kinds, Beatriz represents an ideal foil to the largely housebound Laura

---

45. Jurij M. Lotman, "The Origin of Plot in the Light of Typology," *Poetics Today* 1, no. 1–2 (1979): 167.

who, for political reasons, is confined to the political and ideological spaces of the GDR. These political spaces coincide with the narrative space of the socialist Bildungsroman or the socialist realist novel whose codes determine and define the parameters of Laura's social world as well as the nature of her activities. The netherworld of Greek Goddesses and medieval legends seldom interferes in Laura's life, and yet when it does the divine intervention is always of momentous significance. As the underworld of socialist reality, the chief function of the realm of Greek myths is to lend clandestine support to Laura in her search for self-realization. The presence of this other world is vital, for only with the support of the world of myth and legend are women able to enter into history as autonomous subjects. In *Amanda*, this mythical other world has been expanded into an imaginary magic mountain, a place where utopias are forged but where the utopian potential of the present lies imprisoned. The magic mountain represents an alternative parallel world linked in a symbiotic relationship to the social world and its working women.

In modern post-Romantic fantasy, it has been argued, the desire for "otherness" of a secularized culture seeks alternative means of expression, no longer displacing otherness onto metaphysical regions such as heaven or hell.[46] Modern utopias no longer employ geographical displacement in order to project alternative worlds to the present and tend to use instead the technique of displacement in time rather than space. Alterity in Morgner's texts is expressed by means of displacement onto other geographical, political, and mythical realms: the Blocksberg of *Amanda* and the underworld of the Round Table in *Trobadora Beatriz*. All these realms are exploded out of the continuum of mythical and historical time into the socialist present. They constitute a hidden accessory to the real, a secret resource from the past for the future. In both novels of the Salman trilogy Morgner employs a device peculiar to the earlier spatial utopias of pre-Romantic times. As the world itself became more thoroughly known through navigation and colonization by the world's major imperial powers in the course of the eighteenth century, much of the mystery attached to remote and exotic settings was diminished. Deserted islands and new continents became less appropriate a setting for the creation of utopian worlds as these

46. Jackson, *Fantasy*, 19.

parts of the world became more accessible through new modes of travel. But by the middle of the twentieth century certain geographical regions of the world began to regain some of their earlier appeal. It was not only in the foundation myths of the American popular Western that the existence of impassable frontiers experienced a revival: the iron curtain and the Berlin Wall also came to represent a similar last frontier for those citizens of Eastern Europe whose movements were curtailed by the repressive travel policies of their respective socialist governments. For the majority of East Germans denied travel privileges, the Western world represented an exotic realm of myth and legends, foreign territory as yet uncolonized and uncharted. In many works written in the former GDR, the capitalist West, like the other worlds of the Blocksberg and the Persephonic Opposition in Morgner's works, functions as a repository of alterity, forming a compelling object of desire and curiosity for those confined by geo-political borders. For those denied access to overseas travel, many of whom were women, links between the barred worlds of the West and the familiar terrain of the East had to be forged through the use of intermediaries or emissaries, often male colleagues or husbands, who brought back reports upon their return to the socialist real for the less privileged citizens. Similarly, Laura is reliant on a go-between to establish contact with the mythical power of the Round Table and the Blocksberg.

Jackson has remarked upon the compensatory function of much fantasy, attributing this to the lack of faith in an increasingly secularized world.[47] Modern fantasy attempts to offer compensation for the loss of transcendental realms, yet it does so not by creating supernatural realms but by representing the natural world as one turned into something unrecognizably strange. Fantasy must, according to Jackson, not merely offer solace in compensatory other worlds but suggest the possibility of transforming the real.[48] She is dismissive of fantasy's "transcendental counterparts" to be found in the works of W.H. Auden, C.S. Lewis, and J.R.R. Tolkien, as well as in much recent "faery literature" because of its nostalgic, humanist vision.[49]

47. Ibid., 18.
48. Ibid.
49. Ibid., 2.

Cranny-Francis too is critical of feminist literature of the fantastic that "enables readers to avoid critical engagement with the real."[50] Compensation, understood as unrealistic wish fulfillment or escapist dreaming, has with few exceptions tended to provoke the scorn of feminist theorists. Critical opinion has tended to distinguish between, on the one hand, such popular fiction genres as the romance, which are thought to offer a legitimate form of escape from the drudgery of familial life, and on the other hand more socially critical forms of feminist fiction that are regarded as transformative in their impetus rather than merely compensatory. Within contemporary feminist criticism compensation is generally seen as a justifiable effect of reading women's texts only when dealing with popular literary forms that were considered in the early days of feminism to reinforce traditional gender stereotyping. Serious feminist writing, it is generally thought, ought to offer more than mere compensation or gratification.

In the case of Morgner such distinctions appear arbitrary; her use of fantasy is both compensatory and critical. The element of compensation is vital for the functioning of fantasy in Morgner's works and provides a major structuring device for the novels. The function of the mythical otherworlds in *Trobadora Beatriz* and *Amanda* is first and foremost to offer compensation for the paucity of experience in most East German women's lives. The world of myth and fantasy offers the women of the GDR access to geographical places never before experienced and to historical realms hitherto suppressed or forgotten. It regulates the exchange between women from different realms, in particular the relationship between Beatriz, the time traveler, and Laura, the sedentary East German train driver and mother of one. At the interface between the two antagonistic worlds of fact and fantasy, history and legend, East and West, realist and fantasy narratives, there occurs a crucial life-sustaining exchange. This exchange, which generally takes the form of a friendship between two women, forms the basis of a feminist challenge to phallocentric social practices and their dominant discourses. In the following chapter the function of the figure of Beatriz and the subsequent disruption her "arrival" in the GDR causes to Laura's everyday life and to the practices of socialist patriarchy will be investigated.

50. Cranny-Francis, *Feminist Fiction*, 78.

Feminine Epistemology and the Utopian Imagination

The compensatory impetus underlying Morgner's use of fantasy forms an integral part of the emancipatory and utopian function she ascribes in general to "heretic" prose, in particular to the prose of women. Christa Wolf's celebration of the revolutionary potential of prose fiction in 1968, when she proclaimed that ". . . it [literature] is revolutionary and realistic: it invites and encourages the impossible,"[51] reads as a particularly apt epithet to Morgner's works. Her Munchhausian tales of impossible and unlikely events provide comfort to women weighed down by the burdens of careers and families as well as offering encouragement to women who hope to transcend the insufficiencies of their lives via the contemplation of utopian perspectives. To create a fictional discourse in terms of miracles and the supernatural is to provide a necessary foil to the hardships of daily life, and to reactivate faith in the possibility of alternative utopias to the officially promulgated one of state socialism.

In an interview with Ekkehart Rudolph, Morgner describes the impulse propelling her use of fantasy as utopian:

> The fantastic in my works can perhaps be explained in terms of a utopian moment: it gives me a poetic opportunity of introducing the future via images into the present, into quite intangible events and phenomena.[52]

Women, she argues, are more receptive to utopias and the utopian possibilities latent in the present for the same reasons they are more receptive to the fantastic side of existence; their daily forms of improvisation and their heavy reliance on miracles to survive have meant they have been forced to develop a keener awareness of the latent utopian aspects of the present. This susceptibility to utopian thinking is not grounded in essentialist notions of sexual difference but in the material conditions of the majority of working women's

---

51. Wolf, *Lesen und Schreiben*, 48.
52. Morgner, "Interview mit Irmtraud Morgner," *Aussage zur Person: Zwölf deutsche Schriftsteller im Gespräch mit Ekkehart Rudolph* (Tübingen & Basel: Horst Erdmann Verlag, 1977), 160: "Vielleicht ist das Phantastische bei mir zu erklären aus einem utopischen Moment: Es gibt mir eine dichterische Möglichkeit, Zukunft mit Bildern in Gegenwart einzubringen, in ganz anfaßbare Ereignisse, Erscheinungen."

lives. Women's particularly bleak history has further sensitized them to the importance of clutching at straws or of chasing pipe dreams; since women's collective past seems unsuitable as a viable blueprint for the future, women's main source of hope must lie in the future: "What is of interest to them is the history of their future, that which already, at least in the GDR, extends a little into our everyday lives, but which still requires a great deal of work. And I believe for this reason women have a propensity for utopian thinking."[53] Furthermore, women have become so accustomed to accommodating other people's utopian models and to pinning their hopes on the power of utopias, that it can be argued that they in fact already live with "a real utopia." This "real utopia" is a somewhat ambiguous reminder of the utopian claims of "really existing socialism" and the fact that state socialism was a far cry from the model of utopia it purported to be. Without a utopian perspective, Morgner reasons, women "would not be able to survive the sacrifice that their emancipation requires, if they did not have this sense of the future."[54] Utopias, however distant and unreachable, provide women with an indispensable form of "life support."[55]

Obviously, in light of the many hardships women faced in the GDR, this "sense of the future" often appeared more like a form of blind faith. Women adhered doggedly to the belief that their lot would eventually improve since it clearly could not get any worse. There is, furthermore, a very real sense in which Morgner's focus on the latent utopian impulses of the present can be seen as making a virtue out of necessity. If women are to overcome the hopelessness of the "black chapters" of their past and indeed the bleakness of their present, they have, according to Morgner, little alternative but to cling to the remnants of a lost utopia in socialism's original promise of better conditions for women. She has therefore little

---

53. Morgner, "Das eine tun und das andere nicht lassen," 44: "Was für sie interessant ist, ist die Geschichte ihrer Zukunft, das, was schon, jedenfalls in der DDR, etwas in unseren Alltag ragt, was aber noch viel Arbeit verlangt. Und ich glaube, aus diesem Grunde neigen Frauen zu einer utopischen Denkungsart."

54. Morgner, "Aber die großen Veränderungen beginnen leise," *Für Dich* 21 (1978): 20: "Sie würden die Belastung, die ihre Emanzipation erfordert, gar nicht durchstehen, wenn sie nicht diese Ahnung vom Zukünftigen hätten."

55. Morgner, "Die Perlen des Phantastischen: Interview mit Klara Obermüller," *Die Weltwoche*, 30 March 1977, 35.

choice but to take her state's professed commitment to women's emancipation seriously: "I would be stupid if I did not."[56] Implicit in Morgner's appeal to the utopian possibilities inherent in women's lives is no doubt an oblique critique of the failure of socialist models of utopias to bring about better conditions for women. Yet her dogged insistence on the utopian aspects already existing in the present – no matter how invisible they may be, since "one only has to recognize them"[57] – is nevertheless disconcertingly reminiscent of the similar upright gait adopted by Bloch during the Stalinist years and his steadfast refusal to recognize the failure of his model of a concrete utopia. There must come a time when waiting ceases and the inconsequentiality of the utopian potential of the present must be weighed up against the very concrete dystopian aspects of women's everyday lives. Waiting too long can be just as detrimental as hasty overreaction.

Although Morgner would appear to harbor serious doubts as to the possibilities of realizing utopian visions of the future, she still recognizes the validity of utopian thinking as a means of highlighting social contradictions between the ideal and reality of socialist life (TB. 218). A utopian consciousness is for her one that finds itself out of step with social reality and that constantly measures the insufficiencies of the present against a utopian yardstick. Morgner is not so much concerned with postulating concrete, feminist alternatives to existing social forms as she is with using the force of utopian thinking to demystify existing social relations and to point up the inadequacies of social programs for the improvement of conditions for women. She is not concerned, as is Christa Wolf, with creating utopian models, but with utopian impulses as forms of social intervention. Utopian models very rarely have real equivalents or correspond to social reality, the "lovely Melusine" remarks to Laura, and the most effective utopian models are ones that have no concrete or existing counterparts in the real (TB. 182).

Morgner grounds her hypothesis that women have a greater affinity to the unrealized utopian possibilities of the present in the negativity of women's lived experience. "Extreme circumstances give rise to extreme utopias" (TB. 27), Laura protests in *Trobadora*

---

56. Morgner, "Weltspitze sein und sich wundern, was noch nicht ist," 98.
57. Ibid.

Beatriz. Laura describes the image of the Lady and the Unicorn in the tapestry in the Cluny Museum in Paris as "an image of longing borne out of desperation" (TB. 27). It follows therefore that women must also possess a keen sense of the dystopian aspects of their lives. The use of utopian fictional topoi is motivated by the desire to turn what is essentially a disadvantage into an advantage and takes, as does the deployment of fantasy, its cue paradoxically from the absence of utopian perspectives and tangible miracles in most women's lives. In this way she manages to avoid attributing women's greater propensity for wishful thinking to essentialist notions of women's greater capacity for imagination. The example of Laura clearly demonstrates just how easily the ability to believe in miracles can be suppressed. Openness to utopias and to the fantastic is portrayed as a skill that must be constantly cultivated and maintained; women's greater proximity to other worlds can never be taken for granted and must be repeatedly contested and recontested. As demonstrated in the case of Beatriz, the ability to perform miracles and to participate in magical experiments is also tenuous. The fate of Beatriz after her arrival in the "promised land" of the GDR provides ample evidence of the crippling effects of everyday life on the female imagination and on women's belief in the power of utopias. Yet the key to the transformative power of wishful thinking lies not in the specific trajectory of Beatriz but in the alliance formed between Laura and Beatriz and the complex web of their interrelations and exchanges.

2
Lessons in Socialist Patriarchy

The Socialist Paradise as Feminist Dystopia

As a form of estrangement, fantasy provides alternative ways of looking at gender relations and hierarchies in society; it also allows comparisons to be drawn, lines of continuity and discontinuity to be highlighted between women's past, present, and future. The most popular device in feminist fiction seems to be the intermingling of present and future time periods via the extrapolation of the present into some future society that suggests parallels to the present. Time travelers are a particularly common motif used by feminist writers to point up lost utopian possibilities as well as the dystopian aspects of the present. Less common are time travelers from the past. Feminist fiction seems less keen to remind its readers of the injustices of the past in any way that might inadvertently cast a more favorable light on what most feminist writers agree is an unsatisfactory contemporary state of affairs for women. Morgner, however, chooses to introduce a time traveler from the "black chapters" of medieval Europe for the very reason that it allows her the possibility of reading the present either way: as an improvement on the past, or as equally as oppressive to it. Through comparison with the past, certain aspects of the present may well appear to some readers as a sign of human progress towards greater enlightenment. Equally possible, however, is that the so-called "enlightened" present may reveal rather too many similarities with the dark past for comfort.

It would seem as if it were Morgner's initial intention to introduce a female medieval troubadour into the socialist present in order to stress the positive achievements of socialism in the area of gender equality. But having highlighted the laudable aims of socialist states with respect to women and by comparison with capitalist countries, the rest of the novel is given over to underscoring the immense gap between the ideal and the reality of women's emancipation. Beatriz's surprise at the discovery of a potential feminist paradise rapidly changes to dismay as the country heralded as the promised land for women is progressively transformed into a feminist dystopia. This negative reading of the present is itself a product of the device of the time traveler from the distant past. Beatriz's experiences in the GDR are continuously measured against her utopian yardstick; her naiveté and ineptness at dealing with the realities of life in East Germany reinforce the failure of "really existing socialism" to live up to her idealistic expectations. Any reading that persistently ignores the irony in the use of the term the "promised land" and that sees in the GDR the fulfillment of Beatriz's dreams, is ultimately forced to discredit the experiences of Beatriz altogether. Indeed, this is the way in which most East German critics have dealt with the problem of narrative perspective in the novel. Of course, the reader is encouraged to adopt a standpoint superior to Beatriz's. But since Laura too is the object of authorial irony, the reader is invited to adopt a vantage point superior to both Laura's and Beatriz's. This means that the reader is forced to mediate between the excessiveness of Beatriz's demands on the one hand, and Laura's timidity and pragmatism on the other.

The story of the life and adventures of the medieval troubadour Beatriz de Dia, as told by Laura Salman, train driver and single mother, comes to us via the mediating hand of the author Irmtraud Morgner who is given fictional status in the novel as both the editor and the official author of Laura's manuscript. The manuscript contains the story of Laura's experiences with Beatriz, the medieval Minnesinger, who decides to leave "the medieval world of men" (TB. 11) to await better times for women. With the help of Persephone, the Greek Goddess of the underworld, she goes to sleep for 810 years in return for 2,920 working hours per "sleep-year" to be dedicated to the cause of the "Persephonic Opposition." The Persephonic Opposition, which has held the majority on the Arthurian Round Table since 1871, has co-opted both Beatriz and the "lovely Melusine" into its plans for the return of matriarchal conditions.

Beatriz's decision to leave the medieval world was primarily motivated by the desire to escape the oppressiveness of patriarchy – "this masculine sea of egotism" (TB. 26). She longs for a country that has abolished patriarchal relations so that she may fulfill her calling as a singer of love songs – a vocation not possible under the rigid codes of the medieval "Minnesang" and the conventions of courtly love. She is helped in her quest by magic and women's mythical past. Her flight from medieval history is, however, not a rejection of history per se but of the determinism of patriarchal structures. Morgner employs the device of a time traveler not out of any disregard for history or for the historical nature of women's oppression but as a means of transcending the limitations of a particular historical period.

When Beatriz is rudely awakened from her slumber in the spring of 1968 in France by workers trying to clear away the undergrowth of the rose bushes surrounding her sleeping-beauty hide-away, she believes she has been returned to a world more sympathetic to the practicing of her profession as a troubadour. Her travels to Paris at the time of the student revolts of 1968, and her experiences with misogynistic student radicals, soon disabuse her of these illusions. Disillusionment with the radical left acts as a catalyst for her renewed search for utopian conditions for women. In many ways Beatriz embodies the archetypal second-wave feminist whose pursuit of feminist goals was triggered by collective disenchantment with the radical left of student politics in the late 1960s. Her naiveté and initial blindness towards the real plight of women in the GDR are reminiscent too of those West German feminists who, in the early 1970s, saw in the GDR a genuine incarnation of a feminist utopia.

Propelled by an unflagging optimism and a picaresque-like naiveté, Beatriz continues on her quest for ideal conditions for women. She is finally encouraged through her meeting with East German citizen Uwe Parnitzke, ex-husband of the characters Valeska and Laura, to abandon the world of capitalism and to seek her paradise in the "concrete utopia" of "really existing socialism" of the GDR. Ultimately she is impressed most not by Uwe's exemplary Marxist-Leninist rhetoric, but by the fact that a sensitive man such as Uwe could have been divorced twice: "What a great country that must be, thought Beatriz, where such men are scorned twice" (TB. 72).

Beatriz's arrival in "the promised land" of the GDR is immediately proclaimed by the narrator an "amazing home-coming. Eternally longed for" (TB. 92). But here too the discrepancy between the ideal and reality leads to further disappointments and amusing misunderstandings. Beatriz naively attributes her perturbing experiences with misogynistic East German men to her lack of familiarity with "the ideal conditions" of her newly found Heimat (TB. 100), hoping that the mystery behind the reality of relations between the sexes will soon be revealed to her. What Beatriz had hoped was a trick of perspective turns out to be a fact of life and an unalterable fact of socialism. Beatriz's true ideological arrival in the world of the GDR, or rather, her arrival in the realm of the ideological, is signaled by her decision to renounce the supernatural help of her sister-in-law the "lovely Melusine" and the "ghosts of the past," and to put her faith in the "progressive forces" (TB. 106) of history, that is, in historical materialism. Almost immediately she begins to adjust to the exigencies of socialist life.

Her first mistake is to declare her independence from her mythical past. Her second mistake is to place her trust in the future of socialism. In many respects the education process by which Beatriz's radical ideals are tempered in favor of the forces of pragmatism mirrors the development of the protagonist of the socialist "arrival novel," whose loss of false idealism is compensated for by insight gained into the necessity of putting one's faith in the forces of progress and the future of socialism.[1] Yet the "arrival" of Beatriz into the realities of the GDR must be seen as a parody of this model. Her demands for emancipation and sexual liberation reach an impasse in the novel almost from the moment Beatriz arrives in the GDR. The reconciliation of the demands of the individual and the collective that was still possible in the "arrival novels" of Christa Wolf's *Der geteilte Himmel* (1963) and Brigitte Reimann's *Ankunft im Alltag* (1961) only becomes possible in *Trobadora Beatriz* at the cost of both Beatriz's and Laura's hopes for genuine equality between the sexes.

This is most clearly illustrated at the outset of the novel in the apparent incommensurability between Beatriz's expectations and her actual experiences. Beatriz's initial hopes of producing the sort of love poetry she was prevented from writing in her previous existence as a female medieval troubadour are dashed; her odyssey comes to an end when she begins to channel her creativity into such "pragmatic inventions" as the manufacturing of love

---

1. See Dieter Schlenstedt, "Ankunft und Anspruch," *Sinn und Form* 18 (1966): 816–17.

poetry in a "verse smithy." Her invention is an example of the way in which the creative impulse becomes instrumentalized in the production of socially useful artifacts. At the same time, Beatriz's pragmatic change of direction springs from a real need in the East German population for love poetry, as illustrated by the hordes of people who queue up to buy the products of her highly successful business as they come off the production line. This absurd situation points up the extreme gulf between her demands for free sexual expression and the very limited opportunities for realizing them in the GDR in the early 1970s. Accordingly, GDR critics have concluded that Beatriz's demands are unrealistic and untenable, and that her attempts to reclaim eroticism as "the last domain of men" are ultimately doomed to fail. It would appear, however, that she fails in her mission precisely because the GDR allows very little room for the free expression of sexuality and eroticism.

The first stage in the pragmatic reorientation of Beatriz is her encounter with the pragmatic mother-to-be Laura Salman, train driver and trained Germanist. Once Laura has rescued Beatriz from the circus where she and the "lovely Melusine" have been performing tricks to earn a living, Beatriz attempts to co-opt Laura as her minstrel. Laura has no conception of what Beatriz could mean by the term and immediately thinks in pragmatic terms of baby-sitting and other household duties. She reminds Beatriz that she already has a job and, moreover, that train driving is not just her work but her profession. Although suspicious of Beatriz's idea of a modern equivalent to the medieval minstrel, Laura seems to agree that cooperation between the two women can be productive for both. Laura discovers that Beatriz is lacking in pragmatism and, to this end, delivers her first lesson in the stark realities of relations between the sexes in the GDR.

Beatriz's reaction to the cautionary tale, "Topsy-Turvy Coffee" is to lock herself in the bathroom, a clear signal that she was indeed misguided in her expectations of East German society. The story Laura invents is an empowerment fantasy that constitutes an inversion of stereotyped sex roles. The role of the sexual aggressor is played by a heterosexual woman and worker, and the reluctant, timid victim of her unsolicited attempts at seduction is the male comrade. The inversion serves to highlight the glaring lack of equality between the sexes at the level of personal and sexual relations. It thus identifies one of the major obstacles to the realization of the goals of Beatriz's quest in the antiquated patriarchal sexual and social practices of the GDR. If women are still primarily the passive objects of male desire, as Laura's story seems to imply, the profession of a female troubadour, which presupposes an active subject of desire, still seems a utopian one. And a passive troubadour, Beatriz argues, is a paradox: "an object that sings the praises of a subject is logically inconceivable. Paradoxical" (TB. 112). Beatriz realizes that she may have awakened too soon and considers going back to sleep for a further 800 years. Laura, a champion of Realpolitik and highly skilled in improvising, nevertheless persuades Beatriz to participate in a collective plan to bring about the appropriate conditions under which a female troubadour might still be possible.

As Laura's story has made only too obvious, the first step in the historical "subject-becoming" of women must be the reclaiming of eroticism as the last bastion of male supremacy. This is expressed in terms of the reappropriation of women's nature. Beatriz's departure from the medieval world precipitates a process of enlightenment in which women attempt to gain control over the forces of nature in reclaiming themselves and their own "natures." Beatriz declares her first priority is to "appropriate nature. First of all my own." (TB. 113). Although expressed in analogous terms to the appropriation of nature and the forces of production by the working classes, Morgner's uses the term nature to refer more specifically to female sexuality. Morgner implies that the work of repossessing the world of eroticism is not an individualistic solution to the problems of sexual inequality; it is a project designed to ameliorate the situation of women in general, something that can only be achieved through the collective efforts of women.

Laura's first strategy is to utilize Beatriz's historically proven skills as a troubadour. To do this she must reactivate Beatriz's "inventive genius" and her talents as a writer of love poetry. To this end Laura arranges readings for Beatriz in various factories, eventually forcing Beatriz to abandon production of her strangely mechanical and unerotic love poetry in her "verse smithy" and to produce real stories of her own. But Laura must write the first of the stories that Beatriz is commissioned to tell because Beatriz seems incapable of delivering a story by the agreed date. The parodic element of her activities, which resemble the duties performed by writers during the 1960s, becomes apparent from the inappropriate content of the love story that she tells to the "thirteen male and seven female co-workers of the Berlin Tramways" (TB. 125).

The story tells of a pair of lovers who undertake a trip to heaven and finally to hell in search of a utopian space where they can satisfy their uncompromising thirst for eroticism and love. Although the agitatory intention of the story appears to be little understood by the workers, this first story is clearly conceived as an operative piece to raise awareness among the working population of the lack of eroticism in the world of everyday socialist life. The highly unconventional love story, which contains explicit erotic descriptions of masculine sexuality, serves as a form of agit-prop literature aimed not at increasing workers' political consciousness but at raising awareness of the limitations imposed on the free expression of female desire and sexuality. In this way, the aims of the Bitterfeld campaign are harnessed to the ends of a type of feminist "consciousness-raising." Whereas workers were encouraged to write their own accounts of life in the work place in the form of diaries and reports, Beatriz's intention is to reawaken the workers' stifled eroticism and rekindle their thirst for passion. The story functions in a covert way as a form of feminist consciousness-raising, and Beatriz herself serves as a creative catalyst for both Laura and the other women of the brigades who hear her story.

In the West much of the consciousness-raising work performed by women's groups and feminist literature in the 1970s concentrated on revealing women's status as objects of masculine desire and victims of male power; a critique of women's role as sexual objects frequently took the form of an unconditional rejection of heterosexuality and an affirmation of lesbian sexuality. By contrast, the type of consciousness-raising conducted by Laura and Beatriz does not entail a wholesale rejection of heterosexual eroticism; instead they propose liberating women from their position as passive objects by encouraging female eroticism within heterosexuality. Given the extreme prudery of socialist Germany, with its taboos on sexuality in both the literature and the media, the affirmation of an active female desire, even within heterosexuality, fulfills much the same function as feminist consciousness-raising in the West. However, a crucial step in this process is also to raise awareness of women's status in GDR society as objects of masculine desire and objects of exchange.

Women as Objects of Exchange

To reactivate Beatriz's powers as a love poet Laura decides to arrange a brief love affair with an ex-lover of her own, Lutz Pakulat. This act of exchange, to be discussed in more detail later, has the desired effect and sets into motion Beatriz's creative powers. The first of Beatriz's pieces of creative writing is the product of memory-work from her medieval past. The second of these is particularly significant and warrants special attention. The second story Beatriz tells Laura concerns a medieval aristocratic woman, Marie of Montpellier. The story, described as "not invented," purports, like the first invented story told by Beatriz, to tell the truth about women's status as objects of exchange within patriarchal societies. Although it is only one and a half pages long, the story is central to Morgner's analysis of the status of women in patriarchal societies. Through a comparison with pre-capitalist feudal Europe and the status of women in aristocratic circles, Morgner raises important questions about the gender blindness of traditional Marxist notions of exploitation and property relations. Like many socialist-feminists in the West she questions the Marxist orthodoxy that ties the oppression of women unilaterally to the rise of property relations, indicating the need to conceive of patriarchal relations as broad, all-encompassing structures of domination.

The story Beatriz narrates to Laura tells how Marie of Montpellier is first married at the age of eleven to the Viscount of Marseilles, whereupon she is forced to pass her inheritance rights to her father's property on to her stepmother's children. The marriage contract is sealed between her father and her husband and the deal is presumably clinched with the aid of a dowry and Marie's virginity as an added bonus.[2] On the death of her husband, Marie finds herself without a master at the age of fifteen. At this

---

2. See Luce Irigaray, *Speculum of the Other Woman*, trans. Gillian C. Gill (Ithaca: Cornell University Press, 1985), 122.

point she momentarily comes into possession of his property, but only to convey it back to her original owner, her father. Because, as Cixous remarks, "everything must return to the masculine,"[3] Marie returns back to her rightful owner together with her accumulated property once the property transaction is completed. As the emissary of her father sent out to accumulate capital in his name, Marie becomes herself a capital investment; when she returns home after successfully completing this task, she delivers up the interest and is sent off once again on a further investment mission.

The pattern of exchange repeats itself a second time. Marie is dispossessed by her father and stepmother and is forced once more to circulate between husband and father. This time the father is aiming at higher returns and invests his "capital" with the Count of Comminges, although the count himself already has two other wives. Marie's instrumentality within feudal aristocratic society is emphasized by the use of the passive mode:

> Her riches are taken off her and she is married anew to the Count of Comminges who was married at the time to two other women, which was no cause for embarrassment in those days and was not censured by the church, if one belonged, as did the Count of Comminges, to the persecutors of the Albigenser. (TB. 139)[4]

As the third wife of the Count of Comminges, it would appear Marie can only keep her exchange value if she bears her husband male heirs. After bearing him only two daughters, she fails in both her father's and her husband's expectations of her because she has not produced male heirs to her husband's estate. She has failed in her mission to secure male ownership of property by reproducing heirs for her husband's capital, as well as failing to convey property back to her father. Her father's investment strategy has been unsuccessful with the consequence that Marie forfeits her exchangeability as a commodity and hence her

---

3. cf. Hélène Cixous, "Castration and Decapitation?" *Signs* 7, no. 1 (Autumn 1981).
4. "Man nimmt ihr die Schätze ab und verheiratet sie aufs neue an den Grafen von Comminges, der zur Zeit noch mit zwei anderen Frauen verheiratet war, was damals nicht genierte und auch von der Kirche nicht gerügt wurde, wenn man, wie der Graf von Comminges, zu den Verfolgern der Albigenser gehörte."

desirability to both men. However, once divested of her "exchange value," she still "possesses," as does every true Marxist commodity, "use value."[5] Depleted of all exchange value, she is then forced to circulate ever increasingly between her father and husbands, no longer as an object of exchange or even as a means of exchanging property, but as an object of physical and sexual abuse:

> Marie bore [the Count of Comminges] two daughters, but was treated cruelly by him, which is why she returned home. There her suffering proved so great that she forgot her sorrows in the house of the Count of Comminges and went back to him. But once again she was so terribly tormented there that she was forced to flee a second time. (TB. 139)[6]

The act of returning home to the father is thus repeated a second time. He too recognizes her worthlessness as currency or as an object of exchange, given she has failed in her mission to accumulate capital. She had been unable to circulate capital or to secure – through male heirs to her husband's property – her father's ultimate claim to the count's wealth. The father also recognizes that Marie's sole value now lies in her use value and her treatment at her father's hands is even crueler than at the hands of her previous husband. However, even as an object of abuse she still has limited exchange value and is forced to circulate back and forth between her husband and her father until eventually her father dies and she comes into the rightful possession of her father's property.

The pattern of expropriation is repeated twice, but with the important difference that the second time Marie is the object of sexual expropriation. The violation of Marie's body is represented as the logical consequence of her loss of value on the feudal

5. See Karl Marx, *Capital*, vol. 1, trans. Samuel Moore and Edwards Aveling, ed. by Frederick Engels (Moscow: Progress Publishers, 1954), 43–54. Luce Irigaray, "When the Goods Get Together," in *New French Feminisms*, ed. Elaine Marks and Isabelle de Courtivron (New York: Schocken Books, 1980), 105.
6. "Marie gebar [dem Grafen von Comminges] zwei Töchter, wurde aber von ihm grausam behandelt, weshalb sie heimkehrte. Dort waren ihre Leiden aber so groß, daß sie jene im Haus des Grafen von Comminges vergaß und wieder zu ihm zurückging. Aber aufs neue fürchterlich geplagt, sah sie sich gezwungen, ein zweites Mal zu fliehen."

"exchange market" and her failure to participate in the exchange of capital. No longer the receptacle for the transference of male capital, she now becomes the receptacle for male desire. Displaced from her position within the monogamous family as bearer of male heirs, she is forced to occupy the place of the woman at the other end of Engels's feminine spectrum, that of the prostitute. For Engels, the prostitute was the "necessary correlate" to the wife in monogamy, the logical other half of the opposition prostitute/ housewife-slave.[7] Marie, in failing to conform to her role within the patriarchal family as the bearer of male heirs, is then forced to take the place of the prostitute as the recipient of male desire. As a "reproducer" of male desire, she is forced to circulate within the male "libidinal economy." The transactions do not, however, end with the expulsion of Marie as "prostitute" from inside the parameters of the family. Instead, the narrative takes an unexpected turn when her father dies and she becomes the legal heir to his capital:

> Fortunately her father William died just at this time. And since his marriage to Agnes was not recognized by the Pope because his first wife was still alive, Marie of Montpellier came into her inheritance rights. Which was why the King of Aragon Peter II married her. (TB. 139)[8]

Marie is unable to usurp her father's place or partake of his political and economic power. The place of her father is eventually filled by the King of Aragon, Peter II, who appropriates the entire fruits of her life-long labor. Marie, it would seem, can only represent the father until his place is filled by a substitute father. As Catherine Clément reminds us: "women must circulate, not put into circulation."[9]

But it is here that the system of exchange of women between

---

7. Frederick Engels, *The Origin of the Family, Private Property and the State, Collected Works*, vol. 26 (London: Lawrence & Wisahrd, 1990), 174.
8. "Zum Glück starb ihr Vater Wilhelm gerade in dieser Zeit. Und da seine Heirat mit Agnes, weil seine erste Frau noch am Leben war, vom Papst nicht anerkannt wurde, trat Marie von Montpellier in ihre Erbschaftsrechte. Weshalb sie der König von Aragonien Peter II heiratete."
9. Clément, "The Guilty One," in *The Newly Born Woman*, by Hélène Cixous and Catherine Clément, trans. Betsy Wing, introd. Sandra M. Gilbert (Minneapolis: University of Minnesota Press, 1986), 53.

men breaks down when the King, having decided to marry Marie, refuses to consummate the marriage. The reason given is that his attentions have been captured by the more beautiful and younger Countess Mireval:

> The wedding was celebrated in Montpellier. As night drew near the King refused to consummate the marriage. To the great embarrassment of the guests and the deep pain of the bride. No-one could explain the refusal of the good, young King who was always composing verse and was so chivalrous, because the bride was not ugly. But the young coquettish Countess Mireval, who was present at the wedding, was more beautiful. (TB. 139)[10]

It is not immediately clear why the circulation breaks down and Morgner gives no further reasons why. One plausible explanation would be that the object of exchange, once depleted of its exchange value, eventually becomes depleted of its "ab-use" value as well. Once Marie, as a commodity, ceases to fulfill either of the dual functions Marx ascribes to the commodity, she becomes redundant, reduced to the status of Gustaf the Garbage-Tip Driver's "garbage" in *Gustav der Weltfahrer*: a commodity devoid of function and value. What remains is therefore the mere outer casing or phantasmagoric form of the body of the commodity, which is the specific form the commodity assumes once it has become an object of exchange.[11]

The reason given in the story for the King's rejection of Marie as a legal wife is the greater sexual attractiveness of the Countess Mireval. The rejection of the sexuality of the legal wife amounts to the expulsion of eroticism and sexuality from the site of the legality of the family to outside its boundaries. Marie cannot fulfill both functions of each term of the binary opposition wife/mistress, that is, she cannot simultaneously occupy the place of mistress with respect to her lover's desire and still be mistress of his property. Thus, despite an unwitting consummation of the

10. "In Montpellier wurde die Hochzeit gefeiert. Als die Nacht herankam, weigerte sich der König, die Ehe zu "akkomplieren." Große Verlegenheit der Gäste, tiefer Schmerz der Braut. Niemand weiß sich die Weigerung des guten, jungen, Verse machenden und immer galanten Königs zu erklären, denn häßlich war die Braut nicht. Aber schöner war die junge, kokette Gräfin Mireval, die der Hochzeit als Gast beiwohnte."

11. Marx, *Capital*, 77.

marriage and the outwardly happy unification of both territories, the King continues to display little interest in his new wife:

> Aragon and Montpellier are united by common law, and the dynastic power increases. Admittedly King Peter is now even more irritable towards the Queen. He withdraws from her more resolutely and abandons her to a lonely life in the Castle Mireval. (TB. 139)[12]

The King cannot be persuaded to continue the marriage and files for divorce, although he now has no legitimate case for doing so. To prevent the divorce, Marie turns to the Pope whereupon she mysteriously dies from poisoning: "Marie of Montpellier went to Rome to complain to the Pope and to prevent the divorce. There she died. Of poisoning" (TB. 140). Marie's act of appealing to the rival authority of the church clearly represents a challenge to the authority of the King and to the hegemony of the state and its attempts to establish absolute authority over the church. It is this challenge that would appear to necessitate Marie's death.

The story, although short, raises a number of pertinent questions about Morgner's view of history and her interpretation of Marxist dogma. Morgner's concern with the status of aristocratic women is of interest for three reasons. First, the story of the fate of Marie of Montpellier is one of the first examples in the novel of a failed narrative of self-realization. In its position in the novel, it serves as a warning to women who refuse to participate as objects of exchange within patriarchal societies. As the product of "memory-work" by Beatriz and an example from Beatriz's own experiences as a medieval troubadour, it operates on one level as a reminder of women's long and varied history of oppression and exploitation. Exploded out of the continuum of history in a Benjaminian moment of crisis, the story seeks to point up similarities between the experiences of medieval women and women's treatment in the present. Because it directly precedes an attempt to invert the habitual "economy of sexual exchange" between the sexes, it also serves as a type of cautionary tale to female querulants or dissidents.

---

12. "Aragon und Montpellier sind völkerrechtlich vereinigt, und die Hausmacht mehrt sich. Allerdings ist König Peter jetzt noch gereizter gegen die Königin. Er wendet sich noch entschiedener von ihr ab und überläßt sie einem einsamen Leben im Schlosse Mireval."

Second, the story demonstrates the urgent need for the recognition of sexual exploitation as a determining factor in the history of women's subordination and hence in the continued discrimination of women in the GDR. The story raises the taboo subject of sexual abuse and, in a very displaced form, the question of domestic violence. By focusing on aristocratic women in feudal society, Morgner is also attempting to correct the bias in Marxist and feminist theory towards analyses of the role of bourgeois women in capitalist societies. Finally, the story Beatriz tells suggests the need for a feminist critique of some of the canonical socialist theories of the origins of women's oppression. Morgner's rereading of classical Marxist accounts of the history of patriarchal systems and the nexus between private property and the exploitation of women bears many similarities to the work of Western socialist-feminists as well as to the psychoanalytic critiques of Marxist theory by the French feminists Hélène Cixous, Catherine Clément, and Luce Irigaray. Their post-Freudian analysis of the construction of gender relations in their investigation of the workings of "phallocentrism" is similarly concerned with revealing the inadequacies of an orthodox Marxist position on the "woman question." Although Morgner's story does not discuss women's status in the feudal economy explicitly in these terms, her story contains an unmistakable critique of traditional Marxist concepts of exploitation and property relations, something best elucidated with the help of recent French feminist work that draws on both the insights of Marxism and psychoanalysis.

In raising the crucial question of the interrelationship between patriarchy and private property, the story seems to challenge the thesis advanced by Engels in *The Origin of the Family, Private Property and the State* (1884) that male supremacy is the sole result of the rise of private property and the economic superiority of men. According to Engels's analysis, the abolition of private property and the capitalist mode of production should necessarily bring about the end of monogamy and the economic exploitation of women: "The predominance of the man in marriage is simply a consequence of his economic predominance and will vanish automatically with it."[13] Beatriz's story implies a critique of the economic determinism of Engels's theory of the oppression of

13. Engels, *The Origin of the Family, Private Property and the State*, 189.

women. It achieves this by presenting property relations as more general social structures governing not only economic relations but psychic and sexual relations as well. On the one hand, the depiction of women as objects or commodities of exchange would appear to correspond to Engels's argument that women's status in the family is determined by the dominant set of property relations at a particular historical moment. On the other hand, the text seems to offer sufficient evidence to support the theory that women's status as objects of exchange cannot be entirely explained by the capitalist mode of production, and that women also function as sexual objects of exchange in what Irigaray and Cixous term "a masculine economy of desire."[14]

At first glance the story of Marie reads as an illustration of Engels's thesis that women have been little more than house-slaves since the emergence of private property. Although Engels's primary concern was the bourgeois nuclear family, Morgner has chosen to set her story in the Middle Ages rather than in the nineteenth century. The story would seem to bear out the view that women's principal function in the family under the capitalist mode of production is to further the preservation and inheritance of private property. Engels contends furthermore that the modern nuclear family contains in embryonic form the structures of slavery and serfdom.[15] In locating the exploitative practices of serfdom and slavery between individual members of the family, in this case the bourgeois family, Engels is opening up the way for a more differentiated analysis of power relations along gender lines. However, he fails to draw any parallels between women's status in the bourgeois family and the principle of commodity exchange in the capitalist mode of production, although he does remark that relationships between people in a capitalist economy can display features characteristic of commodity exchange when people and their relationships become reified.[16]

Irigaray and Cixous have analyzed woman's commodity status in symbolic systems of exchange within a psychoanalytical

14. See Cixous, "Castration or Decapitation?" 41–54; and Irigaray, "Women's Exile," *Ideology and Consciousness* no. 1 (1977): 62–76; Monique Plaza, "'Phallomorphic Power' and the Psychology of 'Woman,'" *Ideology and Consciousness* no. 4 (1978): 36.
15. Engels, *The Origin of the Family, Private Property and the State*, 166.
16. Ibid., 274.

framework. Their thesis is that women act as "commodities exchanged between men or groups of men" and that "it is their silence, their silent bodies – but yet productive – which regulates the smooth exchange between men and the social mechanism in general."[17] Irigaray's and Cixous's psychoanalytical approach to the question of female identity and the functioning of female sexuality within a "masculine economy" or a "phallocentric" order challenges Lévi-Strauss's identification of the basic structuring principle regulating social and cultural relations as the exchange of women as goods between men. According to Lévi-Strauss, women act in patrilinear societies as one of many objects of exchange, as a "sign" or a generator of signs in a system of communication primarily conducted between men. Women may serve occasionally as a partner but never as the subject of an exchange.[18] Paraphrasing Lévi-Strauss, Irigaray writes: "The trade that organizes patriarchal societies takes place exclusively among men. Women, signs, goods, currency, all pass from one man to another . . . ."[19] The economy and trade to which Irigaray is referring are not purely social structures but psychic structures, formed through interaction with the "socio-cultural order" or what Lacan has termed the symbolic order of language.[20] The symbolic order and society in general are, according to Irigaray, founded on the exploitation of women's bodies, an exploitation that acts as a form of exchange between men.[21] Accordingly, women never gain access to the symbolic order and are never paid for their task.[22]

Because "woman" has always occupied the place of the "other" in Western metaphysics, she has, according to Irigaray, always been reduced to a specular image of man in a system of representation that can only conceive of the other in terms of the same, that is, as repetition, reflection, or reproduction. She becomes

17. Irigaray, "Women's Exile," 72.
18. Claude Lévi-Strauss, *The Elementary Structures of Kinship*, trans. James Harle Bell, John Richard von Sturmer, ed. Rodney Needham, rev. ed. (London: Eyre & Spottiswoode, 1969), 496.
19. Irigaray, "When the Goods Get Together," 107.
20. See Annette Kuhn, "Structures of Patriarchy and Capital in the Family," in *Feminism and Materialism: Women and Modes of Production*, ed. Annette Kuhn and AnneMarie Wolpe (London: Routledge & Kegan Paul, 1978), 60.
21. See Irigaray, *Speculum of the Other Woman*, 26ff.
22. Irigaray, "Women's Exile," 72.

an object of exchange in a masculine "economy" of representation that requires the woman to reflect the male, in effect to circulate around the center of the male self:

> ... the desire for the same, for the self-identical, the self (as) same, and again of the similar, the alter ego and, to put it in a nutshell, the desire for the auto ... the homo ... the male, dominates the representational economy.[23]

As a commodity, woman is positioned at the center of the economy of exchange but is always excluded from the practice of exchange itself.

Although the narrator in Morgner's story makes no explicit reference to the act of exchange of women among men, the mechanisms of commodity exchange are all too clear to the reader familiar with the passage from *Capital*, where Marx, in a footnote, draws parallels between the formation of the human subject and the constitution of the exchange value of commodities.[24] Morgner's story can be read as a fictionalized account of Irigaray's and Cixous's critique of the gender blindness of Marx's analysis of the mechanisms of commodity exchange within a capitalist economy. It also raises the question of women's status as commodities in order to highlight the insufficiencies of a purely economic approach to the question of women's oppression.

As the representative of her father, Marie can never inherit her husband's or her father's wealth herself; she can only facilitate the transference of property among men of the same class. She can only perpetually redirect, convey, reproduce this property, and she is repeatedly divested of the products of this labor. Irigaray's description of women's role in the economy of "phallocentrism" reads as a particularly fitting description of Marie's function within aristocratic circles. Woman, for Irigaray, is that "matrix – womb, earth, factory, bank – to which the seed capital is entrusted so that it may germinate, produce, grow fruitful, without woman being able to lay claim to either capital or interest since she has only submitted 'passively' to reproduction."[25] Marie is never the active agent of her marriages; she is always the representative of her

---

23. Irigaray, *Speculum of the Other Woman*, 26.
24. Marx, *Capital*, 59.
25. Irigaray, *Speculum of the Other Woman*, 18.

father, "re-presenting" the Father in a system of economic management in which "woman exists only as the possibility of mediation, transaction, transition, transference – between man and his fellow-creatures, indeed between man and himself."[26]

Marie's attempt to usurp the place of her real father by claiming her rights to his inheritance can be read as a threat to law and order as well as a disruption to the whole of the symbolic order. If Marie were reduced entirely to the status of a commodity, it is not immediately apparent why the King should refuse to consummate the marriage. And yet by refusing to consummate the marriage, the King is exercising his patriarchal right over her property and herself as property. Marie is not merely the site of an investment of male desire for the purposes of producing an heir for his capital; her social status, even as rightful heir to her father's estate, is dependent on the readiness or unwillingness, as the case may be, of a male master to appropriate her as sexual object. Such an appropriation of the female body cannot, however, be simply reduced to a function of capital accumulation. By the same token, the rejection of female sexuality is neither compatible with, nor even the result of, a refusal to merge the King's wealth with hers.

Engels's account of the role of women in the capitalist mode of production as a means of ensuring the transference of capital from one male to another seems insufficient to explain why the King could not be brought to form such an advantageous alliance with Marie. The analysis of property relations within the family needs to be complemented by an understanding of the functioning of female sexuality with relation to the masculine libido and the position of woman within the masculine "economy of meaning" or the production of sexual difference. Woman has no function outside this economy and once she no longer serves the purpose of "the repetition – representation – reproduction of sameness," that is, of the masculine, and starts to represent herself, she presents a danger to the smooth exchange between men and, as Irigaray argues and Morgner's story illustrates, she must be removed from circulation.[27]

The medieval aristocratic woman was not only dependent on a man to appropriate her deceased husband's or father's property,

26. Irigaray, "When the Goods Get Together," 108.
27. Irigaray, *Speculum of the Other Woman*, 43.

as the case may be, in order to secure for herself a place in feudal society. She also had to market her sexual favors in order to legalize her social status in marriage. Without this appropriation of female sexuality within marriage, even women of the propertied classes were doomed to remain powerless and propertyless. Just as feudal aristocratic men had the right to dispossess women of the same class of their property, by the same token, the males also had the right to reject women, to devalue women's currency, thereby limiting women's purchase of legal, social, and economic rights. The repression of female sexuality within the borders of the monogamous and polygamous family prevents woman's entry into a social system that effectively diminishes her chances of gaining equal rights to the products of her sexual favors in her amassed wealth. The exhaustion of her exchange value, although due to a failure to circulate capital, is also inseparable from the finiteness of her use value as a sexual object. Although Marie still retains her beauty, the mystery of her sexuality has already been disclosed and the elusive Countess clearly represents new terrain to be conquered in contrast to the well-charted territory of the recycled wife. The depletion of Marie's use value eventually leads to a blockage in the economy based on the exchange of women. A commodity that has no exchange nor use value and therefore no purchase for either owner or receiver, producer or consumer has no function within the economy of endogamous or exogamous exchange and, thus, must eventually be taken out of circulation before it can be allowed to block the free exchange of women among men.

Marie's subordination is indeed largely the result of the need to find a master for her material goods, yet the King's refusal to appropriate her bodily goods obviously runs counter to the aims of capital accumulation evident earlier in the narrative. Women not only serve as exchange values, they must also produce and reproduce use values, as well as produce and reproduce themselves as use values as part of the "natural" sexual division of labor.[28] Woman herself is, according to Irigaray, "held in receivership as a certified means of (re)production."[29] This involves the production of use values for the maintenance of men

---

28. Cf. Engels, *The Origin of the Family, Private Property and the State*, 173ff.
29. Irigaray, *Speculum of the Other Woman*, 18.

– for which women are primarily responsible – and for men's property, which entails the reproduction of male heirs. But this activity also involves the reproduction of male desire. If woman fails to reproduce herself for the male and reflect his desire, then her production of other use values and even her more direct forms of contribution to the accumulation of capital are to little avail. Thus, although the King's motive for sealing the marriage contract was to consolidate his power through a valuable extension to his kingdom, Marie is prevented from remaining the King's legal wife and the inheritor of his wealth through the active rejection of her sexuality on the part of the King. This occurs despite the stated marketability of Marie as an object of desire, since we are told: "the bride was not ugly" (TB. 139).

Engels's notion that monogamy is a function of private property and that sexual oppression will consequently disappear with the abolition of private property was modeled on the bourgeois family and an idealized image of the proletarian family. His conception of the proletarian family as an exemplary site of equality between the sexes bore in fact little resemblance to the reality of his time and to twentieth-century socialist societies where the dictatorship of the proletariat was installed for most of the century. Underlying his analysis of family relations is the assumption that the capitalist mode of production is the sole point of intersection between patriarchal and property relations; his theory thus implies an historical conjuncture between the two sets of relations. Western socialist feminists have argued that it may be useful to see patriarchy as having a relative degree of autonomy with regard to the particular mode of production of a society.[30] Morgner's choice of pre-capitalist feudal society, where the family would seem to be already the site of property relations, raises the question of the possibility of property relations existing within the family both prior to the emergence of fully-fledged capitalism and after its supposed demise with the formation of socialist states such as the GDR. Morgner shares the aims of socialist feminists in the West who attempt to establish patriarchal relations as being somehow independent from class and property relations. But whereas most socialist feminist work has argued that the two sets of power relations have separate but parallel trajectories, Morgner's story

30. See Kuhn, "Structures of Patriarchy," 50.

seems to imply that patriarchy is very much the overarching term in the equation.

If we choose to read the story of Marie not so much as an illustration of feudal gender relations but as an oblique commentary on the gender blindness inherent in Marx's and Engels's analysis of the transition from feudal to capitalist society, we can in fact regard Marie as a rather grotesque representation of gender relations in twentieth-century socialist and capitalist societies. Women are, according to Morgner, the slaves of the twentieth century, compelled to sell themselves as commodities in an economy of exchange that operates around not the exchange of capital but the exchange of women. By implication, women in the twentieth century are like Marie after the death of her father: a woman without a master and a commodity without an owner. Even in the absence of a father or a substitute, women are, as Marie is, never entitled to possess the products of their labor and "own" themselves as property. They cannot, according to Marxist theory, throw off the yoke of feudalism.

The slave only becomes a "free" worker, according to Marx, when she makes the transition from commodity to owner of a commodity, that is, when she can sell her commodities rather than selling herself as commodity. The essential difference between slaves and free workers is that workers who no longer toil under the yoke of capitalism can sell the products of their labor as free agents rather than sell themselves as the embodiment of their labor power.[31] And yet, even as "free" workers East German women are not entirely free of those mechanisms of commodity exchange experienced by Marie under feudalism. Marie does in fact challenge male rights of ownership simply by being without a father or husband. She also threatens exogamous exchange by rebelling against her commodity status in marriage with her refusal to be exchanged for the younger Countess Mireval as well as by her insistence on her legal claim to her property. Yet Beatriz's second true story ultimately tells the story of women's failure to free themselves of their status as commodities and break the feudal ties that have historically determined their position in the monogamous family and in modern society. Marie's expulsion

---

31. Marx, *Capital*; quoted in Sheila Rowbotham, *Woman's Consciousness, Man's World* (Harmondsworth: Penguin, 1973), 63.

from the "market" after her pending divorce is not the positive act of rebellion that Irigaray and Cixous propose as a means of breaking the mechanisms of patriarchal exchange. She cannot simply "refuse to go to market," nor can she resort to "'another' kind of trade."[32] Marie has very little choice but to "go to market" and would obviously prefer to continue to do so, considering that the alternative seems to be death. Marie's fate quite clearly underscores the very limited options open for medieval women, even aristocratic women, who want to resist their expropriation and exploitation by men of their own class.

Like the figure of the hysteric prominent in the writings of Cixous and Clément,[33] Marie also causes a blockage in the family that leads to a breakdown in the system of exogamous exchange with her refusal to vacate her place within the family for the Countess Mireval. She thus refuses to accept her interchangeability as a commodity. But unlike the hysteric of Clément and Cixous, whose resistance to masculine desire represents a positive paradigm of women's rebellion against "phallocentricity," Marie's "blockage" cannot be construed as a conscious rejection of the system of exogamous or endogamous exchange; it is instead the result of market forces, which determine the life span of commodities in circulation. Marie does not refuse to go to market, nor can she, since commodities are, as Marx points out, in fact reliant on the consent of the "commodity owners" who regulate their exchange.[34] The only possibility for rebellion open to the commodity within a Marxist economy once it is depleted of its use and exchange value, and once it has been abandoned by its owner, seems to be for the commodity to reassert itself as "refuse" by "refusing" to be defined solely in terms of its function within a utilitarian economy. As "refuse," the commodity and woman as commodity undergo a redefinition whereby they re-enter circulation on their own terms, refunctionalized. Here we are reminded of the way Gustaf the Garbage-Tip Driver, in *Gustav der Weltfahrer*, reinstates the refuse he finds in his daily visits to the rubbish heap, inscribing the seemingly useless objects of "refuse" with new meaning. Marie functions as a "use" commodity with

---

32. Irigaray, "When the Goods Get Together," 110.
33. Clément, "The Guilty One," 52.
34. Marx, *Capital*, 88.

limited purchase and her fate is inevitably the same as any commodity, which, having exhausted its exchange and use value, becomes superfluous.

Women, the Family, and Domestic Serfdom

Marie's fate as a commodity for exchange becomes metonymically linked to the mode of production associated by Marx and Engels with women's work in the home. Since the sexual division of labor, women have been the producers of use values, whereas men have been engaged in the production of goods primarily for exchange. This sexual division of labor as it is perpetuated in the monogamous family is another of the lessons that Beatriz must learn in *Trobadora Beatriz*.

According to Morgner, women are the twentieth-century equivalents of the slaves of ancient Greece, and domestic bondage the means by which modern industrial societies, in particular socialist societies, sustain progress. In a speech delivered at the VII Writers' Congress, Morgner draws attention to the very real inequalities still existing in contemporary East German society between the sexes, despite the state's public commitment to equality of opportunity. The status of women in twentieth-century industrial societies is comparable, she claims, to the position of slaves in ancient Greece:

> The great culture of ancient Greece was based on a system of keeping slaves. The great artistic, scientific, and technological achievements of our present culture are based on a system of keeping women.[35]

Slavery functions for Morgner as a metaphor for the exploitation of women, their labor, and their bodies, as well as a symbol of the extent of their subordination to men. In *Amanda*, Morgner takes up the theme of slavery once again when she refers to women's situation in the family as a form of modern serfdom. The term bondage (literally "body-ownership") acts as a metaphor for an

---

35. "Die große griechische Kultur basierte auf der Sklavenhalterordnung. Die großen künstlerischen, wissenschaftlichen und technischen Errungenschaften der Kultur, die wir jetzt haben, basieren auf der Frauenhalterordnung." Morgner, "Rede vor dem VII Schriftstellerkongreß," 113.

anachronistic, pre-Marxist set of class relations still upheld and practiced between the sexes within the socialist family. At the same time, bondage or "body-ownership" read literally represents the feminist project of the reappropriation of women's bodies by women, one of the central aims of women's struggle for emancipation in the 1970s both in the East and the West. If women are to break the bonds of serfdom, thus becoming like the free worker, the first step must be to refuse to sell themselves as commodities in order to become their own mistresses. Women must also begin to challenge the division of labor between so-called "productive" work performed in the work place and reproductive work conducted in the home. As long as women continue to be identified solely in terms of their traditional role in society as producers of use values and as long as this work is undervalued, their status in the home will be little more than that of domestic slaves.

In *Trobadora Beatriz*, women are represented as the producers of "use values" in the meals they provide for their husbands and male lovers. For Laura, Valeska, and Berta, the activity of food production in the home is an act of loving and caring (TB. 233). However, it is labor spent in an expression of love that is only appreciated by the women themselves. It is Valeska who realizes that "the form of caring that consists in providing someone with food is not only carried out by women but also only appreciated by women" (TB. 233). The men in the novel, by contrast, regard eating as a necessary but largely unproductive and unpleasurable exercise – "a similar procedure to filling up a car with petrol" (TB. 135; RH. 48). Eating is for Lutz an "act of consciousness" (TB. 135; RH. 47), rather than the act of communication and the declaration of love that it is for the women concerned: "the higher the consciousness the lower the culinary culture" (TB. 135; RH. 47). Katschmann is equally unappreciative of the emotional investment involved in the preparation of meals by his companion, Berta; for him they have merely functional or use value. Eating is on a par with other socially necessary activities such as work: "eating seemed to belong to the incredible work load which he imposed on himself daily. He accomplished it so methodically and thoroughly that it had caused problems with his circulation" (TB. 116; RH. 255). As a consequence, women feel their efforts rewarded most when their food preparation is appreciated and this can be measured in the amounts of food men consume: "The more was eaten the more she [Berta] felt her attentions appreciated" (TB. 115; RH. 254). Only in *Gustav der Weltfahrer* is eating a pleasurable pastime, that is, as far as the two Gustafs are concerned. Here too it is the wife of Gustaf the World Traveler who prepares the soups for the consumption of the two men during their meetings. Although the meal times are heavily ritualized, Gustaf's wife, as the producer of the meals, remains absent from the mealtime rituals conducted exclusively between the two men.

Sheila Rowbotham maintains that it is because women have traditionally been producers of use values, that is, producers of goods for immediate consumption within the family, that this specifically female mode of production has remained outside traditional Marxist analyses of the relations of production. She argues that this is because the production of goods within the family for private consumption is not directly related to the cash-nexus. She also points out the similarities between the relations of production in the family and the relations of production under serfdom. Women function, she argues, within the family like feudal serfs and like Marx's slaves. They are not able to freely dispose of the products of their labor to men or to society and cannot sell them freely as commodities.[36] Their service to society and to men is, because of its feudal nature, largely invisible. Only Uwe Parnitzke in *Trobadora Beatriz,* a sensitive "feminized" male, is appreciative of the invisible service women provide to men in the form of time and emotion invested in preparing meals for the consumption of others. As one of the few male victims of patriarchal culture, Uwe is, however, as Valeska describes him "a rarity among men" (TB. 216).

Beatriz's story to Laura about Marie of Montpellier makes the point that even long before industrialization and the rise of capitalism woman has functioned as a type of "natural" commodity with respect to man. This status as a "natural" object for sexual exchange has been the target of feminist critiques both in the West and in Eastern Europe. Moreover, Beatriz's story deconstructs the markers of sexual difference that have positioned woman on the interstice or dividing line between nature and

36. Rowbotham, *Woman's Consciousness, Man's World,* 58ff.

culture. It is the construction of such binary oppositions that has facilitated the categorization of women's activities in the home as an extension of the "natural" service women provide to men and hence as the product of a "natural" division of labor between the sexes.

In the letter of protest Laura sends to the circus that employs Beatriz and Melusine immediately after Beatriz's arrival in the GDR, Laura decries as reactionary any such theories that posit women as the "missing link between the human ape and man [sic]" (TB. 104). Such theories have, however, found much more reputable proponents than Max Funk and the like, and reassert themselves in such unexpected places as Lévi-Strauss's structural anthropology. While maintaining that woman functions largely as a sign within exogamous exchange,[37] Lévi-Strauss asserts that the essential difference between women and other gifts or goods for exchange lies in their natural function in child-rearing and in their value as a stimulus of male sexual desire.[38] Woman's exchangeability results from her ability to excite "sexual and proprietal instincts" in others as well as in her own proprietor. In pre-Marxist society these "sexual and proprietal instincts" both belonged to the natural order of things and received their legitimation from this order. Marx and Engels were concerned about rescuing only one half of the pair, namely the proprietal instincts, from the realm of the natural in the name of the science of historical materialism. They were content to leave the question of the other codeterminant in the oppression of women, namely their sexual expropriation, unaddressed. If women are to reappropriate themselves as "objects of personal desire,"[39] that is, "appropriate nature. First of all their own" (GW. 157), which is the project Morgner assigns women and women's writing, they must reverse the process of expropriation by which they have become natural stimulants, becoming instead owners of their own commodities. The model she uses corresponds to Marx's ideal of the free worker. The "marriage con-woman" in *Amanda* attempts to do just this by regulating the sale of her labor as housewife and lover for her own profit.

37. Lévi-Strauss, *The Elementary Structures of Kinship*, 496.
38. Ibid., 62.
39. Ibid.

The representation of woman as cash for exchange amongst men as well as a commodity with exchange and use value, which is implicit in Beatriz's story about Marie, can be read as a radical critique of the way in which the theories of Marx, Engels, Lévi-Strauss, and others have done nothing to explode the myth of women's "natural" role as producer of commodities with use value for the maintenance of the family and the reproduction of the work force. The perpetuation of the myth of women's natural role as objects of male desire has meant that women not only have continued to produce use values but have had to produce themselves as commodities for sexual use and abuse. The representation of woman as commodity in this second "true" story told by Beatriz constitutes a crucial point in the novel insofar as it points to the need for an alternative concept of value that can adequately deal with women's work within the family and the less tangible products of women's labor outside the work force. The text also raises questions concerning the possibility of an alternative set of relations between the sexes and alternative sexual "economies" practiced by women.

Feminist Paradigms of Exchange

The novel *Trobadora Beatriz* offers several alternative "economies" of exchange and alternative models of sexual relations that are non-objectifying and aim at freeing women from their commodity status. The first experiment with other modes of gender relations is to be found in Laura's attempt to share her lover Lutz with Beatriz. Although Laura's original intention was to release Beatriz's creative energies, her action is simultaneously a way of testing Beatriz's utopian ideal of an active female subject of desire.

The exchange of men between Laura and Beatriz, posited by Laura as a "measure to catalyze poetry" (TB. 133), highlights the potential for solidarity amongst women. At first glance it seems to be merely an inversion of the patriarchal model of exchange between men as illustrated in the story about Marie. The inversion appears to be a Brechtian alienation technique designed to reveal a particular phenomenon normally considered natural as historically constructed and hence able to be changed. But the exchange of men between women is not solely designed to point up the objectification of women in GDR society. The model postulates the possibility of women becoming active subjects of sexual desire. Whilst the solidarity between the two women could possibly be seen as analogous to the collusion between the father and the husband within patriarchal relations (as indicated by the story about Marie), there are significant differences in the way in which Lutz is "exchanged" between the two women. These differences raise the question of a specifically female form of sexual and social exchange.

What appears to be absent from the act of "gift-giving" between Beatriz and Laura is the compulsion to reciprocate the exchange in some form or another. The concept of a return on the erotic and emotional investment involved in the relationship with Lutz, as well as any ownership claims, seems unimportant in the exchange between Beatriz and Laura. The alternative system of exchange in operation here would appear to be one not based on "returns" of any kind. Once Lutz has failed to have the desired catalytic effect on Beatriz and she fails to continue to produce the stories she has been commissioned to deliver, Lutz, the so-called object of exchange, is not returned to its initial owner, Laura. Instead, both women are happy to relinquish all claims to Lutz, just as he is only too happy to escape the cries of screeching children: "Lutz had fled. Because screeching children cannot be controlled by definitions. So Beatriz had dismissed him" (TB. 147).

The inversion does not appear to modify substantially the mechanisms of objectification and functionalization that typify the position of women in patriarchal societies. However, there is little to suggest that the interlude with Lutz was meant to be more than an alienation effect. Lutz is conceived purely and unashamedly as an object of female desire. This fact alone is sufficient to break radically with sexual and moral taboos on female eroticism, as the example of Beatriz's erotic tale told to the workers of the Berlin Tramways demonstrates. The moral quality of the story was found to be lacking for the reason that, "women writers should not be tempted to describe naked men by the fact that male writers portray naked women" (TB. 126). Belletristic means just that, "beautiful literature" (TB. 126), Beatriz is told. In terms of the overall narrative of the novel, the story of the exchange of men between women serves the specific function of demonstrating solidarity among women and of freeing representations of women from sexual taboos and prudery. It is successful, furthermore, in reawakening Beatriz's dormant erotic imagination and in putting the slow process of feminist consciousness-raising into motion. The relationship between Lutz and Beatriz is, for both parties, an alliance of convenience, each having an ulterior motive for pursuing the erotic involvement. In this sense Lutz is very definitely a willing accomplice in the deal.

Although the experiment with Lutz is an attempt on Morgner's part to break with a set of relations between the sexes that designates one as the beneficiary or subject of the exchange and the other as its object, it offers no real alternative other than the inversion of the relative positions of the terms of the commodity relations between the sexes. It neither upturns the hierarchical structuring of the positions within the "economy," nor does it transgress the boundaries between active and passive positions of exchange. It does, however, challenge assumptions that woman's position within the operations of sexual exchange is naturally that of the object, and thus introduces the possibility of a female desiring subject. An active desiring subject is also the necessary precondition for the realization of the ideal of the active female troubadour.

An alternative form of social rather than sexual exchange explored by the novel, and one which does challenge hierarchical forms of exchange based on the objectification of one of the terms, is to be found in the relationship between Beatriz and Laura. This relationship between two diametrically opposed characters is an attempt to break down fixed subject positions and to posit alternatives to the objectification of women. There is a constant swapping of their respective roles and social functions throughout the novel, which deliberately blurs the boundaries between the identities of the two women. The sliding of subject positions is a direct result of the swapping of social roles; it originates in the need to find pragmatic solutions to Laura's primary concerns of child-rearing and -minding. The confusion of identities, which begins from the earliest encounters between the two women, has, however, far-reaching implications for the personal development of the two women and for their joint strategies for overturning patriarchal relations of domination.

Initially Laura's experiment with Lutz appears to be successful although it eventually has the opposite effect from what was intended. So great is Beatriz's absorption in her new lover that her creativity would appear to be stifled. At least she stops producing stories for the brigades and workers in factories. Sexual gratification is apparently not compatible with her social obligations as a socially committed writer nor with her contract with her publisher, and Beatriz falls behind with her commitments. She fails to deliver literary lectures to the "Society for the Dissemination of Scientific Knowledge" and fails to attend a literary ball given in her honor along with other prominent East German writers such as Sarah Kirsch and Volker Braun. She forgets a reading in a Berlin light bulb factory and simply stops writing. Beatriz is only saved from official censure by a division of creative labor between the two women. This allows her to fulfill her erotic desires as well as meeting her publishing deadlines. She delegates her obligations as an officially registered writer to Laura, who subsequently holds readings to various groups of factory workers in Beatriz's name as Beatriz's minstrel. In return, Beatriz is initiated into the duties of motherhood.

The first story that Laura tells in her new role as minstrel to a women's brigade in an electric light bulb factory takes as its theme the conflict between the two mainstays of official GDR policy concerning women, namely between the sacredness of "marriage, family, and motherhood" (TB. 331) and the full participation of women in the workforce. The role-swapping is therefore a direct response to the inability of one woman to comply with the exigencies of two disparate ideals of femininity. Laura is entrusted with the task of continuing the consciousness-raising work begun by Beatriz. Laura claims to have written the story "at the diaper table. In between the meals of her son Wesselin" (TB. 148). She pretends she has successfully combined the duties of motherhood and those of her profession. Yet Laura's story flaunts its fictionality and its mendacious foundations, much in the same way as do Gustaf the World-Traveler's tall tales. Laura's story is obviously a piece of "fiction," premised as it is on the myth that women can effortlessly meet both of the conflicting demands society imposes on them without the help of miracles. Melusine reminds Beatriz at this point that no real change can occur without recourse to miracles: "without miracles you cannot even help a baby, even less the world" (TB. 147).

The emancipatory effect of the role reversal is in Laura's case indisputable and, once she is relieved of the sole responsibility for child-minding, it seems as if her creative potential has indeed been tapped. In Beatriz's case the effect of the role reversal is, however, more complex. Laura initially conceives of the idea of acquainting Beatriz with the day-to-day realities of child-rearing and pots of diapers as a means of curbing her fanaticism. She is censured by Melusine for attempting to cure Beatriz of her megalomania:

> ... impatience is Beatriz de Dia's unique talent, megalomania her extraordinary virtue. Whoever robs her of her talent and her virtue, as has happened for thousands of years to her sisters, sins in the eyes of God who cannot be a man. Nor a woman. (TB. 181)[40]

To be able to understand fully the significance of both the female protagonists within the structure of the narrative it will be necessary to undertake a detailed analysis of their functions with respect to one other and also with respect to the narrative structure as a whole. An understanding of the relationship between Beatriz and Laura is, moreover, essential if we are to be able to draw conclusions about the problems of female subjectivity and the relative position of the fantastic in relation to the real.

40. "Denn Ungeduld ist das einzigartige Talent der Beatriz de Dia, Größenwahn ihre außerordentliche Tugend. Wer ihr Talent und Tugend abdressiert, so geschehen ist jahrtausendelang ihren Schwestern, macht sich schuldig vor Gott, der kein Mann sein kann. Auch keine Frau."

3
The Quest for Female Emancipation

Female Solidarity and the Sibylline Secret Society

In most of Morgner's larger works from *Hochzeit in Konstantinopel* onward the quest for emancipation, self-knowledge, and self-realization is dependent on the support of another woman. This other woman often takes the form of an editor of the main protagonist's prose as in *Hochzeit in Konstantinopel*. Here the other woman serves as an alter ego who both sympathizes and censures the other woman's excesses and idiosyncrasies. The support may also take the form of editorial guidance or, in the case of *Trobadora Beatriz*, the form of physical help with the demands of daily life. Or, alternatively, the other woman may function in a political capacity as a surrogate for direct feminist action. She generally appears in the form of a friend, although female solidarity among women friends is, as Beatriz remarks, only too rare "among creatures who have been humiliated for thousands of years" (TB. 113). In the early novels and in *Trobadora Beatriz* East German women seldom form alliances or friendships, and in *Amanda* the pacts between two women from the same country are perceived to be highly subversive and conspiratorial. In *Trobadora Beatriz* the alliance between the pragmatic, thoroughly realistic Laura and Beatriz, the medieval time traveler, seeks to overcome "the lack of solidarity among women" (TB. 113), which has had little opportunity to develop between women in a society that sees female solidarity as undermining both male supremacy and the authority of the state. Beatriz and Laura are therefore much more than mere mirror images or the dark, maddened other halves of the heroines in much nineteenth-century English fiction.[1] These

---

1. See the work of Sandra M. Gilbert and Susan Gubar, *The Madwoman in the Attic: The Woman Writer and the Nineteenth-Century Literary Imagination* (New Haven, London: Yale University Press, 1979).

doubles provide a crucial form of support in the heroine's search for self-realization; they are the medium through which the articulation of female desires and the search for selfhood becomes possible. The quest for emancipation is therefore intersubjective, achieved through a dialectical process whereby the experiences and knowledge of one woman modifies and complements those of the other.

After meeting Laura, Beatriz initially perceives her role in the GDR to be agitatory; Laura sees her role in relation to Beatriz as that of mentor and educator. In the course of the novel, however, the respective positions of the two characters in relation to each other shift. Beatriz's original proposal to conquer eroticism as the last frontier of male domination undergoes substantial modifications as she acquires new knowledge about the very real barriers to gender equality in the "promised land" of the GDR. Beatriz's hopes to find a country in which male supremacy has been abolished are progressively dashed with each new experience of existing socialism. The country that had held out the promise of better conditions for women proves to be no better than the one she has left. Having renounced the help of the Persephonic Opposition, Beatriz soon comes to the realization that her aims of revolutionizing relations between the sexes through art are also doomed to fail. Laura's lessons in the realities of socialist life and her attempts at educating Beatriz are initially successful; Beatriz rapidly becomes at once more realistic in her expectations and more determined to see her goals achieved. Yet the process of educating Beatriz does not lead to a harmonious reconciliation of individual aspirations and social reality, with Beatriz becoming instead more fanatical and immoderate in her demands for an immediate solution to the hardships facing women in the twentieth century.

Beatriz's disillusionment is so great that she is willing to resort to more radical means of achieving her ends, and to this end she devises a plan for facilitating women's entry into history through the use of terrorist tactics. When Laura catches Beatriz planning to build a bomb and highjack a jumbo, she realizes Beatriz's fanaticism has gone too far. Laura cannot agree with Beatriz that a terrorist attack on her "Workers' and Peasants' State" is an appropriate means of blackmailing the government into lifting the restrictions of the abortion laws. Laura eulogizes the virtues of

patience in the revolutionary struggle: "Whoever wants to change
the world must have patience" (TB. 166). Yet it is precisely these
qualities of "impatience and megalomania" (TB. 180) that are,
according to Melusine, what is required if Beatriz is to help women
retrieve the lost traces of their as yet unwritten history.
Megalomania, Melusine argues, is essential if women are to throw
off the yoke of oppression and enter into history as true historical
subjects. If Beatriz is generous enough to bring back the history of
women's oppression "that was not written by men," the least Laura
can do, chides Melusine, is to have faith in her. Laura is then forced
to reconsider her appraisal of Beatriz and to think of the best way
of utilizing Beatriz's excessive idealism to achieve their joint ends
by less violent means.

The problem for women's emancipation lies, she realizes, not
in the lack of women who see themselves as active subjects of
desire but in the customs and sexual practices of her country, ones
still dominated and controlled by men. Beatriz's next strategy is
to effect structural changes in society through violent and coercive
means. The work of consciousness-raising by means of erotic
poetry and story telling is insufficient, given the strong resistance
to the expression of female desire at official levels. Beatriz suggests
instead forming an underground organization in the "Sibylline
Secret Society," which can coerce patriarchal governments to
relinquish their hold on power. Laura, who disapproves of
terrorism whatever its ends, must reconsider how she can best put
Beatriz's radicalism to productive rather than destructive use. The
slightest suggestion of terrorist attacks in the GDR shocks Laura
and she immediately protests that her first loyalty must be to
protect her state from terrorist attacks. Furthermore, Laura finds
the suggestion of terrorist tactics unsettling for the very reason that
it is the first open admission that what had hitherto been a
personal affair between two women has wider political
ramifications: that is, that the personal is political.

Laura attempts to defuse the subversive potential of Beatriz's
proposal by attributing it to the excesses of a childish imagination,
thereby rendering it marginal and less threatening. Furthermore,
she dismisses the notion of a secret society as a "poetic absurdity,"
a childish fantasy (TB. 163). Despite her initial horror, Laura seems
to be in tacit agreement with Beatriz that the two women must
bring about structural change in the way in which society

produces and reproduces sexual difference. Women can only realize their potential as active desiring subjects if changes are made to the gender hierarchy and women foster a political awareness of the structural nature of their collective problems. As Laura points out to Beatriz: "The possibility of forcing people into things is dependent on power. That means to this very day: it is dependent on men" (TB. 163). The best way of encouraging awareness of the inequalities in society is by organizing women politically. The precise form the organization of women in such a society as East Germany must take will naturally differ substantially from those strategies developed in the Western world by women's liberation groups. In view of the official constraints on the formation of all alternative or oppositional political organizations in Eastern bloc countries, the experimentation with forms of resistance must necessarily assume a clandestine form.

In all the strategies developed by Beatriz and Laura under the auspices of the "Sibylline Secret Society" the imperative of secrecy and marginality remains constant. Within Western feminism the issue of whether and how women should convert the negative fact of their cultural and historical marginalization within a male-dominated society into a positive means of breaking the hegemony of patriarchal structures has been a contentious issue. Resistance to reclaiming the cultural "center" has often been the result of an unwillingness to participate in hegemonic cultural discourses that are perceived to exclude women. It has been argued that the simple fact of women's exclusion from the dominant discourses in the West has necessitated a struggle from the margins and must continue to do so. Debates have accordingly centered around what constitutes an appropriate marginal or alternative position from which feminism should operate. Where should a feminist discourse position itself in relation to the generality of Western philosophical discourses? As Meaghan Morris has pointed out, debates in the West about the appropriate site for feminist resistance have not always been entirely productive. She contends that the circularity of the argument about women's exclusion from history and cultural production has meant that women have been faced with two mutually exclusive alternatives: either to participate in the dominant culture or to remain in the cultural ghettos, a choice, she argues, that has not proved itself productive in analyzing how femininity operates within these discourses.[2] Marginality often merely reproduces the subordination of women and the feminine and does not address the real inequities that feminism purports to ameliorate.

Laura's search for a suitable revolutionary "lever" for her secret society clearly must be considered within the broader context of debates in feminist theory surrounding the specific nature of a feminine form of subversion. At the same time, however, any comparison with the strategies of Western feminists must be aware of the specific problems associated with the formation of feminist interventions and a feminist politics in the German Democratic Republic. Because it was party policy after 1949 to render women visible in official Marxist discourses – by highlighting their achievements and the measure of their contribution to socialism at every possible opportunity – the strategies adopted by women to challenge their cultural marginalization necessarily differed from those of French feminists or Western Marxist feminists. In the GDR marginality was essential to protect the activities of feminist groups and writings. Marginality does not represent so much a choice as a virtue borne of necessity. Furthermore, because East German women had little alternative but to participate in the public arena on terms that were not their own, the choice of spheres marginal to mainstream society from which to launch a feminist attack on patriarchy must be judged according to the limited range of genuine alternatives available to East German women. It is not so much that East German women rejected public forums for change, but that the public arenas of the work place and the political parties allowed no room for official dissent. The articulation of women's interests other than in the terms prescribed by the party and its officially recognized organizations was simply not permitted as it was in Western countries. Therefore, the decision by Laura and Beatriz to launch their first attack on behalf of the "Sibylline Secret Society" from the privacy of their homes does not constitute an alternative to public engagement but rather a second line of resistance. A feminist strategy that weighs the merits of getting one's hands dirty by lending tacit support to patriarchy against the benefits of refusing

2. Meaghan Morris, "Aspects of Current French Feminist Literary Criticism," *Hecate* 5 (1979): 65.

to become an accomplice in a bankrupt "economy," to take up Luce Irigaray's metaphor once again, can only operate under a system that permits both possibilities. In socialist societies such as the GDR, which guaranteed and enforced women's right to work since its formation, and where women had little option but to participate in the public spheres, the private sphere and those private spaces provided by the family and friendships necessarily assumed an oppositional role. The emphasis on the private spheres in Morgner's writing is, it seems, a far cry from any affirmation of traditional public/private divisions.

For Laura, the most effective site from which to launch a feminist attack on patriarchal structures is the privacy of her kitchen. The importance of private spheres is underlined by Morgner in an interview with Ursula Krechel:

> The immense amount of work that a society and every individual has to do in order to change the thousand-year old customs takes place above all in those so-called private spheres, and cannot be achieved from one day to the next or in 10 or 20 years. It progresses gradually and cannot be enforced by law; it must evolve and is a creative social process.[3]

The attack therefore that Laura proposes launching from amongst the diapers represents by no means a "soft" or even a "wet" option; nor is it a substitute for a political offensive within the public sphere or in the work place. It represents instead a conscious decision to adopt the domestic sphere instead of a public forum as a site of resistance. It is in the private sphere, according to Morgner, that women suffer most from the perpetuation of anachronistic sexual practices. It is in the confines of the family home where social contradictions are most acutely felt; here the discrepancy between public efforts to guarantee equal opportunity for women and interpersonal practices in the home is most blatant. For women keen to change patriarchal practices in the home and

---

3. "Die große Arbeit, die eine Gesellschaft leistet und die jeder einzelne leisten muß, um die jahrtausendealten Sitten zu verändern, die spielt sich aber vor allen Dingen in der sogenannten privaten Sphäre ab und kann nicht von heute auf morgen und auch nicht in 10 oder 20 Jahren geleistet werden. Das geht allmählich, ist nicht durch Gesetze zu erzwingen, muß wachsen, ist ein schöpferischer Prozeß der Gesellschaft." Morgner, "Das eine tun und das andere nicht lassen," 43.

challenge the official narrative of the history of their emancipation under socialism – which barely acknowledged these practices – there is perhaps no better place for an act of subversion than the privacy of women's kitchens, as this is the site where political activity is least expected. The private sphere thus offers a perfect camouflage for activities that question the truth of official narratives or endeavor to undermine official myths.

However, when Laura suggests that Beatriz should be subjected to the effects of pots of diapers in order to curb her fanaticism (TB. 164) and distract her from the more violent methods of a terrorist secret society, she is not suggesting Beatriz should divert her attention away from politics to focus on the traditionally feminine spheres of child-minding. As part of the education of Beatriz, Laura is merely pointing out that women's child-rearing duties are one of the main obstacles to the political organization and mobilization of women. Beatriz must experience the conflicting demands made on women's time and energies at first hand before the secret society can decide where to insert the lever for social change. The pots of diapers appear to provide the perfect cover for the activities of a secret society. Laura's proposal to continue her work for the society from amidst pots of boiling diapers is so absurd as to provide the perfect alibi for political activity from below. The same also applies to the alchemical experiments that Vilma conducts in her kitchen in *Amanda*. Laura's strategy does not so much affirm traditional female values of motherhood as politicize them in a way that transforms their private, personal nature into something far more powerful and socially dynamic. Laura's suggestion resembles the proposal put forward by West German feminist Ulrike Prokop, who incites women to decipher the subversive impulses latent in their everyday lives and convert them into the basis for further feminist action.[4]

The discovery that the personal can be utilized for political ends is a crucial step in addressing the difficulties imposed on women by the "double burden." In many of Morgner's novels the pressures of the dual and incompatible responsibilities in the work force and in the home have necessitated that women lead double

---

4. Ulrike Prokop, *Weibliche Lebenszusammenhänge: Von der Beschränktheit der Strategien und der Unangemessenheit der Wünsche* (Frankfurt am Main: Suhrkamp, 1976).

lives. Their energies are divided between a public and a private life, between an official and an unofficial one, a "real" one and a "fantastic" one. Characters such as Vera Hill, Valeska, and Laura in *Trobadora Beatriz*, Vilma, and Hilde Felber in *Amanda,* and Bele in *Hochzeit in Konstantinopel* all lead lives of apparent conformity either in the work place or, in Vilma's case, in their official capacity as spouse, whilst simultaneously existing in private fantasy worlds of subversion and treachery. Although firmly rooted in GDR reality, these fantasy "other" worlds are incompatible with the women's official function in society as working mothers and wives. These alternative spheres of action, which in *Trobadora Beatriz* are entirely private, and which only later in *Amanda* expand to include select public arenas such as the Hugenottendom and the Blocksberg, provide a necessary foil to the public, official spheres in which women are required to participate. Their role in providing an unofficial, private space for the formulation of alternative forms of self-expression and the testing of conspiratorial methods is all the more important because women have had limited success in effecting changes to gender relations in the public spheres.

The Romance, the Quest, and the Unicorn

As both Beatriz and Laura realize, their search for the ideal conditions under which a female troubadour can be possible calls for the creation of a subject of desire that actively pursues the fulfillment of her dreams. The two women's plans to liberate their fellow women from social and political constraints are complex and multifaceted, ranging from the quest for the ideal man to the quest for mobility and adventure. The novel experiments with a range of narrative possibilities for realizing these aims in the various narrative paradigms its explores and adapts for the purposes of the two main protagonists. Morgner investigates common models of male and female development in narrative, subjecting stereotyped narrative patterns to critical scrutiny. Many of Beatriz's and Laura's adventures are attempts to reveal the limitations these received patterns place on the encoding of women's experience. The most general pattern explored in the novel is the model of the quest-romance.

Northrop Frye has defined the quest-romance as the "search of the libido or the desiring self for a fulfillment that will deliver it from the anxieties of reality but will still contain that reality."[5] Defined in these terms, the quest-romance is a narrative of wish-fulfillment that has as its starting point a deficient reality, which it strives to ameliorate through substitute wish-fulfillment in other spheres. The romance, according to this definition, is anything but an escapist narrative; instead, it is one that is aware of the insufficiencies of social reality and that seeks to remedy these through an imaginary resolution of conflicts. Modifying Frye's definition, Fredric Jameson has termed the romance a "utopian fantasy" that aims at the "transfiguration of the world of everyday reality."[6] For Beatriz and Laura, therefore, the romance provides the appropriate narrative vehicle for the dual goals of self-realization and the eroticization of everyday socialist life. Frye identifies the dominant conflict in the romance as the struggle between the forces of good and evil or heaven and hell. The hero of the romance is "analogous to the mythical Messiah or deliverer who comes from an upper world, and his enemy is analogous to the demonic powers of a lower world." The conflict takes place, however, in "our" world, in the world of the real.[7]

In *Trobadora Beatriz* Morgner examines the suitability of various models of the quest-romance for female patterns of development. The difficulties in applying male models of development to the experiences of women leads Morgner to challenge the very structure of the quest in its cultural and historical variants, along with the gender assumptions underpinning its different manifestations. The following analysis of the quest draws on the insights and methods of analysis developed by structural linguist A.J. Greimas in his generative narratology. Greimas's structural narratology can provide a useful tool of analysis here because it offers a narrative grammar based on structural semantics that analyzes how meaning is organized around sets of binary oppositions present at the level of the paradigmatic axis rather

---

5. Northrop Frye, *Anatomy of Criticism* (Princeton: Princeton UP, 1957), 193.
6. Fredric Jameson, "Magical Narratives: Romance as Genre," *New Literary History* 7, no. 1 (1975): 138.
7. Frye, *Anatomy of Criticism*, 187–88.

than the syntactic level.[8] Along this paradigmatic or semantic axis, meaning is constituted between two lexematic poles that can be broken down into sets of binary opposites such as individual/collective, masculine/feminine, and active/passive, which form the fundamental terms around which the narrative is organized.[9] Greimas's narrative schema can provide us with the tools with which to demonstrate how any particular set of binary oppositions present in any narrative are developed and resolved syntagmatically in the narrative syntax. However, one difficulty in applying methods of the deductive, generativistic tradition of narratology is that they often pay scant regard to the socio-historical determination of the narrative processes.[10] To avoid the reduction of surface narrative patterns to a set of universals, we need to subject Greimas's so-called universal categories, his transhistorical sets of binary pairs, to a further, cultural analysis in order to explicate just how these binary oppositions are themselves the products of their specific cultural and historical contexts.

Much recent feminist criticism has recognized the importance of performing similar analyses on dominant discourses in the West, precisely so as to reveal the operations of binary thinking underpinning much philosophical discourse and its categorization of the feminine in relation to the masculine. Although this work often runs the risk of universalizing the masculinity/femininity dichotomy by hypostatizing the "feminine" as an oppositional category, the deconstructive gesture is perceived by many feminists to be a useful means of analyzing the construction of femininity in discourse. When adapting Greimas's actantial model and the syntagmatic structuring of narrative around binary oppositions, one should remain aware of the ways gender comes to bear upon the use of such oppositions as subject/object, active/passive, and hence the inherently gendered nature of the structure of the quest narrative itself. A feminist critique of the quest and Greimas's structuralist reading of the narrative of the quest must

---

8. See Ronald Schleifer, introd. to A.J. Greimas, *Structural Semantics: An Attempt at a Method*, trans. Ronald Schleifer, Daniele McDowell, and Alan Velie (Lincoln: University of Nebraska Press, 1983), xI.
9. Greimas, *Structural Semantics*, 23–28.
10. See Annette Runte, *Subjektkritische Diskurstheorie* (Cologne: Pahl-Rugenstein, 1982), 73ff.

necessarily read the "actants" in the narrative model no longer as the gender-neutral "everymen" of a universal narrative but as projections of specific cultural perceptions of gender relations in particularized cultural and historical systems.[11]

Morgner adapts a number of variants of the quest in such a way as to point out their structural incompatibility with changing perceptions about women's role in society and in relation to men. The first of these models that she develops is the quest as adventure narrative. One of the first clandestine activities of the Sibylline Secret Society is to send Beatriz on an adventure to the West. Beatriz's travels abroad have a pivotal function in the structure of the novel in terms of the development of each woman and the relationship between the two. Beatriz becomes the active subject of a quest-romance, which Laura has devised as a strategy ostensibly to teach Beatriz the virtues of patience and moderation. But the mission to find Anaximander also serves the purpose of vicariously satisfying Laura's need for adventures and travel. Beatriz, as a non-German-speaking foreigner from the pre-capitalist past, functions as a surrogate for Laura, who because of travel restrictions in the GDR and her duties as a mother, can only experience foreign cultures and countries through the aid of a mediator.

Beatriz thus provides a crucial link between Laura and the outside Western world. She is from the very outset a substitute for Laura long before she starts to resemble her physically towards the end of the book. Beatriz is described by Morgner in literal and figurative terms as someone who crosses frontiers.[12] She violates political and cultural borders as well as transgressing ideological and political boundaries between East and West. By traversing boundaries of time and space through non-scientific means, with the aid of magic and other subversive means, she also challenges the limits of realism and the limits of the "real." Furthermore, she represents those female experiences that cannot be contained by

11. Greimas designs an actantial model for mythical narratives that consists of six components. According to this schema all narratives have a sender who seeks to gain possession of an object through the medium of another subject. The quest is conducted for the benefit of a higher power that Greimas terms the receiver of the quest. This main action is accompanied by a helper and an opponent whose functions are not so much syntactic but adverbial. See Greimas, *Structural Semantics*, 207.
12. Morgner, *Die Hexe im Landhaus*, 17.

conventional realist narratives of self-realization. She provides therefore the perfect counterbalance for the pragmatic Laura, who is firmly rooted in the fictional world of socialist realism. Beatriz's status as a foreigner in the GDR permits her freedom of movement as well as the liberty to be both eccentric and extremist in her demands. It is this privileged status as an outsider or foreigner that allows her her unlimited freedom to question, criticize, and even undermine existing practices and policies on women's status and prevailing taboos on sexuality. She subverts official versions of women's reality and femininity as well as fixed modes of behavior between the sexes. In many ways Beatriz's story is the story of the "other," and more specifically the female "other" and the female as "other." In this sense the quest is also very much Laura's quest.

Because Beatriz's origins are in medieval France rather than the capitalist West, she finds it easier to escape being defined by the ideological rhetoric of the Cold War. Her aims and ideals belong to the ideological grey area of the neither/nor: neither capitalist nor socialist, East nor West. The threat she thus poses to the fabric of East German society defies definition in clear-cut ideological terms. She can also be far less easily contained if her mission cannot be simply dismissed as a capitalist plot or as a typical form of Western sabotage. Beatriz is clearly not the ideological mouthpiece of "capitalist imperialism" or of the Western women's movement; her grievances pre-date the rise of modern capitalist systems and of course the popularization of international second-wave feminism. She represents therefore an ideal impartial surrogate for Laura who is curious to find out how women in the West cope with similar difficulties to her own.

There are several different reasons given for Beatriz's mission in the West, all of which have to do with aiding women in East Germany to articulate their dissatisfaction with the opportunities for women in the postwar era. Laura's initial justification for sending Beatriz on an adventure abroad is to capture the unicorn, who is given the conspiratorial code name Anaximander. This search for Anaximander would appear to be a kind of ruse or a disguise for a mission with quite a different purpose. It seems in fact that Anaximander itself is nothing more than a ploy to disguise the real object of Beatriz's search which is quite different in nature. If the name Anaximander is a code, its meaning then requires decoding. Laura first has the idea of the quest for the unicorn when she is devising a suitable means of utilizing Beatriz's mobility and revolutionary zeal for the collective needs of other women like herself. Unlike the proposal of terrorist activities, Laura's strategy must be effective without drawing attention to itself. The choice of Anaximander as the object of the quest seems therefore to be the ideal solution in as much as it best serves the needs of Beatriz as well as the needs of the GDR.

With respect to Beatriz, Laura devises the quest as part of a therapy aimed at facilitating Beatriz's integration or "arrival" into GDR society. But the procuring of the unicorn appears not to be the primary goal of the "therapeutic adventure" (TB. 175) being instead a type of occupational therapy or theory (TB. 167). At this stage of the narrative it seems as if Beatriz is the sole object of the educational exercise. However, it is unclear whether the objective of the mission is to expand Beatriz's knowledge of the world (TB. 175) or in fact Laura's own. Laura proposes the search for Anaximander as a solution ("Lösung") (TB. 167) to the problem of accommodating Beatriz's radical demands for the emancipation of women. However, what is conceived as a "Lösung" turns out instead to be a "Losung," that is, a code word (TB. 169) or phraseology (TB. 200). If Anaximander is thus not a real solution to the problems facing Beatriz and Laura but instead merely a code name or a secret sign, what does it then signify and for whom?

In a playful letter to Beatriz, Laura reminds Beatriz of the code name, Anaximander, and includes a description of the unicorn. In this story Laura extends the semantic field surrounding the code, Anaximander, on the basis of her childhood experiences with a unicorn. The semantic field regulating the use of the code Anaximander is widened to include meanings more traditionally associated with the figure of the unicorn. As a symbol of her virginity, the unicorn is Laura's invisible companion until her defloration. It figures in the story as the guardian angel of the pre-pubescent girl, as a signifier of childhood dreams and of the as yet unshattered illusion of female subjectivity and wholeness. The disappearance of the unicorn after Laura's defloration heralds not only the loss of Laura's virginity but also the loss of self-confidence and autonomy. The exit of Anaximander marks in other words the initiation into those age-old feminine virtues of "self-sacrifice and surrender" (TB. 203) and thus the loss of her childhood dreams of self-fulfillment as well. The quest in search of the lost unicorn is therefore linked to the desire to regain a sense of wholeness and self-sufficiency. As a mythical figure with no proven existence, the unicorn and its retrieval serve as a perfect means of redressing the fetishization of rationality.

If the rediscovery of the unicorn functions on an individual level as a catalyst to reinstate lost childhood ideals of female autonomy, on a collective level it could be interpreted as encouraging the recovery of women's collective past by retrieving the unwritten text of women's participation in history. The search for Anaximander becomes, therefore, by a process of metonymical substitution, the attempt to write a history that pays tribute to women's participation, a history not written from the perspective of men and the ruling class. This is, however, by no means the end of the chain of metonymical substitutions that the sign Anaximander undergoes within the novel. As already mentioned, Anaximander is also posited as a solution to the specific problems faced by women in the GDR. For Laura, the recovery of the unicorn is associated with the reactivation of the belief in miracles and the impossible. If the GDR is truly "a place for miracles" (TB. 167), it should logically also be a place for unicorns. Laura is forced to admit, however, that "at any rate nobody looks for the unicorn today anywhere else but in the fable. This nobody is me" (TB. 167). To disguise her real agenda of feminist consciousness-raising, Laura conjures up the more traditional mythical properties of the unicorn, in particular its notorious powers as an aphrodisiac (TB. 167).

The aphrodisiac properties of the unicorn's horn are, however, far outweighed by the usefulness of the concentrate of a single unicorn's brain as an alternative to more orthodox means of state propaganda. In the same way that the fluoridation of drinking water was seen by many countries as an effective means of fighting tooth decay, Laura proposes the "monocerosation of drinking water" (TB. 167) as a means of population control. Through the addition of one measurement of "unicorn protein" to the drinking water, the ideological level of the population could be cheaply and effectively raised – those people with a low or "reactionary" level of ideological development could be transformed into "intelligent, kind-hearted, peaceful citizens of this earth of communist persuasion" (TB. 168). Eventually unicorns would have to be cultivated by the state to cover the number of "unenlightened" heads in the population and to continue the fight against the national enemies of the state in "capitalism, wars, hunger, and patriarchy" (TB. 168).

If the parodic intention of the proposal to indoctrinate the masses with unicorn horns were not already clear, the final suggestion that unicorns' horns could also be usefully employed to wage war on patriarchy leaves no doubt about the feminist intention of this critique of the state's use of propaganda. The fight against patriarchy is obviously not one of the officially recognized aims of international socialism and its pointed inclusion at the end of a list of legitimate objectives of the socialist state underscores once again the protracted exclusion of women from the operations of official discourse. This passage is clearly a spoof on the eagerness with which the East German state carried out the education of its populace, its paranoia towards the West, as well as being a comment on the principles of instrumental rationality that governed the state's attitude to its people for forty years. As more than just a critique of state propaganda, the plan to "monocerosize" drinking water reads in fact as a subversive feminist strategy for raising the level of collective awareness of the specific needs of women.

In order to disguise the feminist aims of the "monocerosation" of the drinking water in the GDR, Laura proposes conspiring with the technical apparatus of industrial scientific research to lend her strategy scientific legitimacy. As Laura points out, there should be no great difficulties in arranging collaboration with scientific institutions, provided Beatriz can pretend her project is being conducted in the name of reason, "for what scientist of substance does not long for the world to be ruled by reason" (TB. 168). Thus, if on a superficial level the aims of Beatriz's mission can be made to coincide with the aims of technological progress by privileging "reason" over "non-reason," Beatriz's mission ought to find a perfect camouflage. Laura, however, is using the term reason in a radically different sense from the way it is commonly used in scientific discourse. Within the discourses of science and technology, reason is frequently associated with technological progress and the development of nuclear and military technology. Within the context of Laura's and Beatriz's "plan to improve the world" (TB. 286), reason undergoes a shift in meaning to signify the abolition of all wars and the end of patriarchy. Reason then takes on antimilitaristic, pacifist, and feminist attributes, which would not normally be considered compatible with the aims of reason within scientific discourse.

Through a process of substitutions along the syntagmatic axis of language, Anaximander can be made to serve a range of varying functions that can be classified into narrative functions pertaining to an individual subject of the narrative – as in Laura or Beatriz – and into functions that relate to a collective subject of the narrative. It becomes increasingly difficult to isolate one specific function of the quest for the unicorn without first examining the different variations of the quest motif and the varying quest narratives in some detail. It is not clear at all for whose benefit the quest for the unicorn is being conducted and who is the active subject of this quest. To best answer these questions it will be necessary to undertake an analysis of the various narrative models that Morgner supplies in the form of narrative clues to the reader.

Intertextuality and the Paradigm of the Medieval Quest

When Laura is musing over the reasons for the absence of any mention of Anaximander in Beatriz's letters, she wonders whether Beatriz has correctly understood the real meaning of Anaximander: "A woman who had read the entire works of Chrétien de Troyes ought to know who Anaximander was" (TB. 184). Just why this should be so, given that Anaximander is in fact a Greek philosopher and astronomer, is not immediately apparent. Laura then shifts the focus away from Anaximander and the ambiguity of his identity (is he the white stag in the medieval tale of Erec and Enide, the unicorn, or the Greek philosopher and astronomer?) to Erec and Yvain, both male heroes of medieval courtly romances. At first glance the reference to the medieval courtly romances of Chrétien de Troyes, in particular the romances of Yvain and Erec and Enide, seems somewhat obscure. On closer analysis, however, it would appear that the narrative paradigms of both medieval romances provide crucial models for the development of both heroines, Laura and Beatriz. The use of intertextual references serves as a means of guiding the reader through the narrative, offering textual clues about the purpose and relevance of particular narrative segments. Morgner's choice of the medieval courtly romance is significant because it combines the notion of the quest, the aspect of adventures, and the traditional ingredient of romance and love with an overriding concern for questions of loyalty and balance. Unlike many modern quests, which combine all these ingredients, the medieval quest, it seems, differs in its emphasis on teaching the desiring subject the virtues of loyalty and moderation. Most importantly, the use of the motif of the quest allows Morgner to highlight the limited range of experiential opportunities available to East German women and to point up the dearth of narrative models appropriate to women's needs.

Both Arthurian legends are examples of quest narratives, a generic pattern underlying all the basic types of narratives Propp identified in his study of the Russian folktale.[13] Greimas identifies the relationship between the two syntactic "actants" of the quest narrative, or in Propp's terms between the subject and the object of the narrative syntax, as one of desire that may take the form of the desire for an object or the desire for truth or knowledge. Those narratives that involve a change of state between the subject and the object describe relations of disjunction or conjunction between the subject and the object.[14] Changes from one state to another operate through a transforming function.[15] Greimas isolates another type of narrative that does not focus on the transference of a valued or desired object but on the mediation between two opposite poles, usually between the social order and the individual.[16] This type is in fact the basic structure of the Bildungsroman, although Greimas makes no specific reference to this most common form of a narrative of mediation. He identifies two possible variations of the mediation narrative in which the existing social order is either accepted or rejected by the subject-actant.[17]

The parallels between the figures of Erec and Yvain, and Laura

---

13. Greimas, *Structural Semantics*, 207.
14. A.J. Greimas, *Du Sens II: Essais sémiotiques* (Paris: Editions du Seuil, 1983), 68–69.
15. See Greimas, *Structural Semantics*, 243–45.
16. Greimas, *Structural Semantics*, 245–46.
17. Ibid., 246.

and Beatriz are infinite and will be discussed at greater length in a later chapter. Both the pattern of the medieval courtly romance and the motif of the quest, when applied to Morgner's novel, reveal interesting parallels of their own. The best example of a quest-romance that approximates the trajectory of the medieval quest is, however, Beatriz's search for the unicorn. Beatriz, as the subject of the quest, is sent out by Laura (the sender or the acting subject) in search of Anaximander (the object of the search) with the aid of a "helper" (Laura). Beatriz's mission, like that of the medieval knight, is fraught with hidden dangers and ordeals that appear to be successfully resolved until the point where she thinks she has successfully completed the mission in locating the unicorn. It now becomes clear that Beatriz's quest is indeed a parody of the medieval courtly romance.

As Anthony Stephens suggests, one such way of detecting a parodic intent in a narrative is in the deviations in the syntagms of contract, performance, and their resolution.[18] Initially there seems to be little in the narrative syntax itself to suggest that Beatriz's quest is indeed a parody of the conventional courtly romance. Beatriz has successfully outwitted such opponents to her mission as Professor Leopold Janda and his daughter, who, she is convinced, are trying to put her off the scent of Anaximander (TB. 286). She also eventually successfully completes her mission to find the unicorn. But once she has located the unicorn, she attempts, like Erec, to bring her spoils home to the GDR. In the act of transporting the unicorn, the much sought-after object of desire, back over the border to the GDR, the unicorn itself undergoes a curious transformation. Instead of being the living embodiment of female ideals, it has become transformed into a mere travesty of its former self:

> She espied a small animal next to Beatriz's left trouser leg. Which Laura would immediately have recognized as a dog if a corkscrew-like horn had not protruded from between its ears on its head. (TB. 329)[19]

18. A.R. Stephens, "'Narrative Structures in Karen Blixens' 'The Dreamers,'" *Festschrift für Ralph Farrell*, ed. A.R. Stephens, H.L. Rogers, and Brian Coghlan (Frankfurt/Main: Peter Lang, 1977), 128.
19. "Da erblickte sie neben Beatrizens rechtem Hosenbein ein kleines Tier. Das von Laura gleich als Hund erkannt worden wäre, wenn ihm nicht ein korkenzieherähnliches Horn zwischen den Ohren aus dem Kopf geragt hätte."

The obvious difficulty in transporting the ideal of the unicorn over the border to the GDR parallels the difficulties women in the GDR faced in transporting Western feminist ideals and strategies into the East German context. Ideals and goals, which may have substance in the West, vanish into thin air when applied to the situation of women under state socialism. The homecoming is blatantly intended as a parody of the typical narrative segment of the medieval courtly romance when the knight brings the fair damsel home to the court, as well as of the ideological homecoming of the protagonist in the socialist "arrival novel." In light of this final absurdity – Lenin's idea *reductio ab absurdum* (TB. 166–67) – it now becomes possible to read backwards from this crucial syntagm of performance in search of other significant deviations from the conventions of the quest.

It soon becomes apparent that the parody lies mainly in the incompatibility or incongruity between what can be termed the surface syntactic structure and the underlying hierarchy of binary oppositions traditionally thought by Greimas to be part of the deeper universal structure of narrative. That is to say, there appears to be a disjunction between the actantial model and the casting of Beatriz in the role of subject. At the level of the surface structure *Trobadora Beatriz* displays similar patterns at the syntagmatic level to the folktales analyzed by Greimas and Propp. Yet the quest narrative inverts the usual ordering of binary pairs of oppositions, in particular the gender oppositions that equate femininity with passivity and masculinity with activity. The historically specific content of Morgner's use of the medieval quest lies therefore not so much in the variations on the narrative pattern at the level of the surface structure but instead at the level of those pairs of semes, those universal categories, that Greimas saw structuring all narratives. It is these inversions that in fact prepare the way for the final parody of Beatriz's inability to bring the unicorn home. Whereas Greimas is concerned with identifying the abstract structures underlying the culturally specific surface structure, it is precisely the culturally specific substrata of meaning motivating the use of conventional motifs of the quest narrative that are of interest here. The problem of the historical, cultural, and gender specificity of narrative structures and genres is one Greimas does not address and one that will be the object of investigation in the following section.

Mobilizing Women: The Longing for
Travel and Adventures

The most significant deviation from the narrative structure of the courtly romance to be found in *Trobadora Beatriz* can be located in Morgner's choice of actants in the quest. The subject of Beatriz's quest is not the medieval knight, nor feudal man; nor is it a masculine subject hiding under the guise of the gender-neutral "man," but is instead a woman. Likewise, the role of the sender is filled by a woman, Laura, who is the initiator of the quest, as is the role of the receiver, occupied by either Beatriz or Laura or both, since both stand to benefit from the quest. Women occupy all major roles in the narrative with the exception of the one that has traditionally been their lot, namely that of the object of the quest. Beatriz, in leaping out of history, that is, out of her historical context in which she is prevented from fulfilling her wish to be the desiring subject of love poetry, could be said to have embarked on a mission to find the right historical conditions for the speaking female subject of erotic discourse. One of Beatriz's objectives in the GDR is therefore to reinvent the speaking female subject, or the woman as the singer of love songs, because: "A medieval Minnesinger who is a woman is historically unthinkable. A medieval singer of love songs who is a woman is not" (TB. 33). Both Laura and Beatriz seem to be in agreement that the time of the female troubadour has not yet come, not for want of women who perceive themselves as subjects, but for want of somebody to fill the place of the object of love poetry.[20] If the speaking, or in this case, singing subject has no addressee or object, it cannot yet constitute itself as a subject. The search for a suitable object for her narrative is thus part of the process by which the female subject actively constitutes herself. One additional aim of the alliance between Laura and Beatriz is the invention or creation of someone suitable to love, as well as the creation of a female subject who is

---

20. Compare the pronouncement made by the narrator at the end of Christa Wolf's science fiction story, "Selbstversuch," that women have yet to invent a suitable love object: "Now my experiment awaits us: the attempt to love. Which moreover also leads to fantastic inventions: to the invention of someone that can be loved." Wolf, "Selbstversuch: Traktat zu einem Protokoll," *Unter den Linden: Drei unwahrscheinliche Geschichten* (Darmstadt & Neuwied: Luchterhand, 1974), 169.

the active pursuer in the relationship.

By foregrounding questions of gender in the structure of the quest narrative, the novel raises pertinent questions about the interrelationship between gender and genre. By casting a female in the role of the subject of the medieval romance, the text exposes the ideological assumptions about gender difference that are implicit in the semantic structures of the quest narrative itself. Moreover, Morgner's novel invites a reading of the quest narrative, and in particular the genre of the courtly romance, along that axis that has persistently been ignored by all the masters of narratology: the gender axis. This enables us to produce a reading of the medieval quest along the lines of gender difference. Gender is therefore the hidden semantic category structuring such genres as the classical Bildungsroman and the medieval courtly romance, the hidden variable that aligns activity and subjectivity with masculinity and passivity with femininity. It is precisely the implicit presence of this gender divide that has traditionally provided the rationale for casting the male in the active role of the subject of the quest and the female as the passive, silent object. The binary opposition of active/passive is admittedly one that is grammatically given, that is, one that is structurally inherent in any adventure genre, because without an active subject of the narrative it becomes hard to conceive of a quest narrative at all. What Morgner's use of the genre does question, however, is the gender assumptions that are implicit in the genre of the courtly romance and in variations of this genre such as the modern adventure novel. Thus, by reversing the gender of the actants in the narrative and by inverting the semic hierarchy of the binary pair male/female, Morgner's adaptation of the quest motif reads as a parody and therefore as a critique of the gender blindness of the conventional quest narratives.

The main barrier to the constitution of the female subject of the adventure segment is described as the "sedentary nature" of women. Laura's lack of mobility is primarily attributable to the unequal distribution of child-rearing responsibilities among men and women. This is further compounded by women's poor representation in the better qualified professions that offer travel opportunities through the attendance of overseas conferences. Attendance at international science conferences in *Trobadora Beatriz* is a male prerogative, and even "feminized" males such as Uwe

Parnitzke feel deeply uneasy in such an overtly masculine environment. Alternatively, women function within the context of conferences as men's "minstrels" or playmates, as in *Gauklerlegende* and *Hochzeit in Konstantinopel*.

Laura is effectively barred from accepting all invitations to travel not so much because of prevailing travel restrictions in the GDR, which precluded someone of the politically dubious status of a train driver from visiting Western Europe, but mainly because of the demands on a single parent:

> Child-rearing demands a strict regimen that is normally at odds with adult natures. This regimentation ranks after an enforced sedentary life-style among the penalties of motherhood. (TB. 179)[21]

These were initially the demands that made Laura sacrifice her career as a Germanist, a career that may have offered her travel opportunities to international conferences. It is not in the least surprising that the only figures in *Trobadora Beatriz* who are free to travel are, apart from those fantastic characters such as Beatriz, Melusine, and Persephone, solely professional men, primarily engaged in scientific professions. The major actants of syntagms of contract that involve syntagms of disjunction (for example, a change of place), are therefore either male or, if female, belong to the realm of legend or fantasy.[22] Otherwise the real women of the GDR in *Trobadora Beatriz* are all stationary.

As a rule women barely figure in popular adventure novels of the time as protagonists, usually playing the part of the wife or lover who stays at home. Because adventures are usually something that the protagonist experiences on his travels abroad, women are rarely featured as the subject of the travel or adventure

21. "Kinderaufzucht verlangt strenge, Erwachsenennaturen normalerweise zuwiderlaufende Ordnung. Diese Ordnungsmaschinerie zählt neben erzwungener Seßhaftigkeit zu den Strafen der Mutterschaft."
22. An exception here is the case of Tamara Bunke, a famous Cuban revolutionary, who functions in Eberhard Panitz's novel *Don Juanita* as a male projection rather than as a female ideal, and belongs more to the realm of legend than history. Tamara Bunke makes a brief appearance in Morgner's novel as the deliverer of a letter addressed to Laura from Beatriz, who is holidaying in Split. It is apparent that Tamara Bunke is very much a living legend, especially when Laura recalls having seen a death notice in the newspaper.

genre in East German literature. Exciting and risky adventures are
events that generally occur outside the geographical and
ideological space of the GDR, either in the wild capitalist West or
in outer space, and thus are not accessible to most women. Despite
numerous claims that socialism should also be a suitable setting
for an adventure novel, most examples of the adventure genre
prefer an exotic or foreign backdrop.[23]

In all three of Morgner's earlier works, *Hochzeit in Konstantinopel*,
Gustav der Weltfahrer, and *Gauklerlegende* the concept of travel is
inseparable from the longing to experience something out of the
ordinary, as well as the need to transcend rigid mechanistic ways
of categorizing human experience. In *Gauklerlegende*, the dice that
repeatedly fall into Wanda's lap are a constant reminder of the
elements of chance that have been rigorously excluded from the
male-dominated world of science and mathematics. The dice,
which resurface again briefly in *Trobadora Beatriz*, become a
recurrent metaphor for the longing for a feminine alternative to
male-dominated forms of political and scientific discourse. In
earlier novels, this longing is triggered by the chance to travel. In
all three stories the opportunity to travel, even if as the playmate
of a man, serves as a precondition for women's encounters with
the extraordinary and the fantastic.

The cultural and political constraints preventing the female
subject from accepting the call to travel are duplicated at the level
of the construction of an active female subject of the quest
narrative. When Beatriz asks Laura to join her on her travels to
Split, Laura interprets this as a breach of their original contract
and declares Beatriz crazy (TB. 189). Were she, as the subject of
her own quest, to accept the "contract" now imposed by Beatriz,
who acts here as the sender in Laura's quest, she would be actually
violating the contract she had entered into with Beatriz in their
secret society as well as the conditions of the traditional quest
narrative. Laura's refusal at this stage to emulate Erec and go off
in pursuit of adventures highlights the particular difficulties
women in the GDR had gaining permission to travel. It also stresses
the problems of articulating female subjectivity through the
medium of an adventure narrative. Despite Laura's thirst for

23. See Hans Hofmann, "Historische Wandlungen des Erlebnisphänomens
'Abenteuer,'" *Weimarer Beiträge* 23, no. 1 (1977): 84.

adventure and her craving for an injection of the unpredictable into her life, she is far too fearful of social and political conventions to apply for a visa. Instead, she must experience vicariously the pleasures of traveling through Beatriz. Her longing for travel and risk is clearly a response to the increasing predictability of life in industrial societies.

Morgner's adaptation of the medieval courtly romance and its knightly adventures seeks to reinstate moments of chance and the unknown and lend legitimacy to human longing for the extraordinary aspects of everyday life. By the same token, her use of the adventure motif in connection with female protagonists is intended as a critique of the gender constraints implicit in the use of adventure narratives for women. The casting of women as adventurers is also a reminder of those unofficial adventures and hardships women encounter on a daily basis outside the work place that are either excluded from or smoothed over in official accounts of women's achievements. In making reference to the medieval notion of adventures, Morgner is attempting to gain recognition for the trials and tests of physical endurance women in the GDR are subjected to daily. Laura's yearning for adventure is therefore the desire to experience something that has not been colonized by idealized newspaper and literary reports of women's emancipation and hence something that has hitherto had no legitimate place in a rationalistic technological life-world.

Morgner's rewriting of a medieval adventure story parodies the notion of the test of one's endurance and the socialist concept of adventure as a test of the individual's ideological rather than physical strength. Beatriz's final ordeal, which like its medieval counterpart, is meant to test "the courtly virtues moderation and loyalty" (TB. 184), is a test of her solidarity and loyalty. It is, however, not loyalty to the immediate economic objectives of the factory or to the goals of the "New Economic System" that is being put to the test here, but rather a new sense of female solidarity. What we have emerging in the main quest narrative is the construction of a new addressee or receiver who, in the folktale, is the person who receives the object of the quest or who benefits from retrieving the lost object. The receiver can also be a collective in the broader sense if the quest is conducted in the name of a larger community. In Beatriz's quest it is not only Laura and Beatriz who are to benefit from finding the unicorn but the working women of the GDR, as implied by the "we" and "us" in Laura's discussion with a colleague:

> For example, Laura replied to her one-time work colleague, Grete, who flatly denied the existence of Beatriz as it defied all logic: If Beatriz is big enough to personally deliver *us* [emphasis added] the unwritten history that was not made by men, *we* [emphasis added] should be big enough to believe in her. (TB. 181)[24]

As Beatriz is homing in on her "prey," it becomes increasingly clear that the unicorn is a code not for an individualistic solution to the problems of women's emancipation, but signifies a collective solution aimed at a wider audience than Laura herself. Beatriz remarks on her travels:

> Was the individualistic solution a code? . . . I was certain that Janda wanted to corrupt me shortly before my goal with a personal solution. To prevent a social one. (TB. 284–85)[25]

But before we can complete decoding the actants in Beatriz's quest it will be necessary to outline briefly the general narrative structure of the socialist variant of the Bildungsroman that provides the reference point for Morgner's intertextual allusions.

The central focus of those novels of the 1960s generally regarded as variations of the Bildungsroman has been described by Emmerich as the "daily probation through work in society."[26] The process of the integration of the protagonist into the socialist collective is, in the majority of cases, portrayed as a test of his/her ideological commitment to the socialist cause, to the "Workers' and Peasants' State," and more generally to international socialism. Conflicts between the collective and the ideologically naive or unin- formed individual, which form the basis of the ordeals or trials that

24. "Ihrer einstigen Arbeitskollegin Grete, die die Existenz von Beatriz kurzweg leugnete, da sie der Logik widerspräche, antwortete Laura zum Beispiel: 'Wenn Beatriz groß genug ist, uns die ungeschriebene Geschichte, die nicht von Männern gemacht wurde, persönlich zu überbringen, sollten wir wenigstens groß genug sein, an sie zu glauben.'"
25. "War die individualistische Lösung ein Code? . . . Sicher, daß mich Janda kurz vorm Ziel korrumpieren wollte. Mit einer persönlichen Lösung. Um die gesellschaftliche zu verhindern."
26. Wolfgang Emmerich, *Kleine Literaturgeschichte der DDR* (Darmstadt & Neuwied: Luchterhand, 1981), 100.

the hero must undergo, tend to be resolved with a change of heart of the hero/heroine accompanied by new political and personal insights. Although exponents of the socialist Bildungsroman like to stress the element of historical continuity between the modern socialist variant and its bourgeois humanist precursor, there are significant differences between the two, in particular at the level of the semantic structure of the quest motif. In conclusion, it will be useful to analyze the socialist Bildungsroman in terms of Greimas's actantial model of narrative in order to highlight the significant differences between the socialist variant and its humanist predecessor.

The subject of the quest of the socialist model is no longer simply "mankind" but more specifically "socialist mankind," that is, the son or daughter of the working class. The object of his/her quest is clearly identifiable as the cultivation of a socialist consciousness.[27] The search for this ideal involves not so much physical hardship (although this is certainly a factor in some cases) as an ideological struggle between, on one level, the attitudes and needs of the individual and the needs of the collective, and on another level, the regressive forces of capitalism and the progressive forces of socialism. The sender, or the person in whose name the quest is conducted, is not society or humanity in general, but the "Workers' and Peasants' State." The ideal or historical force that stands to benefit from the education of the individual, or the receiver of the sought-after object, is either international socialism or the socialist revolution, as opposed to humanism or modernity in the case of the humanist Bildungsroman.[28] The role of helper in the quest is filled by either the party or the scientific and technological revolution or both. The chief opponent in the quest is usually the class enemy, the bourgeois renegade, the "deserter of the Reupublic" or the careerist, or, more generally, fascism or capitalist imperialism.

The most important adaptations to the structure of the socialist Bildungsroman that Morgner makes are not located at the level of the narrative syntax but in the choice of actors in the actantial model itself – although ultimately the choice of actors must disrupt

---

27. Ibid., 101.
28. See Peter Zima, *Textsoziologie: Eine kritische Einführung* (Stuttgart: Metzler, 1980), 78ff.

the teleology of the narrative. The subject of Beatriz's quest and of all other quest narratives in the novel becomes a feminized subject. The various narrative strands center neither around men and their relationships to nature, technology, and society,[29] nor the alleged gender-neutral subject of the socialist revolution, but around the female subject and her specifically "feminine" relationship to science and technology, nature, and work. The role of the initiator or sender of the quest is enacted by Laura who can be seen to represent the particular interests of the majority of working women (and therefore eighty to ninety per cent of women of working age), and more specifically of single, working mothers. The substitution of the female subject and female actants for the socialist "Mensch" constitutes therefore an attempt to displace the male subject or the male subject masquerading as "Mensch" as the chief actor in socialist realist fiction and official discourse. Morgner's text thus exposes the working-class subject of the socialist revolution as implicitly male with its masculine concerns, attitudes, and privileges. By displacing the humanist concept of the "Mensch," something socialist aesthetics and cultural politics have unquestioningly adopted, and by highlighting the gender-bias underpinning official party rhetoric on socialist work and society, Morgner's text raises the crucial question of sexual difference and its importance for the constitution of female subjectivity in fiction. If the quest motif functions as a means of transcending the socially and culturally imposed passivity of many working women like Laura, it remains to be seen exactly what the nature of Laura's relation to Beatriz's adventure quest is and what relevance Beatriz's travels abroad and her homecoming have to Laura's daily existence.

---

29. Wuckel, *Science Fiction*, 185.

4
Science, History, and Legends

Obstacles in the Female Quest: The Double Burden and Science

The modifications Morgner makes to the narrative pattern of the quest through the insertion of culturally specific material extend far beyond cosmetic changes made to the surface level of the narrative. She in fact makes substantial alterations to the structure of the narrative by correcting the androcentric bias of many of the pivotal terms organizing the quest. In this way she challenges the very nexus between masculinity and activity underlying the fundamental trajectory of many quest narratives. In choosing a male paradigm as a vehicle for the expression of female desires, Morgner does not simply substitute a female heroine into a narrative heavily encoded as masculine. Certainly the inscription of a female actor in the role of the active subject of the adventure sequences is an important step in breaking down gender stereotyping. But the "feminization" of the quest in fact extends far beyond the choice of an active female heroine for the role of knight errant. The changes Morgner makes to the quest are much more extensive than would initially seem, affecting the entire structure of the quest in all its elements. Women are cast in the crucial roles of sender and receiver of the quest: they represent the hidden collective subject in whose name the quest is undertaken as well as the receiver of the retrieved object, that is, they are also the beneficiaries of the successfully completed quest. In fact, it would seem that all the roles in the actantial model undergo transformations. Parallel to the changes in the roles of sender, receiver, and subject of the quest, Morgner refashions the roles of helper and opponent. In this way, she challenges many of the ideological assumptions inherent in the quest narrative itself, particularly its assumptions of gender.

In the socialist Bildungsroman as well as in most forms of science fiction novels written during the Cold War in Eastern and Western Europe, the role of the helper or friend in the quest is generally assigned to science and technology. Morgner challenges the role of science as humanity's best friend, casting scientific fantasies and inventions in the role of women's worst enemies. Both the major scientists that Beatriz meets on her travels – Professor Wenzel Morolf, a nuclear physicist, and Professor Leopold Janda, a philosopher – prove unsuitable as helpers or even allies in Beatriz's quest for the unicorn. Professor Janda, it turns out, is undertaking his own mission to find the key to the "creativity automaton," a mission that Beatriz suspects is at cross-purposes to her own: "Perhaps Janda wanted to snatch Anaximander away from me. In the name of the Persephonic Opposition. Or for personal reasons . . . ." (TB. 286). The objective of Janda's mission is to develop the necessary technology, not merely to create artificial intelligence, but to reproduce the intellectual and creative abilities of human beings:

> "It goes without saying that the creation of a new generation of problem-solving, or rather creatively active automatons, so-called creativity automatons, would give rise to such far-reaching upheavals in people's way of life that science cannot yet fully grasp its dimensions," said the professor. (TB. 283)[1]

The dream of developing artificial intelligence to the point that much of the work performed by human beings would be rendered superfluous was particularly popular in the GDR in the 1950s and 1960s (as it also was in Western countries), and the figure of Janda is obviously meant as a critique of the general euphoria amongst scientists at the time concerning the limitless possibilities of the computer age and space technology.

Both scientists function within Beatriz's mission as opponents rather than helpers in her quest, despite the fact that both Janda and Morolf are in every way exemplary in their commitment to socialism and, of course, to science. It is, however, not only Morolf's arrogance and self-importance that is satirized in the novel, but also his particular interest in inanimate matter and the

---

1. "'Es liegt offen auf der Hand, daß die Schaffung einer neuen Generation problemlösender beziehungsweise schöpferisch tätiger Automaten, sogenannter Kreativitätsautomaten, solch weitreichende Umwälzungen in der Daseinsweise der Menschen hervorrufen würde, daß die Wissenschaft ihre Dimensionen heute noch nicht voll zu erkennen vermag,' sagte der Professor."

scientific model of antagonistic opposites he is avid to develop. Morolf is portrayed as the living incarnation of these goals he pursues in his research in nuclear physics. He represents, in the words of Dr. Solowjow, a fanatic of a different kind, "the normative, masculine style of thinking that tends towards intellectual fanaticism" (TB. 165). It is this type of fanaticism and excessive dedication to a cause that is seen as providing the norm for men and women employed in scientific professions.

In Morgner's *Hochzeit in Konstantinopel* as well as in *Gauklerlegende*, it is mainly women who are perceived as being the victims of this masculine norm, although in *Trobadora Beatriz* the primary victim of the stereotype of the dedicated, selfless scientist is in fact Uwe Parnitzke. In the first "Intermezzo" in *Trobadora Beatriz*, Morolf describes nuclear physics to a group of scientists convened for a conference as being "a vigorous science for vigorous men. A masculine science therefore" (TB. 78; RH. 249). Here Morolf is merely testifying to the widely held belief in the inherent interconnection between conceptions of masculinity and the discourse of science. The relationship between representations of masculinity and science as perceived by Morolf and Parnitzke is not presented as metonymic, that is, as historically and culturally determined, but as metaphoric, that is, as a relationship grounded in essential similarity. Morolf apprehends the pursuit of science as an essentially masculine profession; he regards the transference of qualities traditionally attributed to masculinity, that is, properties of the subject of inquiry, onto the object of inquiry, here physics, as somehow natural or given. Although Uwe rejects the myth of physics as a masculine science, signified by his rejection of an authoritarian father-figure – "I am a person who does not need a father" (TB. 76,80; RH. 246) – he remains a victim of the immense social pressure to conform to norms of masculinity.

The domain of science is not only dominated by men as we see from the conference Uwe attends – "the men sat around a large square table – exclusively men" (TB. 78); it is also imbued with values that have historically and culturally belonged to the ruling sex. As Uwe observes, the feminine has no place in the realm of science and the merest trace of what has traditionally been regarded as feminine or pertaining to women can be sufficient to damage a scientist's credibility and reputation as a researcher. The perceived lack of authority commanded by the Armenian physicist is attributed to the unsettling combination of a "feminine mouth" with "hard, fanatical eyes": physiognomical features that give his appearance a heterogeneity that by comparison with Dr. Morolf's "intellectual sex appeal" (TB. 79; RH. 251) makes the Armenian, even in Uwe's eyes, a faintly ridiculous figure. The exclusion of the feminine from the site of the operations of scientific discourse clearly puts such progressive, sensitive men as Uwe, who have rejected normative concepts of masculinity, at a disadvantage. For those women, however, attempting to break into traditional strongholds of masculinity, such as the hard sciences, it represents a clear disincentive.

In the novels preceding *Amanda*, the female figures who attempt to enter traditionally male-dominated professions can be divided into two distinct groups. On the one hand, there are those female characters such as Bele in *Hochzeit in Konstantinopel* and Laura in *Trobadora Beatriz* who are unwilling to make the sacrifices required of them in a male-dominated profession. These women are generally forced, either for personal or family reasons, to opt for careers that do not require the same degree of self-sacrifice and subjugation to men as would a scientific career. Driving trains throughout the night is preferred by Laura, for instance, to a career as a Germanist because it allows her to spend more time with her child during his waking hours. There are, on the other hand, a number of women in Morgner's novels who have succeeded in entering into scientific professions, albeit the "soft" sciences, such as the area of dietetics. Valeska, a dietician working on the synthesis of protein from crude oil, has devised her own strategy to cope with the problem of sex discrimination in the work place and the effects this has on her status and reputation as a researcher. To relieve herself of the double burden of working full-time and looking after her children, she shares a house with two other working mothers. She thus manages to avoid the "fragmentation of her forces" (TB. 233), that fragmentation of time and energy that is symptomatic of the lives of single working mothers. This in turn gives her more time for her research.

The theme of women sharing accommodation and child-rearing responsibilities, as unremarkable as it may seem to a Western reader, is conspicuous by its absence in East German men's and women's writing. Alternative forms of living arrangements such as communal arrangements between women, homosexuals, or single parents received little or no attention in East German writing.[2] The desire to experiment with different ways of organizing and distributing household and child-rearing duties in order to escape the double bind of the double burden very rarely found its concrete expression in women's texts in the GDR, as much of the literature did not usually go beyond a critique of existing living and working conditions in offering alternative solutions to the problem.

Valeska's experiment presents a utopian perspective that touches on a subject that has constituted one of the taboo topics in GDR literature. Such solutions as communal living arrangements were generally not encouraged and certainly not practiced at official levels as they were thought to be incompatible with the socialist ideal of the harmonious nuclear family. Morgner includes in her novel an excerpt from a speech given by Professor Dr. Ludwig Mecklinger, the East German minister of health in the early 1970s, on the occasion of the abolition of paragraph 218, which had until then prohibited abortions. In the speech he cites the preservation of harmonious marriages and stable families as one of the prime concerns of socialist policy makers:

> Marriage, the family, and motherhood are under the special protection of the socialist family. This principle is embodied in Article 38 of the constitution of the GDR. The development of healthy, harmonious, and happy marriages, the formation of stable families, the promotion of love for children, the raising of the birthrate are all inalienable attributes and principle objectives of socialist policy. (TB. 331–32)[3]

The primacy of the family in the GDR was further upheld in the family law legislation in the "Family Statute Book" of 1965 as it was in the "Federal Statute Book" at the same time in the Federal Republic. The particular emphasis in the speech given by the

---

2. One exception is Christine Wolter, "Ich habe wieder geheiratet," in *Wie ich meine Unschuld verlor* (Berlin/GDR: Aufbau, 1984), 26–35.
3. "Ehe, Familie und Mutterschaft stehen unter dem besonderen Schutz des sozialistischen Staates. Im Artikel 38 der Verfassung der DDR ist dieses Prinzip verankert. Die Entwicklung gesunder, harmonischer und glücklicher Ehen, die Gründung dauerhafter Familien, die Förderung der Liebe zum Kind, die Erhöhung der Geburtenfreudigkeit sind unabdingbare Attribute und prinzipielles Anliegen der sozialistischen Politik."

minister of health on the stabilization and maintenance of the nuclear family under socialism is further evidence of the ambivalence of state policy concerning women's rights, in particular the individual woman's right to abortion:

> Nor do our responsible young citizens in new marriages want to forego the happy experience of a family and children. They know too well that the family has a secure place in socialist society, that the formation of families is encouraged by society, and that children will earn the great love and protection of the socialist state. The promotion of love for children, the strengthening of the family in socialist society, and the raising of the birthrate will always remain a basic objective of socialist policy in the GDR. (TB. 333)[4]

It is also characteristic of socialist policies on women that the word "woman" rarely appeared without the accompanying appendage "family" or "child." Legislation governing women's rights was formulated exclusively in terms of their rights and obligations as mothers, which were subsumed under policies on the nuclear family. Despite an increasing tolerance of single parenthood, the nuclear family continued to be considered the norm and single parenthood a temporary deviation from this pattern. In the official rhetoric of the GDR, women were defined predominantly in terms of their traditional role within the family unit. Their position in society was determined by their social function as producers of use values in the home and work place as well as their role as reproducers of labor power. In light of this, the fulfillment of the first condition of women's emancipation, seen as the integration of women into the work force, becomes contingent on the resolution of the contradictions of the double burden. Yet patriarchal societies have failed, according to Morgner, to solve the impasse of the double burden. Bele H. in *Hochzeit in*

4. "Unsere verantwortungsbewußten jungen Bürger in jungen Ehen wollen auch nicht auf das glückliche Erleben der Familie, auf das Kind, verzichten. Sie wissen sehr wohl, daß die Familie in der sozialistischen Gesellschaft einen festen Platz hat, daß die Familienbildung von der Gesellschaft gefördert wird und die Kinder die große Liebe und Fürsorge des sozialistischen Staates erfahren.
  Die Förderung der Liebe zum Kind, die Festigung der Familie in der sozialistischen Gesellschaft und die Erhöhung der Geburtenfreudigkeit werden in der DDR stets ein Grundanliegen der sozialistischen Politik bleiben."

Konstantinopel and Laura Salman in *Trobadora Beatriz* are both negative examples of emancipated women who have compromised their career aspirations because of the unreasonable demands of the double burden. But the double burden of a family and a career is not the only problem; the double standards that apply to working women present further obstacles to the emancipation of women. In the case of Valeska it is the double bind of double standards that ultimately stands in her way. Having escaped the problems of the double burden through officially non-sanctioned means, Valeska finally falls prey to those very same traditional prejudices. According to Valeska, there is a high price to pay if women want to take on the traditional bastions of male intellectual activity:

> Of course a woman must be more talented if she wants to achieve the same as a man. This is apparent in professions that demand that a person extends his or herself, in scientific ones for example, but not in others where women merely wear themselves out faster through the double burden, which runs strictly counter to the ideal of beauty. (TB. 233–34)[5]

Helpers in the Quest: Black Magic and Miracles

A consistent theme that runs through Morgner's works is the importance of magic and the supernatural as a form of support for working women who experience the stresses and strains of the double burden. Melusine reminds Laura and Beatriz in *Trobadora Beatriz* of the necessity of miracles in women's daily life and warns them of the dangers of dispensing too readily with the help of the supernatural. In *Amanda*, as well as in excerpts from the unpublished third volume of the Salman trilogy, Morgner stresses the fact that women are given no time for the reproduction of their own labor power because of the second and third shifts they perform outside the traditional spheres of productive labor. The mere fact that they still manage to perform these additional

---

5. "Eine Frau muß selbstverständlich begabter sein, wenn sie das gleiche wie ein Mann erreichen will. In Berufen, die verlangen, daß der Mensch sich ausgibt, in wissenschaftlichen zum Beispiel, wird das deutlich, in anderen nicht, da verschleißen sich die Frauen nur schneller durch Doppelbelastung, was dem Schönheitsideal strikt zuwidergeht."

functions, she argues, must be conclusive proof of the existence of miracles, because how else could women have managed to survive? She reiterates the need for recognition of the value of magic as a legitimate and necessary means of aiding women in the reproduction of their labor power:

> The fact that in a state where almost half of the working population lives and produces without the reproduction of its labor power proves that black magic has long since been integrated into our everyday lives. Let us prove ourselves worthy of this miracle by recognizing it, acknowledging it.[6]

In *Trobadora Beatriz*, Valeska invents a novel way of utilizing the forces of magic to counteract the discrimination she encounters in society. Her reliance on magic to neutralize discrimination in the work place is an expression of the lack of political and social power available to women to effect radical changes to their status in the home and the work force. At the same time, it also represents a strategy of resistance aimed at opposing those patriarchal structures upholding women's inferior status in scientific and other male-dominated professions. To foil the attempts of a fellow scientist, Clemens, who solicits Valeska's sexual favors in order to extract from her the official secrets of the formula for synthesizing meat, Valeska conjures up woman's age-old ally – magic. Through the use of magic to produce samples of synthesized meat for the lovers' consumption she manages to both please her lover while keeping her integrity as a scientist intact. After all, she was only too familiar with the urge to consume the flesh of the other in moments of passion: "In the course of love play Valeska had often had the strong urge to taste Clemens's flesh" (TB. 222). When she manages to conjure up the aid of magic to synthesize human flesh, she is thus able, in a manner of speaking, to "have her flesh and eat it too": to combine "the useful with the pleasant" (TB. 222). Clemens, however, remains blissfully unaware of her supernatural powers: "the occasional wish to be consumed by a woman had hitherto seemed to him only able to be realized metaphorically"

---

6. "Die Tatsache, daß in unserem Staat fast die Hälfte der arbeitenden Bevölkerung ohne Reproduktion ihrer Arbeitskraft lebt und schafft, beweist, daß die schwarze Kunst längst in unseren Alltag integriert ist." Morgner, *Die Hexe im Landhaus*, 55.

(TB. 222). Valeska is well aware of the ideological reservations that she, as a scientist, should have indulging in unscientific, irrational forms of creativity long since discredited in a scientific age:

> For conjuring tricks belong to the order of successful laboratory experiments that cannot be exploited industrially. Nowadays one could at best perform in a circus with fairy-like abilities. Valeska wanted a scientific career. (TB. 222)[7]

Valeska reminds herself that the epistemologies of magic and science are fundamentally antagonistic; her insistence on using magic as the only possible solution to keeping both her lover and her integrity as a scientist still intact obviously flies in the face of the principles of scientific rationality. Yet in practicing magic, she challenges the distinction between the binary pair science/magic, refusing to regard the two as mutually exclusive terms of a contradiction. Magic becomes a metaphor for a form of feminine resistance whose subversiveness lies in its indifference to the binary logic of dominant discourses. Valeska's experiments thus prefigure the alchemical experiments of Laura and Vilma that play a central role in *Amanda*. Valeska's conjuring experiments and her use of "archaic methods" (TB. 222) must not, however, leave any traces or clues because:

> . . . it followed that a female scientist, who could be shown up as a fairy, would also cast her female colleagues under suspicion of mysticism, in view of the often quoted fact that women's brains weighed on average less than men's. (TB. 222)[8]

Valeska's success at synthesizing Clemens's and her own flesh for their communal consumption and erotic gratification fails, however, to elicit any recognition for her ability as a researcher

---

7. "Denn Zaubern gehört in die Größenordnung erfolgreicher, industriell nicht auswertbarer Laborversuche. Mit feenhaften Fähigkeiten kann man heutzutage bestenfalls im Zirkus auftreten. Valeska wollte die wissenschaftliche Laufbahn."
8. ". . . eine Wissenschaftlerin, die als Fee entlarvt werden könnte, würde in Anbetracht der oft zitierten Tatsache, daß weibliche Gehirne durchschnittlich weniger wiegen als männliche, logischerweise auch ihre Berufsgenossinnen mystisch verdächtig machen."

and instead only strengthens Clemens's belief in the myth of the eternal feminine:

> Valeska's abilities, which were designed to show Clemens in a way that was not prohibited that the protein deficit of the world could be met by 15 million tons, increased Clemens's tendency to mythologize women. That is, to set up a division of labor between "man" and nature. Valeska sensed a pedestal. This degradation soon spoiled her appetite and the desire to conjure partial reproductions from fodder yeast cultivated from crude oil fractions. (TB. 223)[9]

The tendency to mythologize women as creatures of nature is seen here as a consequence of the sexual division of labor or the division of labor between humankind and nature, something feminists have long held responsible for naturalizing women's role as child-rearers and men's role as primary makers of the social environment. Valeska refers here to what socialist feminists have often termed the blind spot in Marx's and Engels's theory of the division of labor in the first division of labor between the sexes, which Marx and Engels assumed to be an inevitable outcome of biological differences between the sexes. Official policies furthering the equality of women in the work force reproduce this blind spot in orthodox Marxism and society in general, thus perpetuating traditional Western concepts of femininity and womanhood.

Achieving equality of opportunity for women in scientific professions is, it seems, not simply a matter of overcoming anachronistic prejudices; it also calls for a radical critique of the masculinist ideology underpinning scientific discourse and those gender assumptions that have been instrumental in upholding patriarchal structures in socialist and capitalist societies. Many of the montages in the novel *Trobadora Beatriz* serve to challenge the myth that the pursuit of excellence in science is predicated on intrinsically masculine qualities such as fanaticism and single-mindedness that women by nature allegedly do not possess. Their

9. "Valeskas Fähigkeiten, die Clemens eigentlich auf nicht untersagte Weise zeigen sollten, daß das Eiweißdefizit der Welt von 15 Mill. t gedeckt werden kann, bestärkten Clemens' Neigung zur Mythologisierung der Frau. Das heißt zur Arbeitsteilung zwischen Mensch und Natur. Valeska spürte Piedestal. Diese Erniedrigung verdarb ihr schnell Appetit und Lust, aus Futterhefe, die auf Erdölfraktionen gezüchtet war, Teilwiedergaben zu zaubern."

first and foremost responsibility towards their children is cited by Dr. Solowjow, a Soviet chess champion, as the main biological reason why women can never make good chess players, and by implication, good scientists:

> S.M. [the Lovely Melusine]: In your opinion what constitutes part of the natural life of a woman?
> Dr. S. [Solowjow]: Not her sociologically determined burdens. But children do. Whose presence, demands, claims, poetry protect her against the fanaticization of the intellect. A child's existence connects intellectual objects to reality, relativizes them, sometimes even ironizes them in a drastic way. (TB. 164)[10]

Women's child-rearing responsibilities, classified here as biological constants rather than as the product of the sexual division of labor, are put forward by Solowjow as the fundamental reason why women do not possess the necessary qualities of fanaticism, aggression, ambition, and self-confidence to make good chess players or scientists. They are, in short, considered to be unscientific by virtue of their biological nature.

Women's achievements in the sciences are constantly undermined by the perpetuation of patriarchal attitudes and deterministic theories defining women in terms of their nature and biology. Women are generally doomed to remain second-class workers of mere "local standing" (TB. 164) without due recognition for their achievements, or, alternatively, are presented with the option of adopting male norms and masculine qualities as a means of attracting attention to the fruits of their labor. As a result, women find themselves at an impasse, faced with the false alternatives of either accepting their inferior status as female workers or conforming to masculine work standards as proof of their competence. In *Trobadora Beatriz* Morgner offers several imaginary solutions to the problems of hidden sex discrimination in the work place, the most notable being the metamorphosis of a woman into

---

10. "S.M.: Was gehört eigentlich nach Ihrer Ansicht zum natürlichen Leben einer Frau?
    Dr. S.: Nicht ihre soziologisch bedingten Lasten. Aber Kinder. Deren Anwesenheit, Forderungen, Ansprüche, Poesie sind Barrieren gegen die Fanatisierung des Geistes. Kindliches Dasein setzt geistige Gegenstände zur Realität in Beziehung, relativiert sie, ironisiert sie auch mitunter auf drastische Weise."

a man in the final book of *Trobadora Beatriz*, "Valeska's Glad Tidings."

Morgner's sex change story forms part of a series of stories on the same topic written by a number of prominent East German authors in the 1970s. The stories were originally commissioned by Edith Anderson for the Aufbau publishing house in 1970 to encourage debate about the glaring lack of equality between the sexes in the former GDR.[11] The anthology was finally published by Hinstorff Verlag in 1975 after years of delays and wrangling with the reluctant publishers. Morgner's contribution to the topic was rejected for publication due to its explicit sexual content. Morgner eventually included the story at the end of *Trobadora Beatriz*.

Laura reads Valeska's "Glad Tidings" on the day of Beatriz's funeral where it functions as a revelation as well as a form of feminist gospel. Valeska's transformation into a man is, unlike that of the protagonist of Christa Wolf's science fiction short story on the same theme, "Selbstversuch," an involuntary response to the exclamatory statement, "If only one were a man" (TB. 426). Disturbed at the prospect of being forced once again into the stereotyped role of housewife in her new conjugal life with Rudolf, Valeska finds herself wishing she were a man in order to escape the expectations of housewifely behavior once and for all. Despite sharing the same profession as her husband, she knew that "Rudolf was used to housewives" (TB. 423). Whilst contemplating the inevitable transformation that would occur in their relationship once the couple moved into a common flat, Valeska finds herself once again wishing she were a man. An erotic friendship, she realizes, is only possible between equals, and Rudolf certainly did not love her as a person but as a "representative of her species" (TB. 427). The third time she repeats the wish to become a man, her wish is granted and the transformation takes place.

Valeska flees to Moscow where she has an affair with an old female friend, Shenja. In her new incarnation as a man, but with the memories of her former life as a woman still intact, Valeska is portrayed as the embodiment of every heterosexual Soviet

---

11. See Edith Anderson, "Genesis and Adventures of the Anthology *Blitz aus heiterm Himmel*," *Studies in GDR Culture and Society* 4, ed. Margy Gerber, 1–14.

woman's dreams. For Shenja and her female friends it is the existence of a man without "the desire to dominate and without expectations of submissiveness" (TB. 434) that makes the appearance of Valeska such a miraculous event. The taboo of female homosexuality is thus broached in the story although not entirely broken. Similarly, the matter of male homosexuality is addressed with equal caution. Upon her return to Berlin, Valeska resumes her life with Rudolf, changing back into a woman during love making by drinking valerian tincture. This is presented primarily as a concession to social decorum. The question of homosexuality is thus defused of its subversive potential and contained in a socially accepted form. Morgner's point is, however, that sexuality itself is ultimately a matter of sexual preference rather than of biology, and that the genital constellation in relationships is peripheral to the more important matter of free sexual expression. Since Valeska's transformation back into a man is merely a concession to local mores, the implication is that this does not substantially alter the homosexual nature of the relationship between Valeska and Rudolf.

At the outset of the story, Valeska, like the female scientist of Wolf's story, is very much a victim of social pressures to conform to masculine work norms. Valeska, however, is never merely a victim; she is also an active opponent in the fight to undermine male hegemony in the better-paid, more prestigious professions. Her reactivation of women's dormant magical powers in her successful attempt to transform herself into a man constitutes one form of resistance to the normative power of scientific discourse and its practices. Her harnessing of magic and the forces of the supernatural, far from underwriting essentialist theories about women's closeness to nature or women's intuitive powers, transforms magic into a Marxist form of "appropriating life," something that has historically and culturally been the province of women. Magic therefore offers an alternative form of knowledge and interaction with the world that women can appropriate to subvert oppressive dominant discourses.

By foregrounding magic as the "natural" helper of working women, the novel causes a displacement of science and technology as the logical ally of socialism. The story of Valeska inverts the actantial model of the Bildungsroman and positions science and technology in the role of the opponent rather than the helper.

Likewise in Beatriz's quest narrative, Dr. Morolf, an exponent of the socialist principle of scientific progress at all costs, plays the role of the opponent rather than the helper in her quest. In the Bildungsroman of the 1950s and 1960s the obvious choice for an opponent in the narrative was either the class enemy or the renegade. In Beatriz's quest it is that much-idealized figure of the dedicated scientist who serves as the opponent or obstacle in Beatriz's quest for the unicorn. The structural changes Morgner makes to the actantial model correspond to an inversion of discursive hierarchies within the Bildungsroman as well as a subversion of official Marxist discourse and its main legitimating discourse of the natural sciences. The displacement of science from its key position in official Marxist discourse opens up a space for suppressed "feminine" forms of knowledge. To remember these "subjugated knowledges,"[12] historically disqualified and suppressed by the dominant discourses of science, is therefore to challenge the imperialism of official party ideology and its legitimizing discourses. Morgner's recuperation of the magical powers historically and mythologically attributed to women, in particular the figure of the witch, to be discussed in detail in chapter 7, constitutes a rediscovery of women's historical struggles against the hegemony of scientific, rational thought.

The portrayal of magic and the supernatural as the natural helpers of working mothers and wives can also be read as a polemic directed at the official heroes of popular socialist literature, who are typically idealized as supermen or superwomen in all respects. Although it is often denied that these exemplary heroes are in any way supermen, being instead "socially active personalities whose humanity is tested in extraordinary situations,"[13] that is, representative rather than idealized figures, it becomes clear reading Morgner's novel that women in the GDR indeed had little choice but to become superhuman if they were to live up to the ideal of the socially committed personality, as well as the traditional ideals of

---

12. For a discussion of *Trobadora Beatriz* in terms of oppositional or "subjugated" knowledges, see Biddy Martin, "Socialist Patriarchy and the Limits of Reform: A Reading of Irmtraud Morgner's *Life and Adventures of Troubadour Beatriz as Chronicled by her Minstrel Laura*," *Studies in Twentieth Century Literature* 5, no. 1 (Fall 1980): 60.

13. Wuckel, *Science Fiction*, 185.

motherhood. According to Morgner, it is only with the help of magic that women can survive in male-dominated professions and successfully combine the duties of motherhood and a career. A sex change through the use of magic is the only way Valeska can maintain her integrity as a researcher and paradoxically preserve her relationship with her husband.

Thus, by insisting on the need for magic in women's daily lives, the novel tries to render visible the hidden contradictions underlying the position of women in patriarchal societies and in many fictional representations of women's lives. Magic has, according to Morgner, always been the secret helper of the "supernatural" heroines of socialist realist fiction by virtue of necessity; claiming recognition for the work of magic is one means of drawing attention to these superhuman feats of endurance. The introduction of the supernatural therefore calls for an acknowledgement of the supernatural as being both an essential part of women's existence and a vital tool for women's survival. Morgner's attention to pre-scientific forms of female knowledge such as magic and mythology stems from the need to articulate the "discursive repression of a 'feminine' difference,"[14] and at the same time signals the search for feminine alternatives to dominant discursive structures.

Inverting Scientific Paradigms

As Beatriz comes closer to tracing down the object of her mission, she gradually gains a new understanding of the underlying structures organizing scientific discourse that have provided the main opposition to women's search for equality and self-realization in technological societies. Although Beatriz perceives the mere presence of Leopold Janda as the main obstacle to her search, there is evidence that suggests the main obstacle lies not with the individual, Janda, but more importantly with his masculinist system of values and the discursive principles he represents. If masculine values and representations of masculinity have pervaded the way in which nuclear physics and scientific research in general have been conducted, from their

14. Martin, "Socialist Patriarchy," 60.

epistemological framework to their praxis, it comes as no surprise that these same values have also informed scientific discourse and the formulation of scientific theory.

Dr. Wenzel Morolf provides Beatriz with an exposé of a theoretical model that forms the basis for scientific inquiry into inanimate matter. Beatriz conveys this treatise in turn to Laura in a letter she sends from Genoa. According to Morolf, the organizing principle of matter is that of absolute, antagonistic opposites. Every part of the inanimate world, from the galaxies to the smallest unit of matter, has a Doppelganger, an opposite or a mirror image that has not merely an imaginary existence, but is a real and tangible force. Morolf stresses the fact that the mirror image is no mere phantasm, but is empirically verifiable and quantifiable. The particles and their opposites are essentially antagonistic; they can only exist as the negation of each other. They are in effect mutually destructive: "particles and antiparticles are incompatible and destruct on encounter" (TB. 199). The synthesis of the collision of opposite particles results in their mutual destruction and the release of large amounts of energy. It is this explosive potential of antagonistic matter that, according to Morolf, has made space travel possible, thus opening up an entirely new future for mankind: "that enables us to talk today in scientifically plausible terms of flying to distant stars" (TB. 199).

In a similar fashion to Engels, Morolf argues that the writers of futuristic fiction are concerned with fantasies about antigalaxies, antistars, and the possibilities of living organisms, whereas scientific inquiry is concerned with the more pressing global problems of the age. Scientific discourse may share similar aims with scientific fiction, yet its superiority undoubtedly lies in its empirical method of inquiry. The contents of this treatise on the organization of the inanimate world appear without commentary in a letter from Beatriz to Laura. In her reply, Laura makes no other reference to Beatriz's letter other than this cryptic form of address: "Dear Antilaura" (TB. 200). By casting Beatriz in the role of her own double, Laura raises the question of the nature of her relationship to Beatriz and the issue of female solidarity. Laura's playful reference to Morolf's treatise on inanimate opposites raises the question once again of feminine difference.

If we examine the interconnection between Beatriz and Laura at the level of the narrative structure, it would seem that Laura serves on one level as the sender in Beatriz's quest, as she is the one who is primarily responsible for the initial injunction to travel. Laura is furthermore responsible for the choice of the object of the quest. However, Laura's role in Beatriz's quest is not confined solely to that of the sender; she also reappears in the role of the helper. As Beatriz's minstrel, it is her role to provide a stationary "point of support," that is, a support system for Beatriz's escapades in much the same way as does Laudine in the Arthurian romance. Laura also provides Beatriz, the time traveler from thirteenth-century France, with a solid grounding in the real. Laura provides Beatriz with an essential link to the realities of women's situation in the GDR in the 1970s, and thus supplies that necessary dose of pragmatism that Beatriz's seemingly naive idealism lacks. She also provides the provincial troubadour's revolutionary enthusiasm with a concrete social and historical focus. In other words, she gives her a concrete historical mission to complete. Laura's task is then to facilitate Beatriz's quest for the ideal conditions for female subjectivity.

As part of her first task as Beatriz's minstrel, Laura secures a contract with a publisher for the proposed montage novel that she is attempting to write in Beatriz's name. The swapping of names coincides with a shifting of narrative functions and subject positions within each narrative. The question of the right name, and moreover the proper name on whose behalf the quest is being conducted, is not merely a question of identity: it inevitably impinges on the question of textual authority. Whereas Laura appears to be occupying the position of minstrel or helper, she in fact comes to represent Beatriz as the author of the montage novel in a process of substitution that has Laura "acting," but only in the sense of "deputizing," as the subject of textual authority in Beatriz's place. In the Beatriz narrative, Laura acts as both helper and subject of the signifying process that constitutes Beatriz as the object of that particular narrative strand.

Despite the considerable amount of role-swapping and shifting of functions within the various narrative strands, Beatriz and Laura appear to represent opposite poles of female experience within East Germany. As "Antilaura," Beatriz represents that fantastic other side of Laura's experience: those unfulfilled desires and yearnings that have been afforded no official place in women's daily experience and its representations. Like the narrator of

Christa Wolf's *Nachdenken über Christa T.*, Laura seeks to answer the questions about the possibility and impossibility of existence through the exploration of another woman's life.[15] In *Trobadora Beatriz*, as well as in Wolf's novel, the exploration of questions of female identity via another woman involves a confusion of identities to the extent that it often becomes difficult to discern the separate identities of the various women in the narratives.

The relationship between the subject of the Beatriz narrative and its helper or acting subject, Laura, provides us with a model of feminine interaction based on mutually compatible, non-antagonistic, empathetic opposites. This mode of interaction is presented as an alternative to the scientific model of mutually exclusive and mutually destructive opposites propounded by Morolf. Laura's realization that Beatriz is her double in the other worlds beyond the borders of the GDR, and beyond the stereotyped representations of women in popular fiction, is accompanied by the realization that she needs another half with which to complement herself. Beatriz's experiences and ideals are therefore not a negation of Laura's but are instead a corrective or addition to a one-sided picture. The alternative offered to the male-propagated and - dominated scientific model of matter therefore marks a shift in paradigm to a mode of social and textual interaction that is posited as feminine and is not based on antagonistic but rather on complementary and mutually compatible opposites.

It is therefore significant, if hardly astonishing, that the destructive energy that is released in Dr. Morolf's model when matter collides with antimatter is given a positive reinterpretation in Morgner's feminist paradigm. The outcome of the meeting between Laura and "Antilaura" unleashes Laura's creative potential and launches her career as a writer. In *Gustav der Weltfahrer* there are already the beginnings of such a model of doubles in the friendship between the two Gustafs. Here, as in *Trobadora Beatriz*, the friendship is a source of inspiration for both Gustafs. The fantastic stories that Gustaf the World-Traveler tells Gustaf the Garbage-Tip Driver, his alter ego in the real, encourage

15. See Anthony Stephens and Judith Wilson, "Christa Wolf," *The Modern German Novel*, ed. Keith Bullivant (Leamington Spa: Oswald Books, Berg Publishers, 1987), 285.

both the narrator and his listener to give free rein to their imagination. It is only later in *Amanda* that the release of creative potential is viewed slightly less optimistically when Laura's sudden fame as the author of the novel *Trobadora Beatriz* is marred by the jealousy and resentment of her new husband, Benno. The resistance to female creativity does not stem so much from official levels but from men's inability to cope with their wives' unexpected public fame.

This shift of paradigm has further consequences for the compatibility of the discourses of the real and the fantastic. The constellation of the two main female protagonists, Beatriz and Laura, constitutes an attempt to break down hierarchies between the real and the fantastic and between subject/object positions within discourse. The model presented by the two women would seem to posit the possibility of a non-hierarchical relationship between opposites based on the principle of metonymical contiguity. Such a model allows for the co-existence of disparate, independent terms as opposed to a metaphorical relationship that subsumes difference under the rule of the same. The positions of the terms in a metonymical system are not necessarily fixed and can be subject to numerous substitutions. The relationship of metonymical contiguity is borne out by the constant role-swapping and job-sharing going on between Beatriz and Laura and the shifting of positions within the actantial model of the various narratives.

Although Laura succeeds in displacing Beatriz as author of the proposed montage novel while Beatriz supplants Laura as child-minder, the substitutions in the novel are by no means limitless or arbitrary. Beatriz, it seems, is able to displace and replace all of Laura's functions as working mother. The number of official substitutions that Laura can undergo, however, is much more restricted. It is precisely the substitutions that she is barred from undergoing that ultimately point to the limitations within this paradigm of opposites and the problems associated with constructing real alternatives within the social and political confines of the former GDR and patriarchal systems in general.

Laura's function with respect to Beatriz is to provide stability and support at home during Beatriz's adventures abroad. Laura is also Beatriz's stable point of reference in the realm of the socialist real. Although Laura is described repeatedly as the stationary pole of the dyad, she ultimately comes to displace Beatriz as female troubadour and as creative subject, becoming the author of her own stories. While Beatriz is away, Laura vents her frustration at being left home "holding the baby" in "wanderlust stories," which openly express her longing to travel and escape the monotony of her daily routine. Writing becomes a kind of substitute adventure or a surrogate for traveling since it is only through the act of writing that Laura can traverse the limitations of her socially and politically imposed situation. But Laura can only stand in for Beatriz as author of the montage novel in the same and only way she can transgress the borders of the GDR: in fictional representations. She can only be the sender, the acting rather than active subject of Beatriz's travel adventures, never fully displacing Beatriz as the active subject of her own adventures and her own narrative.

From her holiday in Split, Beatriz writes a letter to Laura inviting her to join her. With this letter, Beatriz is offering Laura a chance to become both the subject in her own quest narrative and the author of her own travel stories. The letter Beatriz sends Laura from Split requesting leave from Laura's employer thus reads as an invitation to Laura to embark on her own adventures. It also reads as a disguised application for a travel visa:

> Dear Colleagues, I herewith apply for a free ticket Berlin-Prague-Budapest-Zagreb for the Tram Driver Laura Salman, who is currently employed with you in a sedentary working capacity. (TB. 189)[16]

Apart from the fact that an application for a travel visa might well blow her cover and create difficulties for her at work, Laura's extreme consternation at Beatriz's request seems to be unwarranted. Laura suspects the misunderstanding stems from diverging conceptions of the "support model" theory: "Laura rummaged around desperately in the support model. Which could be characterized as an off-shoot of the classical heritage fashion" (TB. 189).

---

16. "Liebe Kollegen, hiermit beantrage ich einen Freifahrschein Berlin-Prag-Budapest-Zagreb-Split für die Triebwagenfahrerin Laura Salman, die bei Ihnen in einem vorübergehend ruhenden Arbeitsverhältnis steht."

Laura's acceptance of the invitation would be equivalent to an inversion of the support model. The inversion of this model would thus dislodge Laura as the passive, static pole of the pair, freeing her from her position within Beatriz's narrative as passive bystander. Laura's refusal, then, even to consider Beatriz's request points to a reluctance, or even an inability, to constitute herself as an active subject of her own quest. The attainment of female subjectivity is thus indefinitely deferred. Laura's reluctance to join Beatriz in Split can be read as an affirmation of difference and of a continuing dialectic of identity. If one reads Beatriz's invitation to Laura to travel to Split as an attempt to collapse the opposite halves of a dichotomy, it is then hardly surprising that Beatriz's invitation precipitates something of an identity crisis for Laura. It is after all in the town of Split that Beatriz discovers her true identity, that is, her "split" identity, which is of course reinforced by the name of the city where she makes the discovery. Her holiday is described as a "recovery from myself" (TB. 195), an escape from the self. One can presume that the self Beatriz is referring to is Laura.

The central metaphor of the story of the stronghold or citadel of slavery of the "Diacleties Palace" also provides us with further clues here. Both the palace of Split and the landlady of Beatriz's pension are described as "historical produce," that is, as the organic product of an historical process. Behind the facade of the palace Beatriz sees history in human form: "Behind the palisade is history in natural, almost human manifestation" (TB. 191). Frau Sarić is also likened to the palace; she partakes of the long and turbulent history of the palace in a harmonious fusion of collective and personal identities. Beatriz writes: "For seven days my feet walked over the historically produced remains of the facade of Frau Sarić" (TB. 194). The use of biblical imagery here underscores the immense importance of the creative process underway during Beatriz's stay in Split. As the metaphor of the castle and the representation of subjectivity as "historical produce" seem to indicate, the female subject is presented as the gradual result of a long, protracted process of political struggles. The historical "subject-becoming" of women is seen in analogous terms to the "infiltration of the tyrannical building" of the palace by the "homeless Salonites" (TB. 192). The realization that the foundations for a new historical consciousness cannot be laid down overnight and are the work of centuries marks a crucial turning point in Beatriz's journey of self-discovery. Furthermore, it is the lack of historical roots and precedents that distinguishes Beatriz from Laura and that constitutes a major hurdle in the realization of Laura's hopes for selfhood. Beatriz's search for the foundations of the castle therefore marks the beginnings of the laying down of the foundations for a new female subjectivity. Her explorations in the foundations, or rather in the cellars of the castle, is also a search for Laura, for her absent other self and for the history of that other woman. The woman whom she meets in the cellar, Bele, a character from *Gustav der Weltfahrer*, can be interpreted as a fictional representation of Laura or Laura's representative in fiction.

Morgner's parable is reminiscent in many ways of the Italo Calvino story in *Invisible Cities* where men build a city, Zobeide, in order to capture the lost dream of a woman. Yet the woman for whom the city is built, and who, like Morgner's women, provide its very "foundation and the very condition of representation," remains forever absent.[17] But unlike the lost dream of the woman in Zobeide, Morgner's women are always very much physically present. They are not absent from history, as some Western feminists have maintained, but are instead hidden underground, to be found in the cellars of the castle in Split or at the very foundations of patriarchal history. They too, like the illusive and illusory woman of Calvino's story, a woman who is the city's "foundation" and "the very ground of representation," provide the foundations upon which Western patriarchal culture is built.[18]

The "historical produce" of female subjectivity, although fortified by "protective walls," which are likened to Laura's pragmatism, is also described as an "infiltrated stronghold of slavery." Thus it is simultaneously the historical site of centuries of domination as well as the site of struggles for liberation. Beatriz's discovery of the fragmentation of the female self accompanies the realization that the female subject has always been, and still is, the site of ideological warfare. Subjects are, like the palace in Split that has seen generations of rulers come and go, also able to be invaded and inhabited by ideological and political struggles for domination and control. But by the same

17. Teresa de Lauretis, *Alice Doesn't: Feminism, Semiotics, Cinema* (London: Macmillan Press, 1984), 13.
18. Ibid., 12–14.

token, they can also become the sites for struggles for liberation.

In Laura's case, the invasion of the subject by ideology is described in rather ambiguous terms as the product of a process of alienation whereby the female body becomes the site of the intersection of railway tracks, streets, and rivers: "So it happened that Laura is traversed by streets and by railway tracks and rivers which deposit objects, both animate and inanimate, in the robes of her body" (TB. 195). The female body becomes occupied territory, the repository of introjected objects from the external world. In the case of Beatriz, however, the same process of breaking down barriers between the self and the world and invading the interior of the subject is seen as a positive act of reappropriation as well as an emancipatory move in the historical becoming of the female subject. Beatriz's holiday, moreover, provides a cure for her impatience and her reliance on miracles:

> Impatience fell away. And this urge for cleanliness. Physical and intellectual. I only washed while swimming in the sea. I didn't shower the salt from my skin and mind. Soon I felt myself infiltrated by crystals that were growing, outside and inside. Seven days. (TB. 192)[19]

The laying down of crystals during her seven-day holiday is symbolic of the laying down of foundations for a mythical construction of an organic kind in the "subject-becoming of woman," as well as for the active constitution of a new female identity.

The Assistance of History and Legends

In Split, Beatriz comes to the realization that her real mission is to provide the historical and cultural foundation for the reconstruction of a women's history and a new historical consciousness among women. In the cellars of the palace in Split, Beatriz is approached by the figure of Bele – herself a character resurrected from Morgner's literary past – who reminds Beatriz:

19. "Ungeduld fiel ab. Und dieser Trieb zu Reinlichkeit. Körperlich und geistig. Ich wusch mich nur schwimmend im Meer. Ich duschte das Salz nicht aus Haut und Gehirn. Bald fühlte ich mich außen und innen von Kristallen durchsetzt, die wuchsen. Sieben Tage."

"No-one who is endeavoring to achieve something on a larger scale can dispense with the help of history. The certainty that comes from having roots. An awareness of traditions that creates self-awareness." (TB. 194)[20]

This remark reads very much like a response to Brecht's critique of bourgeois historiography in the poem "Questions from a Reading Worker." Here Bele is advocating a project of recovering and rediscovering women's lost historical remains. This involves the seemingly impossible task of piecing together the nameless and invisible traces women have left behind in history. These traces document the history of the slaves of the slaves.[21] A sense of history and of the history of women's struggles against domination is essential, Morgner argues, for the cultivation of a specifically feminist consciousness. Great achievements, all of Morgner's characters seem to agree, cannot be expected from women if they cannot lay claim to a visible history of resistance as did the working classes in the history of the Peasants' War and the reformation:

> However, historical consciousness is extraordinarily important if you want to understand a historical movement like women's liberation properly. Without historical consciousness we would soon become impatient and possibly experience a nostalgic backlash . . . .. To be able to conceive of oneself as part of a historical context demands of course much effort and strength, it requires intelligence, erudition and unfortunately a great deal of patience.[22]

Morgner's remarks in fact echo a similar comment made by Volker Braun in 1973: "Historical consciousness is self-awareness."[23]

20. "Niemand, der sich müht, etwas Größeres zu wollen, kann den Beistand der Geschichte entbehren. Die Gewißheit der Verwurzelung. Selbstbewußtsein schaffendes Traditionsbewußtsein."
21. See Morgner, "Rede vor dem VII Schriftstellerkongreß," 113.
22. "Geschichtsbewußtsein ist aber außerordentlich wichtig, wenn man eine historische Bewegung wie die Frauenbefreiung richtig verstehen will. Ohne Geschichtsbewußtsein würden wir bald ungeduldig und möglicherweise einen nostalischen Rückschlag erleiden . . . .. Sich in einem historischen Zusammenhang zu begreifen, erfordert natürlich Mühe, Kraft, verlangt Intelligenz, Belesenheit und leider viel Geduld." Morgner, "Die täglichen Zerstückelungen: Ein Gespräch mit Ursula Krechel," *Frauenoffensive* 5 (1976): 39.
23. Volker Braun, "Literatur und Geschichtsbewußtsein (Diskussionsgrundlage auf dem VII Schriftstellerkongreß der DDR, 14. November 1973)," *Neue Deutsche Literatur* 22, no. 2 (1974): 131.

Beatriz also concurs that women need the assurance and confidence that only historical "roots" can provide, because a sense of history and tradition is a key factor in developing a strong sense of self. The project of rewriting women into official historiography shares the same difficulty of documentation as Brecht's project of writing the proletariat into bourgeois historiography. A history of women cannot be concerned with existing recorded historical facts: "because only the history of the powerful appears recorded in the history books" (TB. 193). Because the traces women have left behind are both nameless and invisible, unlike those of the male slaves, which are "nameless" "but visible" (TB. 194), women must venture into the world of legends to discover the history of their oppression. They must then reappropriate these legends as a basis for a new history. Bele describes to Beatriz her first encounter with the suppressed history of the proletariat in the legendary figure of her grandfather. Significantly, the encounter takes place on the day of the historical workers' uprising in the GDR on 17 June 1953:

> A certain Bele H. . . . told me that history appeared to her on 17 June 1953 in the lecture theater 40 of the old University of Leipzig in the form of her grandfather. Due to circumstance in legendary form. (TB. 193)[24]

Although the recuperation of the history of the working class provides the point of departure from which women should start to reappropriate their own history, a history that includes women's achievements and contributions must be distinct from the history of the proletariat. In *Gustav der Weltfahrer*, Bele recounts the story of her grandfather and the tall stories he used to tell as the first step in writing the non-heroic story of the proletariat into history. Morgner's story clearly demonstrates, however, that the project of rewriting history from the perspective of the proletariat cannot do justice to the very different history of women's contribution. Such a history of the proletariat as offered by Brecht in his "Questions from a Reading Worker" fails to take into account women's labor in the home, that is, women's labor outside the spheres of economic production. Bele's account of her grandfather in *Gustav der*

---

24. "Eine gewisse Bele H. . . . erzählte mir, daß ihr die Geschichte am 17. Juni 1953 im Hörsaal 40 der Alten Universität zu Leipzig in Gestalt ihres verstorbenen Großvaters erschienen wäre. Umständehalber in legendärer Gestalt."

Weltfahrer demonstrates that the rebuilding of the legend of her grandfather and his fantasies cannot at the same time take into account the secret desires and creativity of his wife as long as the relations of production within the family retain their feudal character. The process of rendering visible women's particular forms of productivity entails at the same time a process of reappropriation of women's forces of production:

> History records victors. Clara, one of the vanquished, bore 14 children, as well as the World-Traveler. From her body grew and still grow endless numbers of invented flowers. I await the time when she takes what is duly hers. (GW. 87)[25]

The marginal position of Bele's grandmother with respect to the story repeats the marginal position women have occupied even in the history of the working class. Morgner seems to suggest that although a Marxist historiography has been hitherto ill-equipped to take women's productivity into account, particularly in the home, she concurs with Brecht's position that a materialist analysis of history is essential for rendering the productivity of an oppressed group or class visible. Bele argues, however, that Brecht's poem only raises the question of the history of working-class men and is only "concerned with men" (TB. 194). It fails to pay tribute to the slaves of the slaves who have left no visible signs behind them and who were generally women. *Gustav der Weltfahrer* can therefore be read as a feminist pendant to Brecht's poem, and in particular as a feminist reply to Brecht's question: "Who cooked the victory banquet?" As Morgner's story demonstrates only too clearly, it was not the male slave or worker who cooked the feasts for the kings and the patriarchs but generally his wife.

During her stay in Split, Beatriz speculates about Laura's lack of historical origins and reflects on women's need for the backing of tradition and history in their struggle for recognition and autonomy. Beatriz, herself a cross between historical fact and legend, provides Laura with just that sense of historical tradition that Laura needs. The metaphor of the "historical produce"

25. "Die Geschichte verzeichnet Sieger. Klara, eine Besiegte, hat vierzehn Kinder geboren, auch den Weltfahrer. Ihrem ausgemergelten Leib entwuchsen und entwachsen noch und endlos lügenhafte Blumen. Ich erwarte die Zeit, da sie nimmt, was ihr gehört."

expresses the dialectical process between history and legend, art and nature that is needed to free women from the realm of nature with which they are constantly identified. Beatriz sets up a dichotomy between art and nature, on the one hand, and between historical fact and legend, on the other: "I [Beatriz] am rooted in the twelfth century. By virtue of art. Laura is rooted in legends. By virtue of nature. I wonder whether she knows this?" (TB. 193).

Laura's historical and cultural roots are situated along the same axis as legend and nature; Beatriz's historical origins are to be found in the twelfth century and therefore belong to the realm of historical fact. Yet it is only through the medium of art, through the fictional appropriation of the legend, that Beatriz can actually enter into history as an historical and legendary figure. In the case of Beatriz, the boundaries between history and legend are not clearly demarcated. Laura's historical roots on the other hand are shrouded in those literary legends of the 1950s and 1960s about emancipated women who combine effortlessly the new duties of the socialist comrade with the expectations of motherhood. The creation of legends has not always been productive in providing women with a history they can claim to be all their own making, that is, a history that includes all their struggles, both public and private, heroic and non-heroic. In the 1970s a number of works by women tried to redress the imbalance in previous literary legends about women, emphasizing for the first time the degree of personal sacrifice required of the female activist, bringing to light seemingly irreconcilable individual and interpersonal conflicts. As Beatriz demonstrates in her first "Bitterfeld Fruit" about the legend of comrade Martha, the preoccupation of newspapers and official party organizations with the creation of legends and heroic socialist figures led to the creation of dangerous and unrealistic myths about women's superhuman feats for socialism. Beatriz's attempt at a documentary, by contrast, does not aim at a coherent, unifying "picture" of Martha Lehmann for the reason that "she made none of herself" (TB. 356). If Beatriz is ambivalent towards the official version of the legend of Martha Lehmann, it is because Martha is the object of an artificially unifying legend rather than the subject of her own story. If women's entry into history is dependent on their rewriting popular legends from a female perspective, history and legend lose their qualities as fixed categories in the dialectical process of the constitution of the female subject.

Laura's entry into history involves, as announced by Beatriz soon after her arrival in the GDR, the appropriation of her "nature" since Laura's identity was rooted in legends, "by virtue of nature" (TB. 193). The allusion to a female nature, as mentioned earlier, can be interpreted as an encoded reference to female sexuality. Yet Morgner's use of the Marxist concept of nature contains a hidden polemic directed against classical Marxist concepts of productivity and reproductivity. Reappropriating women's nature can also be read as the act of repossessing women's means of production and reproduction. The Western notion of free love thus gains new legitimacy under the mantle of Marxist terminology. The project Bele announces at the end of *Gustav der Weltfahrer* is identical to the historical mission Beatriz proclaims in *Trobadora Beatriz* and centers around the notion of appropriating women's nature as a prerequisite for their historical becoming.

The reference to the appropriation of nature cannot, of course, be read without reference to Marx's history of the working class. Marx argued that if the working class were to appropriate its own means of production this would involve harnessing the forces of nature in much the same way as had the bourgeoisie. Marx's account of the rise of the bourgeoisie gives legitimacy to women's struggle for "body ownership" and functions as a narrative of legitimation. Women's task of appropriating their nature is concerned with reappropriating those means of production specific to women that Marx excluded from his analysis of the forces of productivity. It is also concerned with breaking down the classical Marxist opposition between the forces of production and reproduction. The reappropriation of women's nature, their sexuality, and their forces of reproduction is posited by Morgner as the first step in inscribing women into history. Moreover, it is not until they can write themselves into history and their history becomes written, that women can effect the transition from naturalized objects of sexual exploitation to historical subjects. Laura, whose roots are "by nature" legendary, still finds herself on the side of nature in the nature/culture dichotomy, at the crossroads of her historical becoming. As a member of the working class she has already, at least officially, entered into history, yet as a woman she still finds herself, at worst, on the other side of the demarcation line between nature and culture and, at best, as a type of "missing link" between humankind and nature (TB. 104). It is only in freeing themselves from their natural status, by refusing their natural function as mothers, wives, and lovers, that women can begin to enter into the world as historically constructed and determined beings.

Women's historical becoming is part of a dialectical process whereby women's initial leap out of history as natural objects is followed by a leap back into history as historical subjects. This is what Volker Braun has termed "the dialectical leap of history."[26] Despite the urgency of the project of historical becoming, Valeska, the dietician mentioned earlier, gives voice to her bitterness and frustration in a nostalgic plea for a return to a naive, plant-like, vegetative existence in a state of pre-consciousness. She expresses the desire to escape the painful process of historical becoming in the conceit of the dandelion. As a dandelion she could hide on the "bleaching ground" in the "clay soil": "there it would not be necessary to have deep roots" (TB. 224). She would, as a dandelion, have no need of tradition or history; history and nature would already have taught her how to survive without roots. The dandelion also provides a model of feminine survival and non-heroic resistance with its remarkable ability to survive even the most pernicious attacks on its leaves, flowers, and roots. The dandelion is useful for its medicinal and nutritional value, yet it is generally regarded, especially by those housewives "obsessed with white-washing" who wash on the square, as a noxious weed and an object for extermination. Not surprisingly, the dandelion has developed its own ingenious means of self-defence to survive the various onslaughts it is subject to. First, it thwarts all attempts to root it out by refusing to ever be completely uprooted: "A piece of root always remains in the earth" (TB. 224). And second, its flowers, "fruit with hair-like parachutes," ensure that the dandelion is indestructible: "I am ineradicable: immortal" (TB. 225). To become a dandelion is thus to bleed but to feel no pain: "I may feel the cut but no pain. No desire nor joy, I am" (TB. 224–25). To lead a dandelion's existence may be a reaffirmation of the notion of woman as immanence, but it is an immanence that has not given up striving for transcendence.

Valeska's longing for a vegetative form of existence is also

---

26. Braun, "Literatur und Geschichtsbewußtsein," 131.

associated with a disguised form of homoerotic love: "Sometimes I would like to be a plant, for example a dandelion or a lesbian" (TB. 225). To be a lesbian in the GDR is clearly to suffer a fate worse than a dandelion. The articulation of lesbian sexuality and identity constituted one of great taboo topics, the great silences in East German literature and culture, and the suppression of lesbian sexuality was pursued far more vigorously in the GDR than in the West. Valeska's desire for a homosexual attachment finds no legitimate expression in the text, except in a displaced form of representation in the utopian story of Valeska's sex change at the end of the novel. Homosexuality can thus only be expressed within the sanctioning frame of utopian fiction. By virtue of the fictional device of the sex change it loses its threatening illicit aspect and is made respectable by the fact that when Valeska makes love to a woman she at least assumes the physical shape of a man. Homosexual desire must disguise itself as heterosexual sex. Likewise, the fear of male homosexuality is disavowed by the narrative trick of allowing Valeska to revert back to her original feminine form before she makes love to her husband. Thus, homoerotic desire is channeled through conventional hetero-sexuality and must assume the guise, if only externally, of heterosexuality. A physical sex change becomes the necessary prerequisite for the fulfillment of homosexual desire: the necessary narrative form for the articulation of a literary and social taboo.

The conceit of the dandelion can be read as a general expression of the desperation at the lack of sexual and social alternatives available to women in the GDR: as the negation of all feminine desire – for love between two women, for social mobility, for travel and adventures, and for difference. In its regressive nostalgia, it also provides a somewhat more realistic foil to the naive optimism of Beatriz's project of women's entry into history. For Valeska the story can be seen as an attempt to purge herself through the diuretic of the dandelion of all longing, to become totally without desire and hence without fear of frustration and the pain of waiting. It is also an announcement of defeat; the gap between individual claims to happiness and the objective possibilities for realizing them has become unbridgeable. The conceit of the dandelion ends with the eradication of all longing and the affirmation of a state of being verging on catatonic: "I am waiting for nothing. Am by nature stationary. No thought of traveling and other illusions. Longing is as foreign to me as satiety" (TB. 225). This extremely pessimistic portrayal of the limited possibilities for the self-realization of women in the GDR is only of marginal importance in the framework of the main narrative. It does, however, parallel an increasing sense of desperation on Laura's part; her "wanderlust" and sense of isolation during Beatriz's absence grows more acute and can no longer be placated by the travel reports Beatriz sends home. Laura's situation begins to look more and more hopeless; she cannot travel herself and the travelogues are a poor substitute. And Beatriz has not yet returned with the unicorn.

At this point the narrative enters a new phase. The Bildungs-roman that began with Laura's decision to educate young Beatriz via the medieval notion of the quest may prove to be successful in taming Beatriz's wild and fanciful ideas about women's emancipation, but this solution is clearly not in the best interests of the other working women of the GDR, such as Laura. Laura is literally left pining for Beatriz while the latter cavorts around the capitalist countryside. The solution of Laura being a surrogate subject of the quest romance is not tenable. Laura must actively constitute herself as a subject of her own desires and her own romance narrative. The choice of a quest-romance for Laura is significant. Whereas Beatriz became the historically impossible female subject of the medieval courtly romance, allowed to go in search of adventure, Laura can only become the subject of a modern day love romance that permits her to conduct a search for the ideal heterosexual partner. In the following chapter the role reversals between Beatriz and Laura will be investigated along with the implications of this narrative shift in emphasis from the medieval courtly romance to the modern romance with the goals of emancipation and self-realization in mind.

5
Gender and Genre: Models of Female Development

The Female Bildungsroman

In *Trobadora Beatriz* Morgner experiments with a range of socialist and non-socialist genres, invoking narrative conventions familiar to her readers in order to challenge these reader expectations and plot paradigms at a number of levels. Her explorations of such genres as the medieval courtly romance revive non-traditional and pre-bourgeois narrative patterns that offer alternative narratives of self-development for women. Her choice of medieval topoi stems from a desire to escape the ideological straitjacket of socialist cultural policy with its prescriptive canonization of bourgeois cultural traditions. The courtly romance provides an example of a pre-capitalist narrative that is ideologically neutral in terms of the response it evokes in the minds of socialist ideologues. At the same time, her deliberate decision to eschew conventional models of female development as offered by the nineteenth-century female Bildungsroman or the twentieth-century socialist variant of the "arrival novel" is motivated by a dissatisfaction with the way gender is encoded in these genres – specifically, the way female experience is molded in a restricted range of narrative possibilities. Morgner's inversions of generic conventions effect a feminist critique of what Jameson has called the "allegorical master narratives"[1] and Jean-Francois Lyotard the "grand narratives"[2] underlying and structuring all forms of modern narrative. Steeped in patriarchal value systems, these master narratives are obviously deeply problematic for a feminist point of view.

The modifications Morgner makes in the Bildungsroman in its

1. Jameson, *The Political Unconscious*, 28ff.
2. Jean-Francois Lyotard, *The Postmodern Condition: A Report on Knowledge*, trans. Geoff Bennington and Brian Massumi, foreword Fredric Jameson (Manchester: Manchester UP, 1984), xxiii.

nineteenth-century and twentieth-century socialist variants constitute far more than mere substitutions at the surface level of the narrative or at the level of content. The roles of all actants in the narrative undergo substantial revisions, ranging from the subject and object of narrative processes to the choice of opponent and helper. But most significant of all perhaps is the choice of narrative telos. Here Morgner unravels the link between the representation of gender and the ideal of social integration and harmony characteristic of the socialist and classical male Bildungsroman. Through a number of attempted substitutions in the narrative chain she reveals the telos typical of male patterns of development and maturity to be androcentric in its bias and therefore inimical to female development. As she demonstrates the inappropriateness of male patterns for female maturation, she also seeks to adapt typically female models of the quest to incorporate alternative endings and stories.

In her works she is engaged in a narrative practice that, in the words of Rachel du Plessis, aims to "write beyond the ending" by underscoring the inadequacy of the conventional endings to the "heroine's text" of marriage and death. At the same time she is careful when rejecting conventional female narrative scripts not to posit stereotyped male models as unproblematic correctives to received patterns of female development. In Morgner's works typical male patterns of self-realization remain on the whole inaccessible to women who, for a range of pragmatic, political, and social reasons, are prevented from fulfilling their aspirations for autonomy. Narrative segments in which women attempt to achieve a typically male telos invariably fail or falter due to the personal and political constraints impeding the construction of an active female subject. The impasse this creates for the female protagonist, whose aspirations cannot be adequately met by either traditional female or male patterns, often necessitates an uneasy shifting within Morgner's plots from male paradigms to female models and vice-versa. Rather than constituting a blind spot of the narrator this should instead be seen as a strategy designed to point up the difficulties in forging narrative alternatives that are sensitive to the way gender informs narrative practices.

Traditionally, the plots of male and female Bildungsromane have displayed quite different trajectories. In each of the models the classical ideal of social integration and harmony produces radically different endings. According to Franco Moretti, the classical Bildungsroman with its male protagonist typically strives to synthesize two essentially contradictory and conflicting goals that it presents as complementary and convergent trajectories. The Bildungsroman seeks to harmonize the twin goals of individual self-development and realization with the demands of social integration.[3] The uniqueness of the Bildungsroman form for Moretti lies in its ability to synthesize the dual trajectories of modernity in symbolic form. The Bildungsroman achieves a synthesis of societal demands for order and harmony and the individual's striving for self-fulfillment through the mechanism of internalization, whereby the individual adopts the imperatives of the social order as his or her own. In this way the novel represents the symbolic legitimation of the social order.[4] In its classical configuration, Moretti conceives of it as a synthetic form holding together its inherent tensions in a more or less perfect state of "organic" balance.[5] One typical form that this synthesis takes is the ideal bourgeois marriage that is held out as a model for a new type of "social contract," sealed not by external forces, but by the mutual consent of two willing and supposedly equal partners. A perfect balance is finally struck between the individual's desire for self-realization and the call to duty in "the perfect match."[6]

As feminist analyses of the Bildungsroman have revealed, almost all definitions of the genre presuppose a range of social options in the narrative that are only open to men: the unfettered exploration of the social milieu, access to formal education, and the valorization of social involvement in the linear progression towards maturity.[7] Marianne Hirsch reminds us that the maturity the female protagonist of the Bildungsroman attains can not be equated with the acquisition of wisdom and Bildung of the male hero; for the female heroine marriage invariably increases the

---

3. Franco Moretti, *The Way of the World: The 'Bildungsroman' in European Culture* (London: Verso, 1987), 19.
4. See ibid., 16.
5. Ibid., 17.
6. Ibid., 22.
7. Elizabeth Abel, Marianne Hirsch, and Elizabeth Langland, eds. *The Voyage In: Fictions of Female Development* (Hanover, London: University Press of New England, 1983), 7; Marianne Hirsch, "Spiritual 'Bildung': The Beautiful Soul as Paradigm," in Abel et al., *The Voyage In*, 27.

sense of isolation and confinement, bringing her intellectual and emotional development to an abrupt and often violent end.[8] Heterosexual love and marriage are frequently the female counterparts to the adventures and travels that characterize the development of the male protagonist. For this reason, Karen E. Rowe has argued that the patterns of folktales and the romantic fairytale often exert a persuasive influence on the female Bildungsroman. The fairytale, with its ideals of romantic love, provides a subtext for female growth and a paradigm for female maturation.[9] The development of the female protagonist is shaped according to the dual imperatives of the romantic fairytale and the male Bildungsroman with its emphasis on adventures.

The socialist variation on the Bildungsroman, propagated during the first few decades of the GDR, shares many features of the classical Bildungsroman, in particular the emphasis on the processes of individual legitimation of the social, that is, the socialist order. Yet the social harmony that was still possible in the early 1960s even in such novels as Wolf's *Der geteilte Himmel* had by the 1970s become increasingly implausible and artificial. Like Wolf's *Nachdenken über Christa T.*, perhaps the first of the failed female Bildungsromane to be written in the GDR, Morgner's *Trobadora Beatriz* challenges this increasingly untenable notion of an ideal balance between social norms and pressures to conform and the individual's irrepressible desire for the fulfillment of personal goals. The novel replaces the conventional notion of a perfect process of socialization with an alternative concept of harmony and balance, one that opens up a far greater realm for the realization of feminine aspirations and needs. This utopian ideal is perhaps best expressed in the image of the medieval lady who tames the lion and the unicorn in the tapestry "A mon seul désir" in the Museum of Cluny.

The metaphor of balance serves in *Trobadora Beatriz* as a focal point around which the central concerns of the novel are organized: the relationship between Beatriz and Laura, and hence between idealism and pragmatism; the unresolved tension between the teleologies of the Bildungsroman and the romance,

---

8. See Hirsch, "Spiritual 'Bildung,'" 27ff.
9. Karen E. Rowe, "'Fairy-born and human-bred': Jane Eyre's Education in Romance," in Abel et al., *The Voyage In*, 69–70.

as well as the uneasy coexistence of the real and the fantastic. As previously indicated, the novel *Trobadora Beatriz* exists in a constant state of tension between a dialogic structure and a more rigid, hierarchical arrangement of its contradictory elements. Furthermore, the issue of balance is of paramount importance to the survival of working women in their quest for the ideal balance between the demands of a career and a family.

Emancipation as Balancing Act

In Beatriz's third "Bitterfeld Fruit" she tells the story of a physicist employed at an academic institute. Beatriz's tale, which illustrates the plight of working women, particularly in non-traditional areas, is a satirical look at the barriers women face in overcoming discrimination in the work place and the community. As a single mother and a physicist with a considerable reputation, Vera Hill, like the dietician Valeska, must resort to illegitimate, fantastical means to meet the conflicting demands of a child and a job. In order to save valuable time traveling to her place of work she devises the pragmatic trick of stretching a tightrope from her home to the institute. The time she thus saves on traveling can be more usefully spent with her child and working on her "habilitation" dissertation that will qualify her for promotion to professor. Because she is precluded from drawing on the assistance of a servant or a housewife by virtue of her gender, Vera is at a significant disadvantage to her male colleagues. Unlike most of them, who have at their disposal a wife who caters to these needs, Vera herself is responsible for the reproductive labor required to ensure she is adequately equipped to perform at her peak during her working hours.

Vera Hill's tightrope walk to the physics institute stands as a metaphor for the extreme skill women need to juggle professional aspirations and the daily demands of a family and children. The tightrope is symptomatic of the delicate balancing act women perform daily in order to cope with the exigencies of the double burden and double shifts. During the day women are active as producers in the labor force, and yet they are expected to be reproducers of their own labor power in addition to that of their husbands in the evenings. And if these activities do not call for a delicate juggling act, then the additional responsibilities of motherhood will make it imperative that women develop a keen sense of balance. The tightrope is clearly both a pragmatic and a utopian solution, relying as it does on exceptional balancing ability and extraordinary dexterity. It is a time-saving device borne out of necessity, but one that allows Vera Hill to meet the conflicting demands of both her shifts. It enables her simultaneously to continue to care for her son without sacrificing her desire for success and recognition in her profession. The rope obviates the necessity for further sacrifice and as such it provides Vera with an ideal solution, for as Vera explains to her skeptical boss, she cannot possibly have her dissertation finished on time without her ingenious method of transport:

> After she had gone shopping after work, picked up her son from kindergarten, prepared the evening meal, eaten, painted cars and other requests of her son, washed him and packed him off to bed with a fairytale, had also washed the dishes or clothes or darned a hole or chopped wood or fetched brickets from the cellar, with the help of the tightrope trick she could be thinking about invariants at her desk around nine o'clock, without the trick an hour later. She would have to get up an hour earlier without the trick. She could not come up with any useful ideas on less than six hours sleep. (TB. 394)[10]

The story of Vera's superhuman efforts to cope singlehandedly with the hardships of being a single working mother is a paradigmatic example of the way Morgner reinvests the metaphor of the tightrope with concrete force. By taking a figure of speech literally, she focuses the reader's attention on the superhuman feats women are required to execute in order to preserve a balance between the conflicting perceptions of women's role in society. Vera's tightrope act along the interstices between the duties of motherhood and her career is precarious precisely because there

10. "Wenn sie nach Arbeitsschluß eingekauft, den Sohn aus dem Kindergarten geholt, Abendbrot gerichtet, gegessen, Autos und andere Wunschbilder des Sohnes gemalt, ihn gebadet und mit einem Märchen versehen ins Bett gebracht, auch Geschirr oder Wäsche gewaschen oder ein Loch gestopft oder Holz gehackt und Bricketts aus dem Keller geholt hätte, könnte sie mit Seiltrick gegen einundzwanzig Uhr am Schreibtisch über Invarianzen denken, ohne Trick eine Stunde später. Müßte auch eine Stunde früher aus dem Bett ohne den Trick. Nach weniger als sechs Stunden Schlaf fiele ihr nichts Brauchbares ein."

is only a very fine line between success and failure in the two conflicting spheres of the work place and the family home. The division can only be bridged through a careful tightrope walk requiring such concentration that the slightest distraction or criticism is sufficient to send Vera tumbling to her death. The day following her official censure by the director of her institute, Vera loses her faith in her acrobatic abilities, and on her way home from work she literally loses her balance and falls to her death.

The metaphor of balance proves crucial to a reading of the novel, providing a focus around which most aspects of the narrative are organized. Almost all aspects of the story of the adventures of Laura and Beatriz are concerned with finding a suitable balance: between the desire for a career and motherhood, for pragmatism and idealism, the past and the present, the real and the fantastic. We can therefore read the search for Anaximander, which is after all referred to as a code, as a quest for this perfect balance: an ideal balance between the radical impulses of Beatriz and the pragmatism of Laura. Moreover, the quest is for a synthesis between the conflicting trajectories of the quest for female self-realization and the quest for loyalty to the socialist collective. It is therefore possible to read Beatriz's mission as a search for a compromise between the radical emancipatory ideals she herself espouses and the pragmatism of daily survival advocated by Laura. The "support" model, which initially defines the relationship between the two women within the narrative, is, we recall, intrinsically concerned with the question of balance and counterbalance. Its primary function is to provide Beatriz, a fantasy construct, with a solid grounding in the real, because Beatriz can only maintain a footing in the real and hence contact the women of the GDR if she has the support of Laura. The presence of a real counter-weight is therefore a necessary precondition for the stability of the fantastic. Beatriz's letter to Laura from Split represents one such example of the precariousness of this state of balance between women's ideals and the reality of their situation in the GDR. Thus, if Vera Hill's circus act is indicative of the daily contradictions lived by East German women, then the balancing act Morgner's text must perform is equally symptomatic of the status of the fantastic in mainstream socialist realist fiction and socialist literary theory.

The question of balance is one that impinges on the relationship between Beatriz and Laura. As seen by Laura's response to Beatriz's suggestion that Laura should travel to Split to experience the origins of female resistance to tyrannical systems of oppression, the convergence of tasks assigned to the two women represents a threat to the alliance originally made between the forces of pragmatism and the imagination as represented by the respective women. It therefore seems that the possibility of merging the two aspects of female experience presents a threat to the very nature of difference itself, and that the separation of the two poles of femininity is necessary to maintain the subject/object dialectic. It appears that the ideal state of balance between the two women is a non-hierarchical one in which both terms of the relationship stand to benefit from a separation of functions and roles. In the previous chapter the relationship between Laura and Beatriz, or Laura and antilaura, was identified as one of mutually compatible opposites, capable of peaceful, non-destructive coexistence and of generating a creative and productive union. Is the marriage between the real and fantastic aspects of women's lives in fact as well-balanced as this anti-scientific model of opposites would suggest? Or is the match between the realist forces of pragmatism and the emancipatory powers of the imagination and fantasy in fact an uneven one?

The fundamental ambiguity in Morgner's text, it seems, is the oscillation between a non-hierarchical, metonymical ordering of the real and the fantastic and a more stable metaphorical structuring that clearly privileges the real. There are, however, two breaks in the text where the stability of the support model and the hierarchical ordering of Beatriz's and Laura's respective spheres comes under threat. The first occasion is when Beatriz attempts to free Laura from her sedentary position, beckoning her to give up her position as the fixed term of the relationship. The second example of a threat to the stability of the model comes in the chapter leading up to Beatriz's fatal loss of balance, when Laura's functions in the realm of the real are gradually displaced by Beatriz, ultimately rendering Laura superfluous. But surprisingly it is not Laura who disappears from the novel but Beatriz.

One of the main reasons for the surprising turn of events clearly lies in the lack of balance between the forces of the real and the fantastic. The barriers to the successful integration of the worlds of the imagination and pragmatism are twofold. One of the main

hurdles in all of Morgner's works remains the inability of the
fantastic to make substantial inroads into the spheres of the real.
The major problem, as discussed earlier, lies in the extreme
resistance by men, especially those with scientific training, toward
assimilating any kind of irrational or unnatural occurrence. It has
been noted that it is primarily women who display the greatest
readiness to accept the existence of the supernatural and the
fantastic. In fact, the alarming ease with which Beatriz becomes
assimilated into Laura's world is testimony to women's
receptivity to the extraordinary. Yet it is paradoxically this extreme
willingness to utilize the forces of the supernatural that poses one
of the greatest threats to Beatriz's continued existence. The
assimilation of the fantastic, as Biddy Martin has correctly pointed
out, leads eventually to its domestication and hence to the
domestication of feminine difference.[11]

However, from a quite different point of view the failure of
Beatriz's mission can be attributed to the inability of the real, that
is, of official party rhetoric and those institutions that reproduce
this official rhetoric, to enter into a dialogue with alternative, non-
rational discourses such as the fantastic. Laura's inability to
replace Beatriz as the mobile pole of the dyad indicates a major
difficulty in overturning or subverting existing perceptions of
reality, particularly officially propagated truths. While Laura's lack
of mobility is specifically indicative of the typical predicament of
working mothers in East German society, her inability to cross
boundaries must also be seen as an indication of the general
difficulties involved in subverting official myths and legends
about women. The restrictions on Laura's freedom of movement,
even if partially self-imposed, become spatial ciphers of the
widespread resistance to overturning official versions of the
history of women's emancipation in East Germany and to the
construction of alternative narratives about their struggles for
equality.

The increasing domestication of Beatriz's demands after her
return "home" to the GDR can be read as a parable of the way in
which fantasy, as a literary genre in the GDR, as well as women's
fantasies in general, have often been incorporated into mainstream
canons of realist fiction. In East Germany, writing that transgressed

11. Martin, "Socialist Patriarchy," 62.

generic conventions by cutting across traditions and breaking taboos traditionally remained either outside the canon or, in the case of science fiction, was drawn into the services of the dominant literary aesthetic.[12] Annemarie Auer's reception of Morgner's use of fantasy is typical of the attempts by East German literary scholars to deny the otherness of fantasy fiction. In order to reassure the reader and the critic that Morgner's work deserves its place in the canon of socialist realist fiction, Auer must play down the points at which Morgner's use of fantasy differs from accepted conventions, thus minimizing its emancipatory potential to such an extent that the notion of a difference is almost lost altogether. This becomes apparent when Auer states that Morgner's prose is not fantastic, but is instead "obviously socialist realist."[13] Thus the subsumption of fantasy and other genres under the rubric of realism acted as a means of diminishing the subversive potential traditionally associated with forms of the fantastic, in particular, with the Romantic tradition.[14] Horst Heidtmann attributes the defensiveness in the GDR towards literary transgressions to a fear of the manipulation of needs through popular literature, a fear largely fueled by the negative experiences of German fascism.[15] Rainer Nägele, on the contrary, sees in this extreme disavowal of mass literature and fantasy a refusal to come to terms with real needs and desires.[16] He criticizes the need to dogmatically assert "the firm foundations of reality" as a form of defense against the dangers of irrationalism and fascism; behind those arguments in favor of the necessity for a solid grounding in the real, Nägele detects a disguised act of disavowal. The insistence on firm ground becomes a means of imposing limits on the imagination, freedom, and change: "in each case everything is allowed within the borders of the staked-out ground: boundlessness within bounds, orderly freedom."[17]

If Beatriz represents the unspoken and silenced truths about

12. See Rainer Nägele, "Trauer, Tropen und Phantasmen: Ver-rückte Geschichten aus der DDR," Hohendahl, *Literatur der DDR in den siebziger Jahren*, 196.
13. Auer, "Trobadora unterwegs," 1093.
14. Werner Neubert, "Realer Sozialismus – Sozialistischer Realismus," *Ansichten: Aufsätze zur Literatur der DDR*, ed. Klaus Walther (Halle: Mitteldeutscher Verlag, 1976), 8.
15. Heidtmann, *Utopisch-phantastische Literatur der DDR*, 97.
16. Nägele, "Trauer, Tropen und Phantasmen," 197.
17. Ibid., 196–97.

women's lives, that which has been suppressed from public and private consciousness, the phase of the narrative when Beatriz returns home to the GDR and gradually takes over Laura's domestic tasks represents an attempt to stifle these truths and censor the voice of difference. The domestication of Beatriz thus can be read as a commentary on the processes of colonization of the fantastic as a genre and more specifically of women's fantasies in realist fiction. The disruptive force of women's unrealized desires for more freedom to move and to determine their lives that Beatriz brings to bear on the lives of women such as Laura's is eventually contained in a process of assimilation that sees Beatriz curbed of her radicalism and robbed of her fire. Rather than the passionate singer of love poetry and the impatient harbinger of a new age for women, she becomes instead the perfect housemaid to Laura.

Doubling and the Domestication of
Female Desire

If Laura's initial aim in sending Beatriz off in search of adventures is to curb her excesses and fanaticism, she is by the end of Beatriz's travels abroad more than successful. Upon her return to the GDR a curious transformation takes place that Laura obviously had not anticipated. In the chapter bearing the enigmatic title "The two friends grow visibly closer together, which distances them from each other," Laura learns to her horror that her friend Beatriz is becoming more like her every day. In a further chapter we are told that Beatriz has been so successfully integrated into Laura's daily life that she has effectively outgrown her purpose in providing a fantastic counter-weight to the pragmatic-minded Laura. Beatriz has become so well-assimilated into socialist life that her originality has been compromised and her emancipatory edge blunted. The contradictory nature of this process of assimilation is encapsulated in the title of the chapter, "Beatriz settles down and brings herself into line" (TB. 346).

The process of the integration of the individual into the community, described here as the process of settling in or down, typically marks the final phase in the ideological homecoming of the protagonist of the nineteenth-century classical and twentieth-century socialist Bildungsroman. However, in Beatriz's case, the act of settling down and coming to terms with societal expectations, proves to be the very opposite of a harmonious process of ideological education: it is not a settling down ("ein-richten") but a bringing into line ("sich ausrichten"). The homecoming entails a transformation whereby Beatriz and her radical demands are "brought into line" ideologically. The suggestion is that bringing Beatriz into line with the rest of society is in fact the very antithesis of a happy process of integration. Paradoxically, Beatriz's coming to terms with socialist everyday life spells not her arrival but her exit from the socialist arena. If the price of integration is the fitting of an ideological straitjacket and hence the obliteration of all difference, Laura's original task of educating Beatriz to the realities of the GDR has been so spectacularly successful that it has failed. There has been no gradual unfolding of Beatriz's personality, no individual growth within a sympathetic social context; instead, Beatriz's development concludes with a rather grotesque process of domestication. Her accommodation to the demands of child-rearing is so out of character that even Laura's son Wesselin is confused:

> Because Beatriz took pains to emulate Laura even in small matters, Wesselin soon recognized in her a substitute mother. But did not call her "Mama."[18] (TB. 378)

The price for curtailing Beatriz's radicalness is high; shortly after Beatriz has been brought into line, she loses her balance while cleaning Laura's windows from the balcony and falls to her death. The domestication of Beatriz and her emancipatory aspirations for sexual liberation and the eroticization of everyday life also entails, it would seem, the end of those radical impulses. It also seems to signal the end of the usefulness of the supernatural and the fantastic to women's concerns. But Beatriz's death signifies a loss of balance in more ways than one. Her sudden departure spells the collapse of the support model that assigned to Beatriz the role of a fantastic counterbalance to Laura's experiences in the sphere of official East German reality. Without the guaranteed support of

18. "Da Beatriz sich befleißigte, Laura auch in Kleinigkeiten nachzueifern, erkannte Wesselin sie bald als Ersatzmutter an. Nannte sie aber nicht 'Mama.'"

Beatriz, Laura is left to fill the gap caused by Beatriz's disappearance through the creation of another fantasy figure, the ideal emancipated male.

Beatriz's sudden disappearance from the narrative has been thought by some East German critics to be the logical outcome of Laura's successfully completed plan for the education of Beatriz. Once Beatriz has been tamed, her ideals modified and moderated for the more modest aims of East German working women, she is no longer needed. She becomes superfluous, argues Sigrid Damm.[19] One might ask, however, that if Beatriz has been so successfully domesticated and house-trained, as the text suggests, whether it might not seem more logical to conclude that it is in fact Laura who is now rendered superfluous? As mentioned earlier, Beatriz's homecoming to the GDR causes a gradual displacement of Laura as the working mother and the static pole and stationary partner in the alliance between the two women. The more Beatriz becomes integrated into Laura's domestic sphere, taking over her duties as child-minder, mother, and housekeeper, the greater the physical resemblance between the two women. The chapter entitled "The friends grow visibly closer together, which distances them from each other" marks the beginning of a disturbing shift in identities between the two women. The physical resemblance is therefore an external "reflection" of the more important similarity between the now identical social functions of the two friends. This merging of the identities of Beatriz and Laura obviously signals a crisis point in both the education of Beatriz and the emancipation of Laura. It now becomes apparent that there has been a hidden agenda to Laura's plan to rid Beatriz of her excessive revolutionary zeal and smooth her rough edges through the idea of the quest: to enable Laura herself to eventually take Beatriz's place as the active subject of her own adventures. One of Laura's aims in teaching Beatriz the skills of child-minding was to find a substitute mother for herself, to duplicate herself so that she may quit her "sedentary duty" and replace Beatriz as the mobile rather than mere sedentary subject of the pair. She announces her intention to embark on her own set of adventures to Beatriz on the morning after her wedding:

---

19. Damm, "Irmtraud Morgner: *Leben und Abenteuer der Trobadora Beatriz*," 144.

"You get to keep Wesselin. After all, you have not found out about domestic matters for nothing, have you? I have been stuck at home long enough, now you can take over the sedentary duty." – Beatriz could not think of any objections to Laura's logic. She even admired her; the image the Troubadour had formed of her friend on her travels had in the meantime become an ideal that Beatriz was determined to emulate. The newspapers she read since her return thoroughly confirmed her in these endeavors. (TB. 338)[20]

Beatriz has no objections to her new duties; she has been so well-tamed that she has only the utmost admiration for the heroic achievements of the exemplary socialist mother, Laura. The image that Beatriz had formed of her friend has been transformed into a stereotyped ideal, a positive model for emulation that she finds further reinforced at all official levels. The stereotype of the successful working mother that the media and the party propagate is consequently so persuasive that Beatriz feels encouraged to imitate it. This overly positive image of the working mother, like the idealized images of successful working mothers we find in the Western media throughout the 1980s, particularly in women's magazines, has for Beatriz, a naive reader, strong normative power. In view of the fact that it was Laura's aim to moderate Beatriz's unrealistic expectations of emancipation and educate her into the realities of women's situation in the work place and in the home, Laura's mission has certainly failed if all she has achieved is the duplication of the official myth of the active, tireless working-class heroine and working mother.

Beatriz appears to have misunderstood her brief; she is forced into a situation in which she reinforces the official myths and images of femininity instead of challenging them. Rather than encouraging Laura to satisfy her thirst for travel, Beatriz finds herself discrediting the desire to travel, dismissing it as a means of compensating for "inner emptiness" through greater "consumption of experiences" (TB. 347). Here Beatriz mouths

20. "'Du behältst Wesselin. Hast du dich etwa umsonst hauswirtschaftlich orientiert? Ich hab lange genug daheim gehockt, jetzt übernimmst du den stationären Dienst.' – Beatriz wußte gegen Lauras Logik nichts einzuwenden. Bewunderte die sogar, das Bild, das sich die Trobadora während der Reise von der Freundin gemacht hatte, war inzwischen zum Vorbild geraten. Dem nachzueifern sich Beatriz vornahm. Die Zeitungen, die sie seit ihrer Rückkehr las, bestärkten sie in diesen Bemühungen prinzipiell."

official justifications for not allowing more people to satisfy their urge to travel: the desire itself must not be taken seriously because it only stems from a need to compensate for what are essentially seen as problems of an individual or personal nature. Laura also eventually comes to realize the failure of her plan when it becomes clear that she too, like the circus from which she rescued Beatriz, is guilty of taming Beatriz for her own individual needs:

> On the 28th of January . . . Laura noticed that Beatriz had also come to resemble her in external appearance. "Why are you disciplining yourself like this," she asked shocked, "do you want to duplicate me? Are you trying to make yourself redundant?"[21] (TB. 397)

The growing physical resemblance between the two women signals not merely a merging of their social functions; it further suggests a conflation and confusion of identities. This is perceived by Laura as a threat to her own life as well as to Beatriz's. The process by which their social functions and therefore their social identities merge paradoxically does not bring the two women closer together. It is described instead as tearing them apart: "that distances them from one another." The role reversal, instead of providing an ideal solution to Laura's longing for travel and adventure, upsets the stability of the relationship and the fixed subject-positions of both women. It is this loss of equilibrium, this loss of a suitable division of labor between the two women, that can be seen as responsible for Beatriz's loss of balance on the balcony and abrupt disappearance from the narrative.

Beatriz's loss of balance is attributed to an attack of vertigo; yet it could equally well be construed as symptomatic of an identity crisis. That Beatriz's disappearance is indeed somehow linked to an identity crisis, involving both terms of the dialectic between Beatriz and Laura, is suggested by this very chapter heading that implies that the process of convergence will ultimately tear the women apart. Beatriz's attack of vertigo occurs at that point in the narrative in which the identities and social function of the two women come so precariously close to each other as to merge. The merging or collapsing of those quasi-identities that function in the

---

21. "Am 28. Januar . . . bemerkte Laura, daß Beatriz ihr auch äußerlich ähnlich geworden war. 'Warum dressierst du dich so,' fragte sie erschreckt, 'willst du mich doubeln? Willst du dich überflüssig machen?'"

narrative as dichotomous halves of women's experience causes a disruption to the dialectics of identity by removing one term of the pair. Beatriz's usurpation of Laura's social role effectively closes the dialectic between the two women, the dialectic of identity and subjectivity as well as the dialectic between the real and the fantastic as opposite poles of female experience. The net result is a displacement of the relative positions of the terms. It could reasonably be expected that Beatriz's usurpation of Laura would dislodge Laura from her position as the more housebound of the two. But because the real is always the more stable of the two terms, Beatriz's attempt at taking over from Laura miscarries and it is finally Beatriz herself who is usurped and forced out of the narrative. Laura has the more solid footing in the real, is ultimately on firmer ground, and is consequently more likely to be restricted by real social and political obstacles to her freedom.

Critics in the GDR have tended to take at face value Laura's warning to Beatriz that she may well make herself redundant if she continues to copy Laura. Laura's prediction is then taken as the real reason for Beatriz's abrupt disappearance from the text. Laura's explanation is furthermore generally understood as sufficient proof that the fantastic has served its purpose and that the use of fantasy is henceforth superfluous. It would appear, however, that the real cause for Beatriz's loss of balance could be located instead in Laura's inability to break out of the conventional realist narrative. It is not Beatriz who has become superfluous but Laura who has been made redundant by being caught up in a process that effectively duplicates her. Beatriz's disappearance from the narrative is interpreted by Sigrid Damm as a timely "dismantling of illusions, feminist exaggerations and of the wish for an immediate, radical transformation to the position of women."[22] She reads Beatriz's death as a further sign that Beatriz's radical demands for equality and subjectivity have either been met or sufficiently softened by a deeper understanding of the actually existing state of women's emancipation in the GDR. According to Damm, the diminishing importance of the figure of Beatriz is accompanied by a "consideration of the actually existing complex conditions for change."[23]

22. Damm, "Irmtraud Morgner: *Leben und Abenteuer der Trobadora Beatriz,*" 144.
23. Ibid.

To see Beatriz's sudden disappearance from the narrative that bears her name in such terms is to underestimate the importance of the figure and her role in the novel. By reading the removal from the text of its main protagonist as the logical outcome of the moderation of unrealistic demands, Damm is implying that the disappearance of Beatriz is a necessary thing. To read Beatriz's exclusion from the narrative as the dismantling of false illusions represents an attempt to reclaim the novel for socialist realism and superimpose the narrative structure of the genre of the socialist Bildungsroman and the "arrival novel" on a narrative trajectory that is actually going in an opposite direction. The tale of Beatriz, as told by her minstrel, Laura, is in fact the story of the failure of an education. Beatriz does indeed successfully complete an apprenticeship in child-rearing and other household duties, yet her new-found pragmatism does not seem to hold out any promise for the future. Damm ultimately ignores Melusine's rather stern rebuke of Laura's desire to curb Beatriz's "impatience" and "megalomania." When an exasperated Laura attacks Beatriz with a book, crying, "impatience and megalomania will be your downfall" (TB. 180), Melusine's response is to declare Laura's project to be grossly misguided:

> "You are very mistaken. Recant! Renounce sinful intervention. For impatience is Beatriz de Dia's unique talent, megalomania her extraordinary virtue. Whoever robs her of her talent and virtue, as happened for thousands of years to her sisters, sins in the eyes of God who cannot be a man. Nor a woman.[24] (TB. 181)

Until her disappearance the process of Beatriz's education reads as an exemplary process of integration into society. Just at the point, however, where the "arrival" of Beatriz appears to be achieved, the narrative falters and derails, leaving the task of educating Beatriz unfinished. The final stage in the formation of the female self and the harmonious integration of it into the socialist collective cannot take place, and Beatriz is displaced

---

24. "Du hast schwer gefehlt. Widerrufe dich! Laß ab von sündhafter Einmischung! Denn Ungeduld ist das einzigartige Talent der Beatriz de Dia, Größenwahn ihre außerordentliche Tugend. Wer ihr Talent und Tugend abdressiert, so geschehen ist jahrtausendelang ihren Schwestern, macht sich schuldig vor Gott, der kein Mann sein kann. Auch keine Frau."

instead from the narrative altogether. The retraining of Beatriz for Laura's domestic purposes obviously represents an arrival of a radically different kind, one that had hitherto played no role in the dominant narratives of the 1950s and 1960s. Whereas the site of the process of ideological formation at the center of the socialist Bildungsroman had previously been firmly located in the public spheres of production, the final stage in Beatriz's education takes place entirely in the private, domestic sphere. This topological shift parallels the change in the concerns of women's writing in the 1970s, a shift away from the public arena as the major site of women's emancipation to the private, domestic sphere as the new site of struggle for equality among the sexes. Beatriz's integration into Laura's domestic sphere thus signals the need for a reappraisal of this repressed sphere of socialist women's lives and for due recognition of the invisible contributions to society that women perform daily in the family home. Thus, by illuminating that side of women's reality, Morgner challenges common notions of what constitutes socially productive work.

The story of Beatriz's arrival in the domestic sphere of production is, because it is intercepted at its crucial stage of development, indicative of women's inability to fully appropriate the means of production in the home and extricate themselves from the exploitative relations of production within the nuclear family. At this level Beatriz's disappearance signifies the failure of women to "arrive" fully in this other domestic sphere of production. This is reinforced by Beatriz's repeated acts of arriving and taking up residence in what she believes each time to be a paradise on earth for women. Beatriz's disappearance constitutes an unsuccessfully completed period of probation in women's other sphere of production, the family home, which is the site of the reproduction of the family, the labor force, and labor power.

However, seen from another perspective Beatriz's emulation of Laura is nothing but exemplary, providing Laura, the authorized private tutor, with a great sense of personal satisfaction:

[She] was very satisfied with her diligence. Indeed, she felt a similar satisfaction to that experienced by educators whose instructions are followed. Beatriz's role as a herald nevertheless seemed to her to be an overexaggeration. (TB. 347)[25]

It therefore comes as some surprise that the education of Beatriz should be broken off just at the point when she appears to have attained her ideal of the "well-rounded socialist personality." Beatriz's difficulty seems to lie in the fact that she takes her task of imitating Laura and thus Laura's status as a role model far too literally. The result of her over-eagerness is a complete confusion of identities and social functions in which she not only comes to resemble Laura almost exactly, but becomes a carbon copy, an exact replica of the myth she is trying to explode. It is here that the narrative shifts from the model of the Bildungsroman to a narrative mode more reminiscent of a comedy of errors: the world of mistaken identities, role reversals, and happy marriages.

However, the real problem with Beatriz's usurpation of Laura's domestic sphere seems to lie neither in the confusion of identities, nor in her domestication, but in the sliding of genres within the narratives of which Beatriz is an actor. Up until her return home to the GDR with the spoils of her adventures in the form of a toy unicorn, Beatriz had been both the subject of a medieval adventure novel as well as the object of a socialist Bildungsroman narrated by Laura. But in both instances she causes a disruption to the structure of her respective narratives, both to the narrative syntagms and to the paradigmatic layering of meaning. As the active subject of her own adventures, she inverts the gender oppositions structuring the medieval courtly romance as well as the semic hierarchy the narrative sets up between the opposing ideals of motherhood and emancipation. Moreover, Beatriz's adventures up until her return to East Germany are neither the typical experiences and encounters of the hero of the classical Bildungsroman nor those of its socialist variant. Instead, she resembles far more the figure of the picaro who refuses to be molded by societal conventions and mores. Although the taming of the picaro represents a quite common narrative trope in both the East and West German novel of the postwar period, the most famous examples being Günter Grass's *Die Blechtrommel* and Erwin Strittmatter's trilogy *Der Wundertäter*, the ideology of gender, which has traditionally informed the postwar German picaro novel, the

25. "[Sie] war aber mit deren Studienfleiß sehr zufrieden. Ja sie spürte Genugtuung ähnlich der, die Erziehungsberechtigte empfinden, wenn ihre Anweisungen befolgt werden. Beatrizens Botentätigkeit erschien ihr allerdings als Überspitzung."

medieval courtly romance, and the classical Bildungsroman, has not been conducive to casting a woman in the role of the picaro. The fact that women have been traditionally excluded from playing the role of the active desiring subject in patriarchal societies has made the construction of an active mobile female subject of a narrative particularly problematic. One could in fact argue that the figure of the picaro and the genre of the picaresque is a more realistic genre for women because it charts the repeated failures on the part of the protagonists to find a firm footing in society in the way they desire.

The Search for an Ending: "A Marriage made in Heaven"

While Laura is playing the role of mentor in the education of Beatriz, she is herself the subject of a narrative that is predominantly rooted in the conventions of realism. Apart from the visitation of Laura by the mythical and historical figures of Beatriz and Melusine, Laura's choices in life are mainly dictated by the generic constraints of realism, particularly socialist realism. Beatriz's injunction to Laura to leave the world of pragmatism and realism by embarking on her own adventures requires Laura to step out of the realist narrative and enter into a fantasy world where dreams come true and wishes are fulfilled. Laura's indication to Beatriz that she may venture alone into the Western world would indicate Laura's intention to follow in Beatriz's footsteps. Yet this ending is not in the realist plot; this option is only hinted at and is never realized. Despite pronouncing an ultimatum upon Beatriz's return to the GDR that it is now her turn to embark on an adventure story, Laura shows no further signs of setting off on her own travels, apart from a brief adventure when she is "whisked away" through magic to Paris:

> On the morning after the wedding the minstrel notified her Troubadour that she would soon be going away. "Where are you off to on your honeymoon then?" Beatriz asked. "I am traveling alone," said Laura . . . .. She [Beatriz] did not like to inquire about the destination of the trip. And Laura said promptly, "Almaciz or something like that." (TB. 338)[26]

Instead, Laura finds herself part of a fairytale ending of quite a different kind to the one she anticipated.

The text raises certain expectations at a structural level that Laura will be relieved of her child-minding functions and liberated from the double burden. The structural signs that reinforce this are located at the level of the metanarrative in the allusions to the medieval narratives of Erec and Yvain. In accordance with the narrative patterns of reversals set up by the medieval quests of Yvain and Erec, it can be expected that Laura's prolonged period of stasis will be corrected, as was Erec's, by its opposite in the form of her own adventures. Certainly the ultimatum that Laura herself issues to travel to Beatriz's birth place reinforces this expectation. Yet Laura seems incapable of replacing Beatriz as an active subject of a travel narrative, despite issuing herself an imperative to embark on her own series of adventures as a subject of her own narrative. Laura's inability to switch narratives and occupy different actantial positions within these narratives prevents further substitutions along the signifying chain of a metonymic kind, or further role reversals at the narrative level, despite every textual indication that Beatriz's displacement of Laura should bring about a reciprocal substitution.

Both Erec and Yvain are presented in *Trobadora Beatriz* as embodiments of opposing medieval codes of behavior that only represent ideals when in a state of harmony or balance. The same applies to the figures of Beatriz and Laura. Like Yvain, Beatriz's extended period of adventures is corrected by her return home to the GDR to Laura (who doubles here as her lady-in-waiting, Laudine), and a phase of domesticity. It is during this time that Laura acts out the part of Erec in the Erec narrative during his phase of stasis. It is also possible to map the narrative segment of the bringing-home of the object of the quest, the unicorn, onto the syntagm of disjunction in which Erec returns home to the Arthurian court with Enide, the object of his quest. Beatriz's return home is similarly followed by a period of calm, where it seems as if Beatriz and Laura had collectively found the ideal solution to the

26. "Am Morgen nach der Hochzeit eröffnete die Spielfrau ihrer Trobadora, daß sie demnächst verreise. "Wohin soll denn die Hochzeitsreise gehen?" fragte Beatriz. "Ich verreise allein," sagte Laura . . . .. Sie [Beatriz] erkundigte sich also ungern nach dem Reiseziel. Und Laura sagte auch prompt: "Almaciz oder so."

conflicting demands of the working mother and wife. But, as in the Erec narrative, this period of happiness is in a precarious state of balance and is only short-lived.

These structural parallels between the life and adventures of Laura and the legends of Erec and Yvain awaken expectations that Laura will also be freed from her position in Beatriz's narrative as minstrel or vicarious subject, or what Greimas calls the sender of the quest. By stepping out of this narrative, Laura would no longer need to be the "acting" subject of Beatriz's narrative or even the helper in someone else's narrative but the active subject of her own story. Laura, it would seem, misreads Beatriz's attempts at duplicating the domestic, stationary side of women's experience; she consistently misses her cues and forgets her own ultimatum to travel to Almaciz. Beatriz's usurpation of Laura's role is not an attempt to render Laura superfluous but is instead a cue for Laura to go in search of adventure. Even when Laura realizes Beatriz has already replaced her to such an extent as to render her superfluous, she is still unaware of her failure to fulfill her part in the medieval courtly romance and thus disregards the necessity of countering periods of inactivity with periods of activity.

In a discussion between the fictive author, Laura Salman, and the "real" author, Irmtraud Morgner, in the novel, mention is made of the "suspicion that active relationships to the world are determined by gender" (TB. 28). The repeated references to Laura's "sedentary activity" further reinforce the difficulty in constructing an active female subject of an adventure or even a picaro narrative. The question arises here whether the shift from the structure of the medieval courtly romance with an active female subject to a structure reminiscent of a novel of education with Beatriz as the object of this education does not ultimately signify a capitulation of radical demands for an active subjectivity and sexuality in the text. What seems to occur is a transference of narrative roles from Beatriz to Laura and back, resulting in a switching between narrative patterns. The caesura between the medieval courtly romance with its active female subject, and the ensuing domestication of Beatriz, is also signaled by a radical change in Beatriz's attitude to traveling and a strange reluctance to share her travel experiences with Laura. The inconsistencies in character and motivation serve as a hint to the reader that the narrative has perhaps moved into a different mode. If character is largely a function of narrative – which it appears to be here – then a change in character can serve as an indicator of a shift in narrative function or genres.

The breaking off of the medieval romance and Beatriz's emulation of Laura causes a shift in the construction of female subjectivity from mobile and active to one that is stationary, passive, and housebound. The displacement of social and narrative functions is also significantly uni-directional: Beatriz very successfully displaces Laura as the stationary house-based pole of the alliance, but a reverse substitution, in which Laura would take Beatriz's part as the active subject of a medieval romance, fails to happen. Laura may announce her intention to replace Beatriz in the form of an ultimatum that she will soon be visiting Beatriz's birth place and place of historical origin, but she does not act upon it. Her dreams of traveling never materialize, and she is confined to visiting the Museum of Cluny in her sleep. Apart from this solitary visit, when Laura is spirited away to see the tapestry of the lady and the unicorn in her sleep, she shows no other signs of repeating Beatriz's performance or of taking her place as subject of her own adventure narrative. She does, however, become the subject of a narrative of an altogether different kind – the subject of a thoroughly modern socialist romance. The adventures of Laura end with a fairytale marriage, if not made in heaven, then, at least, in a "winged chariot" ("Himmelswagen") (TB. 185).

Running parallel to the main quest for the unicorn is another quest narrative that has Laura as its subject, and Beatriz, together with her accomplice from the underworld, Melusine, as its sender. The aim of the quest is in this case to find the ideal emancipated man, the perfect father for Wesselin and the ideal husband for Laura. Laura's quest is not without its share of ironic twists, which have to do with a reversal of the actors of the ordeal sequences. In Laura's quest it is the object of the quest, Benno, rather than the subject that must undergo a series of ideological tests of strength to prove himself worthy of Laura. These tests are mainly designed to reassure Laura of the sincerity of his convictions on the equality of the sexes and his commitment to sharing child-rearing duties. Thus, while Laura is subjecting Beatriz to a process of education, she is herself unwittingly the object of an experiment.

If the quest for the unicorn can be seen as the striving for an impossible ideal, the search for Benno is equally a quest for the seemingly impossible in the existence of a suitable object of female desire. Benno, however, like the unicorn, may also be nothing more than a figment of the heterosexual woman's imagination.

Significantly, Benno first appears as a conjuring trick of the lovely Melusine in a winged chariot heralded by a blue light. All three subsequent meetings have a distinct fairytale quality and evoke a sense of the unreal and dreamlike. Benno's unexpected openness to matters of emancipation also seems equally fantastic and is in direct contrast to Laura's subsequent first "real" meeting with Benno in the chapter called "Benno Parnitzke in person," where he is caricatured as a Don Juan figure. Laura is predictably incredulous when he presents himself as a model of the emancipated male and an anti-authoritarian father: a utopian figure in every respect. Laura's decision to accept Benno at face value and "bring him home" parallels Beatriz's bringing home of the imaginary object of her quest, the unicorn. Her first "real" meeting with Benno "in person" shows him, however, to be incorrigibly "macho" and a sexual harasser: a veritable embodiment of all the sexual and social practices discriminating against women. In this story he proves to be a fraud much in the same way as Beatriz's quarry, the pet dog, also turns out to be a fake. The description of this meeting with Benno "in person" is almost the exact inversion of the first story Laura tells to Beatriz called "Topsy-Turvy Coffee" (TB. 111), in which the stereotyped roles of the male as active sexual pursuer and the female as the victim of the male's soliciting are reversed. The story ends with Benno's remark that conventional sexual mores are in fact not only intolerable for the women concerned but also for the men.

Benno's first appearance "in person" reminds Laura of the very real barriers to women's equality in her country and reinforces woman's role as the passive victim and object of male desire. While Laura's early encounters with Benno may well be a projection of women's fantasies of liberation, the meeting in person is a timely reminder of the disappointing reality of life between the sexes and the continuing dominance of men in GDR society. Benno's so-called first appearance in person has the status of a waking nightmare that stands in stark contrast to the fanciful dream sequences of the three nocturnal meetings with Benno on

Laura's balcony. In the chapter immediately following the first real meeting, Benno reappears, this time only "himself" ("persönlich") rather than "in person" ("höchstpersönlich"), as the genuine article, the real object of Laura's dreams or Laura's dreams realized. The re-run of the meeting with Benno "himself" could be read as the synthesis between the dialectics of dreaming and waking, reality and ideal. But precisely because it attempts to synthesize women's fantasies with their reality, their past, and their future, the discovery of the ideal partner never loses its fairytale-like, unreal quality. The reader remains uncertain as to who the real Benno is, wondering in fact whether the real Benno only exists as a product of the female imagination, a fantasy figure with a real existence only in the imagination of those women who invoke him. He is, like Beatriz, a fantasy figure given an independent existence in the real and, like Beatriz, he disappears in *Amanda* as suddenly as he appears. Although Benno has an independent existence in Laura's world, no longer disappearing at the touch of a toe, he retains, like the unicorn, his status as an imaginary construct of the female imagination. His grounding in the real and in women's reality is never entirely convincing – something that only serves to heighten our awareness of the possibility of his disappearing from the narrative at a later stage.

Both Beatriz's and Laura's quest narratives near fruition at the same time. When Beatriz first announces "I am onto Anaximander" (TB. 254), Laura is confused and shocked and loses seven nights sleep – a reaction that is surprising for someone who presumably initiated the quest in the first place. Once she has recovered, she rings Melusine to arrange the first of the "examinations for information purposes" with the "exhibit" Benno. It seems as if the discovery of Anaximander acts as some sort of narrative catalyst for the completion of Laura's own quest for the object of her own desire. The retrieval of Anaximander fulfills therefore the same function in Beatriz's quest narrative as the white stag in the Arthurian legend of Erec and Enide. If the hunting of the white stag serves as a catalyst prompting Erec to go off in search of the ideal lady, then the hunt for Anaximander can be read as the catalyst for locating a different object of desire – that of the ideal male partner for Laura.

Thus, instead of going off in search of her own adventures, Laura's desires for travel undergo a displacement. Her failure to undertake travel and to constitute herself as the active subject of a travel narrative points to her failure to constitute herself as the active subject of her own desires. Laura's lack of mobility begs the question whether the marriage to Benno does not in fact constitute an act of re-objectification of the female in marriage and in narrative. In fact, it would seem as if the explosive potential of female eroticism and sexuality that is unleashed by Beatriz's appearance in the GDR has been effectively contained by the *deus ex machina* of Laura's marriage to Benno. Female desire finally finds its legitimate place in the ideal heterosexual marriage. As Biddy Martin has convincingly argued:

> With the domestication and death of Beatriz, struggle and conflict disappear, unconscious desires are defined as safely conscious attitudes, and the female bonding which has provided the disruptive and critical potential in the text is unconvincingly suppressed in favor of a nervously asserted heterosexuality.[27]

Furthermore, if we accept the view that the disappearance of Beatriz signals the domestication of the radical emancipatory impulses triggered off by Beatriz's arrival, then the happy end can legitimately be read as the appropriation of a feminine difference by a "reformed socialist patriarchy."[28]

At the close of the novel Laura may have been co-opted into the Round Table of the Persephonic Opposition, but her situation has not changed radically in material terms. The problem of Laura's "sedentary position," one of the key difficulties faced by women in their on-going struggle for emancipation, does not appear to have been resolved. If women are to become historical subjects, then the social and moral constraints still operating at the material level of women's everyday lives that reinforce their immobility will also have to be removed. Although Laura is allowed a form of nocturnal escapism when she is whisked away in her sleep to the Museum of Cluny in Paris to view the tapestry of the lady and the unicorn for herself, the mode of production within the new family unit, as well as the division of labor, remains untransformed. There does not seem to be any evidence of a redistribution of child-

27. Martin, "Socialist Patriarchy," 72.
28. Ibid.

minding and household tasks. This suspicion is supported by Laura's remarks in the prologue. There she claims that one of the consequences of her marriage to Benno is in fact the sacrifice of her "actual profession." Her job as train driver, it should be recalled, was one of Laura's main means of compensation for the lack of travel opportunities and mobility in her life. Similarly, Laura's other means of compensation, in her vicarious excursions into the realms of the supernatural and the fantastic via Beatriz's travel reports, would also seem to have been safely limited to the world of dreams. Laura's participation in the realm of the fantastic is therefore confined to the night, a time traditionally allocated to the supernatural and the expression of the unresolved desires of the unconscious through the mediation of dreams. The world of dreams, it would seem, has become the proper place for the enactment of desires and fantasies that have no legitimate place in the conscious, waking existence of a married working mother.

Subverting Censorship: Transference, Reading, and the Other Woman

By way of a slight digression, I shall conclude this discussion of the various models of female development employed by the novel *Trobadora Beatriz* with an analysis of the alternative narrative strategies used by Morgner – other than those of genre – to circumvent the censorship of female desire. By the end of the novel the world of dreams has become the only permissible site for the enactment of women's fantasies. Other forms of vicarious wish-fulfillment previously used by Laura, such as reading Beatriz's letters and sending Beatriz abroad on her behalf, are no longer effective in satisfying her wanderlust; instead, the private and monadic realm of dreams becomes her only means of gratification. Laura's dream of flying to Paris during the night is obviously a displaced act of wish-fulfillment that does offer some consolation in the absence of any real opportunities to travel. The intensity of her desire to travel is no longer transferred onto Beatriz who serves as her proxy abroad, but finds expression instead in Laura's dreams. Because her suppressed longings for travel cannot be lived out in direct uncensored form, they are displaced under the influence of the censor and articulated through the medium of dreams.

The mechanism of transference, however, is far more than a means of circumventing censorship of the contents of the unconscious in dreams as it is in Freud's dream psychology. Transference can also be seen as a narrative principle that, by analogy with the workings of dreams, serves to foil the mechanisms of state censorship of female desire by authorizing another person with the power to act on one's behalf. The object of the transference is another woman, who in the case of *Trobadora Beatriz* is the one authorized to act out the subject's desires. The act of reading another woman's fiction also functions through the same principle of transference to compensate for forms of censorship by allowing wish-fulfillment in displaced form. Through reading another woman's texts, letters, and reliving her experiences, Laura effectively "authorizes" another woman to act and travel on her behalf. Laura thus manages to circumvent the barriers preventing her from traveling by a transference of desire and authority onto Beatriz who is not subject to the same laws of prohibition as Laura herself.

The laws of censorship operating at the level of dreams serve as a hidden principle organizing the complex relationship between Beatriz and Laura, between woman and her other. As a narrative strategy designed to bypass the forces of censorship inhibiting the free expression of women's desires, the principle of transference bears on the relationship between Beatriz and Laura, between reader, writer, and author in *Trobadora Beatriz*. Morgner develops numerous textual strategies as political ploys to overcome both internal and external forces of censorship. We have noted that, after the death of Beatriz, the spaces opened up for the intrusion of the fantastic are considerably reduced. Because Laura is limited to acting out her irrepressible longings for travel and adventure in the realm of her dreams, it may help our understanding of the constraints on the expression of female sexuality and subjectivity to look at the particular way dreams have been conceptualized by psychoanalytic theory as filters or censors of the unconscious and of desire itself.

According to Freud's dream theory, unconscious desires are unable to find direct expression at the conscious level and are subjected to a process of censorship before they can "slip . . . past the barrier of the censorship in an inconspicuous disguise" and find expression at the level of the dream's manifest content.[29] Impulses from the unconscious are only able to enter the preconscious, which is the intermediate state in dreams, by transferring their force and intensity onto another object already present at the conscious level in the "day's residues." For Freud this is the normal and necessary process by which the unassimilable desires of the unconscious are "censored" or filtered. If the transference that occurs in dreams is therefore the "enactment of the reality of the unconscious,"[30] as Lacan argues, then the mechanism of transference could in fact be legitimately viewed as a type of compensatory strategy that circumvents the initial act of censorship of the contents of the unconscious.

Within the analytic situation, Lacan modified Freud's analysis of the mechanism of transference to include the desire of the psychoanalyst himself without which the process of analysis would be "unthinkable."[31] Any discussion of the analytic situation and the dynamics of transference must start with the analyst as the "subject who is supposed to know" who is as much the subject of the transference as s/he is the object.[32] It is in the process of transference that the patient ultimately invests the analyst, or the subject in the know, with authority over the meaning of his/her text and the interpretation of his/her illness. The cure therefore involves the transfer of authority and thus the conferral of power onto the other, whether it be the narrator of a text, the analyst in the analytic situation, the father in the Oedipal triangle, or merely the signifier in the reading process.

If we take the act of transference to mean not only the transfer of authority and meaning but the conferral of authority and power onto the subject in the know as well, then the very act of transference also constitutes an act of authorization. By broadly redefining transference in terms of the authorizing of someone to act, speak, or travel on one's behalf, it then becomes possible to unravel the complex fabric of the interrelationships between Morgner, the "real" author, Laura, the fictitious and fictional author,

29. Sigmund Freud, "Revision of the Theory of Dreams," *New Introductory Lectures on Psycho-Analysis (1933), Standard Edition*, vol. 22, 18.
30. Lacan, *The Four Fundamental Concepts of Psycho-analysis*, trans. Alan Sheridan, ed. by Jacques-Alain Miller (London: Hogarth Press, 1977), 146.
31. Ibid., 253.
32. Ibid., 232–33.

and Beatriz, the object of the narrative. One way of understanding the figure of Laura would be to construe her as a type of Lacanian "barred subject" – a subject who is barred from living out her desires directly and who must seek surrogate forms of wish-fulfillment through the transference of her desires onto a suitable form of substitute, whether it be a substitute object as in Lacan's *object petit a*, or a substitute subject in Beatriz. Beatriz functions then, as do the signifiers from the day's residue, as a medium for the expression of Laura's barred or censored desires.

As the real author of the novel, who is given a fictional presence in the novel itself, Morgner is presented as both writer and reader of the same text. She becomes the official author of the novel when she is authorized by Laura to act on her behalf as writer and thus originator of Beatriz's life adventures. As the appointed author of someone else's text and carrier of another woman's message, she becomes a medium or mediator of other women's experiences, a mere vehicle rather than the source of experience. Instead of authoring the text, she is only a reader of Laura's story of the life and adventures of Beatriz that Laura relays to Morgner in the prologue. The function of the prologue is usually to establish the source of textual meaning and settle the question of authorial responsibility for the text that follows. Morgner's prologue manages instead to confuse the question of authorship and scurrilously evades the issue of responsibility. By posing as a mere reader of Laura's manuscript, Morgner is attempting to defer and transfer authorship and therefore authority for the relayed text onto Laura, the putative author of the chronicle of Beatriz's life. Confusing the origins of a text is here not a ploy to postpone the ultimate closure of meaning, which is so often associated with the notion of the conventional authored text; transference of authority and authorship is instead a deliberate political strategy.

To confuse the origins of a text, to deny authorship, and thereby to refuse authority for the text by collectivizing the responsibility for meaning is also not primarily a denial of the determinacy of meaning. It represents instead a ruse designed to escape accountability and liability for the written word and hence any political repercussions that could ensue from an admission of direct authorial intent. The duplication of the female author is therefore also a means of disavowing intentionality. The story of the resurrection and homecoming of Beatriz is relayed from

Beatriz to Laura who, in turn, relays it to Morgner, in the process of which each account is overlaid with the perspective of the next recipient of the text. As the last term in the narrative chain, and as the reader of both Laura's and Beatriz's texts, Morgner refuses to take ultimate responsibility for the contents of the manuscript, making it plain that she perceives her role as that of reorganizer and hence mere co-writer of the novel.

If reading is then a type of transference whereby the reality of the unconscious is enacted, then it follows that Morgner, in reading and rewriting the text, is living out her desires through Laura, and that Laura in turn is living out her desires through the medium of Beatriz. What occurs between Laura, Beatriz, and Morgner resembles in many ways the signifying processes operating in dreams. In much the same way that desire in dreams becomes displaced from one signifier to another in an attempt to "foil censorship,"[33] in narrative the responsibility for the written word is also displaced from one reader to the next and back in a seemingly endless chain of co-authorship. The origins of the text become obscured through the constitution of a narrative chain, which sets up a system of authorization that confers and defers authority and authorship. Meaning thus becomes the effect of a multiple layering of authored and authorized voices, as each reader becomes in turn a co-writer and the writer a reader. Whereas transference functions to deflect the question of authorship and hence accountability for the written word, it is also the underlying narrative principle by which women's suppressed wishes, like the desires of the unconscious, manage to "foil censorship."

Inherent in this notion of reading is the now somewhat unfashionable idea of reading as identification, involving a projection of the reader's wishes onto various characters in the novel. In the wake of structuralism and poststructuralism, the phenomenological notion of reading as a mere projection of the consciousness of an empirical reader has tended to be replaced by the concept of reading as production rather than passive consumption or escapism. The kind of reading performed by Laura involves both elements of production and empathetic

33. Jacques Lacan, *Ecrits: A Selection*, trans. Alan Sheridan (London: Tavistock Publications, 1977), 160.

identification and transference. Given that we are essentially dealing with the conditions of the possibility of a "barred" subjectivity that is reliant on another for its existence and experience, the mechanisms of transference and identification are paramount in the readings and rewritings that Laura performs on Beatriz's texts. Laura's longing for travel and for new experiences is transferred in the process of reading to Beatriz who acts as her surrogate in the worlds Laura is barred from visiting. But as the production of a reading is always an active rewriting of its content, Laura is able to act out her desires vicariously through the agency of Beatriz's travelogues. This is only made possible because of Beatriz's exceptional status as an outsider, the privileged other of East German culture who, as a rule, escapes the strictures of internal and external forms of censorship. Beatriz, like the "neutral" signifiers from the day's residue, can unashamedly make unrealistic demands for emancipation and is free to pursue her ideals of eroticism, however untenable and excessive they may be. By virtue of her status as Laura's double, Laura becomes not so much the subject in the know as the subject "in the act," that is, the subject who has the authority to act.

Through the process of transference Beatriz is then authorized by Laura to act out Laura's secret desires and yearnings. Laura refers to the travel reports Beatriz sends her during her travels as a substitute form of travel as well as a form of compensation for the tedium of being a housewife and mother: "a substitute for traveling. Compensation for being a housewife. Consolation prize for stationary activity" (TB. 185). Reading these travel reports becomes crucial to the expression of desires that, because of the material constraints of motherhood, would otherwise find no other legitimate means of articulation. However, Laura can only perform readings of the travel reports because she remains barred from enacting them out directly. As indicated earlier, Laura's inability to travel stems from more than political prohibitions. Her refusal to travel has to do with a strategic decision to uphold the imaginary relationship between herself and Beatriz without a total loss of identity. However, once Beatriz begins to close the dialectic of identity by actually taking on Laura's physical attributes in addition to her household duties, the imaginary relationship between the two is severed. Laura is forced to halt the act of transference and, like the patient who after the transference in analysis has taken place must mourn the loss of a love-object in the figure of the analyst, Laura too eventually has to mourn the loss of a friend when Beatriz falls from the balcony to her death.

Because the travelogues take the place of that which the subject is deprived of, they are overdetermined with meaning. The sublimated desire for travel is condensed onto the travelogues themselves, which then become, in Lacanian terms, "fetishized." Laura seems in fact to attribute undue importance to Beatriz's tales from abroad, and her interest in receiving the travelogues comes to replace the urge to travel itself. After Beatriz's death, Laura finds a replacement for Beatriz's stories in the world of her dreams. It is at this stage in the narrative that Laura disclaims responsibility for writing the story of the collaboration between Laura and Beatriz. She relays the manuscript to Morgner, an already acclaimed author, and thus reactivates the processes of transference of authorship again. Morgner then becomes the authorized, legitimate author of Laura's illegitimate stories. They are illegitimate in two senses; first, because they are the product of a clandestine alliance between a subject with no officially recognized existence and a subject with no formal status in GDR society; and second, because Laura as a single working mother certainly officially had no time for creative writing and hence any products of her labor must be thought of as illegitimate. There also seems to be sufficient evidence that, even as a married mother, Laura will have even less time to practice her new-found profession as a writer because she no longer has the child-minding help of Beatriz (TB. 7).

In *Amanda*, the question of authorship and authority over the text of the novel *Trobadora Beatriz* is renegotiated. Beatriz, who is reincarnated once again, this time in the hybrid body of a siren, challenges the authority of Morgner as narrator of the manuscript of the novel *Trobadora Beatriz* that Amanda retrieves for her out of the Blocksberg archives. Beatriz accuses Morgner, as the author and the one who has been authorized with the relaying of Beatriz's message, of being irresponsible. Beatriz decries Morgner's novel as willful "character assassination" (A. 35) and as a distortion of the truth. As the author and a female at that, it should have been her duty to conceal the fact that Laura was in fact the author of many of Beatriz's texts in order to protect Laura's reputation.

Morgner's irresponsibility is due to the fact that she has revealed the truth about Laura's co-authorship without telling the other half of the truth of the story, namely, that it was not even Laura who wrote the stories in Beatriz's name in the first place but Laura's other half, Amanda, who had been vegetating in the dungeons of the Blocksberg for years.

Beatriz claims that this other truth about Laura's other half, Amanda, had not been the subject of official censorship, but the victim of "inner censorship" (A. 23). Beatriz conceives of her task of reading Morgner's manuscript as an imperative to rewrite that part of the story that has been censored by Morgner in the novel *Trobadora Beatriz*. Thus, in *Amanda*, the roles of author and object of the narrative are reversed. In *Trobadora Beatriz* it was Morgner who, as receiver and reader of Laura's manuscript about the life and adventures of Beatriz, the last in the narrative chain, was ultimately held responsible for the contents of the novel. In *Amanda*, the role of receiver and reader of the manuscript is assumed by Beatriz, who undertakes to rewrite the story of the other Laura, the story of the novel's author. Her aim is therefore to reconstruct in part the novel *Trobadora Beatriz* by filling in the censored gaps. Writing then becomes a dialectical process in search not of some absolute truth about the real Laura concealed behind the virtuous exterior of the image of a model working mother, but instead a process in search of self-censored truths and censored truths about the self.

6
Female Sexuality, Technology, and State Control

The Quest for Sexual Liberation and Control

The overarching narrative paradigm uniting the various strands of *Trobadora Beatriz* – the Bildungsroman, the medieval quest, and the modern socialist romance – is that of the quest-romance. The common denominator is the notion of the quest: the quest for freedom of movement, for adventures, and for self-determination. Underpinning all these quest narratives is the master narrative of the quest for women's emancipation with its telos as the feminist ideal of the emancipated female subject of historical processes. All narratives relate back to this one overriding principle; all can be read in some way as allegories of this one master quest. Thus, the ordeals of the female actors, their tests of courage and will, become the means by which the history of women's emancipation is contested. Perhaps the most important phase in this collective quest for better conditions for womankind, and one that has not yet been discussed, is the quest for sexual liberation and for self-determination in matters relating to sexuality and birth control. This concern forms a pivotal point in the novel and represents the final phase in the historical "subject-becoming" of women. This final stage is crucial because it attempts to remove the single most powerful barrier preventing women from attaining control over their forces of production. These quest narratives in turn participate in a more general ideological struggle for a female subject of history and social change.

Feminists have repeatedly pointed out that the ideology of patriarchy cannot be adequately accounted for in a concept of ideology as false consciousness; gender ideology has obvious material effects and is embedded in material institutions such as the family, which reproduce the dominant relations of production in their practices.[1]

---

1. Michèle Barrett, *Women's Oppression Today: The Marxist/Feminist Encounter*, rev. ed. (London: Verso, 1988), 85–90.

It is precisely at this physical and material level of women's everyday lives that the ideological contradictions of socialism were most obvious and most intolerable. But it is not only in terms of the material conditions of women's existence that the effects of the ideology of patriarchy, here socialist patriarchy, can be felt; patriarchy has a corporal dimension and its effects have a concrete physical nature that are experienced by women through the agency of their bodies. The double burden, for instance, is lived by women predominantly through the medium of their bodies. Ideological contradictions in general often have a corporal dimension. For example, the discrepancy between women's role as equal partners in the work force and their traditional role in the nuclear family as providers and nurturers meant that East German women until 1972 were able to dispose of their labor freely but not their bodies. Until the East German parliament introduced changes to the laws restricting free abortion in 1972, women were denied the right to decide for themselves whether or not to terminate a pregnancy.

The coexistence of feudal and socialist modes of production, each with its distinctive spheres of operation yet each dependent on the other for its reproduction, brought with it another form of control involving the exploitation of women's sexuality by their male partners and socialist comrades. However, it is not the mere coexistence, or the non-synchronicity of different modes of production and historical consciousnesses that is of such importance to the female body. What is significant is rather the interdependence of the feudal and socialist modes of production. The feudal relations reproduced in the socialist family provide the very condition of possibility for the consolidation of the socialist relations of production. Women's unpaid domestic labor provides the support not only for the spheres of economic production but also for the technological revolution, whose achievements were still, despite equal opportunity programs, attributable in the main to men. Here we may recall the words of Dr. Solowjow, the Soviet chess world champion, who reminds Melusine in *Trobadora Beatriz* that many of men's achievements in all areas of public life would simply not have been possible if men shared domestic and child-rearing duties equally with women: if not only women but men as well were emancipated, men would only be average in their performance. If women are to be liberated from their status as domestic serfs they must gain control over all their means of production, including their means of "reproduction" in the traditional sense of the word.

At the outset of the novel the liberation of eroticism is posited by Beatriz as the most urgent task facing women in the twentieth century. Because of her adventures, Beatriz is in fact diverted from this mission for the greater part of the novel. As a subtext of the novel, this original quest remains submerged beneath the other more pressing quests in the text. Beatriz's original mission reappears later in the form of a quest for control over women's bodies and means of reproduction. In the narrative the achievement of this vital stage in women's progression towards emancipation is made dependent on the fulfillment of two conditions: the reform of the abortion laws and paragraph 218, and the increased availability of reliable contraception. The changes to the abortion laws are represented in the novel *Trobadora Beatriz* as the final and deciding stage in the struggle for emancipation. The reforms are the essential precondition for the reappropriation of women's bodies by their rightful owners.

The body, as that part of women's "private property" hitherto ignored by the state and by classical Marxist theories, becomes the site of a revolutionary struggle over the possession of what women see as their own peculiar force of production. By analogy with the socialist revolution, which takes as its first and immediate goal the abolition of private property, the feminist revolution Morgner proposes should also seek the abolition of "private property" within the patriarchal family. In this sense Morgner's proposal appears very much a historical Marxist one, which sees the sexual liberation of women as only being possible after a change in the relations of production in the family. At the same time, however, it is critical of traditional Marxist theories of private property that ignore some of the most obvious forms of property relations in men's rights over women's bodies. According to Morgner, it is only when women become controllers and owners of their bodies as property (TB. 336) that they can begin to take advantage of their legal and political rights. And yet the history of Eastern European socialism has clearly shown that the appropriation of the means and forces of production by the proletariat and even a change in the mode of production is by no means the end of the story. It is doubtful, therefore, that a quest for sexual freedom that hinges on the development of oral contraceptives and the liberalizing of abortion laws will likewise be the end of the story of women's emancipation. This becomes apparent in the sequel to *Trobadora Beatriz, Amanda.*

Seizing the "Productive Force of Sexuality"

In *Trobadora Beatriz*, as in the earlier novel *Hochzeit in Konstantinopel*, women are presented as being the representatives of a type of Freudian or Marcusian "pleasure principle" who must oppose the "reality principle" or "achievement principle" that informs the male-dominated socialist work ethic of the first two decades of the GDR. The female principle or pleasure principle is posited as being a corrective to the techno–fetishism that dominates the world of science and technology. In *Amanda*, however, this belief in the transformative power of female eroticism has lost much of its force, and the optimism of the earlier novel is tempered with a good deal of skepticism. In *Amanda* there is good reason to believe that the legal changes in abortion rights alone will not be sufficient to bring about radical changes in the social and sexual practices affecting women's everyday lives. In an interview published in the East German women's magazine *Für Dich* in 1978, Morgner stresses the need to revolutionize people's habits and traditional role behavior so that women can begin to take advantage of their legal rights. Changes in social practices require transformations at the level of collective consciousness, and this is hardly something that can be easily achieved in the short term nor something that can be ordered or prescribed from above: "You cannot force people into developing a new consciousness, everyone has to produce it for oneself. It has to evolve."[2]

The real work of changing the customs or social practices between the sexes can only begin with economic and legal changes in the system, and yet this can only lay the groundwork for changes in public attitudes. Morgner is adamant that changes in role behavior cannot be forced upon the population but must instead develop "organically":

---

2. Morgner, "Aber die großen Veränderungen beginnen leise," 18.

The immense amount of work that a society and every individual has to do in order to change the thousand-year old customs takes place above all in those so-called private spheres and cannot be achieved from one day to the next or in 10 or 20 years. It progresses gradually and cannot be enforced by law; it has to evolve and is a creative social process.[3]

Self-determination in matters of birth control and abortion are therefore expressed in terms of the historical reappropriation of a feminine sexuality that is defined in orthodox Marxist terms as a "force of production." The intended homology with the act of seizing control of the means of production by the proletariat is obvious, yet Morgner's concept of productivity and her notion of what constitutes a force of production is significantly at variance with the classical Marxist definition. Behind Morgner's polemic lies a fundamental refusal to recognize the classical Marxist dichotomy between the productive spheres of social life and the private realm of biological and social reproduction. Her attempt to blur the distinction between the forces of industrial production and biological reproduction is particularly significant given that the East German state in fact came to rely very heavily on women's biological reproductivity as a means of ensuring the future productivity of its economy. It would appear, in fact, that changes to the abortion laws were primarily motivated by the concern to regulate women's reproductive cycle so as to increase their productivity and reliability in the labor force. By classifying sexuality as another force of production, on a par with labor power, Morgner seeks in the first instance to gain recognition for sexuality as a powerful but little recognized and expressed force in women's lives.

Although Morgner talks about utilizing female sexuality as a productive force and harnessing its power for the benefit of humankind, in general sexuality in her writings appears to approximate a form of socially committed creativity that is not

---

3. "Die große Arbeit, die eine Gesellschaft und die jeder einzelne leisten muß, um die jahrtausendealten Sitten zu verändern, die spielt sich aber vor allen Dingen in der sogenannten privaten Sphäre ab und kann nicht von heute auf morgen und auch nicht in 10 oder 20 Jahren geleistet werden. Das geht allmählich, ist nicht durch Gesetze zu erzwingen, muß wachsen, ist ein schöpferischer Prozeß der Gesellschaft." Morgner, "Das eine tun und das andere nicht lassen," 43.

necessarily geared to any specific utilitarian or economically productive ends:

> Women who have been forced by customs for hundreds of years to suppress their sexuality inevitably became crippled and original achievements cannot be expected from cripples.[4]

Sublimated sexuality is, according to Morgner, the driving force behind great creative achievements. As a force of nature associated with the creative act, women's sexuality has been stifled by attempts to channel it into socially productive and acceptable ends and, as such, represents a productive force of a qualitatively different kind from the usual forces of production that can be put to socially useful ends.

On another occasion Morgner speaks of sexuality in terms of a social and historical construct based on biological differences that are largely inconsequential. Whereas the social differences between men and women are great, she argues, "the biological difference is by comparison small."[5] In thus proclaiming the historicity of women's sexual oppression, she appears to avoid the sort of biologistic or essentialist arguments prevalent in many Western feminist debates about female sexuality that appeal to the notion of a natural feminine body or some ideal of a repressed natural or pre-social sexuality. In many such arguments the female body becomes the site of an authentic "natural" existence that can be invoked as a positive foil to the repressive nature of the social. The body is often thought to pre-date the social, existing somehow outside the reaches of the social. Although Morgner does not appear to subscribe in her writing to essentialist notions of woman's nature, she does nonetheless present sexuality as a privileged site of resistance to the deforming effects of modern industrial societies.

Morgner's strategy of reclaiming the power of sexuality is similar in many respects to Western feminist theories that speak of a natural pre-social state of female sexuality. In the context of

4. "Frauen, denen die Sitten jahrhundertelang abverlangt haben, ihre Sexualität zu unterdrücken, mußten verkrüppeln, and von Krüppeln sind keine originären Leistungen zu erwarten." Morgner, "Die Produktivkraft Sexualität souverän nutzen," 334.
5. Ibid.

the former German Democratic Republic, however, the matter of reclaiming women's bodies and sexuality presents a different set of problems and requires slightly different forms of negotiation. In political discourses on women's dual function in the public spheres of industrial production and the private sphere of the family, female sexuality became reduced to a mere function of women's roles as mothers and reproducers of the work force. Morgner attributes this silence surrounding women's erotic needs to a certain puritanical or ascetic streak that she claims is common to all revolutionary movements:

> Generally it can be observed that revolutionary movements often have at first an ascetic streak to them. In this respect we are no exception.[6]

One particularly useful means of challenging prevailing social and literary taboos on sexuality and eroticism, and one that has been usefully employed by Western feminists in the 1970s, is to invoke a pre-social or prior state of existence, which is presented as a natural part of human existence and, by extension, an acceptable part of normal social activity. It has been a particularly useful strategy for feminists to argue that sexuality is in fact something quite natural and therefore has a legitimate place in the social realm. Its absence from the dominant social order is then explained by means of a theory of cultural repression, according to which certain social and historical orders have repressed natural aspects of human behavior.[7]

In general, discourses on "origins" provide a convenient way of presenting certain social formations as repressive or "unnatural,"[8] provided they do not succumb to the temptation to couch historical truths in the form of a dogma or an unchanging given. Morgner's ideal of an undeformed female sexuality inevitably draws on the assumption that the natural state of the female body is one in which women's sexuality is a productive force not yet stunted or stifled by social constraints. Similarly, her

---

6. "Es ist allgemein zu bemerken, daß revolutionären Bewegungen oft zunächst ein asketischer Zug anhaftet. Da haben wir keine Ausnahme gemacht." Ibid., 333.
7. See Martin, "Feminism, Criticism and Foucault," 11.
8. Beverly Brown and Parveen Adams, "The Feminine Body and Feminist Politics," *m/f*, no. 3 (1981): 39–41.

rather nostalgic notion of an original state of pansexuality characterized by the eroticization of all social relations – from sexual relationships to women's relationship with nature – further indicates the expediency of constructing an alternative form of sexuality around some notion of the natural or a lost state of being. In a key interview with Karin Huffzky, Morgner outlines her concept of an undeformed sexuality:

> Sexuality is a precious restlessness that makes erotic relationships possible not only with people but also with landscapes, sounds, colors, smells – with phenomena of this world in general. Without it there is no enthusiasm, no intellectual spark, no wit. No thinker, no composer can function with his/her head alone. S/he functions as a whole: the head is a part of his/her body, not its adversary. The world is created in harmony and in opposition with one's self, inside and outside one's self. That holds for women as well as for men.[9]

This imperative to discover the lost power of sexuality and the suppressed potential of a non-dualistic, holistic approach to the mind and body bears similarities to campaigns within feminist movements in Britain, America, and Europe in the 1970s to rediscover the "suppressed power of female sexuality."[10] But whereas the focus in Western feminist movements was entirely on the liberation of a suppressed female sexuality from the "institution of heterosexuality"[11] and from male oppression and violence, Morgner's project, like those of other East German feminists, explicitly includes men and male sexuality in her plans for reform: "That holds for women as well as for men."[12] Many radical feminist arguments in the 1980s contended that

---

9. "Sexualität ist eine kostbare Unruhe, die erotische Beziehungen ermöglicht, nicht nur zu Menschen, sondern auch zu Landschaften, Tönen, Farben, Gerüchen – zu Erscheinungen dieser Welt überhaupt. Ohne sie gibt es keinen Enthusiasmus, kein Feuer des Geistes, keinen Esprit. Kein Denker, kein Politiker, kein Wissenschaftler, kein Dichter, kein Komponist arbeitet nur mit dem Kopf. Er arbeitet als Ganzheit: der Kopf ist ein Teil seines Körpers, nicht sein Widersacher. Mit sich in Harmonie und Spannung wird die Welt gemacht, in sich und außer sich. Das gilt für Frauen ebenso wie für Männer." Morgner, "Die Produktivkraft Sexualität souverän nutzen," 334.
10. See Lynne Segal, *Is the Future Female?* (London: Virago, 1987), 80.
11. Adrienne Rich, "Compulsory Heterosexuality and Lesbian Existence," *Signs* 5, no. 4 (1980): 633; Segal, *Is the Future Female?*, 80–95.
12. Morgner, "Die Produktivkraft Sexualität souverän nutzen," 334.

women's sexuality was crippled by the enforcement of "compulsory heterosexuality," and that the roots of male dominance lay in men's sexual domination of women. Rape and pornography were considered conclusive evidence that the primary form of domination over women was sexual and that the "heterosexual institution" merely reinforced these structures of domination.[13] Although women in Morgner's works most certainly suffer at the hands of the "heterosexual institution," in particular those representatives of the older generation like Olga Salman – Laura's mother, Morgner generally tends to regard the problems of institutionalized heterosexuality as more the symptom than the cause of women's continued subordination. Thus, while her target is often the institutionalization of heterosexuality in the nuclear family and the role this plays in perpetuating a set of social practices that are sexually and economically exploitative of women, nowhere is the domination of women through the agency of heterosexuality reduced to a notion of coercive or violent male sexuality as is often the case in anti-pornography debates in the West.

Morgner repeatedly insists on the need for an education program for men and argues that the subordination of women is also a problem for humanity: "Emancipation of women is unattainable without the emancipation of men and vice-versa."[14] At first glance this appears consistent with the orthodox Marxist axiom that posits women's emancipation as a historical contradiction that can only be resolved after the socialist revolution and after the resolution of the primary contradiction of class. However, Morgner's adherence to this fundamental tenet of Marxist philosophy and politics does not signify an inability or even a reluctance to think the question of the primary and secondary contradiction through dialectically. It should instead be read as an assertion of difference from Marxist feminist theories in West Germany and as a reaction to anxious but well-meaning attempts by West German feminists to integrate East German feminist impulses into their own theories and practices. But its real significance lies in its employment as a strategy to highlight the unresolved nature of the primary contradiction and stress the importance of women's solving both

13. See Segal, *Is the Future Female?*, 96.
14. Morgner, "Die Produktivkraft Sexualität souverän nutzen," 328.

contradictions. "Do the one thing without neglecting the other" is the motto Morgner gives to her project in an interview with the West German feminist, Ursula Krechel.[15]

In interviews and in her works Morgner consistently eschews any form of feminist separatism. In this respect she has inherited the fear of feminism and purely feminist concerns that was characteristic of early socialist feminists, in particular Clara Zetkin, for whom feminism was equal to separatism. The preoccupation with "women's issues" alone was traditionally considered by early social democrats the bastion of liberal feminism. Women involved in the social democratic movements in Europe devoted their attention instead to the more pressing task of accelerating the downfall of capitalism and agitating for the imminent socialist revolution rather than campaigning for what they regarded as mere cosmetic changes to women's lot in society. In order to avoid the sort of marginalization of women's matters from the political programs of their parties that was initially a feature of early bourgeois feminist movements, socialist feminists have traditionally insisted on the futility of fighting against men for better conditions and equal rights for women.[16] Better conditions for women, they insisted, could only be brought about through the collective efforts of working-class men and women. Female socialists tended on the whole to adopt the contempt their male colleagues felt toward liberal feminist campaigns and, in fact, seemed to regard the extent of their disapproval of bourgeois feminist issues as a measure of their credibility as socialists.[17]

Morgner's insistence that the emancipation of women is far too important to be classified as "only a matter for women"[18] therefore must be understood against the background of the polemics between early bourgeois and socialist feminist movements. Her statement is clearly intended as a means of preventing the sort of political division of labor between women's concerns and the so-called broader political struggles of the day typical of bourgeois

---

15. Morgner, "Das eine tun und das andere lassen," 43–45.
16. See Marielouise Janssen-Jurreit, *Sexism: The Male Monopoly on History and Thought*, trans. Verne Moberg (New York: Farrer, Straus, Siroux, 1982), 114–27.
17. See Jean H. Quataert, *Reluctant Feminists in German Social Democracy, 1865–1917* (Princeton: Princeton University Press, 1979), 114–20.
18. Morgner, "Die Produktivkraft Sexualität souverän nutzen," 328.

and socialist movements at the turn of the twentieth century. Because women's issues were thought to be of relevance only to women, they were not seen as part of the more pressing struggle to bring about the socialist revolution. Thus, by asserting their relevance for the whole of humankind Morgner hopes to prevent this sort of marginalization of feminist politics. Furthermore, her insistence on the centrality of feminist struggles masks an implicit critique of the fate of official East German women's bodies such as the "German Women's League," which tended to trivialize and depoliticize women's concerns.

In *Amanda* the problems posed by such a political alliance between feminists and men along with the specific difficulties of feminist separatism in the German Democratic Republic are frequently the object of satire and humor. The voice of a feminist opposition, embodied in Laura in *Trobadora Beatriz*, becomes at once more diversified and more fragmentary in the later novel. The voice of pragmatism and realism is complemented by the different feminisms of Amanda, Laura's other half, and Isebel, one of the witches languishing in the underground of the Blocksberg. Each represents opposing factions in the Hörselberg opposition, a body of witches/feminists/prostitutes who are plotting to overthrow male rule on the Blocksberg or Brocken. Isebel, the leader of the HUU-Faktion, or the Hörselberg underground, represents a type of militant feminism that is antagonistic towards men and endorses the use of patriarchal means of opposition, such as violence.

In *Amanda* Morgner clearly privileges Laura's particular form of pragmatic, realistic feminism, satirizing the type of radical militant feminist opposition represented in the figure of Isebel. Yet Laura's theoretical guilelessness and political naiveté are as far removed from providing a sound basis for the construction of a feminist politics as is Isebel's radicalism. Her reluctance to step out of line for fear of reprisals is meant to typify the sorts of attitudes shared by the majority of working women in East Germany. Laura clearly provides the East German reader with an object of identification; yet Laura's voice is patently the voice of a conservatism constantly subjected to criticism in discussions with Vilma and Isebel. Isebel is, for example, highly critical of Laura's willingness to enter into a pact with the opposite sex in order to regain control of the Blocksberg. What is at issue here is the official Marxist assumption, which Morgner seems to share, that changes for women can only be achieved with the help of allies. Isebel challenges the need for allies and revives the bourgeois feminist notion of women's emancipation as a "continuation of the war between the sexes,"[19] something Laura has explicitly rejected. Laura's final proposal of an alliance with men is essentially not an endorsement of heterosexuality but a necessary political manoeuvre to ensure the success of the emancipation of both sexes. This is conceived of in the same terms already outlined by Morgner, that is, as a "problem for humanity." This solution is rather a choice between two evils, since her own experiences with the heterosexual institution have been far from satisfactory. Moreover, her strategy stems in part from the purely pragmatic desire to share the duties of parenthood and provide her son with both male and female role models. In a later chapter I shall address the particular problems that Laura's pragmatic approach to heterosexuality poses for a revolutionary feminist politics and for feminist strategies for the future. Suffice it to say here that in *Amanda* heterosexuality is represented as the dominant mode of female sexuality, but that the spaces created in the text for sexual plurality are far greater than in *Trobadora Beatriz*.

Disciplining the Female Body

In *Amanda* the task of regaining control over the female body as a means of liberating women's repressed creativity becomes further complicated by an increased awareness of the fact that the female body is, to speak with Michel Foucault, "directly involved in a political field; power relations have an immediate hold upon it, they invest it, mark it, train it, torture it, force it to carry out tasks, to perform ceremonies, to emit signs."[20] The female body can no longer be thought of unproblematically as a force, or even a property to be appropriated by the female subject in the process of "entering history." Nor does it seem appropriate to women's situation in the 1980s to regard the body as something to be freed

19. Ibid.
20. Michel Foucault, *Discipline and Punish: The Birth of the Prison* (Harmondsworth: Penguin, 1977), 25.

from those material conditions that alienate and objectify it. It has been customary within revolutionary movements for those who see themselves as excluded from power to regard power as something external to the subject, something that only coerces, prohibits, and alienates the revolutionary subject from its forces of production. While this certainly holds true for the way the state in the former GDR wielded power, this repression model seems inadequate to account for other ways in which power operates at the level of the individual. The questions thus remain whether power is something that can be seized or appropriated as "property" and whether the act of repossession is sufficient to free the subject entirely from domination.

The arguments put forward in *Trobadora Beatriz* on the question of the liberation of women's bodies through the act of repossession are, it would seem, not entirely free of a certain amount of what Foucault has termed "juridical schematism"[21] – that is, a type of legalistic reductionism that sees the empowerment of the subject as the logical consequence of legal changes or reforms. Once women legally have become the proprietal owners of their bodies and sexuality, the questions must be asked in what ways the subject is empowered, how this power operates on the body, and what precisely are its effects on the body. We must then ask whether the notion of a progression from domination to liberation, from the object to the subject of power relations, can provide an adequate conceptual framework for examining the ways in which the female body is inscribed in power relations.

In the GDR the female body proved especially productive as an economic and political force, particularly in the immediate postwar years. These years of reconstruction and rebuilding would scarcely have been possible without the large-scale mobilization of female labor power and without women's participation in industrial and agricultural production. The entry of women into the work force, particularly into traditionally male-dominated professions, is well-documented in the literature of the first two decades of socialism. In many stories by male authors, women appear to subject their bodies almost euphorically to the

21. Michel Foucault, *Power/Knowledge: Selected Interviews and Other Writings 1972–1977*, ed. Colin Gordon, Leo Marshall, John Mepham, Kate Soper (New York: Pantheon Books, 1980), 120.

physical hardships of hard manual labor. These tributes to the early heroines of socialism pay in fact meticulous attention to the subjection of the female body to the rigors of the work place as a kind of ordeal that the women must survive if they are to prove their worth as equal members of the work force. The greater the physical trials and degree of physical hardship, it seems, the greater the level of achievement of the heroine in a masculine environment. Physical sacrifice thus appears in these early novels to take on a new meaning of the highest form of female heroism. It was those women who suffered the most and displayed the greatest endurance who formed the role models for a whole generation of women in the 1950s and 1960s. They formed a type of politically and physically superior vanguard of the official feminist revolution. The normative power of the image of the quietly stoic female worker is for instance still very much in evidence in the negative responses of the daughters of the postwar heroines of socialist work such as Barbara, the "Marriage Con-woman" in *Amanda.* Barbara's rejection of her mother's impossibly high work standards is given as one of the main reasons for leaving the GDR:

> My mother was a perfect example of a woman: competent in all her roles . . . . She worked in the first shift as a production manager, in the second and third for free. In 1960 my father left his wife, his bad conscience and daughter behind him and moved from Dessau to Hamburg. I soon followed him because I was fed up with equal rights. I did not want to become a workaholic like my mother. I wanted something different. (A. 319–20)[22]

The issue of the ready availability of oral contraception is best seen in the context of women's entry into male-dominated professions. At the time of its introduction into the GDR, oral contraception was welcomed by most women for the reason that it freed them from those aspects of their menstrual cycle

---

22. "Meine Mutter war eine Frau, wie sie im Buche steht: tüchtig in allen Rollen . . . . Sie arbeitete in der ersten Schicht als Dispatcher, in der zweiten und dritten gratis. 1960 ließ mein Vater Frau, schlechtes Gewissen und Tochter hinter sich und ging von Dessau nach Hamburg. Ich folgte ihm bald, weil ich von der Gleichberechtigung die Nase voll hatte. Ich wollte kein Arbeitstier werden wie meine Mutter. Ich wollte was anderes."

that made them less able to perform the tasks required of them in the work place. It provided women with a means of guaranteeing maximum efficiency from their bodies and hence maximum recognition for their labors. Here Laura's example can be seen as typical of women's responses to the Pill in the 1970s. The Pill, she argues, put women in control of their reproductive cycles and partially in control of their labor power. When Laura recalls in *Amanda* the euphoria she and Beatriz felt at the changes to the abortion laws, it is precisely for the reasons of increased efficiency and productivity that she welcomes the reforms:

> Now we take what is due to us. The repercussions are vast. At any rate, my life would have taken an entirely different course if I had been in control of my body since adolescence. (A. 222)[23]

Laura now confesses to Amanda that her earlier optimism was misplaced and that she is no longer entirely convinced that the Pill and the right to abortion will guarantee women ultimate control over their bodies.

Vilma's attitude to the Pill and its social and economic consequences for women is rather more skeptical. She argues that the Pill may well have freed Laura from excessive pain and discomfort yet it has also made her more productive, more reliable, and more competitive in a male-dominated work force. It has therefore made her socially more useful:

> Laura had become reliable in her performance p.p. [post pilalum]. Physically equally as fit and able to compete as her male colleagues. Socially more useful. (A. 370)[24]

Vilma argues that women have had to deny their bodies to be able to compete in a work force dominated by male work norms and standards, as it is the male body that sets the norms for performance:

---

23. "Erst jetzt gehört uns wirklich, was uns gehört. Die Auswirkungen sind unübersehbar. Jedenfalls wäre mein Leben gänzlich anders verlaufen, wenn ich von Jugend an im Besitz meines Körpers gewesen wäre."
24. "P.p. [post pilalum] war Laura leistungszuverlässig geworden. Körperlich gleichbleibend fit und wettbewerbsfähig wie ihre männlichen Kollegen. Gesellschaftlich besser brauchbar."

In male-dominated societies women always reject their bodies, directly or indirectly . . . are ashamed of them. Conceal its characteristics when it prevents them from attaining certain performance parameters that are supposed to represent the human norm. This norm is set by men. (A. 371) [25]

So while Laura maintains that the Pill has given her the sense of being "doubly liberated" (A. 369) from domination and pain, Vilma regards the Pill as merely another form of subjection and control. The regulation of women's menstrual cycles has not only made them socially more productive, it has also helped to make women more readily available to men sexually. This in effect has meant women have substituted one form of subjugation or exploitation for another:

The Pill has thrown us from one form of physical non-freedom into another. . .. It used to be acceptable for a woman to feel too tired for lovemaking. Today every respectable woman is expected to be in the mood at any time of the day or night. And do the preparation of course. Preparation is suddenly entirely a woman's thing. Is that what you call emancipation? I call it exploitation. A new form of exploitation, which we in our naive belief in progress had not reckoned with. And not a trace of proletarian solidarity. (A. 223–24)[26]

Contemporary women's movements in the West have been only too aware of the negative implications of the sexual revolution of the 1960s and how a masculinist idea of sexual liberation often led to greater access to women's bodies and to different forms of exploitation. In East Germany, the medical technology that in the 1970s had promised women greater sexual freedom is, in the 1980s, made responsible for binding women into another form of political

25. "In Männergesellschaften lehnen Frauen ihren Körper immer ab, direkt oder indirekt. . . . schämen sich seiner. Verbergen seine Eigenschaften, wenn die behindern, bestimmte Leistungsparameter der menschlichen Norm zu erreichen. Diese Norm stellt der Mann vor."
26. "Die Pille hat uns von einer physischen Unfreiheit in die andere gestürzt . . . Früher war es einer Frau erlaubt, sich zu müde zur Liebe zu fühlen. Heute wird von jeder anständigen Frau zu jeder Tages- und Nachtzeit Lust erwartet. Präparation sowieso. Präparation ist plötzlich nur noch Frauensache. Kannst du das Gleichberechtigung nennen? Ich nenne es Ausbeutung. Eine neue Form der Ausbeutung, mit der wir in unserer naiven Fortschrittsgläubigkeit nicht gerechnet hatten. Von proletarischer Solidarität keine Spur."

and social domination with a different set of social and sexual obligations.

In his influential study of the genealogy of the exercise of power in the French penal system in *Discipline and Punish*, Foucault observes that "the body becomes a useful force only if it is both a productive body and a subjected one."[27] According to Foucault, power is not only exercised through direct violence; it can be equally wielded through much more subtle forms of coercion, particularly via technologies and other forms of social control. Certain forms of mastery over the body, which on the surface appear to be more enlightened or lenient in style and form, are therefore not necessarily any less a form of control or an exercise of power. In the same way, the Pill is for Vilma simply another means of exercising control over women's bodies; it has neither given rise to the liberation of women's bodies nor has it succeeded in making the female subject and body the unequivocal center of power and control. Instead, the Pill is what Foucault has called a "technology of power" or a "political technology of the body," a new and different form of social and technological control deployed at a micro-political level through specific discourses and social practices.[28] The discussion between Laura and Vilma makes it evident that the effects of domination on the body are not solely attributable to the operations of "appropriation" or alienation, nor can they be adequately accounted for by an analysis of power in terms of prohibition, interdiction, or censorship. They are instead the result of what would seem to be a "political technology of the body," the result of power relations "that invest human bodies and subjugate them by turning them into objects of knowledge," and therefore into more suitable objects for surveillance, discipline, and regulation.[29]

Foucault's interest in the varying regimes of power/knowledge that invest the social body is significantly at variance with the totalizing theories of power we know from Marxism that tend to pose the problem of power only in terms of the state apparatus and mode of production.[30] Foucault rejects the liberal and Marxist concept of power as a purely negative and repressive force, thus

27. Foucault, *Discipline and Punish*, 26.
28. Ibid., 24–30.
29. Ibid., 27–28.
30. Foucault, *Power/Knowledge*, 115.

opening up a space for a concept of power as a "positive creative force" that produces knowledge through discourses on the body simultaneously with techniques of control and domination. Certainly, when attempting to apply these theories to the realities of state socialism, we should be alert to the dangers of embracing in toto any concept of power that is blind to the repressive nature of the mechanisms of state and party coercion, given that state power in the German Democratic Republic clearly did openly practice prohibition, interdiction, and censorship. However, it is crucial to complement analyses of state or institutional power in totalitarian societies such as the former GDR with an analysis of power in terms of its productive as well as negative aspects.

Many such theories of the socialist state that define the modus operandi of the socialist system in terms of the totalization of social control through a "dictatorship over needs," presided over by the party and its bodies, fail to address the more productive and positive effects of the exercise of power at the level, for instance, of the female body and women's everyday lives.[31] They often fail to take into consideration the ambivalence of the exercise of power at the level of the individual subject, that power can be experienced by the subject as both restrictive and enabling. It is customary for such analyses to ascribe all reformist measures to rationalization processes within the bureaucracies of the state apparatus and processes geared to improving efficiency in the economic functioning of the state. However, such a theory of the dictatorship over needs displays several shortcomings when confronted with the ambivalence of the type of state practices Heller, Feher, and Markus identify as pseudo-pluralism. While they are at times only too aware of the contradictions in state policy and practices, these are too readily explained away in what seems an overly simplistic account of the workings of the party and its various apparatuses. Such a theory, for example, has no answer to Laura's protestations that technological control in the form of the Pill, an extension of party control according to Heller, may well have made her economically more productive for the state, but that it has also afforded her a degree of individual freedom she did not have before.

31. Agnes Heller, Ferenc Feher, and Georgy Markus, *The Dictatorship over Needs* (Oxford: Basil Blackwell, 1983).

By the same token, we as readers obviously must resist the temptation, as does Vilma, to laud the reforms in women's health in the 1970s as unequivocally emancipatory and liberal, or merely as the result of an official "thaw" or period of liberalization. As Beverly Brown and Parveen Adams point out, it has become necessary for feminists to move beyond analyses of the female body and female sexuality that contrast women's lack of control over their bodies with the form of absolute control found in private property, "since our form of control of our body is, like all forms of ownership, itself a matter of partial control and partial non-control."[32] Just as it becomes impossible in *Amanda* to speak of the female body as a unity in need of united liberation, it also becomes increasingly difficult to speak of a totally homogeneous body of working women in the GDR with totally unified goals and interests. In the 1970s it was politically expedient for feminists in East Germany as well as in West Germany to see sexual liberation in terms of regaining possession, and therefore control of their bodies as their rightful possession, and to project an image of a natural, undenatured female body that could re-emerge once the repressive social structures were removed. As Brown and Adams point out, "analyses in terms of unities hold out the prospect of liberation – unities can be grasped and will not finally escape us."[33] However, they also warn against the dangers of a feminist politics of liberation that analyzes female sexuality solely in terms of the negative effects of a repressive exercise of power from above. Such theories tend to place great emphasis on the transgression of this source of power in the reclaiming of a natural, unalienated female body. This critique of the repression of female sexuality is based therefore on a concept of power that inevitably sees the individual body as both inside and outside the workings of a monolithic power, simultaneously oppressed by it yet paradoxically capable of liberation from it.

Here Foucault's theory of power is useful for its critique of theories of liberation – in particular, sexual liberation – and of the humanization processes in modern post-Enlightenment societies. An analysis of how bodies are disciplined through their inscription in discourses of power can help shed light on the techniques by

32. Brown and Adams, "The Feminine Body and Feminist Politics," 42.
33. Ibid., 44.

which the female body is subjected to state control through mechanisms of discipline and normalization. It is the constricting nexus between, on the one hand, increased "aptitude" or productivity, a direct effect of the technological regulation of women's reproductive cycle, and on the other hand the "increased domination," through technological intervention and coercion, that Foucault identifies as the dual aspects of the exercise of power through "discipline(s)."[34]

As Vilma's critique of the new technologies of the body implies, the increased availability of birth control and the reforms in abortion laws have in many respects replaced one form of policing with another. Liberation from one form of regulation can often mean control of another sort, by other social, sexual, or medical practices. In *Trobadora Beatriz* Laura remarks that a physical lack of freedom can be more "crippling" than a political lack of freedom. In *Amanda*, however, women's freedom to control their bodies and their reproductive cycles is overshadowed by the realization that political control, in the form of legal barriers, has been replaced by technological control of women's bodies and sexuality through oral contraception. The body is now the contradictory site of different social and institutional practices that regulate and normalize its functions, directing them towards more diverse ends. Such practices also make the female body the object of new developments in medical and technological knowledge.

This form of control, however, is seen by Vilma as a form of intervention into the "creative workings" of the female body that is crippling in a different way. The female body is referred to as a building or edifice and as a source of stifled or untapped creativity harnessed in the name of technological innovations in the interests of the state and the dominant sex. We are reminded of the edifice of the palace in Split that is described as being "related to Laura" (TB. 191). Here the female body is likened to a "historical product" and female subjectivity to an organic construct. Vilma's critique of oral contraception as a form of rape (A. 369) also draws on the concept of the female body as a fundamentally dynamic structure that has been forced into stasis by artificial means. Vilma is critical of the fact that women are forced to welcome artificial interventions into their menstrual cycles if they want to compete,

34. Foucault, *Discipline and Punish*, 138.

as they indeed must, with masculine work norms and achievement standards. Laura, however, dismisses Vilma's argument as a dangerous standardization of women's bodies based on the idea of a natural female body and of the female body as a preexisting piece of nature. She retorts that Vilma can only worship this "magnificent creative edifice" because she, with her "exceptional belly" (A. 371), represents more of an exception than the general rule. Laura is unable to take any special pride in "this nature that had left her in the lurch like this" (A. 370), this piece of nature that in her "ante pilalum" days (A. 369) made her unfit for carrying out her daily duties as a train driver, thus putting herself and her passengers at risk. What is at stake in Laura's case is not so much her duty to the community but the sense of self-fulfillment she gains from her work and of course from the economic independence this guarantees her:

> Laura had become reliable in her performance P.p. [post pilalum] . . ..
> But privately as well: at last Laura could carry out her job of driving trains that she loved beyond all measure, with confidence, supreme confidence. (A. 370–71)[35]

Thus, Laura defends on personal grounds greater forms of technological control, even if this in turn increases her social efficiency and productivity. She prefers to see in the free availability of oral contraception not a form of technological domination but instead a form of personal empowerment.

Public Power and Private Bodies: Women in Patriarchy

In the novel *Trobadora Beatriz* Morgner draws parallels between the economic and sexual dependency of women in the family and feudal relations of domination through the montage of stories about women's subordination in the Middle Ages. In the story about Marie of Montpellier, Morgner implies that aristocratic

---

35. "P.p. [post pilalum] war Laura leistungszuverlässig geworden. Körperlich gleichbleibend fit und wettbewerbsfähig wie ihre männlichen Kollegen . . .. Aber privat auch: Laura konnte das Triebwagenfahren, das sie über alle Maßen liebte, endlich selbstsicher betreiben. Souverän."

women were disenfranchized under a feudal mode of production, functioning as objects of exchange in a patriarchal "libidinal" economy, and as the conveyors of property and power relations between men of their own class. Moreover, their economic and legal dependency on men guaranteed their instrumentalization as commodities with both use and hence "abuse" value – as well as exchange value.

In *Amanda* the analogy with feudal forms of domination is taken up again, primarily in the chapter entitled "Speech about the Execution of Damiens," which narrates in graphic detail the public execution and torture of Damiens, the regicide of Louis XV of France. What distinguishes this medieval story from those in *Trobadora Beatriz* is the account of torture as public spectacle and thus the corporal form assumed by the mechanisms of absolutist state control. Morgner's version of the legend, like the account that opens Foucault's *Discipline and Punish*, focuses on the description of the seemingly barbaric act of the public dismemberment of the body of Damiens as an act of revenge on behalf of the King. In both accounts the body of the feudal subject is the explicit object of the punitive procedure and the site of the execution of absolutist power. The punishment of the royal subject is effected on the body through elaborate torture techniques and finally through total dissection of the body and its components. The subject's liberty is deprived by radically curtailing the freedom of movement of the subject as physical object. Feudal acts of punishment, unlike modern forms of punishment, do not aim at reform and rehabilitation, but rather at the dissolution of the body as the visible representative of the self. Foucault argues, however, that even the more lenient forms of punishment that entail confinement and correction rather than torture or execution still make the body the target of their punitive techniques: ". . . it is always the body that is at issue – the body and its forces, their utility and their docility, their distribution and their submission."[36]

Like Foucault's use of the Damiens story, Morgner appears to resist any such reading of the feudal procedures of torture that might posit the present as either a more humane or an equally barbaric moment in history. She thus avoids making obvious comparisons between feudal forms of torture and socialist modes

---

36. Foucault, *Discipline and Punish*, 25.

of surveillance and control, although parallels clearly can be drawn. Her interest in the Damiens story has to do instead with the specific function of the public display of the power of the feudal monarch in the art of inflicting graduations of pain on the body of the transgressor. For Morgner, as for Foucault, the prime purpose of torture as a public spectacle is its "juridico-political function" as a public ritual designed to reinforce the power of the regent. Rather than a gratuitous act of cruelty and sadism, the public execution signifies an orderly social ritual calculated to have specific effects on the criminal, the power of the sovereign, and finally the spectators at the execution.[37] The spectacle becomes an important means of publicly reactivating the power of the monarch and reinforcing his strength:

> Although the wound inflicted on the King was very minor and could only be minor because Damiens used a small knife, the assassin was executed in the same way as Ravaillac. In that way Louis XV was supposed to be compared with the best King that France had ever had, which is presumably attributable to an overcompensation due to the feelings of hatred and contempt towards the kingship which were only suppressed out of respect. (A. 93)[38]

Morgner, like Foucault, locates another essential ingredient in the success of the public execution in the ambiguous role of the spectators. Both seem to agree that the spectators play a pivotal role in assisting the King wreak his vengeance on the regicide. Although such a brutal display of might, as manifested here in the asymmetry between the crime and its punishment, must at one level invoke fear in the spectators, it also made them the guarantors of the punishment.[39] According to Morgner, the sheer brutality of the spectacle, the excess of fear produced in the spectators, did not invariably result, as Foucault suggests, in an

---

37. See Mark Poster, *Foucault, Marxism and History* (Cambridge: Polity Press, 1984), 97.
38. "Obgleich die dem König beigebrachte Wunde sehr leicht war und nur leicht sein konnte, weil Damiens ein kleines Messer benutzte, wurde der Attentäter auf dieselbe Weise hingerichtet wie Ravaillac. Dadurch sollte Ludwig XV. mit dem besten König, den Frankreich je besessen hatte, gleichgestellt werden, was wohl auf eine Überkompensierung der Haß- und Verachtungsgefühle gegen das Königtum, die nur durch Ehrfurcht unterdrückt waren, hinweist."
39. Foucault, *Discipline and Punish*, 59.

identification of the crowd with the victim. The more unreasonable the punishment, argues Foucault, the greater the probability that the crowd would recoil from the sovereign's brute display of strength and exhibit solidarity with the victim. Morgner, by contrast, is far less optimistic about the rebelliousness of the crowd at executions and its willingness to disrupt the ritualized proceedings of the ceremony. Morgner's reading of the role played by the spectators makes less of the oppositional force of the crowd and its power to express its disagreement. The public spectacle, she argues, should present itself as a "manifestation of hatred for the King" (A. 92), thus providing an outlet for the pent-up aggressions of the people towards a monarch already rapidly losing favor with his populace. After all, the attempt on Louis XV's life was welcomed by and large by the French, according to Morgner, because of the mounting discontent with the King's various practices, not the least of which involved incurring huge national debts and imposing unreasonable taxes to pay for the extravagant tastes of his mistress. Rumors circulating after the minor attempt on the King's life speculating that the King was dead are furthermore cited as an example of the extent of his unpopularity and the power of wishful thinking on the part of the people:

> The rumor about the assassination attempt spread rapidly and was immediately transformed through the power of wishful thinking: it was said the King was dead. (A. 91–92)[40]

Yet Morgner remains unconvinced that the public spectacle often provided the people with an opportunity to express their outrage at the excessive abuse of royal power and display their solidarity with the victim. She asks: "Can it be concluded from this that Damiens was assured of feelings of solidarity?" (A. 93). She surmises that any such display of solidarity with the tortured victim becomes transformed not into a rebellion against injustice but instead into open complicity with the executive arm of the law. The aggressions, which were directed at the King, are displaced and then projected onto the assassin:

---

40. "Das Gerücht vom Attentat verbreitete sich schnell und wurde alsbald in wunscherfüllender Richtung umgewandelt: Man erzählte, der König sei tot."

Thus the spectators' need to punish the King was openly projected onto his assassin and was emotionally satisfied with his execution. (A. 95)[41]

The collective need of the people for vengeance finds its fulfillment just as easily in the bringing to justice of the victim as it would in injuring the body of the King. The spectacle manages, therefore, to redirect the aggressions of the populace onto the oppressed rather than the oppressor or the real source of power. It does so by encouraging identification with punitive power through the public display of the authority of the monarch: "Identification with the avenging society enables aggressions to be lived out in permissible form" (A. 95).

The crowd becomes an accomplice in the punitive act and, through the medium of the public spectacle, the potentially disruptive force of the people can be sublimated and channeled in such a way as to reinforce and enhance the power of the ruling class rather than to challenge it. Morgner quotes Freud as the source of her speculations about the relationship between oppressed and oppressor and about the processes of transference that prevent clear divisions between those with power and those without: "What one endures passively, one strives to live out in aggressive form" (A. 95).

Yet Morgner is not so much concerned with psychological explanations for the way power is exercised through mechanisms of identification, as with the way power structures are internalized and reproduced at the individual level to enable the identification of the victim with its own oppressors. In raising the question of complicity in the perpetuation of structures of domination, Morgner is at the same time touching on issues of a more general nature about women's implication in patriarchal power structures and practices and the ways in which women living under a patriarchy become unwitting accomplices in the perpetuation of social, professional, and sexual inequalities. The story about Damiens is in fact a speech given to the plenum of witches/

---

41. "Das Strafbedürfnis der Zuschauer gegenüber dem König war also offenbar auf dessen Attentäter projiziert und mit seiner Hinrichtung emotionell befriedigt worden."

feminists who hold their clandèstine meetings in the Hugenottendom to illustrate the following point: "Women do not only live in patriarchy; it also lives in them" (A. 91).

The feudal spectacle of the public execution, like the medieval carnival and official feasts of the church and the state, is as Terry Eagleton suggests, "a prime example of that mutual complicity of law and liberation, power and desire."[42] *Amanda* is particularly concerned with the problems this often unwitting complicity of women with patriarchal structures of domination poses for a feminist liberatory politics and practice. As already indicated in the previous discussion of the female body and technological domination, there is often a fine line dividing a politics of liberation from a politics of cooperation and complicity. Women's complicity in power structures, as demonstrated in the medieval public spectacle, presents one of the main obstacles to the formulation of an emancipatory politics and the trialing of an emancipatory practice, a theme that is taken up later in connection with the witches' Walpurgis Night. As with the witches' sabbat, Morgner displays an acute awareness of the subtle and often devious ways in which state power is exercised at its various levels. She closely dissects the mechanisms by which individual needs and emotions can be channeled to enhance rather than diminish the aura of the totalitarian state. These considerations were of paramount concern for oppositional groups in the GDR such as the alternative peace movement and women's movement and their formulation of strategies of intervention.

Morgner concedes that the public execution not only serves to affirm existing power hierarchies in feudal society by allowing the expression of collective sentiments in permissible form. The spectacle, although like Bakhtin's carnival, clearly a "licensed affair,"[43] also provides an outlet for the venting of frustrations and repressed emotions in a form that is usually prohibited. Unofficially, the public execution provides a forum for the unbridled expression of an unlicensed sexuality that under normal circumstances would be kept firmly in check. The best expression

---

42. Terry Eagleton, *Walter Benjamin or Towards a Revolutionary Criticism* (London: Verso, 1981), 149.
43. Ibid., 148.

of this is to be found in the image of Casanova and his friend
copulating with female spectators at the execution:

> He [Casanova] was in the company of several ladies and gentlemen
> who had placed themselves in two rows on the steps in front of a
> window. In doing so they had moved the skirts of the ladies to one side
> so as not to get them dirty. Friend Tiretto made use of the opportunity
> and preoccupied himself in a manner that needs no further elaboration
> with an old lady who was standing in front of him. Aroused by the
> moaning of the victim the two amused themselves in this manner for
> two hours. (A. 95)[44]

The Carnival and the Power of Laughter

The officially organized spectacle in *Amanda* is thus a contradictory
site of conflictual power relations; it both affirms and negates the
socio-political status quo. In the medieval story about Damiens the
crowd is made an accomplice in the execution of the regicide and
yet, as the example of Casanova demonstrates, there are
possibilities even within this complicity for the transgression of
social and sexual prohibitions. Morgner's account of Damiens'
execution stresses the ambiguous nature of the officially sanctioned
spectacle. The spectacle is "incorporative"[45] because it encourages
complicity with "the avenging society" (A. 95) by providing a
licensed safety valve for sentiments that might otherwise lead to
revolt.[46] The example of how anti-royalist feeling and solidarity
with the regicide is channeled into solidarity with the oppressive
regime itself is indicative of the way the public spectacle functions
to reinforce existing hierarchies and power structures. It is also a

44. "Er war in Gesellschaft einiger Damen und Herren, die sich in zwei Reihen
    auf den Stufen vor einem Fenster plazierten. Dabei hatte man die Röcke der
    Damen beiseite geschoben, um diese nicht schmutzig zu machen. Freund
    Tiretto nutzte die Gelegenheit und beschäftigte sich in einer nicht näher zu
    erörternden Weise mit einer alten Dame, die vor ihm stand. Erregt durch das
    Jammern des Opfers unterhielten sich die beiden so zwei Stunden lang."
45. Eagleton, *Walter Benjamin*, 149.
46. This was a defense of popular festivals employed in the Soviet Union, mainly
    by Anatoly Lunarcharsky, the Commissar of Enlightenment, to which
    Bakhtin's theory of carnival is a critical response. See the prologue by Michael
    Holquist in Mikhail Bakhtin, *Rabelais and His World*, trans. Hélène Iswolsky
    (Bloomington: Indiana University Press, 1984), xvii.

practical demonstration of how power – in particular, patriarchal power – is internalized by the individual and reproduced in sexual and social practices. But, by the same token, carnivals may have, according to Morgner, a liberatory and disruptive aspect, particularly for women, in allowing sections of society to show its other, unofficial face or as Bakhtin has termed, its "second nature."[47] The same can be claimed for the public execution as for Bakhtin's carnival; they both provide "temporary liberation from the prevailing truth and from the established order; [they mark] the suspension of all hierarchical rank, privileges, norms and prohibitions."[48] The non-permissible behavior of the public execution in the sexual licentiousness among the spectators during the execution functions in a similar way to Bakhtin's laughter of the medieval masses that "liberated . . . from censorship, oppression, and from the state."[49]

In Bakhtin's account the medieval carnival is the privileged time of the year when official truths and existing hierarchies are subverted by the popular masses with gay abandon. The inversion of all social hierarchies within the carnival does not merely reveal that all existing social relations are arbitrary and relative, but that alternative truths are possible. Rather than positing the carnival as a utopian ideal and a model for a freer community of individuals that can only be realized during sanctioned periods of license, Bakhtin's notion of carnival is instead "the repeated affirmation of the possibility of alternative relations in the midst of order and control."[50] As the people's most effective and subversive means of defense against all forms of dogmatism, orthodoxy, and official seriousness, laughter remained according to Bakhtin a "free weapon in their hands," never becoming an "instrument to oppress and blind the people."[51]

In Morgner's account of the Damiens' execution, the feudal public spectacle functions similarly to Bakhtin's carnival in permitting the expression of emotions otherwise excluded from

47. Ibid., 75.
48. Ibid., 10.
49. Ibid., 93.
50. David Carroll, "Narrative Heterogeneity, and the Question of the Political: Bakhtin and Lyotard," *The Aims of Representation: Subject/Text/History*, ed. and introd. Murray Krieger (New York: Columbia University Press, 1987), 90–91.
51. Bakhtin, *Rabelais and His World*, 95.

the dominant feudal order in a temporary suspension of social hierarchies as well as social and political prohibitions. Official and unofficial worlds co-exist side by side; the official display of power is the paradoxical condition of possibility for the expression of alternative power relations and other unofficial truths. While Bakhtin's emphasis is entirely on the disruptive and subversive aspects of the carnival, on the unofficial interludes of popular laughter amidst the official feasts and festivals, Morgner's discussion of the role of the carnival and the public spectacle focuses on both official and unofficial displays of culture. A determining feature of the carnival for Morgner is the permissible public representation of power as well as the potentially disruptive elements accompanying any public festivity or officially organized performance of existing power relations.

Yet Morgner's reservations about the efficacy of these "licensed enclaves" does not stem from the fact that they are fully contained within an officially sanctioned festival of the state or church. She does not object to the utopian aspects of the carnival, as does Eagleton, on the grounds that the carnival "is a *licensed* affair in every sense, a permissible rupture of hegemony, a contained popular blow-off as disturbing and relatively ineffectual as a revolutionary work of art."[52] The laughter of the carnival cannot, Eagleton contends, constitute the basis for a revolutionary practice if it is in any way tolerated or licensed by the dominant order. Morgner does not question the liberatory potential of the official carnival with its pockets of unofficial social and sexual transgression on the grounds that it has official state approval. She is concerned instead with the ways in which the official culture is able to appropriate and manipulate the mocking, irreverent laughter of the people for its own political ends.

In the chapter entitled "The Walpurgis Night on the Blocksberg (Intermezzo in Minor)" Morgner composes a thinly disguised satirical allegory of an official East German television report on a feminist demonstration, most probably to commemorate the Year of the Woman in the West. Laura is approached alternately by Chief Devil Kolbuk and Father Maccotino, acting for Chief Angel Zacharias, who both propose marriage on behalf of opposing ideological powers. Both of them forcibly subject Laura to a

52. Eagleton, *Walter Benjamin*, 148–49.

viewing of a video of Walpurgis Night festivities conducted on the Blocksberg, each providing their own radically different commentary on the same ceremony. The fact that Laura takes Chief Devil for a ZDF or a "Südfunk Stuttgart" correspondent is a clear indication that the report of the witches' activities on the Blocksberg is from a Western perspective, and hence the version that Father Maccotino shows is quite obviously an edited official East German version of the same event. The East German version is significantly given the subtitle "Substitute Carnival" (A. 496). Interspersed in the commentary is a section taken from Bakhtin's *Rabelais and His World* on the liberatory function of laughter and the carnival in the Middle Ages and the formation of an unofficial alternative truth "full of ambivalent laughter, of blasphemy and profanation, of indecent speeches and gestures, of familiar contact of all people with all people" (A. 510). Medieval laughter thus signaled a victory over fear of authority and absolutes, a victory,

> . . . over fear of the holy and forbidden, of the power of God and the Devil, and of the power of people, of authoritarian rules and bans, of death and retaliation in the after world, and above all of Hell which is even more terrifying than earth. (A. 507)[53]

This section from Bakhtin quoted by Morgner in *Amanda* concludes with the remark that these carnivalistic safety valves in the Middle Ages, like the feminist demonstrations, were not an expression of the increasing liberalism of a repressive absolutist regime, but a measure of the degree of oppression of the feudal order, a mark of "a surfeit of oppression" (A. 510), which made the need for officially sanctioned outlets all the more necessary. If this still forms part of the Chief Angel's commentary, then this reading of the carnival as a measure of the oppressiveness of a regime rather than of the power of the people is obviously intended as an indictment of the pseudo-liberalism of Western democracies. As officially staged displays of pluralism, modern day equivalents of the carnival such as demonstrations by oppositional groups merely serve, in the eyes of the East German reporter, to lend a repressive

53. " . . . über die Furcht vor dem Geheiligten und Verbotenen, vor der Macht Gottes und des Teufels und vor der Macht der Menschen, vor den autoritären Geboten und Verboten, vor Tod und Vergeltung im Jenseits, vor der Hölle, vor allem, was entsetzlicher ist als die Erde."

or absolutist regime a more tolerant appearance. The first report of the feminist demonstration or the witches' Walpurgis Night by the West German reporter in the chapter entitled "The Walpurgis Night on the Blocksberg (Intermezzo in Major)" concludes in fact with a panegyric to the sort of democratic political order that not only tolerates the open expression of dissention but even welcomes such virulent and aggressive opposition. The reporter remarks at the end of the program:

> . . . the structure of the Blocksberg is the most liberal of all systems. Or do you know of an authority that allows it to be abused in such a way? Nowhere else does such a highly democratic government exist that permits its people to rehearse a revolt against it and which not only tolerates these revolts but even celebrates and rewards them. (A. 411)[54]

Spectacles such as the witches' demonstration in fact trivialize the tyranny of a particular regime in an exhibitionist display of pluralism:

> A pyramid scaffolding as in every year – the hollow regime could not have come up with a more tasteless and exhibitionistic way of trivializing its tyranny. Nowadays absolutist forms cannot be dismissed simply by joking about them and playing them down with a pluralistic holiday. With one single one per year. (A. 499–500)[55]

While the reporter is clearly referring to practices in the West, the same criticism could equally be leveled at official periods of license and carnival in the East. The reporter dismisses the official times of carnival in the West, particularly those organized by feminists, as the "clever staging and self-staging" (A. 510) of capitalism. Yet state socialism was also increasingly keen to improve its international image throughout the 1980s by boasting publicly of

54. ". . . Die Blocksberg-Ordnung ist die freiheitlichste aller Ordnungen. Oder kennen Sie irgendwo eine Obrigkeit, die sich derart beschimpfen läßt? Nirgendwo anders gibt es eine so hochdemokratische Regierung, die erlaubt, gegen sich den Aufstand zu proben und diese Proben nicht nur toleriert, sondern sogar bejubelt und prämiiert."
55. "Pyramidengerüst wie in jedem Jahr – eine abgeschmacktere Form scheint dem hohlen Regime nicht einzufallen, um seine Tyrannei exhibitionistisch zu verharmlosen. Absolutistische Formen lassen sich heutzutage nicht mehr einfach als Witz wegwitzeln und mit einem pluralistischen Feiertag überspielen. Mit einem einzigen pro Jahr!"

its tolerance towards feminists. Officially approved demonstrations and functions in the GDR often served as a means of enhancing its international reputation. Morgner indicates that any such tolerance of feminist "dissidents" the East Germany state decides to display at certain strategic moments similarly masks a tyrannical regime that only tolerates dissidence when it can utilize those with an international reputation for its own gain. As a result, alternative women's movements must be aware of the dangers of co-optation by patriarchal regimes who give the appearance of tolerating feminists in their midst only when it is to their advantage.

As a more or less officially recognized spokeswoman on women's issues in the East, and as the official author of a feminist novel, Laura is being courted by both Chief Devil Kolbuk and Chief Angel Zacharias to lend her name to a new feminist book, which they have given the by now cliched title "A woman without a man is like a fish without a bicycle" (A. 452). Both sides see the political advantage of putting Laura's name to a feminist novel as a means of improving the reputation of their respective regimes. The marriage proposals of the two are also attempts to compromise the integrity of Laura in the name of patriarchal systems with opposing ideologies, to give credence to their particular regimes, and to foil the other in a thinly disguised form of ideological warfare. Yet it becomes apparent in the chapter "Wager on the Blocksberg" that Kolbuk and Zacharias are in league with each other, despite their obvious ideological and political differences, and that both are endeavoring to compromise Laura's integrity and authorial autonomy. Father Maccotino reveals to Laura after attempting to win her hand in marriage: "From time to time the heavenly and infernal hosts do battle until they are reconciled in fraternal solidarity" (A. 522).

Officially licensed periods of feminist dissent and anarchy, confined to isolated days of the year and to discrete social and geographical spaces, appear not only to be tolerated by the opposing patriarchal regimes of Kolbuk and Zacharias but are in fact actively encouraged by them. Indeed, they have become wholly licensed affairs. Yet is the public spectacle merely another means employed by state apparatuses to consolidate their control over the populace? In Morgner's view the relevance of the carnival as a means by which the populace, particularly women, can rehearse strategies of resistance to dominant ideologies is not diminished simply because the carnival can also be deployed by state apparatuses as a safety valve to defuse sentiments that might otherwise lead to revolt. But by the same token Morgner does not wholly endorse Bakhtin's utopianism that views the carnival as an unequivocal manifestation of the emancipatory force of popular laughter and unofficial culture – a force so powerful that it obliged the medieval church and the state to make more and more concessions to the popular masses.

But whether the lack or the abundance of periods of carnival is ultimately to be interpreted as a measure of the power of the people, or as a measure of the repressiveness of a particular regime, is perhaps not the crucial issue here in the context of the formation of feminist strategies of resistance to patriarchal power. Periods of carnival and popular festivals will always, Morgner seems to be arguing, be open to multiple and contradictory readings and appropriations, and will never be the unequivocal site of oppression or liberation. They are instead arenas of political struggle, a criss-cross of practices that are neither entirely liberatory nor repressive. Despite the dangers of co-optation, the carnival remains for Morgner a crucial vehicle for the articulation of an alternative feminist culture. Even the officially approved public spectacle, like the feudal public execution, can provide an outlet for the expression of permitted and prohibited emotions, of official and unofficial cultures. Like the medieval feast, which has two faces, the festival of witches also has at least two aspects, comprising an official and unofficial representation. Like the laughter of the medieval crowd, the laughter of the witches and the torrents of verbal abuse they hurl at representatives of patriarchy signal a victory for the female participants over fear of masculine domination and intimidation. By unleashing women's pent-up aggressions towards men, the witches' invective, like Bakhtin's folk laughter, serves to liberate them from the "great interior censor"[56] and to encourage the expression of alternative unofficial feminist "truths" and life forms:

> By overcoming this anxiety, laughter brightened up the human mind, opened up the world to people in a new way. This victory was admittedly only ephemeral and was limited to special days; after that

56. Bakhtin, *Rabelais and His World*, 94.

there were work days of fear and dejection. Yet from these festive rays of light that formed in the human mind another unofficial truth about the world and humankind emerged which prepared the way for the new self-understanding of the Renaissance. (A. 507)[57]

By allowing a less restrained communication of alternative truths, the witches' invective serves a similar purpose to Bakhtin's medieval folk laughter. It articulates a "less restrictive sense of the social, an alternative idea of community"[58] among women. In this way Morgner's women's laughter is in fact itself, like the official culture it debunks, full of ambivalence. As the epitaph to the *Amanda* novel from E.T.A. Hoffmann's *Seltsame Leiden eines Theaterdirektors* suggests, laughter is also symptomatic of a romantic longing for Heimat or for a lost sense of self, for a lost utopia: "Laughter is only the painful cry of longing for Heimat that stirs in one's soul" (A. 6).

Like Laura's laughter, the tirades of abuse vented by the witches are not merely parodic: they are deadly earnest. It is doubtful that Morgner's witches in their staging of the Walpurgis Night do actually escape appropriation by the ruling regime, given the highly mediated form the reports of their festivities take in the novel as well as the very impossibility of immediate and undistorted representation by the media of both the Kolbuk and the Zacharias regimes. More significantly, however, the witches' Walpurgis Night represents an attempt on the part of the participating women to articulate and perform their own sense of identity and community "in their own way"[59] and not in the terms dictated to them by the dominant patriarchal orders.

---

57. "Indem es diese Furcht besiegte, hellte das Lachen das menschliche Bewußtsein auf, öffnete ihm die Welt auf eine neue Weise. Dieser Sieg war freilich nur ephemer, er beschränkte sich auf die Festtage; dann kamen wieder Werktage der Angst und Bedrückung, doch aus diesen festtäglichen Lichtblicken des menschlichen Bewußtseins bildete sich eine andere, eine nicht offizielle Wahrheit über die Welt und den Menschen aus, die das neue Selbstbewußtsein der Renaissance vorbereitete."
58. Carroll, "Bakhtin and Lyotard," 89.
59. Bakhtin, *Rabelais and His World*, 255.

7
The Witch, the Mother, and Pandora

The Witches' Return

The figure of the witch is by now a familiar one in the discourses of feminist movements around the world. Much of the original power to shock and scandalize that women calling themselves witches were able to wield during the abortion demonstrations and reclaim-the-night marches of the 1970s had by the late 1980s lost much of its impact. In the German Democratic Republic the witches' return, however, was somewhat belated; yet the delay in the appearance of the feminist trope of woman as witch on the East German literary scene does not appear to have lessened the threatening and disruptive aspect of her return. Her reappearance in the works of East German feminists cannot be reduced entirely to earlier moments within feminism nor can her political mission be defined solely by reference to previous struggles within international feminism. While the East German witch is similar in many ways to the image of the witch mobilized by women's groups in the Western world, there are a number of crucial differences that merit special attention.

As in the West, the revival of the image of the witch and the plethora of mythical and historical associations East German women writers invoke in their novels and short stories about witches represent a process of remythification by which patriarchal myths are mobilized and reappropriated by women themselves in an act of self-definition and self-representation.[1] As with much modern day recourse to myth, the act of collective recollection of the history of the oppression of women in the witch trials of the Middle Ages by feminists can be seen to "seize . . . hold of a

1. See Silvia Bovenschen, "The Contemporary Witch, the Historical Witch and the Witch Myth: The Witch, Subject of the Appropriation of Nature and Object of the Domination of Nature," *New German Critique* 15 (1978): 90.

memory as it flashes up in a moment of danger."[2] This memory is the history of the persecution and oppression of women by the church and the state, but it is also the story of active female resistance to patriarchal coercion. Although the persecution of women in the medieval witch trials differs radically from twentieth-century forms of oppression, even those in former Eastern bloc countries, this type of "experiential appropriation of the past" underscores the longevity of feminine myths and the long and intractable history of varying forms of women's oppression. And it does so without losing sight of the fact that today, as Bovenschen has stated, "we are relatively safe from being burned at the stake."[3] It is a memory that does not attempt to reconstruct the objective historical figure of the witch nor to re-enact the historical persecution of women during the witch pogroms of the late Middle Ages. Instead it seeks out lines of continuity and points of conjunction between the black chapters of the past and the intolerable aspects of the present.

In *Amanda*, the role of the witch cannot be defined exclusively by the concept of carnival, nor are her activities contained within officially sanctioned periods of chaos. The image of the witch is central to the concerns of the novel and figures much in the same way as the sorceress in the writings of the French feminists Cixous and Clément, that is, as an "exemplary trope . . . for the female condition."[4] In addition, it symbolizes the possibility of feminine subversion of the cultural and political forms of domination in patriarchy. Like the sorceress of the French Romantic historian Jules Michelet, Morgner's witch is "woman finding her autonomy in . . . a 'counter-culture.'"[5] The witch is to an alternative feminist culture what the medieval jester was to the people of the Middle Ages. She is the herald of another, non-patriarchal, non-official truth and her laughter is an ideological weapon in the struggles for a feminist alternative to socialist patriarchal practices. She presents a site of resistance to the oppressiveness of dominant

2. Walter Benjamin, "Theses on the Philosophy of History," in *Illuminations*, ed. and introd. Hannah Arendt, trans. Harry Zohn (New York: Schocken Books, 1968), 257.
3. Bovenschen, "The Contemporary Witch," 84–85.
4. Sandra M. Gilbert, "Introduction: A Tarantella of Theory," introduction to Hélène Cixous and Catherine Clément, *The Newly Born Woman*, trans. Betsy Wing (Manchester: Manchester University Press, 1986), xiii.
5. Cixous and Clément, *The Newly Born Woman*, 4.

belief systems countering the homogenizing and unifying force of the dominant culture with her own counter-culture. In the figure of the witch, Morgner revives a lost mythology of a feminine resistance to patriarchal forms of coercion and patriarchal forms of knowledge, reinvesting the archetype with a new subversiveness and political force. Morgner's rewriting of the legend of the witches' sabbat resonates with Western feminist recuperations of the traditionally negative figure of the witch as seductress, as well as with feminist appropriations of the positive attributes of the witch as nature healer, wise-woman, and midwife. Her critical use of mythical tradition thus participates in the general feminist project of revalorizing negative historical images of women and femininity. Yet at the same time Morgner resuscitates aspects of the myth that have hitherto played only a minor or subordinate role in other feminist reappropriations, overlaying these feminist rereadings and rewritings with new readings pertinent to the socio-historical context of Eastern Europe.

Like the sorceress of Michelet and Clément, the witches in *Amanda* are simultaneously bearers of a past history of resistance and heralds of new forms of opposition to repressive patriarchal social and symbolic orders. They represent similarly "the return of the repressed," an archaic, anachronistic force that serves as a reminder of what a culture has collectively repressed and censored. According to Freud, this "archaic heritage," although of phylogenetic origin, is present in residual form in the individual unconscious. These forgotten cultural memories become reactivated by a recent repetition of the original act of suppression or repression, which then inscribes the original event with fresh significance.[6] The works of Freud and Michelet show how women have traditionally been the repositories of culturally sublimated desires and taboos that, when resurfaced in the figure of the hysteric, for example, or alternatively when invoked by the witch, have the power to challenge the oppressive social and political systems of the present.[7] The mobilization of the figure of the witch in European feminist movements has frequently expressed an

---

6. Sigmund Freud, *Moses and Monotheism: Three Essays, Standard Edition (1937–1939)*, vol. 23, trans. James Strachey, collab. Anna Freud (London: Hogarth Press, 1964), 98–101.

7. Cixous and Clément, *The Newly Born Woman*, 5–9.

almost romantic desire for "the return of the repressed" in the form
of a return to an unalienated female sexuality undeformed by
patriarchal history.

While Morgner's witches are a striking example of the
subversive power of the "return of the repressed," the East
German witch is simultaneously an example of negative
stereotyping for her reappearance also provides a means of
challenging the traditional "demonization" of the female sex that
was still very much in evidence in socialist patriarchies. The
rebellious woman or female troublemaker in *Amanda* carries
associations of sexual promiscuity and lasciviousness; Tenner,
Vilma's husband and Laura's ex-husband, is quick to accuse Vilma
of unfaithful behavior on her failure to return home one night,
when she has in fact been attending a witches' symposium at the
Hugenottendom. The non-conformist woman is quickly
transformed into the temptress or alternatively the bad mother.
The obverse of the superwoman, the other woman of the GDR,
or the GDR woman's other, who dares to defy cultural norms, is
therefore both witch and whore. Political and social disobedience
becomes associated with sexual licentiousness. Both witch and
whore constitute that which has no proper place within socialist
patriarchy and is afforded no official existence within the
dominant culture. They form the basis of a cultural imaginary that
is confined, like the refractory other halves of East German
witches, to the Hörselberg, that mythical underworld of East
Germany's magic mountain, which in recent times also doubles
as a brothel. Here Cixous's description of the role of this cultural
imaginary seems particularly apposite: "Somewhere every culture
has an imaginary zone for what it excludes, and it is that zone we
must try to remember *today*."[8]

In East German culture, this imaginary zone or magic mountain
is to be found on the Blocksberg in the Harz region. This cultural
imaginary with its hierarchical divisions into upper- and
underworld lies on the periphery of the geographical space of the
German Democratic Republic, along the political borders of a
divided nation at the heart of patriarchal ideology. It forms a space
between two political cultures, a space that has historically been
allotted to those who fall between two stools or cultural systems.

8. Ibid., 6.

The women who inhabit the underworld of the Blocksberg, the imaginary red light district of the GDR, are not only those who fall outside the symbolic and social order and who are thus relegated to margins of the country, they also represent a political other, a group excluded and marginalized from the dominant political order. The legendary Blocksberg becomes the imaginary hideaway, not only for a cultural "fall-out," for the prostitutes, the bad mothers, the witches, and the female troublemakers of the GDR, but also for a political "fall-out," for the heretics, the non-believers, and the potential dissidents.

Morgner's witches are therefore much more than the demonic temptresses and seductresses of, say, the Italian feminist movement. They are primarily heretics, and the history of resistance they draw on is the history of witchcraft as a form of opposition to institutionalized religion and to the orthodoxy and dogmatism of the church. Just as witchcraft practices, pagan rites, and the medical practices of healers and midwives became equated with heresy and heterodoxy during the religious struggles of the Reformation, the witchcraft practices of Laura and Vilma, their "sleep-substitute" brews and conjuring tricks, make them guilty too of heresy and therefore subject to persecution and surveillance by the state. They are saved, however, by the fact that the state and its citizens would least expect to encounter political heresy in the form of witchcraft. For Laura's mother and grandmother, for instance, there can hardly be a place less likely to allow the existence of witches and supernatural events than the GDR. Thus, when Amanda makes an appearance on a witch's broom in their living room on the day of Laura's baptism, they are far from impressed. Amanda's offer of a "conjuring elixir" for the young witch-to-be, together with the name Amanda Laura, is regarded with considerable suspicion, and once the apparition has vanished the child is named Laura instead and the potion thrown away. The annunciation of Laura as the "chosen one" occurs some years later when she is visited by Frau Holle and reminded once again of her calling as both witch and madonna.

Morgner's heretics do not merely re-enact a past history of resistance by reasserting the legendary demonic power of their historical predecessors; they are the bearers of a constantly present utopia and thus anticipate alternative cultural and political possibilities. Like the utopian community of the women in the caves along the river Skamander in Christa Wolf's *Kassandra*, Morgner's heretics and their home of the Blocksberg can be seen as representing a type of "utopian model in a nut-shell."[9] In reviving the impossible of the historical present, they offer a perspective on the possibilities of the future:

> Within an orderly society the possible of today and tomorrow is conceivable. The impossible, that is, the possible of the day after tomorrow is properly experienced as lack of order and is only conceivable on magic mountains. And the visitors of such mountains are called heretics and witches today and tomorrow, and sages the day after tomorrow. (A. 115)[10]

The proper place for heretics and witches in the GDR is in the confined and isolated spaces of the cultural imaginary, on the besieged magic mountains, where their effective surveillance and policing can be carried out. They are banished to the political, cultural, and geographical margins of society, the places Western societies have traditionally assigned to society's deviants, mad people, and medical freaks. This means of maintaining order and cohesion in the social fabric condemns non-believers and prophets of the future to a clandestine existence in the occupied military territory of the Blocksberg on the frontiers of the republic. Yet the Blocksberg itself is no longer solely the mythical and imaginary site of witches' sabbats; its dual status as a military zone occupied by the forces of NATO and the Warsaw Pact *and* a place where utopias are forged makes it a highly contradictory and ambivalent object of feminist interest.

Morgner's utopia of the Blocksberg does not appear to present any such idyllic alternative in the momentary brief existence of "a narrow strip of future."[11] In this respect, her feminist utopia differs markedly from the utopian community of women in Wolf's *Kassandra*. This commune of women living on the Skamander river

---

9. Wolf, *Voraussetzungen einer Erzählung*, 104.
10. "In Ordnung ist das Mögliche von heute und morgen denkbar. Unmögliches, das heißt, das Mögliche von übermorgen, wird ordentlich als Unordnung empfunden und ist nur auf Bergen denkbar. Deshalb heißen diese Berge Zauberberge. Und die Besucher solcher Berge werden heute und morgen als Ketzer und Hexen bezeichnet und übermorgen als Weise."
11. Christa Wolf, *Kassandra: Erzählung* (Darmstadt & Neuwied: Luchterhand, 1983), 152.

temporarily offers a harmonious refuge from the war-mongering of the world of men in a type of time warp, or "hole in time" outside the camps of the Greeks and the Trojans as well as outside patriarchal history.[12] Wolf's narrative ultimately allows, as Sigrid Weigel points out, "for no concrete utopia, that is, no way out of the history of increasing relations of domination and violence" where a feminist alternative to the impasse of militarist ideologies can develop. The focus of the narrative of *Kassandra* therefore shifts away from the "impossible of today" and Troy's social outcasts (the women on the Skamander river) to Kassandra's inner struggle for autonomy;[13] the third alternative – "between killing and dying is a third term: life"[14] – is surrendered and Kassandra eventually succumbs to the obsession with death and dying she so despises in Penthesilea.[15]

Obviously, the enclosing of the Brocken in *Amanda* effects a cultural and political marginalization of the utopian moments within the social sphere. Morgner suggests, however, that this position on the margins of the dominant culture can be put to advantage. To be banished to the margins means that the heretics and dissidents in fact occupy an intermediary position, a space in the interstices between East and West, between antagonistic systems. At the same time this is also the military space of No Man's Land, off limits and out of bounds to the "real" women of the GDR like Laura, accessible only to the privileged few or to the incarcerated other halves of these real women. Yet, in occupying the space between the inhabitants of two political systems, the dwellers of the Blocksberg are themselves frontier crossers, go-betweens between two opposing worlds and potential mediators between conflicting ideologies.

The witches' exile, despite the wasteful discarding of the conjuring elixir, proves not to be absolute and irrevocable. Because Laura's mother and grandmother relinquished Laura's right to call upon the assistance of her severed demonic other half when

---

12. See Sigrid Weigel, "Vom Sehen zur Seherin," in *Christa Wolf*, ed. H.L. Arnold (3rd revised ed.; Munich: Edition Text + Kritik, 1985), 75.
13. Ibid.
14. Wolf, *Kassandra*, 134.
15. See Anthony Stephens, "'Die Verführung der Worte': "Von *Kindheitsmuster* zu *Kassandra*," *Wolf: Darstellung, Deutung, Diskussion*, ed. Manfred Jurgensen (Berne, Munich: Francke, 1984), 135.

they threw away the magic potion, it is left up to Amanda to initiate and maintain contact with Laura, her witch-half in this world. However, when Laura, in sheer desperation at her inability to cope with the demands of being a single working parent, tries to distill a fatal potion for herself and her son, she manages instead to conjure up her other witch-half from the next world. Amanda, thus summoned, leaves the Hörselberg where she is currently "stationed" (A. 161) to lodge the right of veto that every woman's banished witch-half can exercise in matters of life and death. Through her clumsy and naive use of magic potions and herbal brews, Laura has unwittingly remembered the traditional knowledge of her historical predecessors, reactivating the ability of her banished other half to return from exile on the magic mountain to the social reality of the GDR.

The power of Isebel and Amanda, as messengers from the banished cultural imaginary of the Castle Blocksberg, to act upon the realms of the symbolic and the real is further reinforced by the alliances they attempt to forge with their other working halves in the GDR. Establishing a satisfactory working relationship between real and imaginary halves is by no means an easy task; Laura continually resists efforts on the part of Amanda to co-opt her into the struggle for the reunification of the two severed female halves. Laura is also reluctant to cooperate with Amanda's plans for conquering the Blocksberg and toppling its oppressive patriarchal regime, a strategy Amanda insists is essential to the witches' overall project. Laura's concerns are represented as strictly pragmatic and she is adamant that she does not need the help of theory and "lofty ideas" (A. 167) – a cry not unfamiliar to feminists in the West – to solve her immediate practical problems of sleep deficiency. Amanda dismisses Laura's desire to combat tiredness with alchemy as a solution of the "third way," a "piecemeal solution" (A. 274) that fails to address the underlying problem of the fragmentation of East German women. Laura's initial response to theoretical solutions to the pragmatic problems of the double burden is, however, eventually overcome by means of a compromise when she realizes that even practical short-term goals cannot be achieved without Amanda's theoretical guidance:

> Laura knew from long forbidden experience that she could not get by
> without complementation. Since she had to forego the optimal

complementation in Amanda, she pondered how she could achieve another. (A. 167)[16]

Laura eventually reaches a compromise by refusing Amanda's theoretical assistance in favor of more practical help from Vilma. By enlisting Vilma, she is acknowledging the need for doubles, although it is for doubles of a more practical nature.

The Blocksberg, like the sorceress, is the site of "incompatible syntheses."[17] Mythical and historical time coexist simultaneously and are in conflict for supremacy; the military occupation by troops of the superpowers stands in contrast to the mythical occupation by the witches. The highly ambivalent status of the Blocksberg, it would seem, makes it far from the ideal hideaway or haven for female querulants and wise-women. Despite its utopian potential, it is reported to replicate patriarchal relations of exploitation and is described by Amanda as being a "place of double standards" (A. 548). Amanda argues that if the Blocksberg is to be returned to its utopian function it must first abolish male supremacy and the sexual exploitation of women because "socialism that does not abolish male domination cannot erect a communist state" (A. 549). In this sense, the Blocksberg represents a microcosm of the social, in as much as it reproduces existing social and sexual relations as well as being the proper place for utopias. The far from ideal conditions existing on the Blocksberg provide a suitable social space for the witches to rehearse their revolt against patriarchal domination. Because it mirrors the hierarchical structure of society at large, it provides an ideal testing ground for the witches' experiments with feminist alternative life forms derived largely from women's experience of subordination. Here women can experiment with marginalized modes of knowledge such as the "mimetic mode of appropriating the world" (A. 461), which has been in decline since the Scientific Revolution and the enthronment of instrumental reason. Furthermore, it provides a forum for "public reflection" (A. 459) in the imaginary institution of the Blocksberg University and thus offers a substitute for

---

16. "Laura wußte aus längst verbotner Erfahrung, daß sie ohne Komplettierung nicht auskommen würde. Da sie sich die optimale Komplettierung durch Amanda versagen mußte, grübelte sie, wie sie zu einer anderen kommen könnte."
17. Cixous and Clément, *The Newly Born Woman*, 8.

institutionalized forms of cultural criticism: "Since public reflection only occurs to a paltry extent in the real places of this country, the Blocksberg University seems to me to be a useful institution" (A. 459).

The Blocksberg thus remains the ground of a still to be realized utopia, a concrete type of utopia no longer the home of the visionaries of the past and not yet the home of the visionaries of the future. The task of returning the Blocksberg to its original utopian function is left up to the fraction of Hörselberg witches for whom the figure of the owl represents the optimal form of human sexuality:

> The serious work could only be achieved with owls. Only they could fashion the place of double standards into a place for urgent utopias. As the old home of the seers, the Brocken/Blocksberg could become the new home of the saviors: that is the home of the peace researchers. (A. 548)[18]

Although we are invited to see in the witchcraft practices of Laura and Vilma much more than the return of a repressed female sexuality, they are the conscious heirs to the myth of the disruptive and destructive power so often attributed to female sexuality and "the female principle" within Western metaphysics, particularly during the witch trials in the Middle Ages. Laura and Vilma's task, as witches based in the real world and as participants of the "nonsense seminar series" held in the Hugenottendom, is to disrupt and subvert the "performance principle" as the dominant ethics in East German society through the affirmation of a type of Marcusian "pleasure principle."[19] During the Walpurgis Night the witches denounce in virulent tirades the archetypal representatives of the "performance principle" and all forms of patriarchal "bugbears" as embodied in the archetypal heroes of the "performance principle" of Prometheus, Don Juan, and Faust. They epitomize masculine principles of rationality and

---

18. "Nur mit Eulen könnte diese Schwerarbeit geleistet werden. Nur sie könnten den Ort der doppelten Moral zum Ort der dringlichen Utopie modeln. Der Brocken/Blocksberg als alte Heimat der Seher könnte zur neuen Heimat der Retter werden: das heißt zur Heimat der Friedensforscher."
19. See Herbert Marcuse, *Eros and Civilization: A Philosophical Inquiry into Freud*, 159–71.

utilitarianism and all excel in their mastery over external and internal nature and hence over woman as nature. The reification of these principles under late capitalism and Eastern European socialism is seen by Morgner – like the exponents of Critical Theory – as symptomatic of the failure of the project of Enlightenment and modernity.

Here Morgner departs radically from the common reception of the mythical and literary figure of Prometheus by many of her counterparts in the German Democratic Republic. In poems by Czechowski, Maurer, and Bernhof, Prometheus functions as a chiffre for the ideal-typical hero of socialist work. The procuring of fire by Prometheus is frequently employed as a metaphor in East German literature for the advent of the socialist revolution, whereby the conflict between Prometheus and the gods is transformed into a classical class conflict. In these works Prometheus is no longer the supreme individualist in his refusal of all tutelage and dependency on the advice of the gods, and is instead the representative of the oppressed classes in the production process dedicated to the promotion of the socialist work ethic and the principles of socialist production.[20] His main adversary is not the world of the gods but the class enemy. Like the Prometheus of Volker Braun, Peter Hacks, and to a lesser extent Franz Fühmann, Morgner's critical evaluation of the myth amounts to a loss of blind faith in the principles of unlimited technological progress. However, in contrast to Christa Wolf's *Kassandra* which has been read as a radical indictment of the cult of Prometheus in light of the escalating global arms race, and thus as a total "negation of the principle of hope,"[21] Morgner's treatment of the mythology – like Hacks' – marks not a retreat from the principle of hope but instead a redistribution of hope from the figure of Prometheus to Pandora. The aporia of the negative dialectic of the Enlightenment can only be overcome by countering the negative legacy of the ideals of technological progress and rationality, inherited equally by twentieth-century capitalism and socialism, with radically new practices, informed by the oppositional discourses of feminism.

In the figures of the witch and Pandora, Morgner offers

---

20. See Rüdiger Bernhardt, *Odysseus' Tod - Prometheus' Leben: Antike Mythen in der Literatur der DDR* (Halle/Leipzig: Mitteldeutscher Verlag, 1983), 82–83.
21. See Michael Rohrwasser and Michael von Engelhardt, "Mythos und DDR-Literatur," *Michigan Germanic Studies* 8, no. 1–2 (Spring/Fall 1982): 42–43.

oppositional female images in contrast to the heroes of the "performance principle" – Prometheus, Faust, and Don Juan. The witch and Pandora, like Marcuse's positive images of Orpheus and Narcissus, stand for alternative modes of social interaction and peaceful, non-aggressive forms of knowledge. Like the images of Orpheus and Narcissus, the witch and Pandora have the ability to explode objective reality and fixed meaning. But although they too are essentially "unreal and unrealistic" images, their existence is, as Marcuse points out, no more implausible than the very deeds of such superhuman cultural heroes of Western civilization as Prometheus.[22] The difference lies in the fact that they celebrate the "pleasure principle" and the "Nirvana principle" against the repressiveness of the reality principle.

The Feminization of Politics

In *Amanda*, Morgner reinvests the female principle, traditionally regarded as disruptive and destructive, with a new positive, peaceful force. Female pleasure and sensuality, which Marcuse described as anathema to the principles of economic productivity and capital accumulation underpinning the project of modernity, become instead highly productive positive forces in the nuclear age. Morgner contends that the world can only be saved from nuclear disaster by politicians and populations recognizing the fact that patriarchal systems have led the world to the brink of disaster: "thinking exclusively in terms of conquests in society, science, and technology have led the earth to the edge of an abyss" (A. 377). The male tradition of categorizing social change and progress exclusively in terms of struggles for power and domination is, according to Morgner, not something that is necessarily inherent in the male character but is instead a product of cultural and historical processes: "a product of acculturation not of men's natures" (A. 377). The aporia of a politics of deterrence can only be overcome once governments and the men who form them recognize the value of the much maligned and neglected talents traditionally associated only with the female sex:

---

22. Marcuse, *Eros and Civilization*, 165.

Only when men and progressive governments headed by men recognize that they cannot master the problems of world politics and ecology as well as their own without certain abilities and virtues of women, and act accordingly, can the planet be saved. (A. 377–78)[23]

The world situation is so serious through the massive build-up of "military machines with the destructive potential of a million Hiroshima bombs" (A. 378), argues Beatriz, that only a radically new way of approaching matters of such global importance as war and peace can avert the danger of nuclear war. The new feminine philosophy that Morgner puts forward as the key to saving the future for the future extends therefore far beyond a concern with female pleasure and incorporates more aspects of female culture than Marcuse's "female principle."

A major problem of Western civilizations has always been, according to Beatriz, "the evasion of concrete matters" (A. 40). As a result of the sexual division of labor, the concern for "the most immediate and concrete things" (A. 40) has traditionally been the province of women. Originally a quality shared equally by both sexes, "the ability to nurture" (A. 377) has since been cultivated only in the female sex and then exclusively for "private purposes" (A. 377). As a consequence these specifically feminine talents, oriented towards the preservation rather than the destruction of life and culture, have had no impact in the realm of politics and government. As Sirene Katharina remarks to Arke: "High politics has never been so strictly a male affair than in the age of women's emancipation" (A. 379).

For Morgner the ability to nurture, protect, and preserve is neither naturally given nor an innate feminine characteristic; it is a culturally acquired skill, the product of acculturation rather than biology. As the result of increasing specialization in society, nurturing is a skill that has been traditionally developed by women to a high degree of proficiency mainly for the purposes of maintaining the monogamous family. And as Engels argues in his famous treatise on the rise of the bourgeois family and private property, the monogamous family and the division of labor

23. "Nur wenn die Männer und die von Männern geführten progressiven Regierungen erkennen, daß sie die Probleme der Weltpolitik und Ökologie und ihre eigenen ohne gewisse Fähigkeiten und Tugenden der Frauen nicht bewältigen und entsprechend handeln, kann der Planet gerettet werden."

between men and women within the family was consolidated during the rise of capitalism primarily for the purposes of securing heirs for private property. Morgner does not specifically link the cultivation of nurturing skills among women to the development of the capitalist mode of production, but it seems likely, judging by the popularity and currency of Engels's thesis in the GDR, that her remarks on the perpetuation of "nurturing as a department for women for private purposes" (A. 377) are also intended as a critique of the way the socialist state continued to encourage the traditional division of labor between the sexes. However, the mere fact that nurturing has remained a skill only cultivated by women does not make her dismiss its worth as a valuable human activity. In recognizing the ability to nurture as socially and historically produced rather than biologically given, Amanda cleverly bypasses many of the pitfalls of essentialism, grounding her alternative feminist politics and philosophy historically in the sexual division of labor under capitalism. She urges women to reactivate these typically feminine skills and deploy them for direct political purposes, even though doing so will not break with traditional female domains of social life and traditional feminine activities. The skills that women have historically developed in private to sustain the bourgeois family and to perpetuate both capitalist and patriarchal relations of production should not, Amanda argues, be abandoned simply because women would be in danger of replicating the very division of labor that has been the cause of their oppression. She argues that it is not the activities themselves that are inherently demeaning or exploitative but the social purpose to which they have hitherto been employed:

> The inability to nurture – a culturally acquired attribute of men – can suddenly no longer be tolerated as a trivial offense as it has been previously. Suddenly the earth can founder on this inability. Suddenly the ability to nurture – hitherto a quality that in a specialized culture has only been highly developed in women for private purposes – is indispensable for the greatest public purposes. (A. 547)[24]

24. "Die Unfähigkeit zu Hegen – eine durch Kultur erworbene Männereigenschaft – kann plötzlich nicht mehr als Kavaliersdelikt hingenommen werden wie gewohnt. Plötzlich kann an dieser Unfähigkeit die Erdenwelt zerscheitern. Plötzlich wird die Fähigkeit zu Hegen – eine durch die Spezialisierungskultur bisher allein bei Frauen hochentwickelte Eigenschaft für private Zwecke – für die größten öffentlichen Zwecke unentbehrlich."

Because of their traditional concern with child-rearing, women also have, according to Morgner, a more highly developed sense of responsibility and a greater capacity to compromise: "Women are therefore highly trained in bearing responsibility" (A. 378). She maintains that women in fact act irresponsibly when they neglect to apply this well-developed sense of responsibility to the public sphere, remaining content to delegate responsibility to so-called specialists: "If women continue to be content with private responsibility and delegate public responsibility to specialists, they act irresponsibly" (A. 378).

Like Christa Wolf in *Voraussetzung einer Erzählung*, Morgner is not advocating motherhood as a general panacea to the problems of the world as a number of American and West German feminists did during the 1970s and 1980s. Like Wolf, who warns against substituting a form of "femininity mania" in the place of a "masculinity mania,"[25] Morgner too seems careful not to paint an idealized picture of either womanhood or motherhood. Laura is a far from perfect mother and, if her experiences with her first child Juliane in *Trobadora Beatriz* are typical of motherhood under socialism, Morgner certainly does not regard motherhood as a quality or gift that comes naturally. Socialist mothers, like socialist fathers, neglect their children as well, if and when conditions force them to.

Unlike other advocates of a new type of mothering such as Nancy Chodorow, Dorothy Dinnerstein, and Margarete Mitscherlich,[26] Morgner does not draw on object-relations psychology to ground her critique of gender inequality. The prime focus of her discussion of motherhood is not the detrimental psychological effects of mother-daughter and mother-son relationships on the socialization of the infant; nor does she imply that better patterns of mothering would generally improve social relations. She is also not concerned with locating the origin of male dominance in Western societies in the asymmetry in child-care arrangements and the institution of

25. Wolf, *Voraussetzungen einer Erzählung*, 115.
26. See Nancy Chodorow, *The Reproduction of Mothering* (London: University of California Press, 1978); Dorothy Dinnerstein, *The Rocking of the Cradle and the Ruling of the World* (London: Women's Press, 1987); Margarete Mitscherlich, *Die Zukunft ist Weiblich* (Zurich: Pendo, 1987); Mitscherlich, *The Peaceable Sex: On Aggression in Women and Men*, trans. Craig Tomlinson (New York: Fromm International Publishing Corporation, 1987).

mothering itself, nor in the personality structures that current forms of mothering produce in males and females. As Lynne Segal points out, this resurgence in interest in issues of childbirth and -rearing after the early pro-abortion campaigns of the women's movement helped many women to articulate many of the mixed feelings white middle-class women in Britain and America were experiencing concerning the choice of whether to mother or not.[27]

In the GDR women were not faced with such a choice, and even the availability of oral contraception in the 1970s, together with the changes in the abortion laws, in no way affected the continuous pressure on all East German women to bear children. Legal abortions and oral contraception did not alter the inevitability of motherhood for most women, merely the timing. Morgner does, however, share the concern of Dinnerstein and Chodorow that fundamental changes in society's "sexual arrangements," are necessary for the survival of the human race.[28] Substantial modifications to "the division of responsibility, opportunity, and privilege that prevails between male and female humans, and the patterns of psychological interdependence that are implicit in this division,"[29] are essential, they argue, if inequities in the social structure are to be rectified. But whereas Dinnerstein's and Chodorow's primary concern seems to be the detrimental effects of asymmetrical mothering relations and the "female monopoly of child care"[30] on society at large, Morgner chooses to highlight the potential for positive changes in society as a whole if traditional modes of mothering are brought to bear on other social spheres than the family unit. Thus, while Dinnerstein hopes to change society radically through psychosocial relations, mainly the mother-child relation – albeit without specifying how these changes within the family will affect the social fabric – Morgner proposes breaking down the public/private split that Dinnerstein's theory still upholds. The project for joint parenting that forms the mainstay of Dinnerstein's and Chodorow's theses fails to challenge the ideology of the middle-class family and the private institution of mothering in the way that Morgner's critique of the socialist family does.

27. Segal, *Is the Future Female?*, 135–36.
28. Dinnerstein, *The Rocking of the Cradle and the Ruling of the World*, 4.
29. Ibid.
30. Ibid., 40.

Where Morgner's emphasis on maternal values and practices diverges most from the work of Dinnerstein and Chodorow is in the link that she forges between maternal values and the "big questions" of war and peace. Morgner's plan to save the globe from nuclear and ecological destruction hinges on the hope of extending the realm of influence of women's nurturing and mothering skills to the public domain, where feminine values and ways of thinking have hitherto had little or no impact. Women are to form the vanguard in the fight against the "militarist mentality" and in promoting peace between nations. Here Morgner agrees with antimilitarist feminists in the West, who contend that women must play a key role in saving humanity from destruction through nuclear war, and that the specific values and skills associated with mothering such as "nurturing" or "preservative love" must be brought to bear upon the social world.[31]

The American feminists Elshtain and Ruddick also argue for the notion of "maternal thinking" as a means of diminishing militarism and undercutting militarist ideologies. Their arguments, however, rely on the assumption that there is a psychological basis for the association of women with peace. Female peacefulness, they contend, is the result of "early experiences of preservative love expected from and bestowed by mothers and other female caretakers."[32] "Women are daughters," the argument continues, "who learn from their mothers the activity of preservative love and the maternal thinking that arises from it."[33] Why mothering should only be successful where daughters are involved and just why these maternal values should be transmitted only to daughters seems unclear. Equally unclear is the uniform manner in which daughters replicate their mother's behavior and the precise reasons why their moral and cognitive development should be any different from that of their brothers, provided they have the same "good" mothers. Furthermore, such theories that ground the greater peacefulness of women in

---

31. See Sara Ruddick, "Pacifying the Forces: Drafting Women in the Interests of Peace," *Signs* 8, no. 3 (Spring 1983), 471–89; Jean Bethke Elshtain, "On Beautiful Souls, Just Warriors and Feminist Consciousness," in *Women and Men's Wars*, ed. Judith Stiehm (Oxford, New York, Toronto, Sydney, Paris, Frankfurt: Pergamon Press, 1983); and Segal, *Is the Future Female?*.

32. Ruddick, "Pacifying the Forces," 479.

33. Ibid.

universal patterns of mothering are flawed in their attempts to claim not only the higher moral ground for women but also a different "cognitive style." Part of the daughter's heritage, and not the son's, from the mother's activity of preservative love is a "concrete cognitive style and theory of conflict at odds with the abstractions of war" and actually opposed to "warlike abstraction." The culprit in Ruddick's eyes is the tendency to abstract, which she sees as being closely connected to "our desire and capacity to wage war."[34] Women, with their more concrete style of thinking, are accordingly much less likely than men to condone wars and to participate in militaristic activities. As Lynne Segal points out, because peace is itself equally an abstract cause why should women be any more predisposed to supporting peaceful causes than men?[35]

Morgner also makes mention of the need for concrete thinking and the knowledge gained from experience as an important means of counteracting the abstract logic of the politics of deterrence. The phenomenon of the nuclear arms race is only made possible, she argues, because of the lack of concrete thinking. Concrete thinking does not designate here a form of cognition that is holistic and field-dependent, but rather a particular attention to issues closest to the individual's life context. In the past, she argues, humanity has too often concentrated on things far-removed from everyday life at the expense of more immediate and pressing needs:

> There is a striking tendency to tackle things in the distant future and to overlook the things that we continuously come across right under our noses. Blinded by the flourishes of expansive gestures, the audacity and adventurousness of expeditions to distant places, we forget what motivated us. Not infrequently it is a matter of avoiding the most immediate things because we do not know how to deal with them. (A. 40)[36]

---

34. Ibid., 479–83.
35. Segal, *Is the Future Female?*, 197.
36. "Es besteht eine auffallende Tendenz, erst auf das Fernste loszugehen und alles zu übersehen, woran man sich in nächster Nähe unaufhörlich stößt. Der Schwung der ausfahrenden Gesten, das Abenteuerlich-Kühne der Expeditionen ins Ferne täuscht über die Motive zu ihnen hinweg. Nicht selten handelt es sich einfach darum, das Nächste zu vermeiden, weil wir ihm nicht gewachsen sind."

Morgner does not specifically state that women, in particular mothers, have a "cognitive style" that makes them better at concrete thinking than men. Nor does she make the associative leap that equates women's more highly developed capacity for concrete thinking with women's greater peacefulness. She does imply, however, that women must lead the way in cultivating an appreciation of "the most immediate and concrete" needs of humankind and that women are better suited to the task by virtue of their experience with child-minding.

In their discussions Beatriz and Arke both agree that the type of thinking that can best come to the aid of the planet is one that places greater emphasis on life quality rather than quantity. Abstract communication with the life world, which has had the ascendancy since the Renaissance, has valued definitions, material laws, and objectivity over quality of life, interconnectedness, experience, and subjectivity. Enlightenment discourses on mastery have, in their race for supremacy, displaced "the capacity for concrete dialogue" (A. 459) as a valid form of interaction with the environment and the social community. Morgner proposes fostering "mimetic thinking" (A. 460) as an alternative materialist philosophy and thus as a means of challenging forms of instrumental thought. A real materialist, she argues in *Amanda*, is someone who does not merely recognize the material basis of the world but one who perceives herself as part of a whole, as "connected, interconnected, imbedded, responsible" (A. 460).

This particular mode of interaction with the world stresses the individual's connections to the natural and social world and encourages a higher sense of responsibility towards the environment. Only by challenging the claim to exclusivity of the negative legacy of Enlightenment discourses such as abstract thinking, can the ability to think concretely and mimetically be retrieved. As Irene Diamond and Lee Quinby suggest, ecofeminist discourses, with their emphasis on interconnectedness, responsibility, and nurturing, may in fact foster alternatives to discourses on mastery and control while still managing to avoid the traps of essentialism.[37] Unlike Ruddick, Morgner implies that

---

37. Irene Diamond and Lee Quinby, "American Feminism and the Language of Control," *Feminism and Foucault: Reflections on Resistance*, ed. Irene Diamond and Lee Quinby (Boston: Northeastern University Press, 1988), 202–3.

the rhetoric of abstraction is used by both pacifists and the defenders of limited warfare alike. Both employ similar abstractions in the realization "that abstractions are easier to deal with" (A. 460). Abstractions, however, soon lose their power to shock or galvanize people into action unless the ability to identify with those most affected is regained. She appeals therefore to people "with ties" to keep the historical memories alive of the victims of third-world poverty and, in particular, the twenty million Russians and six million Jews who died as a result of the policies of Nazi Germany. While she questions the historical efficacy of such abstractions to change postwar German history, she does not call into question her own use of statistics on the megatons of nuclear explosives that are sufficient to blow up the earth ten times over.

In contrast to Ruddick and Elshtain, who subsume all measures to ensure peace under the rubric of "maternal thinking," Morgner includes writing and other creative activities such as "prognosticating" and singing in her list of means of combatting militaristic tendencies in society. Beatriz reflects on the usefulness of such activities in preventing war: "Was the most immediate and concrete matter that I could turn my hand to singing? Was Arke's means of avoiding the most immediate and concrete thing to puzzle over the oracles . . .?"(A. 40)[38] Yet the urgency of the world situation is such that even the sirens' song, the most immediate form of help that Beatriz has to offer in her present incarnation, seems inadequate:

> Now, in 1980, there are already three tons of explosives stored on it [the planet] per capita. Fifteen grams are sufficient to kill a person. By comparison with the stocks to destroy the world twenty times over, the sirens' song seemed to me ridiculous. (A. 41)[39]

One further traditional feminine art to be co-opted in the name of peace is the age-old "art of whispering." On her world tour to muster support from other remaining sirens, Arke encounters

38. "War das Allernächste und Konkreteste, dem ich mich zuwenden mußte, singen? Konnte für Arke dieses Allernächste und Konkreteste umgehen, orakeln über Orakel . . .?"
39. "Jetzt, 1980, lagern auf ihm [dem Planeten], wie ich von Arke hörte, pro Kopf der Erdbevölkerung bereits drei Tonnen Sprengstoff. Fünfzehn Gramm reichen, um einen Menschen zu töten. Gegenüber Vorräten zur zwanzigfachen Weltvernichtung erschien mir Sirenengesang lächerlich."

Sirene Katharina, the former Empress of Russia, and Sirene Sappho. Both mention independently of one another the usefulness of the art of suggestion or "whispering" in increasing women's influence in the political arena. When women have had no other form of political representation, they have had to resort to exerting their influence over political matters indirectly through their male lovers. At first glance, it may appear that Morgner is denying the need to fight for more direct political representation by resorting to the standard anti-feminist argument that women have in fact always wielded power over men in the bedroom and in the realm of the home. It seems unlikely, however, that Morgner is advocating the art of suggestion as a valid alternative to more direct political power for women and is rather offering a critique of the under-representation of women in political decision-making processes. By the same token, Morgner's polemics underscore the fact that an adherence to a type of "rights" feminism that in the West is often associated with a liberal feminist position, and in the East with the SED's official policy on women's emancipation, is in itself insufficient to increase the influence of an alternative feminine or feminist standpoint on the realm of politics. Moreover, her resuscitation of the art of suggestion should be seen as an attempt to refute the notion that the influence of women upon world affairs can be measured in terms of their emancipation from the private spheres into the work force. Sirene Katharina warns against equating higher participation rates in the work force and greater freedom of speech with greater political influence:

> Could Gaia herself possibly be under the illusion that women automatically have an effect on the course of human history just because in some countries they are allowed to have more say and do more work? Speaking and participating do not automatically lead to the headquarters of power. On the contrary. A lot of talk about emancipation can give rise to aggressions in the form of counterreactions. (A. 378–79)[40]

40. "Ist etwa gar Gaja selbst schon der Illusion aufgesessen, daß Frauen gleich Einfluß auf Menschengeschichte haben, nur weil sie in manchen Ländern etwas mehr reden und arbeiten dürfen? Reden und mitarbeiten dürfen führt nicht automatisch in die Kommandozentralen der Macht. Im Gegenteil. Viel Emanzipationsgerede ruft als Gegenreaktion Aggressionen auf den Plan."

The implication here is that a type of liberal or rights feminism that concerns itself solely with increasing women's representation in the work force and in decision-making processes is in itself inadequate to sufficiently challenge militarist ideologies. High politics, Sirene Katharina reminds Arke, was never more a purely male affair than in the age of women's emancipation. Solutions such as those recently put forward by American feminists that go as far as to condone women's participation in the armed forces as a means of feminizing the military and hence abolishing war, would therefore only be implicating women in patriarchal structures without fundamentally altering their functioning.

The assumption underlying Morgner's call for a feminization of politics is that women are historically rather than psychologically more inclined towards peace. Here she comes closest to the theories expounded by the West German sociologist Margarete Mitscherlich who considers the greater peaceableness of women to be the inevitable result of years of compromise and powerlessness. The quality of peaceableness has become a social role that women have been forced to adopt owing to their inferior social status. Mitscherlich does concede, however, that certain attitudes traditionally associated with female social spheres, such as nurturing and empathy, as well as the Christian values of passivity, compassion, and forgiveness, are inherent to women's "nature."[41] She then goes on to argue that unless women attain power these values so essential to the preservation of life and nature will not come to bear upon the world of politics.[42]

Although Morgner agrees that feminine skills and talents must be mobilized if the destruction of the environment and the human race is to be avoided, she stresses at the same time the fact that the preservation of peaceful conditions is not only a feminist concern but "a common human interest" (A. 634). She pins her hopes for the future on a feminization of the political arena that strives "to change the world in a humane way" (A. 312). Like Wolf, she is anxious to dispel any fears about the sectarian nature of this philosophy by stressing the "human" benefits to be gained. It seems as if Morgner too shares Wolf's "genuine fear of any critique of rationalism that itself culminates in unashamed irrationalism." The

41. Mitscherlich, *Die Zukunft ist Weiblich*, 19–25.
42. Ibid., 34.

critique of the one-sidedness of male rationality, Wolf urges, must not find itself substituting a masculinity fetish with a femininity fetish or idealizing pre-rational or irrational phases of human history. One cannot afford to refuse to engage "rational models of conflict solving" and consequently any attempts to eternalize femininity as an absolute value, she contends, are merely manifestations of "large-scale evasion tactics."[43]

The Uses of Matriarchy and Prehistory

What the two most important East German feminist novels of the 1980s, Christa Wolf's *Kassandra* and Morgner's *Amanda*, have in common is a renewed interest in matriarchy as a primal and dominant phase of human prehistory. This resurgence in interest among East German writers in the possibility of matriarchal societies takes its impetus mainly from feminist inquiry in the West into the origins of patriarchal structures and into feminist alternatives to patriarchal history. Both works can be understood as responses to research into matrilinear and matrifocal societies by feminists in the West at the same time as they can be considered responses to the history of the reception of Greek mythology within the GDR itself. Both Morgner and Wolf look to matriarchal societies for solutions to the aporias of Western civilization, which they see manifested in the ever-escalating arms race and the politics of deterrence of NATO and the Warsaw Pact.

However, both retain a certain skepticism towards feminist calls for a return to the matriarchal life forms that form part of the movement "back to nature," especially when this is accompanied by a romantic nostalgia for primitive or prehistoric forms of civilization. Wolf reminds us of the dangers of the idealization of myth and prehistory as a radical critique of modernity, particularly when it is linked to "a relinquishing and immature jettisoning of achievements and principles . . . that not only make Europeans Europeans but which also make humans human." She presents instead an alternative use of matriarchal prehistory in a Faust-like "pilgrimage to the mothers," which purports not to be an "escape from an analysis of social conditions" nor an "idealization of more

---

43. Wolf, *Voraussetzungen einer Erzählung*, 115–16.

primitive social conditions."[44] But whereas Wolf announces an intention to strip Greek mythology of its patriarchal trappings and uncover the matriarchal genesis of European society, Morgner is far less concerned with questions of aetiology and with such conditions as may have given rise to the patriarchal reappropriation of matriarchal myths.[45] Her treatment of Greek mythology in *Amanda* could thus be said to be more utopian in character than archaeological.[46] Underlying Wolf's search for a turning point when European history might have taken a radically different direction, there is, in addition, a fascination with origins that Morgner's work does not share.

Morgner's use of myth is, in contrast to Wolf's, more purely utopian in its lack of concern for ascertaining the historical and social conditions that gave rise to matriarchy and at which point patriarchal rule supplanted matriarchal rule. Although Morgner grounds the female qualities of nurturing and responsibility historically in the original sexual division of labor, her plea for the revival of other aspects of the "female principle" such as the ability to compromise, "love of the earth," and peacefulness makes no attempt to verify her assertions through the allusion to the actual existence of peaceful conditions under matriarchal societies. She side steps, therefore, the contentious issue of whether women can be considered inherently pacifist or peaceful, as well as the equally controversial question of whether matriarchal societies could be considered to be any more peaceful than their patriarchal successors. In place of speculations about social origins, Morgner offers instead her own revised version of Greek myths of the origins of humanity, narrated in the chapter "Parnass Mythology."

Myth functions paradoxically in *Amanda* as the work of enlightenment, that is, as a way of demythologizing the present through the looking glass of the mythical past. Myth no longer represents a form of false consciousness as it appears to in Wolf's *Voraussetzungen einer Erzählung*, a mystification of reality or a pre-rational and thus irrational form of cognition. Isebel speaks of the prime value of myths as ideological buttresses (A. 61) that women

44. Ibid., 100–1.
45. See Stephens, "'Die Verführung der Worte,'" 141.
46. Gerhard Neumann, "Christa Wolf: *Kassandra*: Die Archäologie der weiblichen Stimme," *Erinnerte Zukunft: 11 Studien zum Werk Christa Wolfs*, ed. Wolfram Mauser (Würzburg: Königshausen und Neumann, 1985), 233.

must erect if they are to attain power. Beatriz reminds her that future generations will require quite different myths and legends; they will find today's heroic ideals and idealized heros or any material that is too overtly didactic in its content indigestible. We are told, for instance, that Laura's son, Wesselin, the only representative of future generations in the novel, would not swallow "stories that are one hundred percent for the purposes of edification," (A. 61) and that his generation will require new myths. Beatriz also questions the need for power to secure its foothold through myths of legitimation that are unashamedly exaggerations of the truth. When Beatriz expresses her reluctance to be forced into the role of court historiographer, Isebel puts an end to this squeamishness by reminding her that not all ideological uses of myth are necessarily incompatible with the historians' pursuit of truth. Beatriz's task, then, as a twentieth-century successor to the court historian, is to create unofficial myths of legitimation for feminists in the East.

Beatriz's unofficial reworking of myth undertakes, as Wolfgang Emmerich points out, a correction of those orthodox Greek myths that had already been revised for socialist readers in the postwar years. This use of mythical material goes beyond the sort of demythologizing and devaluation of mythical material that Brecht demonstrates in three short works written in the year 1933 entitled "Correcting old Myths." Authors such as Morgner, Fühmann, Wolf, Hacks, Grass, and Müller attempt to locate the relevance of myths to the present and rediscover the "logos" in myth.[47] Yet whereas Emmerich follows Blumenberg in classifying myths as successful endeavors to compensate for fears by converting them into stories, I would argue that Morgner's (as well as Müller's and Hacks') treatment of Greek mythology is a far more self-reflective process of civilization critique.[48] The act of tracing negative developments of civilization back to a mythical origin is the work of enlightenment, of freeing the present from the hold of the

---

47. Wolfgang Emmerich, "Zu-Ende-denken: Griechische Mythologie und neuere DDR-Literatur," *Kontroversen, alte und neue*, vol. 10, ed. Albrecht Schöne (Tübingen: Niemeyer, 1986), 217.
48. See Emmerich, "Das Erbe des Odysseus: Der zivilisationskritische Rekurs auf den Mythos in der neueren DDR-Literatur," *Studies in GDR Society and Culture* 5, Selected Papers from the Tenth New Hampshire Symposium on the German Democratic Republic, ed. Margy Gerber (Langham: UP of America, 1985): 181.

mythical past. Like the work of Hacks and Müller, Morgner's fiction is primarily concerned with correcting a naive faith in history and progress. This correction does not take the form of what Thomas Mann termed the rehumanization of myth or of divesting fascist ideology of its mythical underpinnings. What Morgner is attempting is instead a refeminization of myth via the process of demythologizing patriarchal myths and resurrecting matriarchal or feminine equivalents. This involves performing a critical feminist reading of patriarchal myths, as Morgner argues in a paraphrase of Marx's famous Feuerbach thesis:

> The philosophers have until now only interpreted the world from a masculine point of view. The important thing now is to interpret it from a feminine point of view in order to change it for the benefit of humanity. (A. 312)[49]

Like Wolf, Morgner turns her attention to prehistory in hopes of discovering peaceful conditions. The same motive is attributed to Laura Salman who is said to study history "because she wanted to investigate what is generally termed prehistory. . .. As if peaceful conditions were not creative. Or had to be" (A. 141). If war is the father of all things, Laura wants to find out what is "the mother of all things" (A. 141). Laura's rather naive interest in matriarchy and what constitutes prehistory stems from the perceived need to subvert teleological accounts of history that posit a radical caesura between prehistory and history. She implicitly questions the need to construct an a priori historical period dominated by chaotic natural phenomena, the belief in superstitions, and the general "immaturity" of the human subject. In Enlightenment discourses prehistory has generally functioned as a means of distinguishing reason from its other, a way of differentiating the history of the Enlightenment from the irrational, barbaric phase of the history of humanity it is thought to supersede. It is the concept of a radical break with the past that forms the basis of the self-understanding of Western civilization as Enlightenment, and it is this notion of the progression of history towards ever more rational goals that is under attack in Morgner's enthroning of

49. "Die Philosophen haben die Welt bisher nur männlich interpretiert. Es kommt aber darauf an, sie auch weiblich zu interpretieren, um sie menschlich verändern zu können."

prehistory.

Within the East German context the binary opposition between history/prehistory often served as a metaphor for the historical rupture brought about by the socialist revolution.[50] The concept of a prehistory frequently acts as a code for the irrational forces of capitalism and fascism that the entry into a new phase of socialist history is supposed to overcome. Under the influence of Bloch, the concept of prehistory has often been associated with an unenlightened, pre-socialist phase of history and thus with barbarism and fascism.[51] In the GDR prehistory functioned specifically as a chiffre for socialist history's other. A feminist return to prehistory sees itself, in contrast, as a critique of this binary opposition and of the distinctions between the rational and the irrational, the barbaric and the civilized, that the division into history and prehistory invites. Morgner's preoccupation with prehistory functions, as does Wolf's, as a form of rationalism critique and more generally as a critique of "the hierarchically ordered, male-controlled reality principle" underpinning patriarchal history. In the "Greek Prelude" in *Amanda*, Morgner postulates the origins of the patriarchal martial tradition or "what people nowadays call history: private property, class distinctions, exploitation, state violence, wars" (A. 160) as coinciding with the beginnings of Western civilization and history as we know it. Implicit in this account, naturally, is the assumption that matrilinear societies were predominantly peaceful, an assumption shared by Wolf.

Pandora's Return and the Principle of Hope

In the "Parnass Mythology" Morgner offers an alternative account of the Olympian creation myth. For the main part her version of the creation of the first human beings closely follows the Greek sources in Hesiod's *Theogony*, beginning with the creation of Mother Earth from the night, then the birth of Uranos followed

---

50. Bernhardt, *Odysseus' Tod – Prometheus' Leben*, 104.
51. See Bloch, *Das Prinzip Hoffnung*, vol. 3 (Frankfurt/Main: Suhrkamp, 1959), 1628.

by the creation of flora and fauna.[52] Gaia and Uranos beget the first men and women, together with giants with three hundred arms and the cyclops. The eldest son, Kronos, rebels against his father and finally castrates him. Kronos is fated to repeat his father's fate and is dethroned by Zeus, one of his sons. The struggle lasts for ten years and brings about the end of the first human race. Humankind is given a second chance with the arrival of Prometheus who, envious of Gaia's powers to create life, strives to imitate her creativity by fashioning people out of clay: "He admired Gaia. He felt challenged by her. He felt compelled to liberate himself from the overwhelming admiration which Gaia's abilities provoked in him and to test out his own abilities" (A. 79).

Prometheus, as the father of all men, is also the "father" of invention. He teaches his creations the secrets of architecture, astronomy, mathematics, navigation, medicine, metallurgy, and other useful arts and sciences (A. 84). Furthermore this period witnesses the beginnings of agriculture. Perhaps the most significant innovation of all was the discovery of Mother Earth's treasures in the mining of gold, silver, and iron. When Zeus, in search of revenge, decides to withhold fire from Prometheus and his men, Prometheus must devise a ruse to win back the vital facility of fire-making. Soon, however, the destructive purposes to which fire is put begin to outweigh the constructive purposes and Mother Earth notices that "the manufacture of weapons became a favourite occupation with the people and the burning down of dwellings a usual method of settling disputes" (A. 81). Initially the possession of fire is neither wholly negative nor positive until the production of weapons for the preparation of war becomes its main function. This period in the development of the human race bears many similarities to the Bronze Age outlined by Hesiod in *Works and Days*, which is lamented as an age of men completely different from the previous peace-loving races of the golden and silver ages, a race "devoted to doing war's wretched works and acts of hybris."[53]

---

52. Hesiod, *Theogony* in *The Poems of Hesiod*, trans. with Introduction and comments by R.M. Frazer (Norman: University of Oklahoma Press, 1983). All further references to this work will appear in the text as the abbreviation [Theog].

53. Hesiod, *Works and Days*, in *The Poems of Hesiod*, 102. All further references to this work will appear in the text as the abbreviation [WD].

It is here that Morgner's version appears to diverge most noticeably from Greek and German sources. The ever-increasing aggressive tendencies of Prometheus's men are explained by Gaia as the result of "the lack of the ability to love" (A. 81). In order to teach them how to give love, she proposes sending them a woman, Pandora. Whereas Pandora is referred to in Hesiod as a gift sent from Zeus to punish Prometheus for the theft of the fire (WD. 47–85) and for deceiving him with the sacrifice of the ox (Theog. 535–75), Pandora appears in Morgner's mythology as a gift from Mother Earth. She is not the "great plague" (Theog. 592), the "evil which all shall take to their hearts with delight, an evil to love and embrace" (WD. 57–58), but a messenger from Gaia, more beautiful and intelligent than any woman before (A. 82). With the exception of Goethe's central figure in his play *Pandora* (1809), Hesiod's virulent misogynistic denunciation of women as the origin of all evil has tended to influence all subsequent interpretations of the figure of Pandora. Even Robert Graves, who chides Hesiod for his "anti-feminist fable, probably of his own invention," cannot resist adding his own embellishments to the list of Pandora's evils, seeing in her the archetypal demonic woman. In addition to her seductive beauty, Pandora is "as foolish, mischevious, and idle as she was beautiful – the first of a long line of women."[54]

The model for Morgner's Pandora was provided instead by Goethe's fragment *Pandora's Return* (*Pandoras Wiederkunft*). Although Goethe was never to complete the last section of the play in which Pandora returns to save humanity, his portrayal of the figure is significantly at variance with the Greek sources and subsequent versions of the myth. Goethe recast his Pandora with classical grace and beauty and her box, which was once the source of "all the Spites that might plague mankind,"[55] contains "figures of the imagination" and "happiness in love."[56] Similarly, in Morgner's retelling of the myth Pandora's box contains "figures of the imagination and goods with wings: images of the future" (A. 82). The "figures of the imagination" represent "quantifiable riches

54. Robert Graves, *The Greek Myths*, vol. 1 (London: Penguin, 1955), 145–48.
55. Ibid.
56. Johann Wolfgang Goethe, *Pandora: Ein Festspiel, Dramatische Dichtungen II* (Berlin/GDR: Aufbau, 1964), vol. 6 of *Goethe: Poetische Werke, "Berliner Ausgabe,"* 22 vols., 414.

and truths, feelings of omniscience, a sense of justice and profit, the inability to compromise, love of the fatherland, conquests, victories and affluence" (A. 82). The "goods with wings" represent intangible, unquantifiable values. Whereas the figure of Pandora functions in Hesiod's epics as an aetiological myth, introduced to explain the necessity for men to work for their livelihood and the existence of such social evils as hunger and illness, Morgner uses the same mythological figure to explain the loss of human qualities that have traditionally been associated with the feminine. When Epimetheus opens the box, "love of the earth . . . a sense of harmony and a feel for nurturing, the ability to compromise, peace" (A. 83), attributes that have only been cultivated by women over the ages, fly out and leave only Hope remaining. Pandora then sees the necessity to flee in order to preserve her only remaining gift to humanity, hope. Hope is entirely stripped of the negative connotations it has in Hesiod's account and becomes – instead of a synonym for delusions – the key to the salvation of the human race and to maintaining faith in the future. After the disappearance of Pandora with the only remaining contents of her box, the second race of human beings continues to misuse the fire that Prometheus had brought and to travel further down the path to self-destruction, guided by the quantifiable values of "the figures of the imagination."

The return of Pandora becomes associated not only with the revival of a type of realistic hope to replace the kind of blind hope that has driven the human race relentlessly on to its destruction, but also with the maintenance of a perspective on the future. The future, according to Beatriz and Arke, resides in a reconciliation between Prometheus and Pandora, between the destructive and creative tendencies in human nature. Goethe's attempt in *Pandora's Return* at a synthesis between the opposing attitudes of Prometheus and Epimetheus is considered by Arke and Beatriz exemplary. Goethe's play represents a significant modification of his positive interpretation of the Prometheus and the Faust figures of his earlier works with their emphasis on the destructive rather than the "creative and ingenious" aspects of the myth. For the first time the figure of Epimetheus, whose name signifies circumspection and caution, care and contemplation, is seen as the more positive of the two brothers. This revaluation involves not so much a rejection of his earlier Storm and Stress hero, Prometheus, but rather an attempt to temper Prometheus's thirst for action with the thoughtfulness and reflectiveness of Epimetheus. Beatriz writes of Goethe's play:

> Goethe's play combines in substance the hope for salvation and renewal of the endangered human culture with the relationship between Prometheus and Epimetheus.
> "Pandora's Return" deals with the contrast between the active life and the contemplative life as well as with the reconciliation between these two mutually exclusive positions in subsequent and more educated human races. (A. 301)[57]

Significantly it is Epimetheus who is the only one to appreciate the loss to humanity that Pandora's disappearance will involve. Furthermore, he is the brother who is most capable of love. The triumph of Epimetheus represents, according to Hacks, a truly utopian intervention, an "anticipation" of a better future and a victory for the "classical critique of capitalism" (A. 301). According to Arke, Goethe's reassessment of the Prometheus myth occurred at a time of personal crisis that was precipitated by "terrible conditions" (A. 257) in the political arena. The crisis was eventually overcome not by an improvement in the political situation but by a resolution to make "daily hoping" (A. 258) the basis of all future action and thought. In a unprecedented move Goethe transforms Epimetheus's longing for Pandora's return, which Arke regards as a regressive hope (A. 258), a nostalgic and unproductive hope for the restauration of a lost paradise, into a forward-looking form of hope (A. 258). This is the type of hope that inspires and encourages humankind to contemplate and build a better future. Myths about the regaining of a lost paradise are common, Beatriz discovers, but myths about their return are rare (A. 258). Goethe's Pandora figure functions as a "symbol of humanity" (A. 96) as well as an embodiment of hope for a renewal of human culture. Morgner's faith in the return of Pandora and the recovery of the lost "goods

---

57. "Goethes Festspiel verband die Hoffnung auf Heil und Erneuerung der gefährdeten Menschenkultur wesentlich auch mit den Beziehungen zwischen Prometheus und Epimetheus.
    'Pandoras Wiederkehr' handelt vom Gegensatz zwischen dem Tatenleben und dem Leben in Betrachtung sowie der Versöhnung dieser einander ausschließenden Haltungen in den folgenden und belehrteren Menschengeschlechtern."

with wings" also stems from the hope that her return will herald the dawn of a new peaceful age and the birth of a new antimilitarist phase of human history in which the historical and social experiences of women will have a formative influence.

Goethe's use of the Prometheus myth provides inspiration for Beatriz and Arke in their attempts to resuscitate the seductive power of the song of the sirens to silence militarist tendencies. Beatriz, as the only siren already awakened, has the difficult task of coordinating or overseeing the various activities to bring the planet back from the edge of destruction. Sirens, by virtue of their name, have the ability to alarm and warn of pending danger and yet they are not prophets of salvation, Arke remarks, "because the earth is full of them. Most prophets are personifications of human presumptuousness and the inability to love" (A. 97). Sirens are needed to fight against the Prometheus principle or the "destruction" principle. Their song must seduce Prometheus so that he will be diverted from his self-destructive path. He will then recognize his work as fragmentary and without future and recall Pandora and her one remaining gift to humankind. The next human race will then evolve out of a reconciliation between Prometheus and Pandora, born out of love and the first to be peaceloving. The new breed of human being will value the non-violent resolution of conflicts, the importance of compromises, and will place a taboo on war.

This plan can only be executed if the unquantifiable contents of Pandora's box, those "goods with wings" are also retrieved. Although Beatriz's task as a siren is to provide support to earthly witches such as Laura and Vilma in the form of information about the state of the arms build-up and the earth's depleted natural resources, as well as providing theoretical and mythological underpinnings for the activities of GDR feminists, Arke reminds her that her task is in fact profane and must take place in a suitably profane place – in a cage in a zoo. Rather than occupy the Blocksberg, the proper place for utopian models where "the possible of the day after tomorrow" is tried and tested, the sirens must instead give voice to the urgent needs of the present to ensure that the future's utopian potential is kept alive. However, the revival of the sirens' song is not only needed to save "the everyday reality of the planet" (A. 246); it must also be employed in the service of the magical reality of the planet: "since death from a nuclear explosion most certainly also threatens magic mountains" (A. 246). In this way the fate of the magic mountain is inseparably linked to everyday reality and thus to the activities of the earthly witches and rebels.

Arke's and Beatriz's plans, however, are sabotaged when Beatriz finds herself the victim of a terrorist attack in which her tongue is cut off. The chances for reactivating the original agitatory power of the song of the sirens now seem remote and, despite the ever-increasing urge to sing, Beatriz has to content herself with a sirens' voice that only has a written form (A. 258): "the only form of voice that remained open to me" (A. 359). Faced with the impossibility of direct political intervention, Beatriz realizes the worth of literature as a "means of publicizing hurdles" (A. 258). Arke, meanwhile, embarks on a world trip to discover what has happened to the other sirens who have been revived to save the planet from ecological and nuclear disaster. Since the removal of Beatriz's tongue and the attempts to render the peace singer silent (A. 357), Arke is also anxious to find out what other political means are being employed to suppress their activities. Yetunde, the only other siren to have been resurrected, warns Arke that terrorist attacks on sirens and Gaia's daughters are to be expected even in a country such as the GDR, whose constitution outlaws "war-mongering and racial incitement" (A. 249). The style of attack peculiar to "assassins of sirens" does not differ from the usual type of political terrorism in that country, but as Yetunde is not familiar with the usual form of assassination attempts in the GDR she cannot say who was responsible for cutting off Beatriz's tongue nor what their motives were. She suspects, however, that enemies of the GDR may be trying to use Beatriz's tongue as a form of economic blackmail. Morgner is quite obviously parodying the motif of economic blackmail so common in the literature of the reconstruction phase. The fact that Beatriz has only lost her tongue and hence her ability to speak freely and publicly is perhaps to be understood as a comment on the more subtle means employed by the GDR to silence dissenting voices, and more specifically its writers, within its population.

At the end of the novel Pandora has not yet been persuaded to return and there is no real evidence that the Prometheus principle has been defeated. Of all the pragmatic and ideological strategies of the real and fantasy figures in the novel, Pandora's return is the most abstract and possibly therefore the least successful. However, Beatriz reminds Arke that her account in *Amanda* only represents half the victory for the witches and the first part of the overthrow of the Blocksberg regime, a long story (A. 656).

8
The Quest for Peace

From a Feminist Politics of the Body to the Body Politic

The unqualified enthusiastic response that the removal of legal barriers to sexual freedom elicits in *Trobadora Beatriz* meets with a cooler and more skeptical response from the various characters in *Amanda*. As the final obstacle in Laura's quest in *Trobadora Beatriz*, the freeing up of women's rights to abortion represents the final victory over male domination and state control. It thus provides the starting point for future narratives of female emancipation and is the very condition of possibility for the narratives in the later novel, *Amanda*. As demonstrated, the project of the subsequent novel is much more ambitious in scope; the emancipation of women becomes incorporated into a broader narrative that has as its focus the emancipation of the entire human race. The history of women's emancipation, which constitutes the major hurdle in the emancipation of humanity, no longer appears as a continuous, linear progression towards an easily definable goal. Instead, the sequel displays a greater awareness of the multiple contradictions inherent in solving the "woman question" in the late 1970s and early 1980s. Indeed, one of the major themes of the novel appears to be the emerging rifts and disputes among feminists themselves. As a sequel to *Trobadora Beatriz*, *Amanda* traces the lives and rebirths of the two main characters of the earlier novel, Laura and Beatriz, from the period between 1980 and 1983. At the same time it is also a rewriting of the events in the lives of Laura and Beatriz as presented in the earlier novel. *Amanda* therefore reads as a revision of the history of the 1970s and the goals of the feminist movement at that particular historical conjuncture. The novel thus attempts a critical reappraisal of many of women's concerns in the 1970s in light of political and historical developments in the early 1980s, both on a local and a more global level. There is, furthermore, a discernible shift in focus in the novel, away from purely sexual political concerns to matters of a more global nature that were perceived in the 1980s to be a matter of increasing importance for women.

In *Amanda*, Beatriz, the medieval troubadour from Provence, is reincarnated for the second time in the figure of a siren, half animal, half woman. She is entrusted with the mission of securing peaceful conditions in a world threatened by the arms race and the possibility of nuclear disaster. As in *Trobadora Beatriz*, when Beatriz, the emissary of the Persephonic Opposition, campaigns to overthrow patriarchy, in *Amanda* Beatriz functions similarly as the agent of a mythical figure, Arke, one of Gaia's serpentine daughters. As Arke's representative in the real, Beatriz is called upon to rediscover her lost abilities as an active pacifist and campaigner for peace, qualities that Morgner attributes to the mythical figure of the siren that were forgotten or ignored in the patriarchal rewriting of the legend. "That is a long story," the serpentine Arke tells Beatriz, reminding her that "singing is the sirens' mother tongue" (A. 14). Morgner's version of the myth purports to tell the story of what happened to the sirens once Odysseus and his ship had disappeared and the sirens' last hour had come. According to her version, the sirens' particular talent for suppressing bellicose tendencies in society by "singing them down" got lost as a result of the patriarchal reappropriation of earlier matriarchal myths:

> At that time there were many sirens. Then men usurped power and introduced what people call today history: Private property, class distinctions, exploitation, state violence, wars. Sirens could silence bellicose songs effortlessly. (A. 16)[1]

This act of appropriation occurred in Morgner's mythology at the point of transition from a matriarchal to a patriarchal society. As almost all women then led double lives as sirens, with the song of the sirens was also lost a specifically feminine trait and a significant feminine myth. Morgner's mythical sirens were able to regain their ability to sing down war only in prolonged times

---

1. "Damals gab es viele Sirenen. Dann übernahmen die Männer die Herrschaft und führten ein, was die Menschen heute Geschichte nennen: Privateigentum, Klassentrennung, Ausbeutung, Staatsgewalt, Kriege. Kriegslieder konnten die Sirenen mühelos niedersingen."

of peace, and as peace grew less and less frequent their talents
became lost forever:

> In wartime the creatures fell silent. Then they remembered and
> regained their voice. However, when the periods of time between the
> wars grew shorter and shorter the sirens no longer had any time to
> remember. Wise women also became rarer and rarer. Kitchens are not
> the place for them to appear. And wartime is not the time for them to
> rise from the dead. (A. 16)[2]

In Morgner's version of the siren myth, Odysseus's success in
overcoming the temptation of the sirens' song is not due to his
"courage in battle," his "will to conquer," or even his "thirst for
victory" (A. 14). Nor is it due to his trick of blocking his crewmen's
ears with wax and tying himself to the mast of his ship. Odysseus's
survival and subsequent elevation to hero status was instead only
made possible because the sirens were in fact already mute,
rendered speechless by the ever-increasing number of wars and
patriarchy's increasing deafness to the sirens' pleas. Robbed of any
real power, they lay dormant, living on in the myth of the power
of their song long after they had ceased to sing:

> The legend of the original abilities of the sirens must have still been
> alive so that the war hero did not dare trust in reality entirely. (A. 14)[3]

Morgner thus creates her own counter-myth of Enlightenment in
the legend that Odysseus's feats of technological mastery over
nature were founded on the myth of the seductive power of the
sirens' song. The Enlightenment's suppression of the myth of the
sirens' song became the precondition for the creation of a new
patriarchal myth in the myth of technological mastery and
progress.

Morgner's critical use of Greek myths, in particular the legend

---

2. "In Kriegen verstummten die Wesen. Danach erinnerten sie sich wieder und
   gewannen ihre Sprache zurück. Als jedoch die Zeiträume zwischen den Kriegen
   kürzer und kürzer wurden, blieb den Sirenen keine Zeit mehr zum Erinnern.
   Auch wurden die weisen Frauen immer seltener. In Küchen können keine
   wachsen. Und in Kriegen können keine auferstehen."
3. "Die Sage von den ursprünglichen Fähigkeiten der Sirenen müsse damals
   offenbar noch derartig lebendig gewesen sein, daß der Kriegsheld der Realität
   nicht gänzlich zu vertrauen wagte."

of Odysseus's victory over the sirens, follows in the tradition of Brecht, Kafka, and the Frankfurt School, all of whom have used the saga of the sirens to highlight negative developments in modernity and twentieth-century capitalism. Perhaps most influential for Morgner's critique of the strain of Western thought initiated and sanctioned by the mythical figure of Odysseus has been Horkheimer and Adorno's *Dialektik der Aufklärung*. In their account, Odysseus appears as the paradigm of the enlightened, rational, bourgeois subject who interprets his ability to employ the qualities of "cunning" and "deception" as unequivocal proof of his superiority over the world of myth and nature.[4] Consequently, the emancipation of bourgeois man and his "ratio" from domination by nature and myth required a dual form of mastery over both internal and external nature. It was only by overcoming the power of external natural forces and by denying the power of his own natural inclinations that the enlightened individual could assert his superiority over the pre-enlightened, pre-rationalistic world of myth and nature. The price for the preservation of his sense of identity and the creation of "that self, the self-identical, purposeful, masculine character of human nature" has been high.[5] For, at that moment when man severed knowledge of himself as part of nature and suppressed the nature in himself and others, he enthroned instrumental reason and technological domination of man over nature, man over man, and man over woman. At this point rationality turns into irrationality, liberation into domination, and enlightenment into myth. The project of the Enlightenment, rather than the overcoming of mythical and irrational thought, reverts to myth when it replaces "natural" force with social and political coercion.

Adorno and Horkheimer see the sirens as the epitome of the seductive forces of nature that had to be overcome in the quest for mastery over the natural world. The temptation of the sirens' song represents the temptation to transcend the self and the boundaries between the self and others. To fall prey to the seduction of the sirens' song is to succumb to a promise of happiness that is incompatible with the capitalist work ethic.[6] The

---

4. Horkheimer and Adorno, *Die Dialektik der Aufklärung*, 42–73.
5. Ibid., 33.
6. Ibid.

beauty of the sirens' song becomes forgotten with the need to warn of its inherent dangers and its potential destructiveness to technological progress. Thus, with the increasing automation of the constraints of reason and "purposive-rationality," the Enlightenment has become increasingly detached from its original goal of freedom from immaturity. It is guided instead by a negative dialectic, the products of which can be clearly seen in the rise of fascism, the events of the Second World War, and the history of Stalinism.

Morgner shares the pessimism present in the *Dialektik der Aufklärung* and a similar distrust of the achievements of science and technology. She also sees them as the products of instrumental reason and new systems of domination rather than of any real concern for the welfare of humankind. Yet her revival of the original mythic power of the sirens does not simply represent the "return of the repressed," or the use of older myths to combat new myths of Enlightenment. It implies a further critique of the nexus between female sexuality, nature, and irrationality that informs Adorno's reading of the victory over the song of the sirens to be an act of domination of nature. For Morgner, the sirens' song is not synonymous with the seductiveness of the female sex, but with other historically determined female qualities, in particular women's ability to oppose male aggression and bellicosity. But, like Adorno, Morgner also suggests that the history of rationality and the Enlightenment is founded on deceit and trickery and willful falsification and myth-making. The reliance on illusion and deception, she implies, had already started much earlier with Odysseus's trick with the wax and the mast:

> Yet the serpentine maintained that the sirens had already been silent during Odysseus's life time. Proof: the earplugs. Such a ridiculous means of defense against the song of the sirens discredited the legend. (A. 14)[7]

Whereas in Adorno's account the sirens' song still had the power to entice men and break their resolve, Morgner sees the sirens as already having been rendered powerless prior to Odysseus's

---

7. "Doch die Schlange behauptete, daß die Sirenen zu Odysseus' Zeiten bereits stumm gewesen wären. Beweis: die Ohrstopfen. Ein derart lächerliches Mittel gegen den überwältigenden Sirenengesang strafe die Überlieferung Lügen."

heroic act. His feat of overcoming the legendary power of the sirens' song, which in Adorno's account is reduced to mere trickery and cunning, becomes in Morgner's version a deliberate distortion of reality. The myth of the Enlightenment originates not with the development of capitalism and capitalist rationality but with the emergence of patriarchy and its legitimizing myths of domination.

Beatriz's first mission in her resurrected form as a siren is to reactivate the original political force of the song of the sirens as the primary means of rescuing the human race from the threat of a nuclear holocaust and ecological destruction. In this particular quest Beatriz is no longer an active agent in search of the ideal political and social conditions for women. The quest for ideal material conditions for the sexually liberated female subject, which broke off rather unsatisfactorily in *Trobadora Beatriz* with Beatriz's abrupt disappearance from the text, appears to have been integrated into the more pressing quest for the survival of the human race and the future of the planet. Certainly the sexual and political concerns of the earlier novel and the issues of birth control and abortion are still relevant in *Amanda*; it seems, however, that the earlier feminist issues have given way to a broader discussion of the implications of scientific and technological advancement for women both locally and globally. In East Germany, as in the West, this shift in focus appears consistent with the emergence in the 1980s of oppositional peace groups, particularly women's peace groups. The scope of a feminist politics has been extended through a "shift from a feminist politics of the body to feminist strategies for the body politic."[8] In contrast to women's peace movements in Britain and America, where opposition to the nuclear arms race has often – and certainly not unequivocally – been considered a purely feminist issue, in East Germany the task of saving the world from the arms race and self-destruction was perceived as a feminist issue, but not solely an issue for feminists. It remains to be investigated what makes peace a specifically feminist issue for Morgner and how the political strategies put forward in the text compare to and converge with similar feminist arguments in Western Europe.

As already indicated, the reincarnation of Beatriz as a siren, with the memories of her experiences as a medieval troubadour and as

8. McNeil, ed. *Gender and Expertise*, 56.

a tourist in the GDR still intact, is a means of providing a critical reassessment of the concerns of women's movements in the late 1960s and the 1970s. This is most obvious in Beatriz's decision to rewrite the version of Laura's life that appeared in *Trobadora Beatriz*. In *Amanda,* Beatriz accuses Morgner of deliberately and irresponsibly falsifying her portrayal of Laura. Beatriz's rereading and rewriting of the life history of Laura is then a form of "memory-work," intended as a preliminary exercise in preparation for the real work of singing for peace. The process of rewriting the character of Laura from Beatriz's perspective entails a rewriting of the history of women's emancipation in the GDR and a critique of the overly naive and optimistic image of the officially emancipated working woman in Laura. Beatriz accuses Morgner of creating a falsely harmonious and heroic picture of Laura who in retrospect appears as an idealized repository of all socialist feminine virtues – as "modest – willing – inconspicuous – willing to do without – self-sacrificial" (A. 29). The act of writing then is for Beatriz a dialectical process that constantly questions the validity and truth value of its products.

Alchemy and Feminine Science

In *Amanda* the traditional feminine skills of mothering and nurturing and the ancient art of suggestion are by no means the only feminine capacities to be enlisted in the name of peace. The new pragmatic skills originally developed by women for private purposes are alone insufficient to change the way of the world and must be complemented in turn by the help of the supernatural. The art of conjuring and mixing magic potions, also cultivated by Laura for personal reasons, represents an additional historical female experience to be remembered by women in the name of peace. In *Trobadora Beatriz* the use of magic by women was sporadic and yet strategic. Women scientists such as Valeska employed the long-forgotten art of magic, albeit somewhat hesitantly, as a counter-weight to the heavily masculinized world of science and research. The strategic use of magic had the potential to become a crucial weapon in women's struggle for recognition for their achievements, particularly in male-dominated areas of research. In *Trobadora Beatriz* and *Amanda* the cultivation of pre-scientific, pre-rational discourses enables women to challenge the gender-bias in scientific institutions and undermine perceptions of gender that perpetuate women's subordinate status in scientific professions. The practice of white magic by women represents a significantly different form of feminine interaction with nature based on a specifically feminine mode of production of knowledge. These strategies therefore effect a critique of the gender politics of scientific knowledge in addition to questioning the association of women with nature as one of the major stumbling blocks to women gaining equality in scientific professions. Magic provides women with an individualistic means of defense, something that in *Amanda* is channeled into organized political ends with the invention of the "Barbara Method" and the use of the "magic hat" to disguise women's subversive activities. In *Amanda* the future survival of the female half of the population is made dependent on the acknowledgment of witchcraft as a valid force. Morgner exhorts historians to study the laws of witchcraft and raise the "necromantic reserves for the preservation of the planet."[9] She recommends the study of "Universalsorcery" as a palliative to the plight of women in the industrial age. Black magic and sorcery are needed to free women from the double burden of multiple shifts in the work place and in the home. They are furthermore necessary to overcome the difficulties encountered in the transition from "patriarchal societies based on exploitation to a peaceful humane system."[10]

Carolyn Merchant[11] and Sandra Harding[12] have argued that the identification of women with "natural magic" has its roots in the Renaissance identification of women with nature and the metaphoric representation of the earth as nurturing mother. With the Copernican revolution, the organicist concept of nature with its emphasis on the earth as the active nurturing force in the cosmos was replaced by a cosmology that supplanted the earth-centered and female-dominated universe with a sun-centered and male-dominated one. It was this notion of the earth as the active

---

9. Morgner, *Die Hexe im Landhaus*, 55–56.
10. Ibid., 55.
11. Carolyn Merchant, *The Death of Nature: Women, Ecology and the Scientific Revolution* (New York: Harper & Row, 1980).
12. Sandra Harding, *The Science Question in Feminism* (Ithaca: Cornell University Press, 1986).

force at the center of the universe that was undermined by the Scientific Revolution and the Copernican view of the universe as revolving around the sun.[13] The new cosmology, in turn, was to have consequences for women and the status of the feminine.

In their studies of the gender politics of the Scientific Revolution, Merchant and Easlea[14] have argued that because women have traditionally always been identified with nature and nature has always been thought of as feminine, the new science needed to suppress traditional forms of female knowledge such as herbal cures, witchcraft, midwifery, and white magic as discernible proof of its mastery over the natural world. Accounts of the history of science as the history of the domination of women and nature have enjoyed increasing popularity in America and Europe, particularly among eco-feminists. Although Morgner implicitly draws on this account of the gender politics of the Scientific Revolution, her critique of scientific rationality seems more indebted to the Frankfurt School and its critique of Enlightenment discourses of mastery and domination.

Morgner seems to share the opinion of Merchant, Easlea, and Fox Keller[15] that science is not only dominated by men but that its very thinking is masculine. To elucidate this idea, she uses the mouthpiece of Konrad Tenner who is masquerading as a feminized male. Tenner confesses to Laura: "there is no feminine science . . . there is only masculine science – to say nothing of human science" (A. 271). Alchemy then is, according to Laura's necromantic studies, "the only not exclusively masculine science" (A. 139). She posits an alternative to masculine forms of knowledge in the form of pre-scientific traditions practiced by women prior to the Scientific Revolution and the Enlightenment. Laura concedes that alchemy was not the exclusive province of women but appeared to be the last form of socially useful, scientific knowledge in the history of Western civilization that women had access to. Closely linked to the disappearance of alchemy as a significant form of production of knowledge about

13. Ibid., 114.
14. Brian Easlea, *Witch Hunting, Magic and the New Philosophy: An Introduction to Debates of the Scientific Revolution 1450–1750* (Sussex: The Harvester Press, 1980).
15. Evelyn Fox Keller, *Reflections on Gender and Science* (New Haven and London: Yale University Press, 1985).

the world is the history of the brutal suppression of this knowledge in the persecution of women as witches. This is given as one of the reasons why no female alchemists of note have been recorded in scientific histories, because "all prominent female alchemists ended up burnt at the stake" (A. 139). It remains the task of rebellious women to remember the practices and objectives of an alternative "feminine" alchemy as a form of suppressed oppositional knowledge. This act of remembering is not a nostalgic attempt to retrieve a lost feminine affinity with a nature untainted by scientific knowledge or untampered with by technological intervention, but is instead utopian in its attempt to free the future from the ideological waste products of the Scientific Revolution.

The aim of the alchemical experiments conducted by women was – according to Morgner – the distillation of the small elixir or drinking silver from the "stone of the wise people of the second order" (A. 140). The traditional aim of masculine alchemy or official alchemy was to obtain the "greater elixir" or drinking gold from the "stone of the wise people of the first order." Among its known and sought-after properties were the ability to preserve eternal youth and to heal all illness and infirmity. Drinking silver, by contrast, when taken as medication, had the ability to "spirit women away" and to restore unity and a sense of wholeness to its adepts. Female adepts, who believed they had found their arcanum, were not known as adepts but as witches, and were persecuted as heretics. The discovery of drinking gold placed the whole world at the feet of the adept, the procuring of drinking silver merely an island.

It is the prospect of an island "as a sort of Orplid" (A. 141) and as a hinterland for women that initially spurs Laura on to remember the alchemical talents of her mothers in order to distill one such hinterland for herself. The idea to create a hinterland is at once the desire for a utopian space where female creativity can flourish and a place where it is possible for women to rest and replenish their energies expended on their first and second shifts. The longing for an island expresses Laura's discontent at the lack of material and historical support available to women and the absence of a long historical and mythical tradition to lend legitimation to their struggles for independence and knowledge. This is because women were traditionally expected to provide the hinterland for their men. Laura is accordingly outraged to discover that even under socialism men can continue to rely on and exploit the material and emotional support of women in the privacy of their own homes, all the while preaching the new discourses of emancipation and equality in public. She is shocked to find that the old militarist dictum that the woman provides the hinterland for the soldier still applied in the immediate postwar years in the GDR, especially considering, "Laura had imagined a socialist family to be different" (A. 139). Upon discovering that the exemplary socialist figure of Kurt Fakal behaves in private like a petty feudal despot, Laura resolves to distill her own hinterland as her own form of imaginary material and emotional support.

While Laura's alchemical experiments are primarily designed to have practical effects at the level of everyday life, the search for the drinking silver is eventually co-opted by Amanda into her plan for conquering the Blocksberg and for rendering women whole again. In the meantime Laura concentrates her efforts on distilling a sleep-substitute elixir that will temporarily solve her problems in reconciling her child-minding responsibilities with the demands of her career. It is only when by mistake she distills a phoenix elixir, granting herself, like Beatriz, a second life, that she is more receptive to Amanda's larger-scale plans for wresting the drinking silver from the hands of the male ravens occupying the Blocksberg.

The Gender Politics of Science

In *Amanda*, Morgner addresses in greater depth the gendered nature of scientific discourse and scientific modes of inquiry. She also investigates how androcentric practices in the family and society inform the norms of scientific institutions. The norms of scientific pursuit are steeped in images of masculinity that masquerade as the post-gendered or universal axioms of science held to be the putative objective pursuit of knowledge. In *Amanda*, Morgner looks at the ways masculinist dichotomies and ideologies contribute to maintaining the gender politics of science in the postwar era. Morgner's main object of attack is therefore less the masculinist assumption that all science is hard and objective,[16]

16. See Harding, *The Science Question in Feminism*, 121–26.

than the gender politics of the popular image of the scientist as dedicated, single-minded, and eccentric. The qualities valued in science and in the scientist himself, such as eccentricity, originality, genius, and passion, have traditionally been associated only with masculine forms of knowledge production and masculine forms of genius. The same qualities in women have tended to signal social or sexual deviancy or outsidership. Passion, says Morgner, has only ever been granted women in the world of love:

> Good passionate decisiveness which is officially to the credit of every man while officially the ruin of every woman. Because we women are only permitted passion in love. (A. 226)[17]

While passion within the private sphere is encoded as female, within the public sphere, the domain of politics and science, it is strictly masculine. Women who display the same fanaticism towards their professions as men are immediately considered bad mothers as well as bad wives. Extreme dedication to one's career is valued in males but condemned as "irresponsible" in women. Husbands expect "relaxed features, an even temper, restraint, conformity" (A. 226) from women, qualities that are certainly not the mark of genius and that traditionally have not been considered to be conducive to great scientific discoveries. Scientific activity and the norms of scientific professions are therefore founded on the exclusion of the feminine and on attributes traditionally associated with motherhood.

Not only have the positive terms within scientific discourses traditionally been encoded as masculine, they are in addition bolstered by social practices that in turn guarantee the reproduction of these gendered ideologies within scientific discourses and throughout scientific institutions. The admirable attributes of the stereotype of the talented, dedicated scientist are grounded in the traditional sexual division of labor within the home and the labor force. They are therefore predicated upon the maintenance of the feudal mode of gender reproduction. The eccentricities and original achievements of a Konrad Tenner, for example, are only made possible by a strict division of labor within the family that frees men

17. "Schöne leidenschaftliche Entschiedenheit, die jedem Mann offiziell zur Ehre gereicht und jede Frau offiziell ruiniert. Denn uns Frauen wird Leidenschaft nur in der Liebe zugebilligt."

from any daily responsibility for the immediate needs of their wives and families. The ideologies informing scientific practices are produced and reproduced within the private spheres and help to legitimize the perpetuation of misogynistic practices in the home. If intellectual fanaticism is the precondition for great scientific breakthroughs, then the sacrifice women and children are required to make is considered by men a small price to pay. The general consensus appears to be that:

> . . . intellectual quality manifests itself as originality, that is, in trains of thought that deviate from well-trodden paths: in oddness therefore, in eccentricity. Only passion can lead off the beaten track. Such thought processes therefore are by no means exercises that tax the brain alone. The whole personality is affected by them and bears their mark. (A. 225)[18]

Morgner cites the processes of gender symbolization as a further example of the gender politics of science in modern patriarchal societies. As Sandra Harding and Fox Keller have consistently argued, the metaphors scientists use in describing their practices are further evidence of the link between masculinity and scientific discourse. Harding also contends that gender politics have in fact "provided resources for the advancement of science, and science has provided the resources for the advancement of masculine domination."[19] Harding recalls the rape and torture metaphors permeating the works of the founding father of modern science, Sir Francis Bacon, as an example of discursive processes of legitimation of the new science. But whereas the gender metaphors underpinning the new science were modeled on "men's most misogynous relationships to women – rape, torture, choosing 'mistresses,'"[20] the new socialist science of the scientific and technological revolution was careful to avoid such blatantly misogynistic metaphors within scientific discourse. That is not to say, however, that gender metaphors did not

18. ". . . geistige Qualität sich als Originalität zeigt, das heißt in Denkbewegungen, die die Normgleise verlassen: in Absonderlichkeit also, in Exzentrizität. Nur Leidenschaft kann aus den Gleisen tragen. Solche Denkbewegungen sind also keineswegs Unterfangen, die allein den Kopf strapazieren. Die ganze Persönlichkeit wird von ihr ergriffen und gezeichnet."
19. Harding, *The Science Question in Feminism*, 112.
20. Ibid.

provide significant resources for the scientific and technological revolution and for the way in which socialist science was conceived of as masculine. Popular conceptions of the "hard" sciences as virile and masculine, as presented by Paul in *Hochzeit in Konstantinopel* (HK. 121), Wenzel Morolf in *Trobadora Beatriz* (TB. 78) and his predecessor Dr. Kai M. in *Rumba auf einen Herbst* (RH. 249), appear to be the direct heirs to the idea of an active virile science proposed by Francis Bacon in *The Masculine Birth of Time*.[21] The metaphors used in *Amanda* by Konrad Tenner are more subtle and seductive than the rape and torture metaphors used by Bacon. They represent nevertheless a more subtle use of gender politics to exclude women from the active areas of scientific research and reinforce the notion of the creative realm of the sciences as an exclusively male domain.

Vilma comments that her husband Konrad Tenner has personified history as his "Frau Queen." His relationship to the science of history, that is, to the object of scientific inquiry, is expressed both in terms of the relationship of a feudal subject to his queen and a king to his wife. The relationship is both one of submission and domination:

> For him [Konrad Tenner] history is the queen of the social sciences and he treats it like a man of his character would a queen: regally. His colleagues know that he virtually loves and reveres history personified. And no-one smiles when Doctor Tenner speaks of "Frau Queen." (A. 224–25)[22]

The incongruousness of the term "Frau Queen" also suggests that Konrad envisages himself very much as the king of science, so that even if history may well be a "queen" that makes her in fact only his wife. The reverence that Tenner brings to his object of research appears to be little more than a ruse to disguise the strictly hierarchical nature of the relationship of the male scientific subject to its feminine object. Tenner's desire to anthropomorphize history and encode it as female and hence himself as male, lays bare the

---

21. See Fox Keller, *Gender and Science*, 38–40.
22. "Für ihn [Konrad] ist Geschichte die Königin der Gesellschaftswissenschaften, und er geht mit ihr um, wie ein Mensch seines Charakters mit Königinnen umgeht: königlich. Seine Mitarbeiter wissen, daß er Geschichte geradezu personifiziert liebt und verehrt. Und keiner grinst, wenn der Doktor Tenner von 'Frau Königin' spricht."

hidden agenda of sexual politics that informs both the practices of
the natural sciences and the human sciences. Tenner's mode of
thinking about science presupposes furthermore a set of gender
assumptions shared by the scientific community. A woman
researcher would have greater difficulties regarding the object of
her study as female when she herself is female. Vilma questions
the association of women with the science of history, finding the
personification of history as a queen incomprehensible, given that
women have in fact always been excluded from official versions
of history:

> History would certainly be inconceivable to me even as a queen. For
> historiography has historically expropriated women. And the history
> not deemed worthy of documentation is a history of crimes
> perpetrated against the female sex. (A. 226)[23]

Tenner adds insult to injury when he insists that the scientific
male gaze is only a form of compensation for men's inability to
match women's innate gift for creating biological life. All male
forms of creativity can therefore be reduced to the compensatory
desire to find a substitute for child-bearing:

> Science and technology have hitherto produced nothing of the
> magnitude of what develops in a fertilized hen's egg in twenty
> days . . .. Because we know we come off second best in comparison
> to nature, we disregard it. (A. 270)[24]

The comparison that Tenner makes between male creativity and
female reproductivity takes yet again as its basic premise the
identification of women with nature and the view that women's
reproductive role in society is primarily a biological fact of life
rather than a socially and politically motivated activity. Tenner
contends that because men's imitations can never match nature's

23. "Die Geschichte wäre mir freilich auch als Königin undenkbar. Denn die
    Geschichtsschreibung hat die Frauen historisch expropriiert. Und die nicht
    als aufschreibenswürdig erachtete Geschichte ist eine Geschichte von
    Verbrechen am weiblichen Geschlecht."
24. "Wissenschaft und Technik haben bisher nichts Annäherndes von der
    Größenordnung hervorgebracht, das in zwanzig Tagen in einem befruchteten
    Hühnerei sich heranbildet . . .. Denn da wir wissen, wie blaß wir aussehen
    bei einem Vergleich mit der Natur, sehen wir über sie hinweg."

creations and hence women's "creations of nature," the history of civilization has had to devalue the miracles of nature to be able to appreciate men's poor imitations at all:

> We have to have scant regard for the wonders of nature to be able to admire the inventions of science and technology as wonders. It is not the creations of nature that are worshipped but the imitations in which humankind seeks to emulate recognized natural laws. We do not adore and nurture what nature gives to humanity but instead that which is artificially created by humanity at immense expense. (A. 270)[25]

Tenner continues to argue that men's feelings of apparent superiority in fact stem from deep-seated feelings of inadequacy regarding their lesser creative capabilities in comparison to women. Modern science becomes a type of "male uterus envy"[26] or, at best, a rather clever ruse designed to conceal men's basic sense of inferiority. In this way the history of modern science since Bacon reads as an ill-conceived and rather pitiful trick that men have tried to pull off to overcompensate for being second-class biological citizens. Men's greater technological mastery is thereby nothing more than:

> A cleverly devised means of converting inferiority complexes into superiority complexes. For how should a man compete with someone who can give birth. Our kind are poorly off in comparison to women who each and every one, whether stupid or smart, ugly or beautiful, small or large, can be a creator. Every one of them is capable of bringing something visibly unique into the world. What about me? (A. 270)[27]

---

25. "Wir müssen die Wunder der Natur gering achten, um die Erfindungen der Wissenschaft und Technik als Wunder anbeten zu können. Nicht die Schöpfungen der Natur, sondern Nachschöpfungen, in denen der Mensch versucht, erkannten Naturgesetzen folgend nachzubauen, werden verehrt. Angebetet und gehegt wird nicht das den Menschen natürlich Geschenkte, sondern das von ihnen mit ungeheurem Aufwand künstlich Geschaffene."
26. See Phyllis Chesler, *About Men* (New York: Simon and Schuster, 1978), 38.
27. "Eine gerissen ausgedachte Weise, Minderwertigkeitsgefühle in Überwertigkeitsgefühle zu modeln. Denn wie steht ein Mann da gegenüber einem Menschen, der Menschen gebären kann? Arm steht unsereiner da unter den Frauen, von denen jede, dumb oder gescheit, häßlich oder schön, klein oder groß, eine Schöpferin sein kann. Jede ist fähig, Einmaliges aller Welt sichtbar hervorzubringen. Ich dagegen?"

What we have here – male superiority masquerading as inferiority – is an extreme example of the naturalization of power in the interests of the dominant sex and culture. Tenner's confession to Vilma, superficially aimed at eliciting sympathy from her, is nonetheless a thinly veiled attempt to reinforce the traditional feminine spheres of social activity by revalorizing women's role in biological reproduction. This is one way of ensuring that the traditional male domains of science and technology remain bastions of male power. Tenner's argument hinges on the qualitative distinction between unmediated natural modes of creation of biological life, which are seen as the province of women, and mediated, artificial modes of creation as practiced by men that merely reproduce or imitate the wonders of nature. This distinction purports to privilege the natural and feminine over the "man"-made, and therefore to value female reproductivity over "mere" male productivity. The adulation of the wonders of nature turns out in fact to be its converse: the fetishization of science and technology and its mastery over nature. As feminists have repeatedly pointed out, the price for the elevation of female creativity to a higher plane than male creative activity is of course the exclusion of feminine forms of productivity from the realm of the social. This then has as its consequence the reaffirmation of the traditional association of women with nature and the natural. It has repeatedly and persuasively been argued that it is this linking of women with nature that has been responsible for the protracted historical subordination of women to the cultural achievements and institutions of men.

By the same token, Tenner's speech offers a critique of modern science that feminists might nonetheless welcome. Whatever reservations Vilma and Laura may have about Tenner's ulterior motives for dethroning his queen and following Laura's crusade to the Blocksberg,[28] Tenner's critical position vis-à-vis scientific practices and institutions enables the women to find in him their first male ally. Notwithstanding Tenner's misogynist relationship

28. See in particular chapter 67, where Tenner uses the discussion to win sexual favors from Vilma, and chapter 80, where he manipulates feminist arguments and critiques of contemporary masculinity to sexual ends. It is also suggested that Tenner is interested in the alchemical talents of Vilma and Laura because of the promise of distilling an aphrodisiac that will enable him to satisfy two women at the same time.

to history, he announces to Laura that he has dethroned his queen. Taking Laura's words right out of her mouth, he now proclaims the importance of investigating prehistory. Nevertheless, he remains impervious to any alternative modes of knowledge and methods of scientific inquiry, particularly when practiced by women or by one of his ex-wives. Vilma reassures Laura that they can conduct their alchemical experiments in the safety of the kitchen, because Tenner would never dream of taking women's work in the kitchen seriously.

It now becomes apparent that it is not simply a matter of the gender of the subject producing the scientific knowledge that determines the weight attributed to the discourse and its truth-claims. If the public spaces in which scientific activity is conducted and in which the scientific subject is constituted are gendered, then it becomes crucial to investigate the discursive processes by which gender comes to bear on the ideology of science and its methods and objects of inquiry. The private sphere of the family home is not the proper place for scientific research, nor are homes considered by men the proper sites for "cooking up" politically subversive activities. It is, of course, precisely these reasons that make Vilma and Laura decide to use their kitchens to try and concoct a potion that will solve Laura's sleep-deficiency problems and eventually distill the drinking silver that will make women whole again.

Utopian Experiments in Irrationality

Tenner is not the only male scientist in *Amanda* to begin to express doubts about the fetishization of science and technology. Heinrich Fakal, Laura's school friend, represents perhaps the best example of a dogmatic scientist whose extreme reliance on principles of empirical rationality earned him from his youth the name "iron Henry" (A. 136). The son of a miner and a communist, Fakal was encouraged during the early years of the GDR to adopt the role of ideological guardian and role model with respect to his peers. His uncompromising attitude towards his school friends when conducting what he calls "operations to clear away the ideological rubble" (A. 604) is only matched by his self-denial and "emotional rigor" towards himself, as his motto "hard on others and even tougher on yourself" (A. 136) indicates. As the director of the section for economic planning at the Institute for the Philosophy of Science, Fakal has been entrusted with the task of intensifying production and rationalizing work processes at his institute. The scientific and technological revolution, which played a key role in the ideological struggle for supremacy between the East and West in the 1950s, functioned as a yardstick by which the success of socialism and in this case the success of Fakal's institution could be measured. The catchwords "science and technology," now little more than clichés, became synonymous with the intensification of production and output:

> The concept of "science and technology" had become synonymous with intensifying production. Citizens were told daily in the factory and after hours that the social system that could best utilize the results of the most advanced science and technology to raise productivity would be guaranteed victory in the world-wide struggle between capitalism and socialism. The co-workers in the Institute for the Philosophy of Science, in which Fakal managed the work section for Economic Planning, were reminded of the fact that the time factor and hence the degree of organization and purposefulness in scientific methodology was of unprecedented importance in the historical race for the mastery of the scientific and technological revolution. (A. 567–68)[29]

The principles of rationalization of time and organization, when applied to the production of scientific knowledge, arouse in Fakal a sense of panic and bewilderment because "naturally he found the popular demand for intensifying work directed at himself. But how does a scientist intensify his work?" (A. 568). Fakal finds his scientific work ethos, based on the principles of reason, diligence,

29. "Der Begriff 'Wissenschaft und Technik' war zum Synonym für Intensivierung geworden. Täglich wurde den Bürgern im Betrieb und nach Feierabend dargelegt, daß in der weltweiten Auseinandersetzung zwischen Kapitalismus und Sozialismus letztlich der Gesellschaftsordnung der Sieg zufiele, die die Ergebnisse der fortgeschrittensten Wissenschaft und Technik zur Erhöhung der Arbeitsproduktivität optimal nutzen könnte. Ständig wurde den Mit-arbeitern des Instituts für Wissenschaftstheorie, an dem Fakal die Arbeitsgruppe Wirtschaftsplanung leitete, bewußt gehalten, daß im geschichtlichen Wettstreit um die Meisterung der wissenschaftlich-technischen Revolution dem Faktor Zeit und damit der Organisiertheit und Zielstrebigkeit im wissenschaftlichen Vorgehen ein bisher nicht dagewesener Wert zukäme."

and patience, in conflict with the institutional demands for instant solutions to pragmatic problems. He has become "oversaturated with rational concerns that had amounted to nothing" (A. 567), "oversaturated with certainties that had lead nowhere" (A. 571). Surrounded by "plans, programs, directives, competitive goals, resolutions" (A. 571), he is the victim of processes of rationalization and short-term economic concerns that he sees as anathema to the goals of long-term research. The principles of instrumental rationality have led him so far from the original scientific precepts of reason that he is eventually willing to resort to the "non-kosher means" of putting his faith in reason's opposite, "non-reason." If instrumental reason sanctions all means provided the ends are worthwhile, then it follows that even those means that are incompatible with a scientific world view must too be legitimate. Fakal is thus forced to consider even pre-scientific, pre-rational methods of inquiry such as magic, and to summon up the belief in miracles as a final means of solving the impasse in which he finds himself. The catalyst for such radical considerations is the discovery of a flying woman:

> Why had Fakal not been able to arrive at the logical conclusion to experiment with non-reason? Non-reason or the belief in miracles or magic – did not worthy ends justify all means, even those that were not reconcilable with a scientific world view? (A. 571)[30]

The intellectual and emotional dilemma that the sight of a woman flying upwards from her balcony in the middle of the city of Berlin causes Fakal and his rational world view on April Fools' Day precipitates his decision to experiment with reason's opposite. Fakal is clearly a pathetic victim of what Habermas has termed the total "colonization of the life world"[31] by science and technology and the principles of instrumental reason.

In the 1970s the theme of the dehumanizing effects of technology became more common in the literature of the GDR, particularly

30. "Warum hatte Fakal den naheliegenden logischen Schluß, mit Unvernunft zu experimentieren, nicht längst vollziehen können? Unvernunft oder Wunderglaube oder Zauberei – heiligte der gute Zweck nicht alle Mittel, selbst solche, die mit einer wissenschaftlichen Weltanschauung nicht in Übereinstimmung zu bringen waren?"
31. Jürgen Habermas, *Theorie des Kommunikativen Handelns*, vol. 1 (Frankfurt/Main: Suhrkamp, 1981).

among women writers such as Christa Wolf and Helga Königsdorf. Often it is the male scientist himself who is the object of scrutiny, as in Wolf's sex change story "Selbstversuch" where a female scientist agrees to undergo a sex change experiment in the hope of gaining recognition for her work and ultimately the love of her professor. Only capable of seeing in the female protagonist an asexual object of his experiment, the male scientist is characterized as lacking in emotions, sensitivity, and warmth. The debilitating effects of the rational, scientific world view are most obvious in his private life, in his treatment of his wife and daughter, but also in his attitude towards his colleagues and women in general. Wolf identifies the inability to love as the major consequence of a thoroughly over-technologized, over rationalized, and – masculinized life world.[32] She also suggests in "Selbstversuch" that the inability to love may even be the cause of many scientific achievements:

> Your artificially constructed system of rules, your unholy work mania, all your manoeuvers to evade the issue were none other than the attempt to protect yourself from the discovery that you are incapable of loving and know it.[33]

This is further evidence of the processes of colonization, whereby the social practices of the life world become progressively subordinated to systemic imperatives and to economic and bureaucratic concerns. The experiment is eventually declared a failure and, after a horrifying look at the male-dominated world of "the three big principles of economics, science, world politics,"[34] "Anders," the object of the unfortunate experiment, decides to reverse the operation, but not before she announces an alternative experiment in the "invention of the person one can love."[35]

32. See Anna K. Kuhn, Christa Wolf's *Utopian Vision: From Marxism to Feminism* (Cambridge: Cambridge UP, 1988), 12; and Helen Fehervary and Sarah Lennox, "Introduction to Christa Wolf's 'Self-Experiment: Appendix to a Report,'" *New German Critique* 13 (Winter 1978): 111.
33. "Ihre kunstvoll aufgebauten Regelsysteme, Ihre heillose Arbeitswut, all Ihre Manöver, sich zu entziehen, waren nichts als der Versuch, sich vor der Entdeckung abzusichern: Daß Sie nicht lieben können und es wissen." Wolf, "Selbstversuch," 167–68.
34. Ibid., 163.
35. Ibid., 169.

In the *Frankfurter Vorlesungen,* Wolf elaborates further on the alienating, dehumanizing effects of masculine science, describing science and also philosophy as a means of shielding the individual from reality, of "keeping reality at bay, protecting oneself from it."[36] Progress in the sciences and the arts, she argues, has been bought at the expense of the extreme alienation and de-personalization of the individual.[37] The main cause of the disregard for human needs and emotions that is characteristic of industrial societies in the nuclear age, she argues in a speech to the Südwestfunk in 1982, is the positivist orientation of the natural sciences and their dependence on quantifiable, verifiable values: "What is not measurable, ponderable, quantifiable, verifiable is as good as not there. It does not count."[38]

In a letter written after the death of her husband to the journal *New Philosophical Papers,* included in chapter 39 of *Amanda,* Laura complains that the principles of Marxist-Leninism have failed to provide adequate answers to the non-material problems of everyday life, in particular the need for forms of support in metaphysical matters to help people cope with death and grieving. This was the sort of support previously provided by religion in pre-socialist times. But when the materialist world view dispensed with metaphysics these basic human needs and emotions could no longer be adequately met:

> We have abolished God, well and good. But we cannot do away with the things that religion deals with. Death, illness, chance, fortune, ill-fortune – how can the inexorable vicissitudes of life be handled on one's own? Whoever lives without God cannot delegate responsibility. He always has to bear this burden alone. (A. 152)[39]

---

36. Wolf, *Voraussetzungen einer Erzählung,* 150.
37. Ibid.
38. "Was nicht meßbar, wägbar, zählbar, verifizierbar ist, ist so gut wie nicht vorhanden. Es zählt nicht." Wolf, "Ein Brief," *Mut zur Angst: Schriftsteller für den Frieden,* ed. Ingrid Krüger (Darmstadt & Neuwied: Luchterhand, 1982), 154.
39. "Wir haben Gott abgeschafft, schön und gut. Aber die Gegenstände, mit denen sich Religion beschäftigt, konnten wir nicht abschaffen. Tod, Krankheit, Zufall, Glück, Unglück – wie lassen sich die unerbittlichen Wechselfälle des Lebens eigenverantwortlich meistern? Wer ohne Gott lebt, kann Verantwortung nicht delegieren. Er muß diese Last immer allein tragen."

Laura's demand for a substitute for metaphysics and hence for an adjunct to the historical-materialist world view expresses a commonly felt dissatisfaction with the hegemony of the discourses of dialectical materialism and Marxist-Leninism and the central role they attribute to science and technology. Her request for an alternative to metaphysics is also intended as a critique of the way dialectical materialism has become in effect a new type of religion with science its new priesthood. More generally then, Laura's demand for a reconsideration of the functions of religion and metaphysics represents a significant critique of the ideal of unlimited technological progress. Technological progress, which in the 1950s and 1960s was regarded as the *sine qua non* of the progress of socialist society and of socialism itself, is no longer a precondition for the progress of humanity, becoming instead a hindrance to the "subject-becoming" of humankind.

The literature by Morgner and Wolf is more critical of the effects of the scientific and technological revolution on human relationships and needs than most of the socialist literature written before the 1970s and 1980s, particularly the works of science fiction. Instead of being a "means of self-liberation,"[40] in Morgner's works the world of science and technology begins to take on those diabolical traits that East German literary critics were so quick to condemn in Western science fiction. Morgner's female characters are not able to establish the positive relationship to the world of science and technology that the male figures do. The euphoria of Rita in Wolf's *Der geteilte Himmel* at the launching of the Sputnik and the dawn of a new technological age is replaced in the 1970s with a general disappointment at failed career opportunities and a well-masked despair at the future of the human race. Morgner's working women by contrast suffer from considerable alienation in the work place as well as in the home, an alienation only matched by the lack of understanding from their male colleagues. We are not told why Bele in *Hochzeit in Konstantinopel* has given up her career at a scientific institute, only that she prefers the work of a taxi driver, a ticket collector, or a train driver to that of a laboratory assistant. In these jobs she at least has the satisfying illusion that she is in control and not subservient to men. In response to Paul's question why she gave up her job in the laboratory, Bele replies that

40. See Sckerl, *Wissenschaftlich-phantastische Literatur*, 126ff.

she "was not cut out for domestic work" (HK. 44). Paul, however, fails to understand Bele's pointed comment, which is clearly aimed at the under-utilization of her abilities in her job. But it is Laura who offers us the most striking example of a failed scientific career.

Morgner presents perhaps the most convincing indictment of the dehumanizing, anti-feminine effects of the work of knowledge-production when she outlines the circumstances under which Laura finally gives up her job as a historian. It is only after the death of her child from pneumonia – for which Laura feels personally responsible – that she chooses a profession that does not demand the sorts of long hours that could lead to her neglecting the needs of her child. Increasingly in the literature of the 1970s and 1980s, the utopia of the humanizing effects of technology gives way to the dystopia of a deformed, dehumanized society that still adheres steadfastly to the now empty catchwords of science and technology, preferring to see in them the only hope for the future rather than as a recipe for disaster. Apart from emphasizing the obvious inaccessibility of scientific careers to women, Morgner stresses in *Amanda* the failure of the techno-fetishist world view to adequately account for the subjective factor – those unquantifiable human needs that are generally regarded as the province of women. The subjective factor plays an important role in criticizing the negative effects on the individual of a too heavy reliance on the methods of scientific empiricism. Subjective feelings and emotions, like the world of dreams and the imagination, can be easily ignored or dismissed as incidental to the main social activity of accelerating production because they are not as easily verifiable or quantifiable. Like the quirky 1,001 goodnight stories that Bele tells Paul, which fail to impress him, and the passionate love affair that Wanda has with the invisible medieval jester, Rade, to which Wanda's scientific lover, Hubert, also remains blissfully oblivious, women's calls for an injection of eroticism and fantasy into the stultified world of everyday life are often overlooked or simply denied a voice.

In *Amanda*, Morgner's critique of the interface between masculinity and science, exemplified in her earlier works in such male figures as Paul in *Hochzeit in Konstantinopel*, Hubert in *Gauklerlegende*, Dr. Kai M. in *Rumba auf einen Herbst* and Wenzel Morolf, Rudolf Uhlenbrook, and Clemens in *Trobadora Beatriz*, comes full circle. Although these figures are not all entirely negative examples of the way masculinity informs and shapes scientific practices – Paul for instance proves to be a surprisingly good lover despite his otherwise consistent lack of concern for his fiancee's well-being – the picture Morgner presents of the interconnections between masculinity, rationality, and science is predominantly negative. All utopian impulses concerning the future of masculinity are focused on the fantasy male figures such as Rade, the medieval jester, and Benno in *Trobadora Beatriz*, who can be said to represent the radical other of the rational scientific male. Not until *Amanda* do we find these utopian impulses actualized in the creation of new images of masculinity. Thus the rational male researcher who, despite wife and child, is "only married to science" (A. 564) and who is renowned for his dogmatism and unrelenting analytical gaze, becomes, instead of purely an object of ridicule, the object of a utopian experiment.

Unlike his literary predecessors, Fakal's "scientific gaze" has not made him totally blind to reason's underside. As the first adult male in Morgner's works to actually witness a fantastic, supernatural event, he finds himself forced to admit the empirical existence of the supernatural. Yet the conversion of Fakal is not the result of an empirical observation but ironically the condition that makes such an observation possible. Paul, in *Hochzeit in Konstantinopel*, and Hubert, in *Gauklerlegende*, are blind to any experience, figure, or event that lies outside their scientific world of empirically verifiable certainties. Likewise, Rudolf and Lutz in *Trobadora Beatriz*, and Tenner in *Amanda*, have no appreciation of the extraordinary because their belief in the rationality and predictability of the world has not yet been shattered. What distinguishes Fakal from the others is not any latent skepticism or lack of commitment to the principles of reason, but a sense of increasing desperation at the inadequacy of these principles as the sole means of interpreting the world. The aporia of scientific positivism and rationality is nowhere more evident than in Heinrich Fakal's eventual willingness to embrace mysticism in the form of numerology.

After observing, along with numerous other eyewitnesses, the phenomenon of a flying woman – originally thought to be Laura but who is in fact Amanda – Fakal makes the dubious decision to experiment with "non-reason, miracles or magic" (A. 571), although he is aware that the belief in miracles of the non-economic kind is not compatible with a scientific *Weltanschauung* (A. 571). He undertakes this despite announcing to his son, also an eyewitness: "everything in nature and society proceeds in accordance with laws" (A. 565). Ironically, his reputation and self-confidence as a rigorous researcher enables him to pass off even the most unscientific, irrational practices as the result of sound empirical experimentation, although he admits that:

> He must not allow himself to be caught out off on an obscure tack. If successful, however, it would be an easy matter to produce the evidence. A philosophical mind like Fakal's could prove anything if he wanted to. And in this case he would not even have to be particularly finicky. If he could come up with a viable scientific strategy all would be forgiven. The outcome would speak overwhelmingly in his favor. (A. 571)[41]

In connection with this, Fakal recalls a remark by the Marxist utopian thinker, J.D. Bernal, who in the twenties and thirties developed a vision of a scientific utopia governed by an aristocracy of scientific intelligence. In his work Bernal stressed the importance of epistemological ruptures or ground-breaking in all scientific revolutions:

> Fakal remembered the well-known remark made by Bernal: "The greatest difficulty when making a discovery does not consist in making the necessary observations but in detaching oneself from traditional ideas when interpreting it." (A. 572)[42]

A paradigm-shift, however, that would allow the "detection of an object of a mystical order" and permit the existence of "magic or even a witch" (A. 572) would necessitate a radical departure from Bernal's Marxist vision of a utopian state dominated by a scientific

---

41. "Auf obskuren Suchpfaden durfte er sich nicht erwischen lassen. Erfolgreich aber würde es für ihn eine Kleinigkeit sein, den Beweis zu führen. Ein philosophischer Kopf wie Fakal konnte alles beweisen, wenn er nur wollte. Und in diesem Fall müßte er gar nicht mal besonders spitzfindig sein. Wenn er jetzt eine handhabbare Wissenschaftsstrategie auf den Tisch legen könnte, würde ihm alles verziehen. Der Erfolg spräche überwältigend für ihn."

42. "Fakal erinnerte die bekannte Bemerkung Bernals: 'Die größte Schwierigkeit bei einer Entdeckung liegt nicht darin, die notwendigen Beobachtungen zu machen, als darin, sich bei ihrer Interpretation von traditionellen Vorstellungen zu lösen.'"

elite constantly engaged in perfecting man's scientific and technological mastery over the natural world.

Yet while Fakal is ruminating on the epistemological, philosophical, and indeed even the political implications of his conversion to magic, mysticism, and astronomy, he becomes unwittingly the object of a transformation of a quite different kind. A few days after sighting the flying woman Fakal notices a mysterious long red plait growing from his otherwise slightly balding head. It is this plait that convinces Laura that Heinrich Fakal was just the man she was looking for.

Recruiting Male Allies: Transforming Masculinity

In the chapter titled "Laura's Annunciation," the thirteen-year-old Laura receives a visit from the underworld from the daughter of Frau Holle. Laura is given the advice that, if she is to continue to put her faith in men, she must then rely on a type of revolutionary artfulness so as not to succumb to the pressures of a male-dominated world. She must look for men with copper hair – even a few hairs are sufficient – delouse them, and save the red hairs in the hope that she can eventually use them to regain entry to the utopian imaginary of the Blocksberg. As the current regime on the Blocksberg only grants red-haired men entrance to the Brocken, women must use the red hairs of men to bribe the door keepers to gain entry. Men are, by necessity, women's secret allies, says Frau Holle's daughter, and gives Laura the advice: "So marry soon and often and properly so that you may be granted insight. Yet do not forget to dye your hair beforehand" (A. 131).

By the same token, the search for red-headed men is designed as a tactic to subvert the authoritarian structures of patriarchy from a position of apparent complicity and cooperation. The red hairs are the secret pieces of information that Laura collects about the internal workings of masculinity and male domination, the key pieces of evidence she needs to mount her case against the authoritarian structures of patriarchy and to storm the Blocksberg. Yet, just as the mere presence of a few red hairs signifies in women witch-like capabilities and potential – as it does when Laura delouses her friend Vilma – the discovery of red hair in men signals their potential for feminization and for co-optation as allies in the witches' cause. So when Laura discovers the red plait growing down Heinrich Fakal's back, she is in fact witnessing an unprecedented transformation of a man into a witch.

Yet Laura's realization that Fakal is recruitable comes not in that moment when she discovers the red plait but when she looks in the mirror and finds that Heinrich has a Doppelganger. Her discovery of Heinrich's secret double in Henri, whom he tries to conceal by stashing away in the cupboard, accompanies the realization that some men, like Laura and most other GDR women, have also been severed in two. Yet whereas the division of women was either the work of customs or the result of a violent act of Satanic aggression, executed to ensure women's subservience and loyalty to male authority, the division of men, as in the case of Heinrich, was due to a more or less voluntary act of self-mutilation. Laura writes of Heinrich in her diary, known in her childhood as "Marie's Heiner":

Marie's Heiner has been living divided longer than I have. He must have chopped himself up. Voluntarily? At any rate after 45 I only had contact and troubles with the one half: with iron Heinrich. The deloused Fakal called the other half, which is now stored in the corner cupboard, 'Henri.'" (A. 608)[43]

Heinrich's sensitive, passionate other half remains stored in a cardboard suitcase along with other useless emotions and unfulfilled wishes that Heinrich, out of sheer desperation, hoards with his secret other self. When the young Heinrich, a passionate mathematician, fails to be accepted for a university course in mathematics and is allotted one in philosophy instead, he hides his desperation and his disappointment along with Henri in the cardboard case and resolves to adjourn his real life as a mathematician until later:

What should he do with his despair? Heinrich Fakal stashed it away in the cardboard suitcase along with Henri. And he postponed the beginning of his real life. And with the motto that he adopted from his

43. "'Maries Heiner lebt noch länger geteilt als ich. Er muß sich selber zerhackt haben. Freiwillig? Jedenfalls hatte ich nach 45 nur mit der einen Hälfte Kontakte und Reibereien: mit dem eisernen Heinrich. Die andere Hälfte, die jetzt im Eckschrank aufbewahrt wird, nannte der gelauste Fakal 'Henri.'"

father: "Hard on others and even tougher on yourself" he achieved
exemplary results in his studies in all his philosophical subjects and
his managerial positions. Only on Sundays and holidays he regularly
used to sit on his case bent over mathematical literature and hoped for
a second chance to study. (A. 609)[44]

Only the socially useful halves of men that can be best adapted
to the short-term pragmatic concerns of the socialist state have been
allowed to survive. The non-conformist, rebellious other halves lie
dormant, locked up in cases with other trivial memorabilia like
Henri, or imprisoned in the Hörselberg underground like Amanda
and the other halves of GDR women. These are the "useless" parts
of the socialist personality that, like Henri, are impatient and
uncompromising in their ideals, and selfish in their demands for
self-fulfillment. These unruly other halves are not only
unproductive in a limited economic sense, they furthermore
present a threat to the smooth workings of the state and to the
processes of rationalization. The banished other halves of East
German citizens act as a repository for those dreams and ideals of
the individual that the state does not acknowledge and cannot
harness for its own rational and economic ends. The wishes of the
other halves are therefore economically and ideologically
unproductive for the state and threaten to block the smooth
exchange between individual and state apparatus and to disrupt
the symbolic reproduction of the socialist system.

---

44. "Wohin mit der Verzweiflung? Heinrich Fakal stopfte sie zu Henri in den
    Pappkoffer. Und er vertagte den Beginn seines eigentlichen Lebens. Und mit
    seiner vom Vater übernommenen Lebensdevise: 'Brutal gegen sich, hart gegen
    andere' erreichte er vorbildliche Studienergebnisse in allen philosophischen
    Fächern und führende Funktionen. Nur sonntags und in den Ferien saß er
    regelmäßig auf seinem Koffer über mathematischer Literatur und hoffte auf
    ein zweites Studium."

9
Conclusion: Female Subjectivity

Patriarchy and the Divided Self

In many respects the treatment of questions of subjectivity in *Amanda*, and to a lesser extent in *Trobadora Beatriz*, appears to be indebted to the theories of subjectivity postulated in the poststructuralist discourses of psychoanalysis, linguistics, and philosophy – that is, the female subject in Morgner's works is conceived as radically split, non-unified, and decentered. Almost all of Morgner's women are in need of a suitable complement, an unreal or fantastic double, which can form a counter-weight to the deficiencies in most women's daily lives. In Morgner's earlier works the fragmentation of women is initially only metaphorical, such as Beatriz's representing Laura's "better half" (TB. 126). Increasingly, the reliance on a double becomes essential for survival in everyday life, the double eventually becoming a surrogate for a whole range of activities the subject is precluded from enjoying. When Beatriz disappears, Laura is optimistic about surviving without the help of magic and Beatriz's historical wisdom. The support of the female double is replaced by the companionship of the heterosexual couple, which has been given renewed impetus through the creation of a new emancipated man. The role of the female Doppelganger thus becomes usurped by the utopian male and the ideal marriage, which Laura seems to think will obviate the necessity of self-duplication. In *Amanda*, however, these hopes prove to be illusory. The ideal male is revealed to be a sham; Benno is deeply resentful of Laura's fame from the publication of the novel *Trobadora Beatriz* and is killed in a car accident after over-indulging in alcohol. Furthermore, it is revealed that the female subject is not merely deficient, but is now literally divided into two separate parts. Laura, while appearing more or less whole although in need of support nonetheless, is now revealed to be one half of a female subject that has always already been fragmented. Separated since birth from her other witch half

Amanda, Laura finds herself increasingly unable to cope with the exigencies of daily life under socialist patriarchy without recourse to the conjuring tricks of her other half. Even when she renounces the assistance of Amanda in a largely misguided attempt to reassert her autonomy, Laura finds alternative support in the needs-oriented friendship with Vilma. While Laura's concerns are primarily pragmatic, she soon realizes that the need for complementation extends much further than the distilling of a sleep-substitute elixir. She then recognizes that the ability to duplicate oneself can prove to be a skill of the highest order, serving a multitude of political and practical purposes.

Notwithstanding the obvious similarities between current poststructuralist theories of the destabilized non-unitary subject, the model Morgner employs in the later novel is borne out of a deconstructive gesture that is more feminist in gestus than poststructuralist. But like much poststructuralist thought, her primary concern is the destabilization of essentialist humanist categories of the self and human change. Where the impetus of her critique is decidedly feminist is in the nexus she establishes between forms of humanism and patriarchy. She deploys postmodernist techniques in an attempt to expose the logic of patriarchal systems of representation and practices and their complicity with humanist values and attitudes. Yet the link between any such subversion of humanist categories and a feminist cultural politics is not one that is a priori given. Feminist strategies that subvert forms of patriarchal orthodoxy differ depending on the context in which they are hatched and can vary greatly according to the prevailing aesthetic and philosophical dogma they seek to oppose.[1]

The marriage between feminism and poststructuralist theories has certainly proved productive even if it has been a deeply uneasy and highly contentious alliance. The problematic nature of the relationship of the non-identical, non-present subject of poststructuralism to feminism has only recently been addressed in ways that fruitfully scrutinize the fundamentally androcentric bias of the celebrated "Death of the Author"[2] and its relation to

1. See Janet Wolff, *Feminine Sentences: Essays on Women and Culture* (Cambridge: Polity Press, 1990), 6.
2. See Roland Barthes, "The Death of the Author," *The Rustle of Language*, trans. Richard Howard (New York: Hills and Wang, 1986), 49–55.

feminist politics. In recent years many feminists have challenged the validity of poststructuralist theories that declare the death or disappearance of the author of texts and the subjects of discourses as part of the project of uncovering the "biographical fallacy" in literary criticism.[3] Many feminists have consistently argued that any position that unequivocally proclaims the redundancy of notions of authorship must be revealed as inherently problematic for women, whose relationship to the privileged positions of author of texts and subject of philosophical discourses is fundamentally different from men's. As Rita Felski argues: "The assertion that the self needs to be decentered is of little value to women who have never *had* a self."[4] However, Felski goes on to argue that "the recognition of subjectivity as a central category of feminist politics and culture does not imply its unconditional affirmation."[5]

An appeal to an alternative notion of a female self can indeed constitute an important cornerstone in the feminist project of defining a politics of difference in opposition to dominant categories of subjectivity. It may therefore be politically expedient for feminism to posit the existence of a unified female self as a utopian model within certain historical and political contexts, while decrying the very same unity as oppressive and monolithic in others. In the case of Morgner and Wolf, the prevalence of a split female subject of narrative in their works from the late 1960s onwards constitutes a significant critique of the unified masculine subject of patriarchal discourses, particularly the discourses of Marxist humanism. As such, the invocation of a non-unified, thoroughly fragmented subject that is female signals a departure from homogenizing, totalitarian discourses, which seek to suppress the question of gender difference. This desire for a different sense of self, which is wholly self-defined, assumes in the case of Morgner and Wolf the form of a rejection of the notion

3. For a discussion of the relevance of postmodernist theory for feminism, see Felski, *Beyond Feminist Aesthetics*, especially chapters 1 and 2; Chris Weedon, *Feminist Practice & Poststructuralist Theory*; Nancy K. Miller, "Changing the Subject: Authorship, Writing, and the Reader," *Feminist Studies/Critical Studies*, ed. Teresa de Lauretis (Bloomington: Indiana UP, 1986), 102–20; Andreas Huyssen, "Mapping the Postmodern," *New German Critique* 33 (1984): 5–52; and Janet Wolff, *Feminine Sentences*.
4. Felski, *Beyond Feminist Aesthetics*, 78.
5. Ibid., 75.

of a whole or undivided self.

Of course, the phenomenon of the split subject is by no means confined to the early twentieth century and postwar social movements alone. Indeed, there are a number of significant literary precedents in the German tradition, most notably the works of Kleist, Jean Paul, E.T.A. Hoffmann in the eighteenth and nineteenth century, and Kafka and Rilke in the twentieth.[6] Popularized in the English-speaking world in the 1960s by the anti-psychiatry of R.D. Laing, and in France by Jacques Lacan and members of the "école freudienne," the concept of a divided subjectivity, understood as the displacement of the Cartesian transcendental ego, is in fact a rehearsal of themes that are much older than many critics would have us believe. Morgner's debt to the works of Jean Paul and E.T.A. Hoffmann is frequently made explicit in her citations of Romantic writers as well as in her use of the Doppelganger motif. The centrality of the theme of subjectivity in Morgner's later novels is confirmation of the widespread political relevance of these themes to feminist struggles. The model of female subjectivity delineated by East German writers such as Morgner provides a pertinent and productive contribution to current debates around the status of subjectivity and female subjectivity in particular. Likewise, the textual strategies she implements to subvert the discourses of patriarchal humanism may prove instructive to feminists who are concerned with the relationship between subversive social practice and textual politics. Morgner's approach to questions of individual identity, it would appear, is not as idiosyncratic as it may seem. Rather, her response to the issue of the nexus between ideology and subjectivity could serve as a timely reminder of the need in any theory of the subject for a consideration of the importance of cultural differences and the role of historical and political determinants in the production of literary texts.

Morgner's treatment of the issue of female subjectivity displays an awareness of the deeply gendered nature of the traditional discourses of humanism and its Marxist variants. In her works she aims to uncover the androcentric bias that underlies the dogma of the self-identical, non-alienated (proletarian) subject of historical processes. The dismantling of the official subject of

---

6. See, for example, Anthony Stephens, "'Er ist aber zwei geteilt': Gericht und Ich-Struktur bei Kafka," *Text & Kontext* (1978): 215–38.

Marxist humanist discourses, in evidence in much East German feminist literature in the 1970s and 1980s, is a direct response to the increasing perception that the socialist paradigm of the humanist subject was patently inadequate as a model for women, given the conflicting and contradictory demands being placed on women in all aspects of their lives. In Morgner's works women are portrayed as radically divided between so-called "real" public images of the idealized heroine of socialist work and the "unreal" images that speak of their tireless efforts to present a brave and optimistic face to the outside world. Split between the needs of families and the requirements of the work place, between conflicting expectations of motherhood and economic independence, the ideal of the all-rounded well-adjusted personality of the discourses of socialist humanism came to represent an unattainable ideal for the majority of East German women. Self-realization through the formative experience of work and through productive engagement with the social environment proved impossible for those women struggling to juggle the competing demands of full-time work and running a household and a family. The humanist ideal was revealed instead to be a debilitating myth that overlooked the harsh realities of women's lives and experiences. It perpetuated an androcentric model of selfhood that remained blind to the lack of opportunities for self-realization available to women and to the real barriers preventing them from attaining this ideal.

All of Morgner's heroines experience this fragmentation and dispersion of self from the relatively unrebellious, conciliatory citizen Laura of *Trobadora Beatriz*, to the openly refractory Vilma of *Amanda*. As the victim of historical processes of specialization and the division of labor, the female subjects of her novels are alienated in several senses: from the products of their work, from the forbidden products of their imagination, and from their innermost desires. Morgner's insistence on the fragmentation of the female subject is therefore most certainly anti-humanist in its rejection of the ostensibly universal subject of orthodox Marxism. This rejection of the concept of a unified subject does not necessarily mean, however, that subjective experiences are not a valid means of contesting stereotypes and falsely unifying ideals of femininity. As Chris Weedon has argued, feminists who align themselves with poststructuralist theories that refute the notion of coherent subjectivity do not automatically find themselves condoning a misogynistic or anti-feminist position that denies the validity of the subjective experiences of women altogether.[7] The recognition of a new feminine paradigm in the notion of a split subject that is divided physically as well as morally and ideologically does not amount to a devaluation of women's experience, nor is it a denial of women's claims to a different kind of subjectivity. Instead, it constitutes a powerful tool for understanding and uncovering the ideological underpinnings of both socialist and humanist ideals of femininity and subjectivity.

Morgner explicitly refers to the subjective experiences of working women in order to reveal the constructed nature of official subjectivity and the diverse nature of experience itself. She does so, moreover, without appealing to a belief in subjective experiences as the unmediated guardian of the truth. Although women's personal experiences are often a more accurate and authentic means of gaining access to the truth, Morgner is careful not to construe subjective experiences as a guarantor of the absolute truth value of a particular woman's account of her life. When Laura and Vilma write or speak of their individual experiences with patriarchal conditions, they purport to present the reader with a more real or authentic account of the truth. Yet this truth is never the whole truth and never wholly the end of the truth because there is always another truth that comes into play, which serves to relativize and modify the initial truth claim. Laura's account of her creative endeavors in *Trobadora Beatriz* is overlaid in *Amanda* with the story from another source that reveals the initial account to be only partial. Experientially-based story telling is significant not because these stories can offer unmediated access to the truth and to women's true selves but because they are able to correct, modify, and challenge less appropriate and ideologically motivated accounts of women's lives. In *Trobadora Beatriz*, Laura's stories of fragmentation are presented as more authentic and truthful than officially propagated versions of the life of the average working woman, but in *Amanda* even these accounts of Laura's are revealed to be gross distortions of the truth and already censored constructions of subjective experience. Subjective experience is in itself no guarantee of the truth value of

7. See Chris Weedon, *Feminist Practice*, 74.

literature or its authenticity.

Against the official Marxist ideal of a true unalienated nature, Morgner proposes a female nature as a contradictory site of conflicting, antagonistic forms of subjectivity. Against the stereotype of the female nature or subject, Morgner proposes the existence of multiple female natures and subjectivities. Women's experiences in the work place and the home may have many features in common, but they are not reducible to a common experience of womanhood nor to the experiences of their male comrades. Similarly, just as women's experiences of oppression and alienation can differ markedly, as demonstrated by a comparison between Hilde Felber and her secretary, Vilma, it also follows that their lived relationship to their sexuality and bodies will be equally heterogeneous. The discrepant attitudes of Vilma and Laura to the so-called "creative building" of the female body are a prime example of this. In appealing to experiences hitherto excluded from the dominant representations of femininity in the GDR, Morgner is not postulating a notion of a female nature deformed and alienated from itself. Instead, she sees subjectivity, as well as women's experience, as discursively produced, the product of contradictory cultural and political meanings assigned to femininity under patriarchal systems. The subject thus becomes the ideal site to contest alternative meanings, alternative ideologies, and mythologies.

By stressing the heterogeneity of women's experiences in the private and public spheres, Morgner's works also challenge the official claims of socialist literature to realism. The realism of the literature about women can only ever be a contingent realism, mediated by prevailing ideologies about femininity, subjectivity, and the value of work in the formation of the socialist personality. Literary realism is always highly crafted, a sensitive balance between permissible and non-permissible, objective and subjective aspects of women's experiences. In *Amanda* the obligation of the author to the imperatives of a realist aesthetic is presented as a type of sleight-of-hand or myth-making. Generally, the mythologizing of women in realist literature has served to limit the range of possible representations and self-representations open to women writers and readers. Morgner suggests realism should be understood instead as responsible or sympathetic myth-making, a difficult decision-making process whereby the author must weigh up the possible consequences of her writing for herself and her subjects with her commitment to the truth.

In this context the basic axiom of socialist realism of partisanship acquires a new feminist dimension. The notion of partisanship is modified to signify a particular kind of feminine or feminist solidarity existing between writer and reader, as well as the writer and her subject. Realism is therefore characterized not by a faithfulness to an objective idea of reality or truth but by an awareness of the intersubjective nature of all conceptions of the real. The partisanship of the female author is enlisted in the service of female solidarity to ensure the maintenance of a necessary fictional illusion. Lying becomes preferable to truthful reporting in order to protect the reputation of the empirical author against charges of subjectivism or voluntarism. In *Amanda*, Laura Salman accuses the author of *Trobadora Beatriz* of not taking sufficient care to hide the truth about Laura's clandestine activities as a member of the Sibylline Secret Society out of an inflexible regard for the truth. Laura chides Morgner for not seeing the necessity of occasionally trying to "put one over the reader." Laura asks why the author does not know "that it is the dammed duty of an author – not to mention a female author – if need be, to kid people into thinking an X is a U for as long possible" (A. 36). The role of the "responsible" author is similar to that of the illusionist in *Gauklerlegende*: too strict an adherence to reality can result in "character assassination," too little adherence in only half-truths.

Morgner's point is that the representation of women's experiences in literature is a precarious balancing act between responsible and irresponsible reporting, that is, between an uncompromising loyalty to a notion of the truth and a prudent adherence to the truth that may only be an approximation of the truth but one that is under certain circumstances politically more judicious. The notion of women's experience is a shifting category that is not only subject to revision by changing ideologies but also to re-editing and reinterpretation by women themselves in repeated acts of self-representation and -determination. The version of Laura's life that appeared in *Trobadora Beatriz* as a more or less authentic account of the adventures of Laura and Beatriz, allegedly recorded realistically by the pen of Laura, is discredited in the next novel of the trilogy as a falsification and distortion of reality by Amanda. In *Amanda* the eponymous heroine is revealed to be the real author of *Trobadora Beatriz*. What appeared to be a real and subjectively authentic account of Laura's life is subject to review by a further subject, in what seems a potentially endless dialectical process of subjective review and revision of women's experiences. What Morgner seems to be advocating here is a type of subjectivity-in-process or, alternatively, a theory of subjectivity as a process of permanent review and revision – a model that bears some similarity to Kristeva's concept of the "sujet en procès" – the subject in process and the subject on trial – but without the underpinnings of psycholinguistic theory. At the same time, however, Morgner is interested in creating an appropriate voice for this new subject to be, a voice that gives adequate expression to its fears and anxieties as well as to its hopes for the future. This voice is not the unmediated expression of an unproblematic subjectivity or "inner being." Rather, it is the voice of a ventriloquist, a "belly-speak" ("Bauchreden"), decentered and displaced, non-identical with itself, elusive and highly devious.

Yet this destabilized and shifting subject is not entirely free of a residual humanism and indeed of a certain idealism often identified with forms of Romantic nostalgia. This becomes most apparent in the ideal of a female subject entirely reconciled with its separate and disparate halves that pervades both of Morgner's major novels. Despite the overriding emphasis in Morgner's works on the fragmentary nature of female subjectivity and identity, there is undoubtedly a discernible sense of nostalgia running through *Amanda* for the reunification of severed halves of the female self. This is most obvious at the level of plot in the struggle for unification of the two halves of Amanda and Laura. It is also manifest at a symbolic level of the text in the rich tapestry of metaphors that resonates with longing for a return to an original state of grace and wholeness. The account of the Satanic splitting of women in the early years of the SED regime reads for instance as a secular feminist version of the Fall. Furthermore, the violent division of women into two antagonistic halves invokes a political reading. The splitting of Amanda Laura coincides roughly with the political division of Germany into separate states in the postwar era. The nostalgia to be reunited with one's lost other half is inseparable from a certain nostalgia for a unified Germany. Although this is never made explicit at a textual level, the careful use of topographical detail associated with the building and fortifying of borders between the two Germanies, together with the centrality of the frontier territory of the Harz and the Blocksberg mountains in the plot, all unmistakably lend the struggle for reunification an undeniable political dimension. The desire for wholeness must also be seen in the broader political context of the Cold War and the division of Germany. In this context, and in light of the unexpected fulfillment of these dreams in 1989, the longing to be reunited with women on the other side of the border cannot be termed humanist or even regressive. At the time of writing the novel, however, the merest allusion to the debates on the future reunification of the two Germanies – issues that had long been laid to rest in both halves of Germany – broke with ideological orthodoxy. Because socialism had effectively solved the problem of women's subordination to men, women had no need to form alliances with their "other halves" in West Germany. Officially, they had no need of support or complementation from any other source outside the national borders. Women who expressed the desire to be reunited with one's other suppressed female half and defied the prevailing orthodoxy of public opinion were likely to be considered highly subversive and dangerous.

Feminist advocates of poststructuralist theory have at times displayed a disdain for any feminist textual practice that mobilizes the notion of an inner female self or essence without realizing that this essential self may constitute a crucial political strategy within certain political contexts.[8] Textual strategies need to be considered in relation to the dominant practices they are attempting to subvert or uphold and not in isolation from questions of audiences and reception.[9] Rita Felski has convincingly argued for the need for feminist critical theory and politics to retain some concept of the female subject, despite the profoundly ambivalent status of the subject in poststructuralist and antihumanism theories. The concept of a subject is useful not as the "archetypal female subject which provides an ultimate grounding for feminist knowledge," but as a necessary fiction: "For women, questions of subjectivity, truth and identity may not be outmoded fictions but concepts

---

8. See ibid., 83.
9. See Janet Wolff, *Feminine Sentences*, 6–7.

which still possess an important strategic relevance" in the articulation of an oppositional culture and politics. Feminist discourse must itself construct a "necessarily streamlined conception of subjectivity which can address the politics of gender as relevant to its particular strategic concerns."[10] This thus raises the question whether poststructuralist feminist critiques of humanism that are of the liberal, Marxist, and radical-feminist kind have not tended to underestimate the importance, indeed the necessity, of asserting and *constructing* a utopian ideal of an undivided subjectivity within particular historical and political contexts.

In the chapter "Brocken Mythology" Morgner offers her own version of a creation myth of Western civilization that attempts to account for the original division of labor between the sexes and the splitting of the sexes into two separate halves. The creation of an alternative mythology serves here as a type of Barthian act of demystification performed on socialist myths and ideologies. With the ascendancy of Chief Devil Kolbuk to the Brocken, which we can take to mean the victory of the socialist revolution, the women who have been imprisoned on the Brocken see their chance of gaining access to the "white magic stone" and drinking silver. The Kolbuk regime, like the SED, promises to make women whole again with the help of the drinking silver. Yet the Kolbuk regime is also anxious to keep female troublemakers away from the Brocken and institutes the "Satanic partition" as a precautionary measure against the female querulants. The procedure of severing women in two, which we see practiced on Laura, is essentially a means of taming the unruly elements of women's personalities by dividing them into useful and non-useful halves:

> Kolbuk brought peace to his ravens by instituting the Satanic partition. He deposited the unusable halves, which were left over after the partition, and which had not died off, in the Hörselberg. (A. 118)[11]

---

10. Felski, *Beyond Feminist Aesthetics*, 70–73.
11. "Kolbuk schaffte seinen Raben Ruhe, indem er die teuflische Teilung einführte. Die unbrauchbaren Hälften, die bei dieser Teilung abfielen und nicht vergingen, deponierte er im Hörselberg."

Yet in dispensing with women's unproductive other halves through violence, Kolbuk is merely harnessing a form of cultural and ideological splitting that already occurs at the hands of the local customs:

> Kolbuk had a look around on earth and was convinced that sooner or later the customs had halved almost all women. The unusable halves of these normal women wilted and died off without leaving any traces. The useable ones made themselves useful without getting in the way. Only a few women who were normal and who therefore were called troublemakers resisted the moral division. (A. 118)[12]

Here it is the customs that are held responsible for the fragmentation of women's energies and time. We can read the customs here as either a synonym for the double burden or to mean those dominant practices (from attitudes towards femininity to more material practices) both inside and outside the home that support the continued subordination of women. But the gradual fragmentation of women through social practices and customs refers to more than just the negative effects of irreconcilable conflicts between the family and the organization of labor; the prevailing customs of the country have led to a further splitting of women into mutually exclusive images of femininity, into good mothers and bad mothers, into diligent selfless heroines and seductive demonic witches. The split here is ideological in nature and although peculiar to the workings of socialist patriarchy, this split is also typical of the construction of femininity in patriarchal systems in general.

In *Amanda* the existence of a unified female subject is located neither in the mythical matriarchal past nor in an equally mythical golden age or Arcadia. In the novel, the myth of the socialist female self as non-divided is located historically in the immediate postwar years after the establishment of the socialist state. Yet the possibility of attaining full subjectivity resembles more Bloch's notion of a "concrete utopia" than a fully realized entity. From the

12. "Kolbuk sah sich um auf der Erde und konnte sich überzeugen, daß die Sitten fast alle Frauen früher oder später halbierten. Die unbrauchbaren Hälften dieser normalen Frauen verwelkten und vergingen ohne Rückstand. Die brauchbaren machten sich nützlich, ohne zu stören. Nur wenige Frauen, die also unnormal waren und deshalb Querköpfe genannt wurden, widerstanden der sittlichen Teilung."

vantage point of thirty, forty years later, the utopia of an unalienated female subjectivity reveals itself to be a myth and consequently has come to function much in the same way as creation myths and other nostalgic myths of a lost paradise. This phase of history and official East German mythology corresponds to Laura's childhood. It is the time when everyone believed in miracles; the miraculous survival of the human race fostered the belief in the impossible, in the existence of economic miracles but also in the existence of miracles of a personal kind:

> When the Second World War was over in the middle of the twentieth century many survivors believed: that was the last one on earth. Particularly the young survivors believed this. The miracle of having escaped the inferno unscathed was conducive to the belief in miracles. (A. 19)[13]

Laura's euphoria after the war, expressed in the exclamation: "Now you can openly say what you think" (A. 102) and "Now you can openly do what you want to" (A. 103), points to the specific hopes of women and girls for a radical new start after the war. For Laura, the socialist state encouraged faith in miracles as well as the practice of wishful thinking. In is not surprising, therefore, that Laura's role models, Don Juan and Faust, are all famous men of genius, and her ideal profession as a child, a "locomotive driver," is correspondingly a traditional male profession. These masculine ideals that fuel her hopes for self-realization all seem within the realm of the possible amidst the emancipatory rhetoric of the immediate postwar years. Laura reports in the first of her reports on her childhood ideals and role models:

> In the afternoon after the unconditional surrender when I had conquered the bleaching ground without resistance from the previous authorities and was soaking up the sun, I thought the world was won. From then on the masquerade of submissiveness and other tricks I had

---

13. "Als in der Mitte des zwanzigsten Jahrhunderts der zweite Weltkrieg zu Ende war, glaubten viele Überlebende: Das war der letzte auf Erden. Besonders junge Überlebende glaubten es. Das Wunder, dem Inferno heil entronnen zu sein, begünstige Wunderglauben."

adopted, which are classified today as revolutionary cunning, seemed to me to be superfluous. (A. 101)[14]

The reunification of women's two halves thus comes to be linked to the survival of wishful thinking and the preservation of a utopian perspective.

The division of Laura is in fact not attributed to the local customs but is said to be the work of the devil, the legacy of a "Satanic partition" effected to make the recalcitrant Laura both a more manageable citizen and a more compliant wife. The amputation of Laura's other half enhances her usefulness both as mother and wife. This form of violent splitting is preferred by Laura to the slower, more gradual kind caused by customs because it is obviously a more expedient and less painful operation. The fragmentation of women by Kolbuk is welcomed by Laura, as was indeed the guillotine, as a more "humane" and enlightened form of "torture" and is far preferable to the fate of her medieval sisters on the pillory:

> The division would be by contrast comparatively painless. Brief in any case, one blow and it was over, better to be divided abruptly than gradually. The precision work of Chief Devil Kolbuk was better than the work of improvisation of customs. Ordinary ladies could be served by any old gentlemen. But Laura was a troublemaker. That was why a representative of Satan was standing by to try his luck himself. (A. 147)[15]

An end with a little terror, Kolbuk announces smugly, is infinitely preferable to terror without end. Bereft of her headstrong, mischievous other half, who is left vegetating in the Hörselberg,

---

14. "Als ich mittags nach der bedingungslosen Kapitulation den Bleichplan ohne Widerstand der bisherigen Autoritäten gewonnen hatte und Sonnenbad nahm, hielt ich die Welt für gewonnen. Ich glaubte also, daß ich nicht mehr beim Wort nehmen müßte, um ihm zu entgehen. Mir erschien der Mummenschanz der Untertänigkeit und andere Tricks, die mir zugekommen waren und die heute von gewissen Theoretikerinnen als revolutionäre Verschlagenheit kategorisiert werden, nunmehr für überflüssig."

15. "Die Teilung dagegen wäre vergleichsweise schmerzlos. Kurz sowieso, ein Hieb und fertig, besser abrupt geteilt als mählich. Besser Präzisionsarbeit von Oberteufel Kolbuk als Improvisionsarbeit von den Sitten. Gewöhnliche Damen würden von x-beliebigen Herren bedient. Laura aber wäre ein Querkopf. Deshalb stünde ein Stellvertreter Satans bereit, sich persönlich zu bemühen."

the now compliant and malleable Laura is willing to fulfill her motherly role. Paradoxically, however, her husband Tenner now leaves her, preferring her previous willful and unruly self. Laura lives in relative harmony with herself until she encounters her other half in Amanda, a meeting that awakens dormant childhood dreams and memories of her lost sense of self (A. 149).

The Satanic splitting of women is explicated in general terms as a byproduct of modernity, the result of increasing specialization and processes of rationalization instituted to increase the productivity of subjects for society. As a modern form of discipline it represents a means of regulation and control, which is simultaneously a way of enhancing the performance of the human body. The Satanic splitting is patriarchal societies' modern day heir to the medieval guillotine. Like Foucault's modern penal system, which conceals its real punitive function beneath the guise of a more humane and enlightened system of correction, the form of discipline effected by totalitarian patriarchies is simply an ostensibly more enlightened and humane form of population control. The Satanic splitting has dispensed with the gruesome bloodletting of the public execution and has abolished pain. Yet for Morgner it clearly represents a more insidious form of punishment and a reprehensible example of the exercise of state power. In this she follows Foucault, who also implies that modern penal systems in no way diminish the power the state wields over individual subjects.

Like Laura, Hilde Felber, the party functionary who answers Laura's advertisement for "mad help" and who is found resting in a psychiatric clinic, also suffers from the fragmentation of her energies because of the incompatibility of her professional obligations and her "household and children" (A. 180). In the case of Hilde, this conflict has resulted in a type of professional schizophrenia that necessitates regular visits to a clinic where she can replenish her dissipated energies. As a member of the party and the ruling bureaucratic elite, Hilde enjoys privileges most women do not. Vilma, her secretary, has no such access to extended periods in hospital, although she too is suffering from a similar professional illness. The contradictory demands of a family and the work place have produced in both women a type of split consciousness that is not only ultimately unproductive for society but is detrimental to women's sense of identity and self-worth. In a petition to the head of a psychiatric clinic Vilma declares herself to be suffering from schizophrenia, not the clinical variety, she argues, but an ideological form of "splitting of the soul." To repair this fragmentary sense of the self Vilma has invented her own division of labor that at least allows her to fulfill one half of herself at a time, or alternatively, to realize different aspects of her personality in succession. She manages to combat the fragmentation of her life by dividing her existence into consecutive phases. She sees the specialization of women as a diachronic as well as synchronic process, a succession of different lives each distinguished by a different division of labor between herself and her husbands. In her first life she specialized in self-denial and services provided to men. Her second life, which is only just beginning, will be dedicated to herself and science, she announces in *Amanda* (A. 191).

Sigrid Weigel has noted that the contradictory images of femininity and motherhood have led to "a latent schizophrenia" in women.[16] The schizophrenia that Vilma suffers from is more specifically the result of the contradictions between old and new ideals of femininity, between the pre-socialist objectification of women as sex objects and their post-revolutionary role as comrades-in-arms. This becomes most apparent while accompanying a work delegation to the decadent capitalist West, where Vilma discovers to her horror that her male colleagues and comrades in fact share their capitalist brothers' pleasure in the sexual objectification of women in pornography. Vilma is shattered to learn that the equality of women has been achieved in rhetoric only. Thus, while socialist women may perceive themselves to be equal partners by day, once outside the spheres of production traditional attitudes about sexuality and femininity are firmly entrenched. These are nowhere more in evidence than in men's attitudes about pornography and sexuality.

Women's lives are characterized by a fundamental dualism that splits them into godlike and devilish halves, into good and bad mothers, and into socially useful and aberrant halves. The effective policing of this dualism has forced them to deny the existence of the non-productive halves and to cultivate only the socially useful

16. Weigel, "Der schielende Blick: Thesen zur Geschichte weiblicher Schreibpraxis," in *Die verborgene Frau*, ed. Sigrid Weigel and Inge Stephan (Berlin: Argument, 1983), 120–21.

halves. However, this dualism has also fostered a form of existence best summarized by Sloterdijk in *Critique of Cynical Reason* (*Kritik der zynischen Vernunft*) as the life of a "kynik." The "kynic" leads a life of critical non-conformity and resistance, taking it upon himself or herself to become the feared and despised other of the dominant value system.[17] Sloterdijk argues that from the Middle Ages to modern times those groups such as "heretics, magicians, homosexuals, Jews, wise women" who refuse to conform to the prevailing ideology are identified with the demonic or the negative term of a transcendental dualism. According to Sloterdijk's thesis, the demonic only manifests itself when dualism itself is under threat, as exemplified for example by the outbreak of Satanic acts and incidents of Satanism at the end of the Middle Ages.[18] Seen in this light, the separating off of the evil term of the opposition in the splitting of women into good and heretic/witch aspects is tantamount to a modern form of exorcism executed by patriarchal regimes in crisis.

The draconian measures introduced by Chief Devil Kolbuk to pacify female heretics represents a particularly virulent form of suppression of ideological and sexual difference. At the same time, these measures signal a legitimation crisis of the reigning regime, which in turn fuels the hopes of those heretics for transformation. The existence of semi-autonomous halves can thus be turned to women's advantage in a productive division of labor between the real and imaginary parts of women. Amanda reminds Laura that effective resistance is only possible when both halves are reunited. Isebel, however, the leader of the HUU fraction, claims that any such ideas of reunification are opportunistic and that it is better to struggle on "halved" than "ideologically softened up" (A. 542). In *Amanda*, Morgner delineates a strategy of resistance rather similar to that of Sloterdijk's kynik. The particular strategy she invents seeks to overcome patriarchal practices that marginalize and silence women's speech through recourse to sheer cunning and inventiveness. Through the invention of the art of "body-speak" she constructs a blueprint for action that is grounded in the notion of a split subject. Such an invention is thus able to take

17. See Peter Sloterdijk, *Kritik der zynischen Vernunft*, vol. 2 (Frankfurt/Main: Suhrkamp, 1983), 659–71.
18. Ibid., 666–67.

into account the difficulties of organizing forms of resistance when women's attentions and energies are dispersed. In making a virtue out of necessity, Morgner converts the paradigm of female subjectivity as alienated from itself into a "positivity."

Ventriloquism and the Art of "Body-Speak"

In the model of "body-speak" Morgner effects a displacement of the speaking subject, transferring her site of enunciation to a position off-center: a position strategic to women's role as outsider, witch, heretic, and dissident. Like French feminists Kristeva, Irigaray, and Cixous she thus attempts to transform the negativity of the heretic's marginality into a positivity by redirecting the force with which her speech has been suppressed into a form of explosive energy possessing the power to disrupt and dislocate the dominant order. The female body becomes theorized in the process as a site of utterance and a locus of resistance to male power. Despite significant areas of overlap, however, there are significant differences in the ways the female body is produced as an instrument of opposition and subversion in the novels of Morgner and the work of French feminists. The model outlined by Morgner effects a critique of the mind/body split and the ways this dualism has been implicated in the suppression of women's desire and corporeality. Yet the particular model to be analyzed here does not resort to a mere inversion of the mind/body opposition through the affirmation of a female corporeality. Morgner thus manages to avoid the pitfalls of essentializing a feminine difference in the hypostatization of the feminine.

French feminist theory, in particular the work of Irigaray and Cixous, represents an endeavor to resist "phallocentric" modes of thought through the postulation of a new feminine paradigm that emphasizes the irreducible nature of the feminine and the elusive, diffuse nature of female desire. Irigaray's model of femininity is one that attempts to deconstruct the mutual exclusivity of binary oppositions by positing the female sex as indivisible. By way of analogy and reaction to Freud's theory of human sexuality, based on the Phallus as the central organizing term and metaphor, Irigaray's model takes the female anatomy as its point of departure. She posits the female body's potential for autoeroticism as an original site of resistance to "phallo-morphism" and monolithic modes of phallocentric thought. It is the two lips of the female "sexe" that suggest to her ways of challenging the unifying, exclusive power of the master signifier of Western philosophy, the Phallus. The systems of exchange set in motion by these two lips that perpetually touch, yet are never divisible, poses a threat to masculine sexuality and systems of representation that are organized around masculine desire and the law of the Phallus.

Irigaray's model of femininity, which is simultaneously a philosophical paradigm, emphasizes the self-sufficiency of the female sex and its inexhaustible potential for reproducing itself without reliance on another and without dominance over the other: "She is infinitely other in herself." Irigaray's polemic is clearly directed at Lacanian and Freudian notions of female sexuality as lack or as "the sex which is not one/ which isn't one," as suggested by the title of one of Irigaray's works.[19] The economy of exchange of the female sex is democratic in its refusal to privilege one term over the other and its avoidance of imperialistic acts of mastery in which the second term of the binary pair is subsumed under the logic of the first and in which female desire is subordinated to masculine. Despite the limitations of such an anatomical model – based as it is on an abstract idealized theory of female sexuality – for a feminist aesthetics and politics,[20] the writings of Irigaray and Cixous have found a resonance among American, Australian, British, and West German feminists that has proved productive for the development of other forms of feminist critiques of phallocentric discourse and for the articulation of specifically feminine forms of speech and writing.

In *Amanda* we find an analogous attempt to formulate a feminist aesthetics and politics founded on the female body in Vilma's technique of "body-speak" or "swallowing words." The art of "body-speak" ("Leibreden") is, as the name suggests, a particular

19. Irigaray, "Ce sexe qui n'en est pas un," in Marks, *New French Feminisms*, 103.
20. See in particular Felski, *Beyond Feminist Aesthetics*, 1-50; and Ann Rosalind Jones, "Writing the Body: Towards an Understanding of 'L'écriture féminine,'" in *The New Feminist Criticism*, ed. Elaine Showalter (London: Virago, 1985), 367; and Mary Jacobus, "The Question of Language: Men of Maxims and 'The Mill on the Floss,'" *Writing and Sexual Difference*, ed. Elizabeth Abel (Chicago: University of Chicago Press, 1982), 37–52.

form of ventriloquism or "belly-speak" ("Bauchreden") performed by women. "Body-speak" allows the female self to speak through the body while using the body as a buffer zone. The body is the repository of women's speech but not in the sense that women's speech is guided and shaped by their sexuality or corporeality. The body is the processing and storing ground of women's speech acts, the clearing house of all linguistic transactions. It regulates the traffic of words, controlling their flow and force. Ventriloquism permits women to produce politically effective speech at the same time as producing themselves through speech. But above all the voice of a ventriloquist is the voice of deception. It disguises its origins and covers its tracks. It is always somewhere and someone else, never who it seems or where it seems.

As a means of speaking the body ventriloquism represents, as does Cixous's aesthetic strategy of *s'écrire, parler femme*, or writing the body, a means of articulating sexual difference through the materiality of the body – a form of material life strangely absent from most materialist accounts of history. Like Cixous's proposal to invent a new "insurgent" writing, Morgner's art of utilizing the body in speech is not only a form of self-expression; it also doubles as a means of producing and reproducing the female self in the liberating, explosive act of writing. In this way women can project their repressed and censored sexuality into their texts and into history by externalizing themselves in the world. If women are to realize their "decensored relation" to their sexuality, Cixous argues, women must make their bodies heard.[21] However, unlike the project of *écriture féminine*, which privileges the experimental formalism of the literary avant-garde over oral forms of communication and more common forms of everyday speech, Morgner's attempt to make the body speak is grounded in the praxis of women's everyday lives. Instead of being the legacy of a literary elite, the practice of body-speak is an extension of women's everyday communicative experience, based on the widespread practice among women of swallowing one's words or biting one's tongue.[22]

The invention of the art of swallowing one's words therefore represents an emancipatory art form. Vilma manages to turn an

---

21. Cixous, "The Laugh of the Medusa," in Marks, *New French Feminisms*, 250.
22. See Felski, *Beyond Feminist Aesthetics*, 62.

essentially negative activity of suppression into a productive act of resistance and creativity by declaring necessity the mother of invention: "The best inventions are borne of necessity" (A. 227). Where some French feminist psychoanalytic theory identifies the "partition" of femininity as the inevitable result of women's narcissism – thereby offering a psychoanalytic justification for the perpetuation of the current status of femininity in psychoanalytic discourse as lack – Morgner's strategy is one that sees the splitting of women as the product of a particular set of historical circumstances. She thus manages to avoid the traps of enshrining existing conceptions of feminine sexuality as transhistorical, cross-cultural constants.

In *Amanda* the body becomes a site of opposition to the silencing of a specifically female voice by an unsympathetic environment. The art of "body-speak" is, however, much more than an aestheticized form of that very mundane activity of "swallowing one's words." It activates a habit formed through centuries of patriarchal domination, converting what for years was a vital means of survival for an oppressed and disenfranchized group into a form of defense against further acts of domination. Traditionally, as Vilma remarks, women have learned to refine the art of ventriloquism in the face of social expectations that demand women subordinate their personal needs and opinions to those of their families and spouses. Well trained in deferring to masculine authority in all matters and suppressing their real opinions, women have stifled all utterances of a personal nature, driving expressions of discontent inward. Vilma describes the different ways the sexes relate to their environment in terms of opposing activities of externalization and internalization:

> Konrad had made great sacrifices in order to rid himself of his basic abilities. I made great sacrifices in order to acquire my basic capabilities. Most of the energy that I required for living I had to expend on conforming. (A. 227)[23]

23. "Konrad hat große Entbehrungen auf sich genommen, seine wesentlichen Fähigkeiten aus sich herauszutreiben. Ich habe große Entbehrungen auf mich genommen, meine wesentlichen Fähigkeiten in mich hineinzutreiben. Die meisten Kräfte, die mir das Leben abverlangte, hab ich für Anpassung aufbringen müssen."

Whereas Olga Salman, Laura's mother, merely suppresses her speech by sending her replies down to the gall bladder where they form a repository of bitterness, Vilma has developed the art of regurgitating her speech, or re-embodying swallowed "truths" as a foreign body. This then provides a means of doubling the self in the projection of the self as other or an-other self into the external world. The self as other, unlike the male other, can furnish the subject with a valuable conversation partner – something that Vilma complains is denied many women in marriages – a conversation partner, moreover, who takes women's words seriously. Borne out of women's suppressed need for communication, the art of projecting or doubling the self acts as an important form of self-help, suggesting possible ways of actively overcoming women's isolation in the home. Vilma describes the emancipatory potential of her invention in the following way:

> I have become an inventor because my need for communication is similar to that of Konrad. The invention of body-speak allows me and all women to satisfy their need to communicate by themselves. No accumulation of false wealth, no pies in the sky. But no symptoms of abstinence either because social customs do not begrudge women having ideas as long as the outside world is not bothered by them. (A. 228)[24]

Although Vilma refers to the invention of body-speak as liberating because it releases energies that women would otherwise expend on conforming to social norms, ventriloquism also has a critical dimension because it facilitates self-examination and -policing. It does this in a convivial atmosphere of mutual trust and sharing. In this way women can discuss their ideas and share their experiences with another, even if the other is only oneself: "swallowed speech, inspected speech. Self-inspection may not be able to replace examination by another or intellectual company but it can help you keep your sanity" (A. 228). This model of substitute communication is, despite its utopian impetus, a savage indictment

---

24. "Ich bin eine Erfinderin geworden, weil mein Kommunikationsbedürfnis dem Konrads ähnelt. Die Erfindung der Leibrede erlaubt mir und allen Frauen, ihr Kommunikationsbedürfnis selbst zu befriedigen. Keine Anhäufung von falschem Reichtum mehr, keine Kopfwolken. Aber auch keine Abstinenzerscheinungen, weil die Sitten den Frauen Ideen nur dann nachsehen, wenn die Umwelt damit nicht belastet wird."

of patriarchal societies that necessitate the invention and cultivation of circus tricks and superhuman skills as an aid to survival. As a model its primary motivation is pragmatic, aimed at overcoming the isolation of women in industrial societies, a problem not only peculiar to socialist societies. Although Vilma presents her strategy with considerable pride, it is patently a desperate measure designed to compensate for the lack of opportunities available to women in the GDR to share common experiences – opportunities that have been provided in some measure in the West by the autonomous women's movement and other community services to women. The severity of the problem becomes most evident when Vilma, despite the jocular understated tone, hints that without the help of body-speak she would have long since committed suicide. The critical polemics of Vilma's invention now become evident: in the absence of alternative non-party support mechanisms, women must rely on miraculous or fantastical inventions in order to survive. To circumvent the criticism that hers is an individualistic solution to a collective problem, Vilma cynically parades her temporary solution as an art that has potential benefit to the collective as a whole: "My thesis: women's ventriloquism – a stabilizing factor of our Workers' and Peasants' State" (A. 229).

But ventriloquism is clearly also a form of self-censorship to control imprudent outbursts of emotion or dissatisfaction that could have negative repercussions for the women concerned. As such, Vilma's theory reads as a polemical attack on the need for self-censorship, reminiscent of Christa Wolf's remarks on the widespread tendency among women to censor their own thoughts and actions to avoid public censure.[25] Self-censorship has the added advantage over other forms of collective or official censorship in that it involves a minimal element of choice at the individual level. Self-censorship, rather fatalistically, becomes equated with individual empowerment. Vilma, for instance, is in the habit not only of swallowing unwanted words but also swallowing her disruptive other half. She has patented this invention which is practiced by some of the other witches who

---

25. See Wolf, "Die Dimension des Autors: Gespräch mit Hans Kaufmann," in *Lesen und Schreiben*, 84.

attend the "Nonsense seminars" in the Hugenottendom. The other witches swear allegiance to the Barbara Method and employ natural magic and a "magic cap" to conceal their other unruly halves:

> "For instance I have swallowed my unruly half," Vilma warbled proudly. "She is located where my body speeches are: safe. Ventriloquism and word swallowing are inventions of mine that have even been patented by the Round Table." (A. 351)[26]

Vilma even claims that her method is safer than Barbara's method because her other half is constantly at hand and can be readily regurgitated whenever required. Laura, however, regards the technique as potentially divisive, stressing the dangers inherent in the trick. Such reliance on acrobatics, she argues, could contribute further to women's already acute sense of fragmentation. She asks Vilma whether this can be a viable means of solving the conflicts in women's lives, or whether not instead it will lead to further disruption. Vilma reassures her that the reabsorption of her heretic other half is only a temporary measure and that she can be reinstated at any time.

Much more than being merely a political strategy, Vilma's invention contains in embryonic form the beginnings of an aesthetic practice that incorporates the materiality of women's daily lives into the creative process in a far more comprehensive fashion than do other feminist attempts to "write the body." The act of making the body speak involves a dual movement; the socially useless and subversive aspects of women's personalities and lives are first internalized and subsequently regurgitated when the occasion warrants. In this way those particularly personal experiences that women endure at first hand can be articulated in a suitable and sympathetic environment. In *Trobadora Beatriz* we have a prototype of the invention of body-speak in Olga Salman's trick of suppressing her contradictory remarks by swallowing them. For thirty-four years she has swallowed her pride and her innermost desires, forcing them down into her gall bladder where they have

---

26. "'Ich zum Beispiel hab meine störende Hälfte verschluckt,' trillerte Vilma stolz. 'Sie ist dort, wo sich meine Leibreden befinden: sicher. Das Leibreden und das Hälftenschlucken sind Erfindungen, die mir sogar von der Tafelrunde patentiert wurden.'"

formed a repository of bitterness and resentment. Vilma too has perfected the art of swallowing her dissatisfaction and discontent to maintain the appearance of a happy marriage. In *Amanda*, however, we are told by Tenner that the practice of swallowing one's anxieties is in fact a typical "male virtue," reactivated by men in response to the stresses of the "humanization of men" (A. 334):

> The heroes of the present have to swallow their fears. "Always swallowing . . . always being eaten up, always being consumed by one fear after the other and then one day when you are totally consumed by a neurosis or psychosis you even have to keep quiet about these illnesses for as long as possible. Because they are not respectable like a stomach ulcer or an alcoholic liver or any other proper sickness . . . "(A. 335)[27]

Tenner's professed experiences with the art of swallowing, however, have failed to make him more sympathetic to the swallowed silences of Vilma and Laura, and his expressed sympathies here instead appear to be a dangerous diversionary tactic on the part of Tenner to seduce Laura.

Vilma attributes her talents as a ventriloquist to her refusal to suppress her energies with antidepressants or "couldn't-give-a-damn tablets" and oral contraceptives (A. 227). Thus, the invention of this type of female ventriloquism is directly linked to the sexual emancipation of women, not through the availability of the Pill, but by women's decision to take charge of their bodies in other ways. When Laura has finally perfected the art of ventriloquism, she also finds it helps to reinforce her decision to maintain her independence from men at all costs. "I will never marry again," she exclaims in her newly discovered voice, "while swallowing it in different registers and volumes" (A. 421). Women's ability to use ventriloquism is thus portrayed as the culmination of a long process of reappropriating women's "bellies" as the primary site of both female reproductivity and productivity.

How the technique of making the belly speak differs from

27. "Die Helden der Gegenwart hätten die Ängste zu schlucken. 'Immer schlucken . . . immer fressen, immer eine Angst nach der anderen in dich reinfressen, und wenn du dir dann eines schönen Tages deine Angstneurose zusammengefressen hast oder deine Angstpsychose, mußt du auch diese Krankheiten noch verschweigen solange irgend möglich. Denn sie kann sich nicht sehen lassen neben einem Magengeschwür oder einer Säuferleber oder einer ähnlichen ordentlichen Krankheit . . .'"

women's traditional practices of self-censorship is in the way the art of body-speak attempts to break the cycle of oppression and suppression by turning an age-old technique into a liberating act of self-expression and self-production. By becoming ventriloquists, women can speak with two voices, one that is their own and one that is their own rendered "other." The other voice of the ventriloquist is therefore at the same time hers but not hers. It is the voice of the self that has no detectable origin, that cannot be traced back to its source. The strategic use of ventriloquism as a means of subversion now becomes apparent. The technique allows women to store either unwanted criticism or inappropriate comments until a suitable occasion when they can be voiced. Women can then unburden themselves of their stored up resentments, their unarticulated feelings and experiences by disseminating their innermost desires among other women also initiated in the art of ventriloquism without fear of detection. As Vilma remarks, "Put off is not put aside" (A. 255).

Furthermore, the technique of ventriloquism provides women with a particularly unique means of outwitting an oppressive authoritarian regime intent on containing all forms of female dissidence. While Laura and Vilma increasingly use the speech of the ventriloquist to disguise the real intentions of their activities, Morgner herself also writes with the pen of a ventriloquist, turning the speech of others back on itself. The writer too is a ventriloquist making use of intertextual references to mythological and fictional figures from medieval times to the present as a means of using the past to interrogate the present. The author, like the ventriloquist, uses the speech of others as mouthpieces, quoting out of context and creating new contexts for the utterances of others. Hers is a form of speech that Bakhtin termed dialogic speech. Dialogic speech is not merely speech that enters into dialogue with the speech of another person, nor is it a simple narrative strategy of allowing opposing voices or perspectives to compete for supremacy.[28] It is speech that is similar to indirect speech, "populated – overpopulated – with the intentions of others,"[29] continually overlaid with multiple social and historical

28. See Dale M. Bauer, *Feminist Dialogics: A Theory of Failed Community* (Albany, N.Y.: State University of New York Press, 1988).
29. M.M. Bakhtin, *The Dialogic Imagination*, trans. Caryl Emerson and Michael Holquist, ed. Michael Holquist (Austin: University of Texas, 1981), 294.

contexts. Dialogic speech, like the voice of the ventriloquist, always belongs to someone else, is always speech within speech, a quotation within a quotation. It enables the speaker to disguise her own authorial voice by speaking through other people's speeches. She can pay lip service to the ideology of the addressee while at the same time covertly subverting this same ideology. Vilma, for instance, can speak with forked tongue when engaging in debates with Tenner while also conveying highly controversial feminist speeches to the other witches who meet in the Hugenottendom.

Moreover, the art of ventriloquism allows Vilma to turn inner speech into outer speech, that is, to give voice to speeches she has internalized or censored because of their inappropriateness in certain social contexts. In more appropriate moments she can then activate those suppressed speeches stored in the gall bladder and in her belly that, like Bakhtin's unuttered discourse of inner speech, lie dormant in the individual, forming "foreign bodies" until they can be exorcised and ejected into the outside world. Inner speech, as the language of the "unofficial conscious," can only be openly shared with others if it is made to conform to patterns of outer speech.[30] Outer speech is that already censored form of speech that inhabits the ideological realm of the "official conscious" or official discourse. If the gap between official and unofficial consciousness, and hence between inner and outer speech, is too great, the ideologically subversive speech of the individual cannot find a suitable form of expression. It then turns into a foreign body in the psyche, unless it can externalize itself and convert its interiority into an external challenge to official ideology.[31]

Vilma's speeches from her body, which are stored in her belly waiting for a suitable opportunity to be projected into the outer world, are forms of inner speech: censored utterances in contradiction to official discourse. They belong to the repository of a suppressed, collective, unofficial consciousness. Like the illicit, taboo contents of Freud's unconscious that are censored and

---

30. See Michael Holquist, "The Politics of Representation," in *Allegory and Representation*, ed. Stephen Greenblatt (Baltimore: John Hopkins, 1981), 163–83.

31. V.N. Vološinov, *Freudianism: A Critical Sketch*, trans. and ed. I.R. Titunik in collaboration with Neal H. Bruss (Bloomington, Indianapolis: Indiana University Press, 1987), 89–90.

sublimated by the conscious mind or superego, Vilma's stored, inner speeches are also subject to internal and external censorship and are therefore unable to be verbalized in the public realm. In the same way that the unconscious desires and drives attach themselves to the day's residue in an effort to express themselves, Vilma's inner speech also assumes an ideological disguise by attaching itself to already censored utterances in circulation in public discourse in order to overcome censorship. She resorts to quotations and citations of ideological material that has already passed into outer speech, "ventriloquizing" the already censored speech of others so as to disguise her sources. Morgner, too, employs literary allusions and mythical material in the form of direct quotations; she "recycles" elements from the German cultural heritage as a means of externalizing suppressed inner speech. By attaching themselves to other literary products, the censored utterances of the author are able to assume a guise that can safely allow the expression of controversial opinion in mediated form. The author thus engages in oblique fashion with official dogma and orthodoxy, covering her tracks and confounding her pursuers as she constantly shifts mouthpieces.

In the model of the female ventriloquist, Morgner has developed Bakhtin's notion of "other-voicedness" as part of a specifically feminist textual strategy that can both disrupt male authoritarian discourse and give voice to an alternative feminist discourse. But because this voice is never what it seems, or where it seems, it cannot be pinned down and tied to any one meaning or intention. The ventriloquist is a conjurer who uses a "false bottom," someone who stands on constantly shifting ground. In this way the voice of the ventriloquist disorients the listener, confuses and surprises the addressee. The voice of a ventriloquist always pays lip service to the dominant discourses and frequently operates with forked tongue. As Vilma remarks, body-speak may well be a stabilizing factor of the "Workers' and Peasants' State," but it is also, like the "mad" activities of the witches who congregate in the Hugenottendom, highly subversive.

The voice of the ventriloquist is innately scurrilous and cunning; by denying its origins it divests itself of all responsibility for its words. The abrogation of authorial responsibility, inseparable from political responsibility, does not mean that ventriloquized literary texts are unauthored or write themselves. As Christa Wolf has remarked, it still holds that "the author is after all a very important person."[32] To speak with forked tongue is not to deny the author the possibility of speech; nor is it to deny the subjective authenticity of her discourse. The author is not dead, she is just elsewhere, always someone and somewhere else. The female subject of Morgner's works still has difficulty – fifteen years after Wolf's succinct diagnosis of the problems besetting the writing female subject – in "saying I." Whereas there are signs that Wolf may have overcome this difficulty in speaking in her own voice in her works after *Kassandra*,[33] it seems that Morgner instead sees political and aesthetic advantages to be gained in keeping the dialectic of female subjectivity – and thus the narrative dialectic – open. Indeed, in the course of her writing there is a proliferation of contradictory positions and irreconcilable view points that seem less and less able to be synthesized into a homogeneous pattern. Unlike Wolf who, according to Weigel, harks after an "original mythological utopia of unity,"[34] Morgner resists the temptation to mythologize an original prelapsarian state of subjective wholeness. The longing articulated in *Amanda* for a reconciliation, or reunification, of the two divided halves of the female self is ultimately relativized by the fragmentary device of ventriloquism that sees merit in a diffusion of subjectivities and standpoints.

The novel *Amanda* offers a curious example of the problem of "saying I," originally diagnosed by Wolf, in Vilma's strange "narrative behavior" (A. 219). After the first few meetings with Vilma it appears to Laura that Vilma seems incapable of using the first person pronoun. Instead of introducing herself, she narrates one story after the other about her superior, Hilde Felber, about Hilde's mother, Hilde's grandmother and grandfather, until finally Laura protests. Laura decries this type of narrative behavior as a "cursed personality cult" (A. 219) and demands that Vilma speak with her own voice and give "Vilma answers" instead of "Hilde answers." Instead of sublimating her own identity in biographical

---

32. Wolf, "Lesen und Schreiben," in *Lesen und Schreiben*, 41.
33. See Kuhn, *Christa Wolf's Utopian Vision*, 213.
34. Weigel, "Vom Sehen zur Seherin: Christa Wolfs Umdeutung des Mythos und die Spur der Bachmann-Rezeption in ihrer Literatur," in *Christa Wolf*, ed. Heinz Ludwig Arnold (3rd rpt.; Munich: Edition Text + Kritik, 1985), 80. (Text + Kritik 46)

snippets about Hilde's life, Vilma should speak about her own life, using the voice of subjective authenticity. Vilma argues:

> After all any old fool could empty his own head. There was no skill in pouring out one's own soul. Nor in interpreting one's life. But interpreting others – that required education. Higher education. Vilma had learned hermeneutics and exegesis at university and had the opportunity to perfect these arts on the editorial staff of the journal "New Philosophical Papers" on a daily basis. . . .. She performed Felber-exegeses . . . (A. 219–20)[35]

Because Vilma has little opportunity to apply her hermeneutic skills to the classics of German literature and philosophy, she turns to lesser known female "classics" such as Hilde herself. As a product of the push to increase the number of women in the upper echelons of the party bureaucracy and in managerial positions in the 1960s and 1970s, Hilde is a classic example of a failed superwoman. As a member of the ministry with four children, she spends much of her time recovering in hospital from the debilitating effects of her career. Vilma's inability to speak of her own experiences demonstrates the normative power of such role models as Hilde. When Laura rebukes Vilma for her obsession with interpreting Hilde's exemplary life, Vilma retorts that for want of someone else, she had chosen Hilde as an unknown classic to interpret. Shamed into silence, Laura accepts this explanation, realizing the importance of "interpreting" little known and publicized lives such as Hilde's.

Vilma's technique of ventriloquism is thus able to perform the important task of reappraising women's hidden contributions to society. The ventriloquist practices a type of gynocritics in rediscovering forgotten female "classics," just as the author, as the "master ventriloquist," speaks through the silenced voices of others in order to express his or her true intentions."[36] Yet, in *Amanda* the

---

35. "Den eigenen Schädel entleeren könne schließlich jeder Dummkopf. Sich auskotzen wäre keine Kunst. Sich auslegen auch nicht. Aber andere auslegen – das verlangte Schule. Hochschule. Vilma hatte Hermeneutik und Exegese an der Universität gelernt und in der Redaktion der Zeitschrift "Neue Philosophische Blätter" täglich Gelegenheit, diese Künste zu vervollkommnen . . . .. Sie triebe Felber-Exegese . . . .."
36. Carroll, "The Alterity of Discourse: Form, History, and the Question of the Political in M.M. Bakhtin," *Diacritics* 13, no. 2 (1983): 72.

ventriloquist herself is also the object of acts of ventriloquism performed by others, as well as being the site of conflicting voices and ideologies.[37] Morgner's author is simultaneously ventriloquist and ventriloquist's dummy, as exemplified in Vilma's "body-speak" and her strange "narrative behavior." While it is true to say that Vilma's peculiar habit of quoting Hilde in place of her own opinions arises out of what Wolf correctly diagnoses as the "difficulty in saying I," the impasse cannot simply be solved, as Laura soon realizes, by advocating the use of the first person, or by prescribing the use of autobiography as a more authentic form of expression.

Morgner appears not to share Wolf's idealism, whose female subject, although torn, has not yet relinquished the hope of rediscovering an authentic position from which an "I" can speak. But like Wolf's aesthetic of dual subjectivity, Morgner's dialogic model of subjectivity and authorship has dynamic and radical potential as a model for a feminist aesthetic. As a means of both projecting censored utterances and interrogating the utterances of others by speaking through and across them, it represents a unique narrative device designed to foil the workings of the internal and external censor. Furthermore, concomitant with such a model is the realization that a feminist aesthetics and politics may well have to relinquish the telos of a unified subjectivity and of reuniting the two ends of a feminine continuum if it is to continue to interrogate fixed notions of identity. A dialogic model of subjectivity that emphasizes the importance of intersubjectivity rather than subjective unity, by contrast, is one that is best able to give consideration to the importance of sexual and cultural difference in the formation of new subjectivities. Female subjectivity continues to be reliant on another woman and on the need for a productive engagement with opposites and contrasts; it is constantly in flux, being reformed and revised in a dialectical struggle for identity and selfhood with woman's other.

The question of female identity remains unresolved at the end of *Amanda*, as does the outcome of the offensive on the Blocksberg. The reunification of women's real and fantastic halves, the precondition for attaining more peaceful conditions, appears to have been adjourned. Obviously, as Amanda remarks, the reunification

37. Ibid., 74.

of the halves of the earthly witches with their other worldly halves
no longer takes priority over the more urgent need to storm the
Blocksberg and introduce conditions that are more conducive to
women's self-realization. The close of the novel anticipates a
partial victory for the witches, yet the narrative breaks off before
the victory of the collective strategy has been ascertained. As with
Trobadora Beatriz, which closes on the utopian story of Valeska's
sex change, *Amanda* ends on a carnivalistic note with the retrieval
of Beatriz's tongue during a fantastical New Years' Eve celebration
conducted by the Blocksberg witches. The victory of the witches
and Beatriz therefore remains confined to the imaginary realm:
the domain of the still to be realized utopia. Here the pressures of
the real are suspended in a phantasmagoric display of utopian
longing and feminine power. The fantastic spaces of the narrative
expand to engulf the real and the realm of the social. In both of
Morgner's major novels, the realist narrative strand is suceeded
in a utopian finale that relativizes and partially negates the ending
of the realist narrative strands. In the ultimate act of
ventriloquism, Morgner mobilizes the grand masters of German
classicism in a wealth of allusions to Goethe's *Faust*; she literally
storms the heights of the German literary tradition, as Honecker
once encouraged writers to do, turning the ending of *Faust* I into
a militant and triumphant display of feminist power. For this brief
but joyous moment the oppressiveness of the present is forgotten,
and the tyranny of patriarchy negated; the shackles of the political
status quo are exploded out of the continuum of time into an
imaginary realm of freedom and justice.

Bibliography

Irmtraud Morgner

Novels

Morgner, Irmtraud. *Hochzeit in Konstantinopel*. Berlin/GDR: Aufbau, 1968. Darmstadt & Neuwied: Luchterhand, 1979.

———. *Die wundersamen Reisen Gustavs des Weltfahrers: Lügenhafter Roman mit Kommentaren*. Berlin/GDR: Aufbau, 1972. Darmstadt & Neuwied: Luchterhand, 1981.

———. *Gauklerlegende: Eine Spielfraungeschichte*. Berlin/GDR: Eulenspiegel, 1970. Darmstadt & Neuwied: Luchterhand, 1982.

———. *Leben und Abenteuer der Trobadora Beatriz nach Zeugnissen ihrer Spielfrau Laura*. Berlin/GDR: Aufbau, 1974. Darmstadt & Neuwied: Luchterhand, 1976.

———. *Amanda: Ein Hexenroman*. Berlin/GDR: Aufbau, 1983. Darmstadt & Neuwied: Luchterhand, 1983.

———. *Der Schöne und das Tier: Eine Liebesgeschichte*. Frankfurt/Main: Luchterhand Literaturverlag, 1991.

———. *Rumba auf einen Herbst*. Hamburg: Luchterhand Literaturverlag, 1992.

Interviews, Essays and Speeches

Morgner, Irmtraud. "Interview mit Irmtraud Morgner von Joachim Walther." *Weltbühne* 32 (1972): 1010–13.

———. "Rede vor dem VII Schriftstellerkongreß." In *Protokolle*. Vol. 2. Ed. Schriftstellerverband der DDR. Berlin: Aufbau, 1974, 112–15.

———. "Das eine tun und das andere nicht lassen: Interview mit Ursula Krechel." *Konkret* 8 (1976): 43–45.

———. "Die täglichen Zerstückelungen: Ein Gespräch mit Ursula Krechel." *Frauenoffensive* 5 (1976): 35–41.

———. "Die Produktivkraft Sexualität souverän nutzen: Ein Gespräch mit Karin Huffzky." In *Grundlagentexte zur Emanzipation der Frau*. Ed. Jutta Menschik. Cologne: Pahl-Rugenstein, 1976, 328–35.

———. "Interview mit Irmtraud Morgner." *Aussage zur Person. Zwölf deutsche Schriftsteller im Gespräch mit Ekkehart Rudolph*. Tübingen, Basel: Erdmann, 1977, 157–77.

———. "Die Perlen des Phantastischen: Interview mit Klara Obermüller." *Die Weltwoche*, 30 March 1977: 35.

———. "Aber die großen Veränderungen beginnen leise." *Für Dich* 21 (1978): 18–20.

———. "Weltspitze sein und sich wundern, was noch nicht ist." *Kürbiskern* no. 1 (1978): 95–99.

———. "Rede vor dem VIII Schriftstellerkongreß." In *Protokolle*. Vol. 2. Ed. Schriftstellerverband der DDR. Berlin: Aufbau, 1979, 64–71.

———. "Gewissensfragen." In *Mut zur Angst*. Ed. Ingrid Krüger. Darmstadt & Neuwied: Luchterhand, 1982, 160–61.

———."Der Planet braucht Hexen: Interview mit Gabi Swiderski." *Rote Blätter* no. 4 (1983): 65–68.

———. "Interview mit Irmtraud Morgner von Eva Kaufmann." *Weimarer Beiträge* 30 (1984): 1494–1514.

———. "Frauenstaat: Interview mit Harrie Lemmens." *Konkret* no. 10 (1984): 54–61.

———. "Gespräch mit Irmtraud Morgner von Doris Berger." *GDR Monitor* no. 12 (Winter 1984/85): 29–37.

———. *Die Hexe im Landhaus: Gespräch in Solothurn: Mit einem Beitrag von Erica Pedretti*. Zürich, Villingen: Rauhreif, 1986.

———. "Jetzt oder nie! Die Frauen sind die Hälfte des Volkes!: Interview mit Alice Schwarzer," *Emma* no. 2 (1990): 32–39.

Recommended Secondary Literature on Morgner
Auer, Annemarie. "Gedanken beim Lesen: Trobadora unterwegs oder Schulung in Realismus." *Sinn und Form* 28 (1976): 1067–1107.

Bammer, Angelika. "Woman's Place in the GDR: Irmtraud Morgner's *Leben und Abenteuer der Trobadora Beatriz nach Zeignissen ihrer Spielfrau Laura*." *Alternative Futures: The Journal of Utopian Studies* 3, no. 1 (1980): 13–25.

Clason, Synnöve. "Auf den Zauberbergen der Zukunft: Die Sehnsüchte der Irmtraud Morgner." *Text + Kontext* 12, no. 2 (1984): 370–86.

Clason, Synnöve. "'Mit dieser Handschrift wünschte sie in die Historie einzutreten.'" *Weimarer Beiträge* no. 7 (1990): 1128–45.

Damm, Sigrid. "Irmtraud Morgner: *Leben und Abenteuer der Trobadora Beatriz nach Zeugnissen ihrer Spielfrau Laura*." *Weimarer Beiträge* 21, no. 9 (1975): 138–48.

Damm, Sigrid, and Jürgen Engler. "Notate des Zwiespalts und Allegorien der Vollendung." *Weimarer Beiträge* 21, no. 7 (1975): 37–69.

Gerhardt, Marlis, ed. *Irmtraud Morgner: Texte, Daten, Bilder*. Frankfurt/Main: Luchterhand Literaturverlag, 1990. (Contains comprehensive list of Morgner criticism)

Herminghouse, Patricia. "Die Frau und das Phantastische in der neueren DDR-Literatur: Der Fall Irmtraud Morgner." In *Die Frau als Heldin und Autorin*. Ed. Wolfgang Paulsen. Bern: Francke, 1979, 248–66.

Kaufmann, Eva. "'Der Hölle die Zunge rausstrecken . . .': Der Weg der Erzählerin Irmtraud Morgner." *Weimarer Beiträge* 30 (1984): 1514–32.

Lewis, Alison. "The Politics and Poetics of Feminist Fantasy: A Study of the Novels of Irmtraud Morgner." Ph.D. diss., University of Adelaide, 1989.

———. "Fantasy and Romance: A Feminist Poetics of Subversion and the Case of Irmtraud Morgner." *Southern Review* 22, no. 3 (1989): 244–55.

Martin, Biddy. "Socialist Patriarchy and the Limits of Reform: A Reading of Irmtraud Morgner's *Life and Adventures of Troubadour Beatriz as Chronicled by her Minstrel Laura.*" *Studies in Twentieth Century Literature* 5, no. 1 (Fall 1980): 59–74.

Nordmann, Ingeborg. "Die halbierte Geschichtsfähigkeit der Frau. Zu Irmtraud Morgners Roman 'Leben und Abenteuer der Trobadora Beatriz nach Zeugnissen ihrer Spielfrau Laura.'" In *DDR-Roman und Literaturgesellschaft*. Ed. Jos Hoogeveen and Gerd Labroisse. Amsterdam: Rodopi, 1981, 419–62.

O'Brien, Mary-Elizabeth. "Fantasy and Reality in Irmtraud Morgner's Salman Novels: A Discursive Analysis of *Leben der Trobadora* and *Amanda.*" Ph.D. diss., University of California, 1988.

Püschel, Ursula. "Von dem Buch *Amanda* zu sprechen." *Kürbiskern* no. 1 (1986): 86–97.

Reuffer, Petra. *Die unwahrscheinlichen Gewänder der anderen Wahrheit: Zur Wiederentdeckung des Wunderbaren bei Günter Grass und Irmtraud Morgner.* Essen: Die blaue Eule, 1988.

Schmitz-Köster, Dorothee. *Trobadora und Kassandra und . . .: Weibliches Schreiben in der DDR.* Cologne: Pahl-Rugenstein, 1989.

von Soden, Kristine, ed. *Irmtraud Morgners hexische Weltfahrt: Eine Zeitmontage.* Berlin: Elefanten Press, 1991.

Wolf, Christa. "Der Mensch ist in zwei Formen ausgebildet: Zum Tode Irmtraud Morgner." *Die Zeit,* 18 May 1990, 71b.

Wolter, Manfred. "Trobadora Startbereit." *Kritik 77: Rezensionen zur DDR-Literatur.* Ed. Eberhard Günther. Halle: Mitteldeutscher Verlag, 1978, 93–96.

Recommended Reading

GDR Literature, History and Culture

Ahlings, Gabi, and Ingeborg Nordmann. "Arbeiten wie ein Mann und wie eine Frau dazu: Frauen in der DDR." *Ästhetik und Kommunikation* 37 (1979): 85–95.

Dölling, Irene. "Social and Cultural Changes in the Lives of GDR Women – Changes in their Self-conception." In *Studies in GDR Culture and*

Society 5. Selected Papers from the Tenth New Hampshire Symposium on the German Democratic Republic. Ed. Margy Gerber. Langham: University Press of America, 1985, 81–92.

Emmerich, Wolfgang. _Kleine Literaturgeschichte der DDR_. Darmstadt & Neuwied: Luchterhand, 1981.

Engels, Frederick. _Socialism: Utopian and Scientific_. Trans. Edward Aveling. In _Collected Works_, Vol. 24. London: Lawrence & Wishard, 1989, 285–339.

——. _Die Entwicklung des Sozialismus von der Utopie zur Wissenschaft_. In _Marx und Engels Werke_. Vol. 19. Berlin/GDR: Dietz, 1962, 189–228.

——. _The Origin of the Family, Private Property and the State_. Trans. Edward Aveling. In _Collected Works_. Vol. 26. London: Lawrence & Wishard, 1990, 129–276.

——. _Der Ursprung der Familie, des Privateigentums und des Staats_. In _MEW_. Vol. 21. 1962; Berlin: Dietz, 1984, 25–173.

Feyl, Renate. _Der lautlose Aufbruch: Frauen in der Wissenschaft_. Darmstadt & Neuwied: Luchterhand, 1983.

Hanke, Irma. "Probleme berufstätiger Frauen mit Kindern als Thema der DDR-Literatur." In _Lebensbedingungen in der DDR: Siebzehnte Tagung zum Stand der DDR-Forschung in der BRD 12. bis 15 Juni 1984_. Ed. Ilse Spittmann, and Gisela Helwig. Cologne: Edition Deutschland-Archiv im Verlag Wissenschaft und Politik, 1984, 111–21.

Heidtmann, Horst. _Utopisch-phantastische Literatur in der DDR: Untersuchungen zur Entwicklung eines unterhaltungsliterarischen Genres von 1945–1979_. Munich: Wilhelm Fink, 1982.

Helwig, Gisela. _Frau und Familie in beiden deutschen Staaten_. Cologne: Wissenschaft und Politik, 1984.

Herminghouse, Patricia. "Die Wiederentdeckung der Romantik: Zur Funktion der Dichterfiguren in der Neueren DDR-Literatur." In _DDR-Roman und Literaturgesellschaft_. Ed. Jos Hoogeveen and Gerd Labroisse. Amsterdam: Rodopi, 1981, 217–48. [Amsterdamer Beiträge zur Germanistik. Vol. 11/12]

——. "'Der Autor ist nämlich ein wichtiger Mensch': Zur Prosa." In _Frauen. Literatur. Geschichte: Schreibende Frauen vom Mittelalter bis zur Gegenwart_. Ed. Hiltrud Gnüg and Renate Möhrmann. Stuttgart: Metzler, 1985, 338–54.

Hohendahl, Peter Uwe, and Patricia Herminghouse, eds. _Literatur der DDR in den siebziger Jahren_. Frankfurt/Main: Suhrkamp, 1983.

Lemke, Christiane. "Women and Politics in East Germany." _Socialist Review_ no. 81 (1985): 121–34.

Lennox, Sara. "'Nun ja! Das nächste Leben geht aber heute an': Prosa von Frauen und Frauenbefreiung in der DDR." In _Literatur der DDR in den siebziger Jahren_. Ed. P.U. Hohendahl and P. Herminghouse.

Frankfurt/Main: Suhrkamp, 1983, 224–58.

Milfull, John. "Die Literatur der DDR." In *Geschichte der deutschen Literatur vom 18. Jahrhundert bis zur Gegenwart, 1945–1980.* Vol. III/2. Ed. Viktor Žmegač. Königstein/Ts.: Athenäum, 1984, 591–694.

Nägele, Rainer. "Trauer, Tropen und Phantasmen: Ver-rückte Geschichten aus der DDR." In *Literatur der DDR in den siebziger Jahren.* Ed. P.U. Hohendahl and P. Herminghouse. Frankfurt/Main: Suhrkamp, 1983, 193–223.

Rüß, Gisela, ed. *Dokumente zur Kunst-, Literatur- und Kulturpolitik der SED, 1971–1974.* Stuttgart: Seewald, 1976.

Schlenstedt, Dieter. "Ankunft und Anspruch: Zum neueren Roman in der DDR." *Sinn und Form* 18 (1966): 814–35.

Schubbe, Elimar, ed. *Dokumente zur Kunst-, Literatur- und Kulturpolitik der SED, 1949–70.* Vol. 1. Stuttgart: Seewald Verlag, 1972.

Sckerl, Adolf. *Wissenschaftlich-phantastische Literatur: Anmerkungen zu ihrem Wesen und ihrer Entwicklung: Überlegungen zum Umgang mit ihr in unserer Gesellschaft.* Berlin/GDR: Akademie der Künste, 1976.

Stephan, Alexander. "Die wissenschaftlich-technische Revolution in der Literatur der DDR." *Der Deutschunterricht* 30, no. 2 (1978): 18–34.

Wolf, Christa. *Lesen und Schreiben: Neue Sammlung.* Darmstadt & Neuwied: Luchterhand, 1980.

———. "Ein Brief." In *Mut zur Angst.* Ed. Ingrid Krüger. Darmstadt & Neuwied: Luchterhand, 1982, 152–59.

———. *Voraussetzungen einer Erzählung: Kassandra: Frankfurter Poetik-Vorlesungen.* Darmstadt & Neuwied: Luchterhand, 1983.

Wuckel, Dieter. *Science fiction: Eine illustrierte Literaturgeschichte.* Leipzig: Edition Leipzig, 1986.

Feminist Theory and Criticism

Abel, Elizabeth, Marianne Hirsch, and Elizabeth Langland, eds. *The Voyage In: Fictions of Female Development.* Hanover: University Press of New England, 1983.

Bovenschen, Silvia. "The Contemporary Witch, the Historical Witch and the Witch Myth: The Witch, Subject of the Appropriation of Nature and Object of the Domination of Nature." *New German Critique* no. 15 (1978): 83–119.

Brown, Beverley, and Parveen Adams. "The Feminine Body and Feminist Politics." *m/f* no. 3 (1981): 35–50.

Cixous, Hélène. "The Laugh of the Medusa." In *New French Feminisms: An Anthology.* Ed. and Introd. Elaine Marks, and Isabelle de Courtivron. New York: Schocken Books, 1980, 245–64.

Cixous, Hélène, and Catherine Clément. *The Newly Born Woman.* Trans. Betsy Wing. Introd. Sandra M. Gilbert. Minneapolis: University of

Minnesota Press, 1986.

Dinnerstein, Dorothy. *The Rocking of the Cradle and the Ruling of the World*. London: Women's Press, 1987.

Elshtain, Jean Bethke. "On Beautiful Souls, Just Warriors and Feminist Consciousness." In *Women and Men's Wars*. Ed. Judith Stiehm. Oxford, New York, Toronto, Sydney, Paris, Frankfurt: Pergamon Press, 1983, 341–48.

———. *Women and War*. New York: Basic Books, 1987.

Felski, Rita. *Beyond Feminist Aesthetics: Feminist Literature and Social Change*. Cambridge, Massachusetts: Harvard University Press, 1989.

Gilbert, Sandra M. "Introduction: A Tarantella of Theory." Introduction. *The Newly Born Woman*. By Hélène Cixous and Catherine Clément. Trans. Betsy Wing. Manchester: Manchester University Press, 1986, ix–xviii.

Harding, Sandra. *The Science Question in Feminism*. Ithaca: Cornell University Press, 1986.

Hartmann, Heidi. "The Unhappy Marriage of Marxism and Feminism: Towards a More Progressive Union." In *Women and Revolution: A Discussion of the Unhappy Marriage of Marxism and Feminism*. Ed. Lydia Sargent. Boston: South End Press, 1981, 1–42.

Irigaray, Luce. "Ce sexe qui n'en est pas un." In *New French Feminisms: An Anthology*. Ed. and Introd. Elaine Marks, and Isabelle de Courtivron. New York: Schocken Books, 1980, 99–106.

Irigaray, Luce. "Women's Exile." *Ideology and Consciousness* 1 (1977): 62–76.

———. "When the Goods Get Together." In *New French Feminisms: An Anthology*. Ed. and Introd. Elaine Marks, and Isabelle de Courtivron. New York: Schocken Books, 1980, 107–10.

———. *Speculum of the Other Woman*. Trans. Gillian C. Gill. Ithaca: Cornell University Press, 1985.

Keller, Evelyn Fox. *Reflections on Gender and Science*. New Haven and London: Yale University Press, 1985.

Kuhn, Annette. "Structures of Patriarchy and Capital in the Family." In *Feminism and Materialism: Women and Modes of Production*. Ed. Annette Kuhn and AnneMarie Wolpe. London: Routledge and Kegan Paul, 1978, 42–67.

Lacan, Jacques. "Intervention on Transference." In *Feminine Sexuality: Jacques Lacan and the école freudienne*. Ed. Juliet Mitchell and Jacqueline Rose. London: Macmillan Press, 1982, 62–73.

Elaine Marks, and Isabelle de Courtivron, eds. and introd. *New French Feminisms: An Anthology*. New York: Schocken Books, 1980.

Merchant, Carolyn. *The Death of Nature: Women, Ecology and the Scientific Revolution*. New York: Harper and Row, 1980.

Mitscherlich, Margarete. *Die Zukunft ist weiblich*. Zurich: Pendo, 1987.
——. *The Peaceable Sex: On Aggression in Women and Men*. Trans. Craig Tomlinson. New York: Fromm International Publishing Corporation, 1987.
Rowbotham, Sheila. *Woman's Consciousness, Man's World*. Harmondsworth: Penguin, 1973.
Rubin, Gayle. "The Traffic of Women: Notes on the 'Political Economy' of Sex." In *Toward an Anthropology of Women*. Ed. Rayna R. Reiter. New York, London: Monthly Review Press, 1975, 157–210.
Segal, Lynne. *Is the Future Female?: Troubled Thoughts on Contemporary Feminism*. London: Virago, 1987.
Stephan, Inge, Sigrid and Weigel ed. *Die verborgene Frau*. 2nd ed. Berlin: Argument, 1985, 35–66. [Argument-Sonderband AS96]
Weedon, Chris. *Feminist Practice and Poststructuralist Theory*. London: Basil Blackwell, 1987.
Weigel, Sigrid. "Mit Siebenmeilenstiefeln zur weiblichen All-Macht oder die kleinen Schritte aus der männlichen Ordnung: Eine Kritik literarischer Utopien von Frauen." *Feministische Studien* no. 1 (1985): 138–52.
Wolff, Janet. *Feminine Sentences: Essays on Women and Culture*. Cambridge: Polity Press, 1990.

Marxism, Critical Theory, and Literary Theory

Bakhtin, M.M. *Problems of Dostoevsky's Poetics*. Trans. R.W. Rotsel. Ann Arbor: Ardis, 1973.
——. *The Dialogic Imagination: Four Essays*. Ed. Michael Holquist. Trans. Caryl Emerson and Michael Holquist. Austin: University of Texas Press, 1981.
——. *Rabelais and His World*. Trans. Hélène Iswolsky. Bloomington: Indiana University Press, 1984.
Foucault, Michel. *Discipline and Punish: The Birth of the Prison*. Harmondsworth: Penguin, 1977.
——. *Power/Knowledge: Selected Interviews and Other Writings 1972–1977*. Ed. Colin Gordon. Trans. Colin Gordon, Leo Marshall, John Mepham, Kate Soper. New York: Pantheon Books, 1980.
Freud, Sigmund. *Civilization and its Discontents*. Trans. Joan Riviere. London: Hogarth Press, 1930.
——. *New Introductory Lectures on Psycho-Analysis (1933)*. Standard Edition. Vol. 22. Trans. James Strachey. Collab. Anna Freud. London: Hogarth Press, 1964.
Frye, Northrop. *Anatomy of Criticism*. Princeton: Princeton University Press, 1957.
Greimas, A.J. *Du Sens II: Essais sémiotiques*. Paris: Editions du Seuil, 1983.

——. *Structural Semantics: An Attempt at a Method.* Introd. Ronald Schleifer. Trans. Ronald Schleifer, Daniele McDowell and Alan Velie. Lincoln: University of Nebraska Press, 1983.

Horkheimer, Max, and Theodor W. Adorno. *Die Dialektik der Aufklärung.* Frankfurt/Main: Fischer, 1969.

Irwin, W.R. *The Game of the Impossible: A Rhetoric of Fantasy.* Illinois: University of Illinois Press, 1976.

Jackson, Rosemary. *Fantasy: The Literature of Subversion.* London: Methuen, 1981.

Jameson, Fredric. "Magical Narratives: Romance as Genre." *New Literary History* 7, no. 1 (1975): 159–63.

——. *The Political Unconscious: Narrative as a Socially Symbolic Act.* London: Methuen, 1981.

Lacan, Jacques. *Ecrits: A Selection.* Trans. Alan Sheridan. London: Tavistock Publications, 1977.

——. *The Four Fundamental Concepts of Psycho-analysis.* Trans. Alan Sheridan. Ed. Jacques-Alain Miller. London: Hogarth Press, 1977.

Marcuse, Herbert. *Eros and Civilization: A Philosophical Inquiry into Freud.* 1955; Boston: Beacon Press, 1966.

Moretti, Franco. *The Way of the World: The 'Bildungsroman' in European Culture.* London: Verso, 1987.

Todorov, Tzvetan. *The Fantastic: A Structural Approach to a Literary Genre.* Trans. Richard Howard. Ithaca: N.Y.: Cornell University Press, 1975.

Vološinov, V.N. *Freudianism: A Critical Sketch.* Trans. and Ed. I.R. Titunik in collaboration with Neal H. Bruss. Bloomington, Indianapolis: Indiana University Press, 1987.

Index